Invisibility Studies

CULTURAL HISTORY AND LITERARY IMAGINATION

EDITED BY CHRISTIAN J. EMDEN & DAVID MIDGLEY

VOL. 23

PETER LANG

Oxford · Bern · Berlin · Bruxelles · Frankfurt am Main · New York · Wien

Invisibility Studies

Surveillance, Transparency and the Hidden in Contemporary Culture

Henriette Steiner and Kristin Veel (eds)

PETER LANG
Oxford · Bern · Berlin · Bruxelles · Frankfurt am Main · New York · Wien

Bibliographic information published by Die Deutsche Nationalbibliothek
Die Deutsche Nationalbibliothek lists this publication in the Deutsche Nationalbibliografie; detailed bibliographic data is available on the Internet at http://dnb.d-nb.de.

A catalogue record for this book is available from the British Library.

Library of Congress Cataloging-in-Publication Data:

Invisibility studies : surveillance, transparency and the hidden in contemporary culture / Henriette Steiner and Kristin Veel (eds.).
pages cm. -- (Cultural History and Literary Imagination ; 23)
Includes bibliographical references and index.
ISBN 978-3-0343-0985-1 (alk. paper)
1. Architecture and society. 2. Space--Social aspects. 3. Privacy. I. Steiner, Henriette, 1980- editor. II. Veel, Kristin, editor.
NA2543.S6I58 2015
720.1'08--dc23
2014039324

Cover image: *within* (2013) © Nina Lund Westerdahl, zURBS.
Reproduced with permission.

ISSN 1660-6205
ISBN 978-3-0343-0985-1 (print)
ISBN 978-3-0353-0671-2 (eBook)

Hochfeldstrasse 32, CH-3012 Bern, Switzerland
info@peterlang.com, www.peterlang.com, www.peterlang.net

This publication has been peer reviewed.

Contents

Illustrations

CHAPTER 6

CHAPTER 7

CHAPTER 16

Acknowledgements

The contributions to this volume originate in papers presented at conferences held in Copenhagen and Zurich throughout 2012 and 2013 as part of the research network *(In)Visibilities – A Network for Studies on the Seeable and the Hidden of Contemporary Culture*. The editors would like to acknowledge the generous financial support received from the Danish Council for Independent Research and the Swiss National Science Foundation, without which this project would not have been possible. Participants at the conferences included art practitioners and academics from areas including literature and film studies, philosophy and art history, architecture, sociology, geography and urban studies. Thematically, the conferences covered a range of topics spanning surveillance and voyeurism, architecture and visibility (especially glass), censorship and security and questions concerning spatial and archival practices. The editors would like to thank everyone who took part in the network's activities and who, in many different ways, therefore contributed to shaping this volume and the contributions included in it, in both direct and indirect ways. We would also like to acknowledge institutional support from the University of Copenhagen, ETH Zurich and Churchill College, Cambridge: each of these institutions facilitated different stages of the collaboration in distinct ways. We furthermore would like to thank Henrik Reeh and Claus Bech-Danielsen for their continuous support for the project. At Peter Lang, we are indebted to the our editor Laurel Plapp, and we would like to thank Rachel Malkin for more help with language and with preparing the text than she probably herself imagines as well as Jesper Nielsen for editorial assistance. We also would like to thank the series editors Christian J. Emden and David Midgley for their help, feedback and encouragement. Finally, we would like to thank the authors for their time, patience and enthusiasm.

HENRIETTE STEINER AND KRISTIN VEEL

Negotiating (In)Visibilities in Contemporary Culture: A Short Introduction

The highly debated yet oft-repeated dictum 'if you have nothing to hide, you have nothing to fear' is usually used as an argument for accepting increased surveillance. But it raises fundamental questions about what privacy actually entails in a society that, with the proliferation of ubiquitous computing seeping into every corner of our everyday lives, challenges existing perceptions of human subjectivity and the place of the individual in the world. Occasionally, new revelations – such as the exposure of global surveillance programs by former NSA employee Edward Snowden and, before that, the persistent rumours about the existence of a signals intelligence collection and analysis network by the name of *Echelon* – reveal snippets of the technological capacities available for those who want to find out about the lives of others through state-of-the-art surveillance technologies. However, the response to such revelations seems divided. While some people react strongly and demand political intervention, the reaction of many citizens rather seems to be a shrug, implying that 'when the technology exists, this is to be expected'.[1] In this book, we propose that the widespread, existence and acceptance of the increasingly ubiquitous, and often unnoticed, surveillance technologies in our daily lives is one example of processes of negotiation that take place in contemporary culture on a wider scale: processes that are indicative of changes taking place in the relationship between what is considered visible and what is invisible – between what remains hidden and what comes to the surface – in contemporary culture. The existence of these changing perceptions is

1 <http://www.youtube.com/watch?v=2HWbReAlblI> accessed 17 October 2013.

what we call an ongoing negotiation of (in)visibility in contemporary culture.[2] If we have nothing to hide, it might not be because we do not fear anything, but rather because we believe there is nothing to see. This book develops the idea of what it means that 'there is nothing to see' and sets out to investigate the consequences of the shifting relationship between visibility and invisibility in contemporary culture.

Negotiations of what is visible and invisible, which are the topic of this volume, take place beneath the surface of a culture that seems to share everything openly, for example, in the form of the traces we leave when we use the internet or, more explicitly, through social media. Our claim is, however, that these negotiations are reflected in a wide range of cultural phenomena, from society's hard infrastructures, such as the computer technologies or architectural and spatial structures of public or political institutions, to much more fleeting cultural practices that concern the more mundane level of everyday life – and that they are shaped by complex interactions of technological, spatial, cognitive, cultural, economic, and political factors. The changing (in)visibilities of contemporary culture thus come in many forms and shapes, not all of them explicitly politically inflected, although their impact on the way we live and think is significant. The different contributions to this volume set out to show how they make their mark on the world in which we live at the same time as they are taken up in, reflected by, and processed through cultural products, be these technologies, discourses, or aesthetic forms.

An example of how the changes in question are discussed in contemporary academic discourse can be found in Hal Foster's architectural criticism. In *The Art-Architecture Complex* (2013), Foster argues that recent architectural practice has witnessed a shift in the direction of artistic practice. This entails a movement from architectural modernism's active separation between architecture and art to a merger of the two. This has the notable effect on the discipline, and on the buildings it produces, that architecture

2 This is also the name of the research network, the activities of which have laid the groundwork for the present volume. See <http://ni.ikk.ku.dk/> accessed 17 October 2013.

is becoming more and more characterised by the use of two-dimensional images, a surface-orientation that tends towards superficiality of signification and spectacle. At the same time, however, simultaneous changes in architectural practice, what Foster calls the emergence of 'a global style', have considerable effects on the kinds of cultural environments produced according to this measure. The surface-orientedness of the global style is dominated by flat, repetitive imagery of sleek surfaces in large-scale developments, and the use of glass, steel, and extensive openings into the interiors. This is presented in a way that distracts us from recognising what is in fact a highly developed technologically based architecture, which we may see as involving an intrinsic use of spatial control-mechanisms, introducing new forms of spatial orderings and visual regimes of everyday life. Foster draws parallels between the architecture in question and movements in art, such as minimalism or the pop art of the 1960s, but laments the loss of critical content by which these art movements were originally characterised, given the way contemporary architecture instead merely dwells on the preoccupation with surface and image within these movements. This suggests that we are dealing with an architecture that negotiates traditional notions of visibility and invisibility, surface and depth, in new ways.

Another recent example can be found in *24/7: Late Capitalism and the Ends of Sleep* (2013), in which cultural critic and historian of visual culture, Jonathan Crary, investigates the recent development of an interminable 'non-time' that blurs the separation between an intensified, ubiquitous consumerism and emerging strategies of control and surveillance. This is connected to the emergence of what social scientists have termed 'surveillance society'. New technological possibilities have allowed surveillance technologies, which formerly belonged to the world of intelligence services and covert operations, to permeate our everyday lives. These technologies are in operation for example in the widespread use of CCTV surveillance cameras in both public and private areas. But they can also be found in everyday phenomena such as motion detectors in public toilets, which, in the name of hygiene and energy efficiency, turn the lights on and off, operate the water tap, or flush the toilet. Crary further describes how concomitant effects on individual attentiveness and impairments of perception arise within the compulsory routines of contemporary technological culture, what may be seen as lying beneath everyday life as 'calm technologies'. One aspect of this, according to Crary, is that human sleep, as a restorative withdrawal from the world, is intrinsically incompatible with this '24/7' culture, in which everything is constantly potentially visible. Crary presents a variety of examples that point to changes in the way in which the categories of the visible and the invisible are at work in, and are potentially changing, the contemporary cultural imagination.

This book develops from the understanding that when it comes to visibility, the process of seeing and being seen is not something that merely takes place between an observer and the observed. It is an exchange conditioned by a physical and social setting, one that creates certain possibilities for visibility and visuality, and excludes others. This makes the cultural framework, in which questions surrounding visibility and invisibility are embedded, significant. A central thesis joining the different chapters of this book is thus the idea that changes in the relationship between what is considered visible and what is considered to be hidden can currently be observed in several areas of contemporary culture. The aim of the book is to trace these changes, and to investigate the cultural significance of how they are expressed in different cultural fields, such as the architectural fabric of cities, new technologies, everyday life situations and the aesthetic, in both literature and visual culture.

This book thus brings together questions that are currently being investigated separately in different corners of the academic landscape. By combining a variety of disciplinary viewpoints, we aim to broaden our understanding of the way in which processes of seeing, being seen and hiding from view are negotiated in contemporary culture and cultural imagination. The individual chapters contain enquiries into these themes and interpretations of their related cultural negotiations in technology, art and architecture, from the points of view of architectural history and theory, art, film and literature, philosophy, cultural theory and contemporary anthropology. Rather than reflecting these disciplinary groupings in the structure of this book, we have arranged the contributions in four thematic clusters: 'Transparency, Refraction and Opacity', 'Urban Topography, Void and Display', 'Surfaces, Secrets and Interior Spaces', and 'Screens, Cameras and Surveillance'. In what follows we shall outline the significance of the book's four parts and of the foci of the individual chapters.

Transparency, Refraction and Opacity

When exploring changes in what is considered visible and invisible in contemporary culture, the faculty of sight, in relation to the material structures of the built environment that facilitate vision and suggest transparency, is an obvious place to start. Two central materials in this context are the glass window and the mirror – these are objects which, apart from enhancing vision, may also give rise to optic phenomena of refraction and opacity.

In his essay 'Glass Glimpsed: In, On, Through and Beyond' English literature scholar Charles Lock takes us on a journey through the literary history of glass, in the form of windows and mirrors respectively. His chapter traces developments in the concrete ways in which glass has been used as the techniques to mould it have become refined, alongside the changing literary connotations of glass that these developments have provoked. His chapter thus teases out the many different connotations of glass as a motif that mediates different spaces, temperatures, and times, oscillating between mirror and window, transparency and reflection, metaphor and metonymy, from St Paul to Vladimir Nabokov.

In 'Mirroring the Invisible', art historian Slavko Kacunko takes us from literature into the realm of art, architecture and science, and explores the cultural history of glass – and in particular the mirror – as medium and material. Rather than discussing the mirror as a motif, he focuses on the science of its materiality, as well as its qualities as a medium. Through a series of examples of modern architecture, Kacunko places the mirror in a contemporary media and surveillance culture as part of the cultural production of invisibility and opacity that takes place there.

Architectural and art historian Mechtild Widrich's chapter '"I'll Be Your Mirror": Transparency, Voyeurism and Glass Architecture' takes as its starting point the use of glass and mirror effects in two contemporary projects at the intersection of art and architecture: VALIE EXPORT's *Transparent Cube* (2000) and Monica Bonvicini's *Don't Miss a Sec'* (2003/04). Widrich uses her reading of these works to question the relation between transparency and reflection, and the position of subjects and the role of gender in public space. She thus tests the way in which modernist and postmodernist stances on transparency inform the works in question, and points to issues of gender, privacy, and control as they are performed in contemporary urban settings, reminding us of the changing relationships between self, other, and the architectural fabric.

In 'Transparency: Effable and Ineffable' architectural historian and theorist Lorens Holm takes the discussion of transparency further by revisiting Rowe and Slutsky's seminal text 'Transparency Literal and Phenomenal' (1963). Holm turns to the concepts of 'space' and 'self', using these as a starting point for an exploration of how architecture constructs subjectivity. Reading Rowe and Slutsky against the grain allows for an exploration of the relation between space and subjectivity, and it is in this dynamic that Holm locates the interplay between visibility and invisibility as an interplay between the effable and the ineffable, in and of architecture.

This first part as a whole brings together different interpretive vantage points for exploring the material of glass itself (be it in the form of glass windows or mirrors) as well as its changing aesthetic connotations (in literature, art and architecture) in modern culture. However, these chapters also seek to draw attention to the implications of this for the viewer's engagement with that material. This raises fundamental questions with regard to our understanding of subjectivity; its historical roots in modernity as much as the changes it seems to undergo in the present suggest that subjectivity appears in a culturally constituted, and instituted, relational structure. Apart from this common orientation, these chapters lay out the scope and aims of the volume as a whole by touching upon central keywords that will be picked up and explored further in the three parts to follow, such as urbanity, transparency, surface, screens, secrets, surveillance and display.

Urban Topography, Void and Display

This part takes us from a concern with visibility as connected to the material of glass to the configuration of visibility within specific architectural settings, a configuration that can take different forms and shapes depending on the urban topography and history in which it is embedded.

In 'Mendelsohn and Libeskind: A Hidden History', art historian Bernd Nicolai discusses Berlin as a place where we must decode and re-contextualise the visible, and, in particular, the invisible, in order to gain awareness of the city's past. He discusses spatiality and memory, arguing that memory can be approached metaphorically through absence and emptiness and architectonically through voids as non-spaces that stand away from time and commercialisation, yielding numerous ways of perception ranging from delight to horror. Nicolai approaches his subject through a comparative reading of two projects in the city by the architects Erich Mendelsohn (1887–1952) and Daniel Libeskind (1946–).

In 'Urban Bottles and Green Glass: Display and Transparencies in Post-Industrial Tuborg', urban scholar Henrik Reeh explores the transformation of post-industrial sites in contemporary cities by focusing on the development of a former brewery site north of Copenhagen. The area was previously an industrial site, but has since the 1990s given way to a new urban and suburban topography consisting of corporate headquarters, upscale housing blocks and a marina. Reeh argues that the transition we see here implies a redefinition of display and transparency that can be identified as a negotiation of visibilities on the urban scale as well as on the surface of buildings.

Anthropologist Mark Vacher looks at another derelict post-industrial site that has gained a new function in his chapter 'Spaces of Difference, Different Spaces: A Study of Urban Transformations at Play in an Old Paint Factory'. By coupling the example of the urban reconfiguration of an old paint factory into a centre for cultural events with Henri Lefebvre's approach to space as a product of human conception, perception and bodily activity, Vacher shows how different notions of space and invisibility have succeeded each other at this particular site. This space has been transformed from a factory to a 'void' site, and has now become a cultural and artistic centre. The space, and Vacher's analysis of it, bring together the historical situatedness of space so important to Nicolai with the interest in a transformation of spaces, which Reeh investigates in Chapter 6. As such, it also points to current changes in memory culture as engraved in and made visible through what are in effect defunct sites in the built environment of the contemporary city.

This is precisely the starting point for Germanist Dora Osborne's chapter 'Negotiating (In)Visibilities in German Memory Culture'. Osborne investigates how the memorial in contemporary culture works through an oscillation between visibility and invisibility. By focusing on the two-part installation *The Missing House* and *The Museum* by artist Christian Boltanski, as well as on the project *Stolpersteine* which artist Gunter Demnig initiated in a number of German cities, she points to the archive as a central trope for a contemporary memory culture that works in the space between private and public, visibility and obscurity, presence and void, remembering and forgetting.

Surfaces, Secrets and Interior Spaces

The third part of this book approaches the issue of visibility and invisibility with regard to the relation between an inside and an outside. In different ways, these chapters both capture and unsettle the surprisingly fragile boundaries separating buildings – here private homes and prisons – from the outside world. By investigating the underlying mechanisms of cultural phenomena such as art and architecture, we may enquire into how these boundaries are both formulated in and challenged by the way in which contemporary culture pictures itself.

In her chapter 'Surface Encounters: On Being Centred, Decentred and Recentred by the Works of Do-Ho Suh', architectural historian and art critic Jane Rendell gives an example of what she calls 'site-writing'. This practice is based on the view that criticism involves a double movement between inside and outside, insofar as a work may take the critic outside herself, but also may work inwards from the critic's own biography. Rendell's reading of a series of installations by Do-Ho Suh is thus a methodological example of such site-writing which, with a starting point in the work of psychoanalyst Jean Laplanche, focuses on the use of tactile surfaces to simultaneously locate and dislocate the viewer's personal engagement with the artwork and to address issues such as identity, duplication, replicas and home.

Duplicate homes, scale models, replicas and identity-formation are also at issue for architecture scholar Claus Bech-Danielsen, who in 'The Secret

Suburb: Second Lives in Second Homes' looks at the perceived forms of the secret lives led both in and by Danish summer houses. While these houses are curiously similar to the suburban environments in which their inhabitants live their daily lives, the qualities of being out of sight and making the everyday invisible are the main characteristics that summer house owners mention with regard to the lives they live in these homes, thus illuminating different strategies of escape, but also of curious self-deception. This other kind of life involves an absence of modern amenities such as telephones, laundry, internet, street lightning, people, watches, rules, etc. Here, invisibility becomes something to be desired, possibly the more so as digital technology makes this eclipse of the everyday an illusion, insofar as we are just as reachable and traceable in the summerhouse as we are everywhere else.

In 'Cool Critique Versus Hot Spectatorship: Jelinek/Haneke's Voyeur around Vienna, a Return', Germanist Annie Ring shifts the viewpoint from those wanting to hide to those who want to penetrate that which would otherwise be considered private. Ring takes the view of those looking in – focusing on pornography and critical spectatorship – by addressing the engagement with pornography in Elfriede Jelinek's *The Piano Teacher* and in Michael Haneke's film based on the novel. She argues that Jelinek's and Haneke's aim, in their renditions of often violent sex scenes in which humiliation and pleasure are intricately interwoven, is to move their readers and viewers to a reaction that facilitates critical agency.

The question of critical agency in the face of images that involve humiliation and shaming is also the issue in cultural theorist Devika Sharma's chapter 'Visions of Punishment: On Susan Crile's Abu Ghraib Drawings'. Sharma looks at the visual dramatisation of punishment and the publication of shame relating to the Abu Ghraib scandal. Through a reading of the American artist Susan Crile's series of pastel drawings and paintings *Abu Ghraib: Abuse of Power*, Sharma explores the representation of the human body under circumstances where it is treated inhumanely, and where an interplay between surface and invisibility becomes central.

All four of these chapters deal with interior spaces that actively renegotiate the culturally determined understanding of boundaries between surface and interior. In each of them, we thus find responses to what it means to be looking in, and to being looked in on, in what might otherwise be considered realms of secrecy, remoteness and covertness. Looking *in* can be experienced with critical awareness or immersed pleasure, while being looked *at* may cause a whole spectrum of emotions: the desire to escape, enjoyment of the lingering gaze, or crumbling in shame.

Screens, Cameras and Surveillance

The final part raises questions regarding surveillance and its media implications. It contains a movement from fundamental questions of what is seen and how one sees to the technological and architectural ways in which our attention is being directed and controlled.

In 'To See the World as It Appears: Vision, the Gaze and the Camera as Technological Eye', theologian and surveillance studies scholar Susanne Wigorts Yngvesson explores the faculty of sight in surveilled and non-surveilled situations. Yngvesson turns to Merleau-Ponty's analysis of perception in *The Visible and the Invisible* and combines this with film and surveillance theory in an effort to understand the faculty of vision in a contemporary culture of surveillance. This chapter thus combines the interests of this volume in the fundamental faculty of seeing, the implications of a technological enhancement of this human ability and the cultural consequences it carries for how we see and what is being seen.

Sociologist David Murakami Wood takes the investigation of the technological gaze a step further in 'Vanishing Surveillance: Ghost-Hunting in the Ubiquitous Surveillance Society'. Wood points out that at the same time as we are made increasingly visible in contemporary societies dominated by ubiquitous surveillance technologies, surveillance itself is becoming invisible. He examines four such tendencies of surveillance technologies: to decrease in size, increase in mobility, mimicking other things and to become embedded in the landscape. Wood argues that these tendencies point towards a change in the position of the visual in Western culture, towards a world that is only fully readable and visible to machines.

Cultural theorist Nanna Bonde Thylstrup follows up this idea in her chapter 'The Invisibilities of Internet Censorship'. In parallel to Wood's suggestions about surveillance technologies, Thylstrup begins from the way digital information infrastructures are increasingly pervasive in our lifeworlds at the same time as they also become increasingly invisible. Her chapter identifies the different forms of recent digital censorship, the advent of which, Thylstrup argues, calls for a rethinking of the very concept of censorship. Invisibility in this chapter is thus a question of what comes up on our screens and what remains black-boxed by technology.

Finally, in the last chapter 'Visible in Theory: Perceived Visibility as Symbolic Form – A Photo-Expedition into a Contemporary Urban Environment', we, the editors of this book, attempt to bring together the focus on surveillance, so predominant in this final part, with the observations on glass and glass architecture with which the book opened. From the perspective of a concrete and situated photographic expedition through a recently developed urban area in Copenhagen – not dissimilar to the urban environments discussed in Part II and addressing some of the same issues concerning interior and exterior that can be found in Part III – this chapter maps out the book's central themes while making an argument for what we propose to call 'perceived visibility' as a symbolic form in contemporary culture.

The Emergence of an Interdisciplinary Field

The groundwork for this book was laid by the international research network *Negotiating (In)Visibilities – A Network for Studies on the Seeable and the Hidden of Contemporary Culture*.[3] This network is co-convened by the editors and has received funding from the Danish Council for Independent Research and from the Swiss National Science Foundation to host a series

3 <http://ni.ikk.ku.dk/> accessed 17 October 2013.

of conferences and workshops, part of the outcome of which is this volume. The contributions in this book have thus been shaped by discussions at these meetings, to which the authors of the individual chapters (and in particular we as editors) are very much indebted. At present, membership of the network surpasses one hundred contributors, and the chapters in this book thus represent only a small part of the interests that bring this network together as a both dynamic and heterogeneous group.

One aim of the network has been the inclusion of non-academic methodologies. The conferences and workshops have been accompanied by a film screening, art exhibition, literary salon and excursions to specific localities where the negotiations of (in)visibility that interests us could be experienced physically. The aim of this approach was to cut across academic specialisations and divides as well as to bring into play other forms of knowledge production than those belonging to traditional disciplines. This book also reflects that multiplicity of perspectives. While the sixteen contributions outlined above provide different inroads into academic discussions of the changing relations between the visible and the invisible in contemporary culture, one slightly different contribution, which makes an equally valuable contribution to this volume, is included in the book: that of the social-artistic group zURBS.

The aim of Zurich-based artist group zURBS is to make people look at and re-think their city in new ways 'by researching, re-viewing and reacting to city life through a social-artistic performative approach that provides new perspectives on the urban debate'.[4] Their contribution to this volume can be found not only in the picture on the front cover, but also on the four double spreads that are placed at the beginning of each of the book's four Parts. These double spreads consist of visual compositions that combine photographs of urban environments, quotations from Italo Calvino's seminal work *Invisible Cities*, solid typeset theorizing statements, large block letters shouting questions to the reader, as well as fragile pencil drawings that weave in and out of these other elements. These different components offer a statement and a very literal illustration of how the

4 <http://www.zURBS.org/> accessed 17 October 2013.

negotiations that take place between what is visible and what is invisible can be captured in a way that both is reliant on and suggests a reluctance to adopt academic discourse. Their contribution is thus an important and intrinsic part of the book's mapping of an interdisciplinary field of inquiry that we propose to call 'Invisibility Studies'. Such an area of study would bring together the many academic and non-academic aims, methodologies, and approaches currently dealing with negotiations of what is considered visible and what remains invisible in contemporary culture. We hope with this book to have set out some pointers for further research into the current changes in this relationship.

PART I

Transparency, Refraction and Opacity

zURBS
Prelude I

Valdrada's inhabitants know that each of their actions is, at once, that action and its mirror image, which possesses the special dignity of images, and this awareness prevents them from forgetfulness.

—ITALO CALVINO, *Invisible Cities*

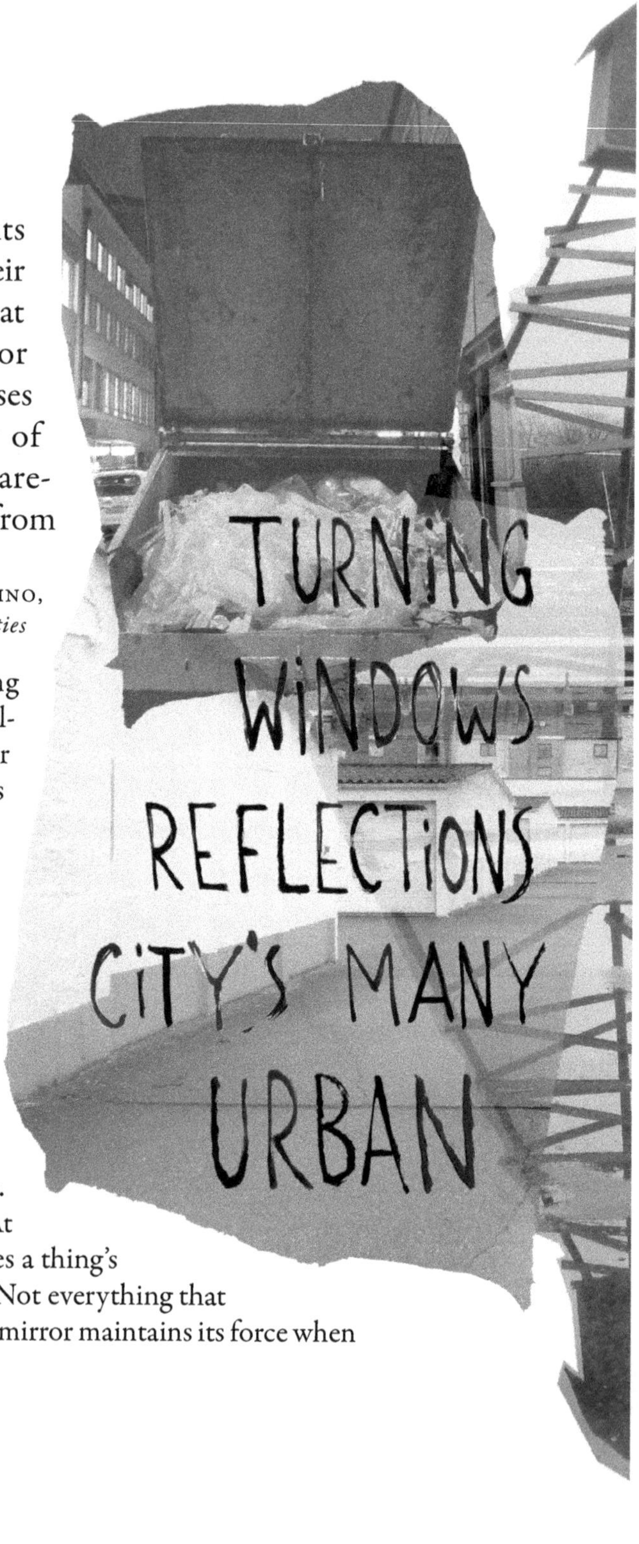

There is no such thing as one given urban reality. The countless mirror images and reflections enveloping us in our day-to-day lives remind us of that: what we perceive as reality can be multiplied in several different forms an exponential amount of times. We could say that the mirror doesn't only reflect the world, it also changes it. As Calvino points out: 'At times the mirror increases a thing's value, at times denies it. Not everything that seems valuable above the mirror maintains its force when mirrored.'

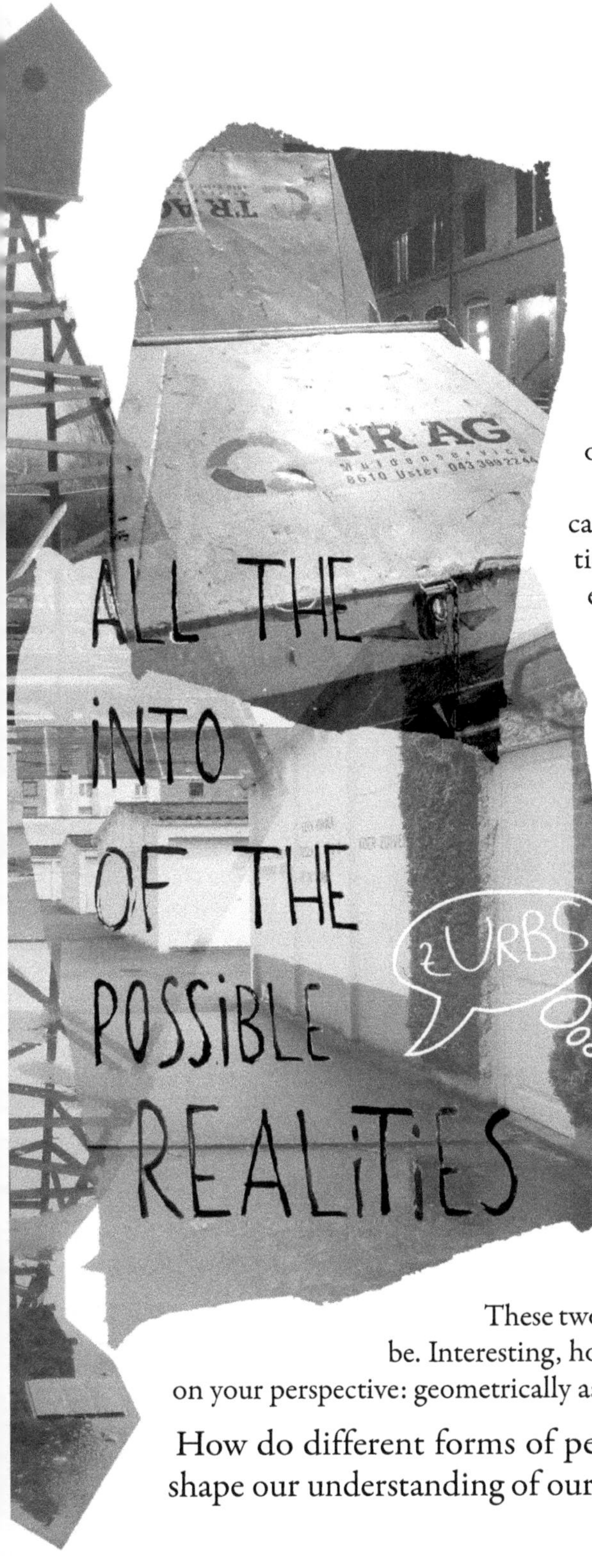

Thus, the mirror not only reflects reality in terms of replicating it in a mirror image, it also helps us *reflect upon* reality, by offering a sensory and critical interpretation that makes us question and further understand our environment.

Mirroring space, then, can reflect many possible realities and provide many different perspectives on the city: mirrors with reflections that make enemies become friends, subversive mirrors with reflections that make left become right, and right become left. Mirrors turning all the windows in a city into reflections of its many possible urban realities, dreams and futures. The person looking out through these windows expects that what he sees is reality. The person looking at the mirroring window questions what reality she is currently looking at. These two visions are as different as can be. Interesting, how reflection always depends on your perspective: geometrically as well as philosophically.

How do different forms of perception and reflection shape our understanding of our environment?

CHARLES LOCK

1 Glass Glimpsed: In, On, Through and Beyond

—in memory of Linda Munk

Inserted in a wall, a sheet of glass brings together two spaces, inside and outside; or, silver-backed and itself acting as a wall, glass creates an illusion of two spaces, both of them inside. Like a wall, glass blocks physical access between one space and another; it prevents touching and smelling, and to some degree inhibits hearing and heating. But unlike other materials used in a wall, glass admits visual exchange. One can see through glass, though one cannot walk through it, nor reach through it. This may seem the merest platitude, yet glass was not always thus: its transparency is of recent date. The mirrored space is inhabited by the body that looks. By the mid-nineteenth century, the quality of both the glass and the reflecting surface was sufficiently refined for one to see an entire world in a mirror, a reverse image of our own, a 'looking-glass world' as in Lewis Carroll's *Through the Looking-Glass* of 1871.[1]

A Metaphysics of Glass

Two thousand years ago neither the glass nor its backing were of such reflective power or optical scope. Thus the mirror could be invoked by St Paul, not as affording access to a parallel universe, but as illustrating the

1 See Isobel Armstrong, *Victorian Glassworlds: Glass Culture and the Imagination 1830–1880* (Oxford UP, 2008); Mark Prendergast, *Mirror/Mirror: A History of the Human Love Affair with Reflection* (New York: Basic Books, 2003), 247–49.

impairment of our vision of the Divine: 'For now we see through a glass, darkly.'[2] The Greek phrase suggests that a mirror would offer only a defective and inadequate resemblance of what it reflects.[3] There is no reference in Paul's Greek to *glass* as a substance; Paul's *esoptron* would have been an unglazed metal sheet. The adverbial phrase *en ainigmati* is rendered in the Authorised Version as *darkly*, an 'enigma' implying not only a riddle but also an analogy: not a clear one, but a weak or obscure analogy whose import has to be inferred. That a mirror gives a poor image is conveyed in the English of the Authorised Version not only by the adverb *darkly* but by the comma that precedes it: *, darkly*. This does some of the work of a non-restrictive clause: 'a mirror, in which one sees no better than darkly'. The comma adds a delicate touch of syntactical resistance to match the optical opacity.

Yet an enigma remains, even *on* the surface: when we look *at* a mirror, are we looking *in* it or *through* it? This is a perpetual riddle, for depending on the degree and proportion of light on either of its sides, we can see *through* glass, or *in* it, or even *on* it. The sequel to *Alice in Wonderland* is entitled *Through the Looking-Glass*, without 'Alice'; the absence of a subject makes for a better play on the idiomatic sense of *through*: our eyes seem to go through the glass and see objects and our own faces beyond, though we who are looking cannot ourselves pass through: the self as object is there, though I as subject remain here. Alice as subject passes through, though this is not learnt until the reader has passed through a comma: *Through the Looking-Glass, and What Alice Found There.*

St Paul presents us with a further enigma: 'For now we see through a glass, darkly; but then face to face: now I know in part; but then shall I know even as also I am known.' The face that we can barely discern in the mirror must be our own, but whose face is this that we shall meet face to face? For 'face-to-face' indicates two persons.[4] Even in the best of mirrors

2 Bible (Authorised Version), I Corinthians 13:12: βλεπομεν γαρ αρτι δι εσοπτρου εν αινιγματι (*blepomen gar arti di esoptrou en ainigmati*).

3 For the sense and etymology of Paul's words I rely on Strong's Concordance of the Bible, first published in 1890, whose latest version is available online.

4 I Corinthians 13:12: *πρόσωπον πρὸς πρόσωπον (prosopon pros prosopon).*

I do not think of meeting myself face to face. Nor do I see 'eye-to-eye' with myself in the mirror. If we are to recognise ourselves even in the least effective mirror, it must be by eyes and face. Paul's sense depends on the obscurity of what a mirror shows: a clear glass would not so tease the vision. The logic of the verse is that of an analogical chiasmus in which only the first and fourth terms are stated: 1) now, we can see our own faces only obscurely, 2) just as we can know God only indirectly; 3) then, however, we shall be able to see our own faces clearly, 4) just as we shall then see God face to face. The final analogy depends – crucially and chiastically – on the mirror becoming a window: *glass* is a most apt translation for the transformation thus enacted: from my own face seen in a mirror to the Divine Face seen 'through a glass'.

Both enigma and chiasmus may be said to characterise the mirror. The spatial inversion of reflected positions can be mapped as chiasmus, and it is an enigma as to whether what we see in a mirror is *on* its surface, or *through* it, or *in* its own depth of space, or even *beyond*. And there is a third characteristic: neither depth nor surface has any power of retaining or recording the image. It is indeed a property of the enigma that the reflected image must be fleeting and impermanent, for whether surface or depth, both or neither, there is no *where* for its retaining. This is recognised elsewhere in the New Testament: 'For if any be a hearer of the word, and not a doer, he is like unto a man beholding his natural face in a glass: For he beholdeth himself, and goeth his way, and straightway forgetteth what manner of man he was'.[5] These three properties of mirrors – the enigmatic, the chiasmatic, the transience of its image – can be traced through literature in a dialectic of optical thinking and specular technology. The fascinations of the mirror may be presented on the axes of metaphor and metonymy, as may the lesser fascinations of the window, whose very name enacts a diachronic contradiction: the window was first designated as an opening in a wall – 'the wind's eye' – to let in the air. Subsequently filled with glass, it lets in light but excludes the wind; by a further refinement windows can be opened and closed at will. We thus confront an enigma of glass as

5 Epistle of James, 1, 23–24.

either mirror or window; both work by likeness, whether of the object or of the subject: either we see our own likeness reflected in the mirror, or through the window we see objects in the outside world refracted in such a way that they retain their likenesses. The myth of Narcissus plays on the possibility of the subject reflected being mistaken for an object refracted; significantly, it was not in any dark glass such as was known to St Paul, but only through a reflection in still water, that the ancient world could experience such a powerful and convincing illusion.

The enigma of the mirror itself is that of the difference between depth and surface: is the location of the objects we see, including ourselves, on or beyond the surface? Chiasmus with left-right reversal figures the relations between the space of the viewer and the space depicted. The transience of the image insists on the metonymy of viewing: only proximity yields likeness, and only by metonymy can this metaphor be produced. There is no lasting likeness, no likeness that endures beyond its moment, or in the absence of its prototype.[6] Lewis Carroll invites us to speculate as to which then would be the prototype, and which the type, which the original and which the image. Does a person cast a shadow, or is it the shadow that makes the man? The one cannot be conceived without the other, and thus the question of priority is suspended, rendered enigmatic. Just as the man straightway forgetteth his own likeness, so the mirror – though it retains Alice – straightway forgetteth the man. A photograph of myself always shows me as I was when young, or at least younger even by moments than I am now; a mirror never flatters, for it keeps no memory of how you were, but insists on displaying you exactly as you are.[7]

6 See, however, Gottfried Keller's novel *Der grüne Heinrich* (1855) in which the hero explains an optical anomaly of visionary force: 'Since then I have been told that copper-plate engravings or drawings which have lain undisturbed for a great many years behind a glass communicate themselves to the glass during those years … and leave behind upon it something like a reflected image.' Cited by W. G. Sebald, *A Place in the Country*, trans. Jo Catling (London: Hamish Hamilton, 2013), 106.

7 See Thomas Hardy, 'I look into my glass, And view my wasting skin ….' [1898]; no. 52 in J. Gibson ed., Thomas Hardy, *Complete Poems: Variorum Edition* (London: Macmillan, 1979), 81.

For poetry, windows seem less interesting than mirrors, in that they merely refract an external metonymic object. As the technology of glass develops, the degree of refraction is minimal, and the interference of the glass is barely registered. Yet every window is a potential mirror; when at dusk and before the drawing-down of blinds we turn on the light, what we see in the window is suddenly transformed from the world outside into our interior space, reflected. A mirror can never be a window onto a world that differs from what it reflects, though it is always teasing us into spatial depths. Yet a window can always become a mirror, or serve as one: refraction turns to reflection; the metonymy of outside yields to the metaphor of within.[8]

In 1611, the mirror of St Paul was translated as 'glass'. Mirrors by then were glazed, though the glass tended to be curved or bubbled, not for humorous or archaic effect, but because this was the best that technology offered: like *esoptrou* 'glass' could still serve as a type of obscurity and distortion. Plate-glass was invented in the late seventeenth century, though its use was restricted to wealthy residences; in the nineteenth century, bow-windows and bay-windows made 'looking out' a common pastime of those at home, and such windows came to characterise the domestic architecture of the urban middle classes. The first-floor bow-window over a high street or an esplanade is a place for informal surveillance (or a form of class-surveillance, by which the middle-classes could observe the working-classes off-duty, even at leisure), and thus also a rich source of gossip. Modern shopping, with its window-displays and arcades, could not have developed without glass at once adequate to the imperatives of display and secure against vandalism and the weather. Until the second half of the nineteenth century clear glass remained a rarity; only with sheet-glass and its mass-production in the first years of the twentieth century did domestic windows become normatively transparent. The usual purpose of a window in earlier times was not for those within to look out, but for that within to be illuminated. Windows for such a purpose are still to be found above

8 See Charles Lock, 'Debts and Displacements: On Metaphor and Metonymy', *Acta Linguistica Hafniensia* 29 (1997), 321–37.

doorways, leading puzzled children to ask why a window should be placed too high up for anyone to look through. That these features are known as 'transom lights' or 'fanlights' is indicative of their purpose: exclusively to give light to the interior, not, as is normal these days, to provide visual access to the exterior.

A Poetics of Glass

Descartes transformed the science of optics with his *Dioptrique* in 1637. In 1633, George Herbert, alluding to St Paul, takes up the enigma of glass:

> A man that looks on glass,
> On it may stay his eye;
> Or if he pleaseth, through it pass,
> And then the heav'n espy.[9]

The poet appears to be at one with his eye: both can pass through the glass, and the very rhyme of *pass* and *glass* says much for the freedom of optic rays. And yet clearly 'a man' cannot pass through glass any more than he can pass through the eye of a needle – the etymology of *eye* refers to an opening, an aperture, as a window is the 'wind's eye' – or pass through earth to heaven, as Gertrude phrases it to Hamlet: 'All that lives must die, Passing through nature to eternity.'[10] The passage through nature cannot be forced, unless by the self-slaughter that church and society alike condemn. Yet without giving passage out of nature, glass can offer us a glimpse of eternity by the sheer marvel of its translucency, even though it is still far from what we would reckon adequately transparent. Heaven is what one can imagine or conceive, and is that to which one can and ought to aspire; in Herbert's figure, to see through the glass is thus analogous to seeing, not the world

9 George Herbert 'The Elixir' [1633].

10 Shakespeare, *Hamlet*, Act I, scene ii.

outside, but the heaven beyond. Our mortal condition, bound in flesh yet capable of heaven, is figured by the limiting power of glass: through the best glass we can see what we can neither touch nor reach. Glass is thus figured as a type of the enigma of the imagination and its negotiations with reality: opening on to limitless possibilities, it yet shuts the body out (to keep it with the living).[11]

One of the exemplary stories of the Romantic imagination opens with Jane Eyre's distress that 'There was no possibility of taking a walk that day.' Curbed and confined by the weather, Jane finds solace, an 'outlet' for her imagination, in reading, yet first she makes her protest, and is thus rebuked: 'Jane, I don't like cavillers or questioners; besides, there is something truly forbidding in a child taking up her elders in that manner. Be seated somewhere; and until you can speak pleasantly, remain silent.' Immediately we are introduced to a scene of reading newly shaped and conditioned by the latest technology in glass:

> A breakfast-room adjoined the drawing-room, I slipped in there. It contained a bookcase: I soon possessed myself of a volume, taking care that it should be one stored with pictures. I mounted into the window-seat: gathering up my feet, I sat cross-legged, like a Turk; and, having drawn the red moreen curtain nearly close, I was shrined in double retirement.
>
> Folds of scarlet drapery shut in my view to the right hand; to the left were the clear panes of glass, protecting, but not separating me from the drear November day. At intervals, while turning over the leaves of my book, I studied the aspect of that winter afternoon. Afar, it offered a pale blank of mist and cloud; near a scene of wet lawn and storm-beat shrub, with ceaseless rain sweeping away wildly before a long and lamentable blast.[12]

Jane finds security behind the curtain, through which nobody can see yet anybody could pass, while enjoying the weather on the other side of the 'clear panes of glass': plate-glass, we assume. Reading a book with illustrations of

11 Sometimes we do try to walk through glass, not out of hubris but through optical error. Such accidents are a consequence of 'non-reflective' coated glass; see note 20.

12 Charlotte Brontë, *Jane Eyre* [1847], Chapter One.

the Polar regions, Jane strengthens her imagination of its setting by looking through the window. The outside world, denied her by the authorities on account of the weather, is now available to her as a spectacle.

'Protecting, but not separating': this is the peculiar and special function of glass. If from a metaphysical perspective glass might be figured as allowing optical passage while acting as a barrier against death and what lies beyond, from a Romantic perspective glass protects us from the temptations of the imagination while enabling its optical indulgence. Jane is kept by glass from the consequences of her imagination and its elemental longings.

A Climatics of Glass

The opening of *Jane Eyre* affords a memorable instance of glass as separator of climates: Jane reads in comfort while the storm rages. Such a division of climes was first devised without concern for optics, but specifically for horticultural reasons. The glass in a glass-house (or a greenhouse) serves the older architectural purpose of glass: not to be looked through, but to let light in. The window extends to every side and aspect so that a building is all window, a vitrine on an architectural scale. However efficient it might be at letting light in, the glass is not meant to be looked through. A glass-house has no interior view-point, nor is it necessary that anyone outside should be able to see in. The significant difference between inside and outside is not optical at all; it inheres only in the temperature.

In distinguishing disparities of heat from disparities of light, we discover yet another remarkable property of glass. It can do more than mediate between two spaces; it can also mediate between two times. Time, that is, in the sense implied by temperature, and indicated by zones. Inside a glass-house one can be amidst summer foliage while outside all is winter: hence the winter garden. Outside is where we live, while inside is an exotic place, with palm-trees and other signs of a world elsewhere. The palm-house is a development of the 1840s, and belongs to the railway age. Their botanical interest aside, palm trees, when full-grown, show off impressively the architectural possibilities of iron girders: the Crystal Palace itself began as a horticultural device. In Roman times there were glass-houses for rearing cucumbers; the *orangerie* was designed to nurture the fruit in France, slightly to the north of the orange's natural clime. Improvements in glass and in the heat-preserving technologies of sealing a glassed-in space made possible a significant contrast in temperature between inside and outside. No longer was the greenhouse merely a prosthetic device for gardeners seeking to extend the growing season, or to cultivate plants slightly outside their latitudinal or climatic range: now the greenhouse could enclose a space utterly alien from what surrounded it, in a time quite different from its own.

An early articulation of the distinction of climes is to be found in William Cowper's *Task* of 1785:

> Who loves a garden, loves a green-house too.
> Unconscious of a less propitious clime
> There blooms exotic beauty, warm and snug,
> While the winds whistle and the snows descend.
> The spiry myrtle with unwith'ring leaf
> Shines there and flourishes. The golden boast
> Of Portugal and western India there,
> The ruddier orange and the paler lime
> Peep through their polish'd foliage at the storm,
> And seem to smile at what they need not fear.[13]

Glass thus separates zones, and affords spectacular contrasts between the winds whistling without and the exotic beauty warm and snug within. Beyond the contrast between inside and outside that Jane Eyre enjoys, there is a peculiar negation at work here. These exotic plants are unaware of their own displacement; they are 'Unconscious of a less propitious clime' than that to which they have been horticulturally accustomed. By contrast, the poet is fully aware of the work performed by glass in yielding the most striking metaphors and metonymics: 'The ruddier orange and the paler lime / Peep through their polish'd foliage at the storm'. Perception is ascribed

13 William Cowper, *The Task* [1785], Book III: lines 566–75 (London: Scolar Press Facsimile, 1973), 120.

to the fruits, which peep, curious but cautious, at the world outside their own clime, 'And seem to smile at what they need not fear.'

They peep, for many flowers have 'eyes', and are named for them, though they merely 'seem' to smile. This is a significant moment, for it turns the glass, whose purpose is only to admit and retain the sun's warmth, into a window for the pleasurable looking out of those within: that is, the plants themselves. And their putative pleasure is not unlike Jane Eyre's some sixty years later: the fruits 'know' that they are protected even while they are in contiguity with the storm. Yet we must ask what sort of contiguity this is: what here is the work of metonymy? Clearly the flowers are not like Jane, whose physical contiguity is mediated by optics, and whose sense of the difference between inside and out is understood in terms of the imagination: the fervour of the imagination means that the Polar regions are to her 'warmer' than the coldness of those on the other side of the curtain. By contrast, the flowers are peeping at an impossible world, contiguous to, but absolutely not continuous with their own. To call flowers 'unconscious' is to assume that consciousness is normative; these plants are both granted and denied the consciousness usually accorded to those within, looking out.

Familiar as such contrasting contiguities may be today in any atrium or mall in northern climes, what Cowper identified was a striking challenge to the work of metonymy. Temperature goes by degrees and gradually, and so must its metonymies: whatever is next to something must be of similar temperature, the difference measured by degrees. Yet since the late eighteenth century, this need no longer be the case, and that fundamental spatio-temporal disruption is the work of glass. Where there is a metonymic anomaly, there is also one in metaphor. The flowers in an orangery or conservatory are hardly different from those in the garden; probably not different at all, though blooming earlier or lasting longer. Cowper, however, is disturbed in a new fashion, by the contiguity of plants that simply cannot be grown in one clime. The British Empire may have been granted, in Kipling's phrase, 'dominion over palm and pine,' but that does not license a palm to look at a pine, nor the reverse. Yet it is precisely through Empire and its exigencies that palm and pine were first brought together in the glass-houses of Kew, where the Royal Botanic Gardens were established in 1759.[14] Allen Paterson, a contemporary historian of Kew, celebrates a visit in winter:

> To go into any of the great glasshouses ... can be an unnerving and disorienting experience. There is that same sudden waft of humid and almost textural air that greets anyone descending from a plane at the start of a tropical holiday. Open the Palm House door and spectacles steam up and at once the hats, coats and gloves so necessary a minute ago ... need to be thrown off.[15]

That Cowper's flowers are 'peeping' suggests their own sense of impropriety, a disruption in the order of things, something unnerving and disorienting, perhaps a little shameful or even illicit.

Windows as Mirrors

Divergent climes can be unnerving, as can divergent degrees of luminosity. Both are achieved and realised by glass. It is unnerving when, out in the dark, we happen to see through a window into a lit interior, and to observe people who are quite unaware of our attention. We who are outside must surely avert our gaze and move on. Such an inhibiting sense of impropriety seldom occurs when we are looking out through a window, for open spaces are subject to observation. But to look in through a window is to invade another's privacy. The window has become an unintended two-way mirror, and we, unwitting Peeping Toms. Looking into lit houses was hardly possible before the nearly synchronised installation of electric lighting and plate-glass. Candle and gaslight offer only a restricted area and degree of luminosity, as Gerard Manley Hopkins acknowledges in 'The Candle Indoors', a sonnet from 1879. 'Some candle clear burns somewhere I come

14 See Richard Drayton, *Nature's Government: Science, British Imperialism and the Improvement of the World* (New Haven, CT: Yale University Press, 2000).

15 Allan Paterson, *The Gardens at Kew* (London: Francis Lincoln, 2008), 47.

by', the poet writes, though it shows nothing, merely setting him to muse: 'By that window what task what fingers ply/I plod wondering'.[16]

Electric lighting entered into widespread use, domestically, between the two World Wars. During the Second World War there was need for a black-out in Britain, not only because of the aerial bombardment of civilians (which Londoners had first experienced in 1916) but because by 1939 the houses of the general population were brightly lit. Two English poems from the decade after 1914 exemplify the sense of something new in the work of the eyes, and of something vulnerable in the lives of those comfortably at home. The last poem Edward Thomas wrote, 'Out in the Dark', turns on the technology of the light-switch, by whose almost silent click darkness can be eliminated, or produced. When the light is turned on the window goes black; the outdoors can no longer be seen. This transformation in an instant from seeing to being reflected is a challenge to metonymy matching that of the Palm House: light, like temperature, had hitherto worked exclusively and strictly by gradation. While a candle can be lit in a moment, it is lit from a lesser flame and its light does not eliminate the darkness but merely pushes it to a certain distance. By contrast, an electric light fills the room, and expels the darkness. While the electric light is on, whatever is outside is invisible, hidden behind the window's reflection of the interior. This gives rise to a new sort of apprehension, of what is not visible out there, while all's visible within:

> Out in the dark over the snow
> The fallow fawns invisible go
> With the fallow doe;
> And the winds blow
> Fast as the stars are slow.
>
> Stealthily the dark haunts round
> And, when the lamp goes, without sound
> At a swifter bound

16 Gerard Manley Hopkins, 'The Candle Indoors' [1879], in N. H. MacKenzie, ed., *The Poetical Works of Gerard Manley Hopkins* (Oxford: Clarendon Press, 1990), 158 (no. 133).

Than the swiftest hound,
Arrives, and all else is drowned;

And star and I and wind and deer
Are in the dark together, – near,
Yet far, – and fear
Drums on my ear
In that sage company drear.

How weak and little is the light,
All the universe of sight,
Love and delight,
Before the might,
If you love it not, of night.[17]

The sense of anxiety and speed is achieved by separating subject from verb, 'the dark' from 'Arrives,' by four lines and seventeen words. The deer had been invisible, and thus could be only imagined or supposed; now that the light is out and the dark has arrived inside the house, all are in the dark together, no longer in any significant way separated by the window. The poet does not say that he can now see the deer, for that is not the point; rather, he is no longer worried about them seeing him, for now they are all together, sharing one darkness that glass does not divide.

'Out in the Dark' was first published one year after Edward Thomas's death on the Western Front in 1917. In 1922 it was echoed by an older poet, Thomas Hardy, whose concern is not with the sublime antithesis between light and dark, but with the personification of animals. As Cowper to the flowers, Hardy ascribes an ambivalent sort of peeping to 'The Fallow Deer at the Lonely House':

One without looks in to-night
Through the curtain-chink
From the sheet of glistening white;
One without looks in to-night
As we sit and think
By the fender-brink.

17 Edward Thomas, 'Out in the Dark' [1918], in Edna Longley, ed., *Poems and Last Poems* (London: Collins, 1973), 134–35.

We do not discern those eyes
Watching in the snow;
Lit by lamps of rosy dyes
We do not discern those eyes
Wondering, aglow,
Four-footed, tiptoe.[18]

A new source of apprehension has arrived with electric lighting, a sense that, in the latest comforts of home, we have lost some control over who looks at us. We are lit up in our houses as though on stage, flood-lit for spectators outside. It's an apprehension rather than a fear, beautifully sensed by both these poets when they ascribe 'looking' not to criminals or spies or voyeurs, but to the most vulnerable and timid of wild animals. The curtain-chink had never mattered before electric lighting; now one can become rather obsessive about making sure that no light shows, whether to observe the rules of the black-out or simply to protect one's privacy.

Snow figures in both poems, or rather it grounds figures: when there's snow we can sometimes see outside even from within a lit room; voyeurs should avoid a 'sheet of glistening white' for it maximises the visibility of the watcher. But in Hardy's poem there's no looking at all; we sit by the fire and think, and we may suppose that what we are thinking about is precisely what we are not looking at, but could, if we looked, see: the snow. Here we are, sitting, lit by lamps whose rosy dyes indicate the effect given by coloured lampshades, and not discerning what we must somehow know to be the case. The eyes that are watching us are indicated by a startlingly cinematic synecdoche: 'Four-footed, tiptoe.'

18 Thomas Hardy 'The Fallow Deer at the Lonely House' [1922], no. 551 in J. Gibson, ed., Thomas Hardy, *Complete Poems: Variorum Edition* (London: Macmillan, 1979), 598. That Hardy knew Thomas's poem – as has long been suspected – is confirmed by a newly published letter from Hardy to Helen Thomas, Edward's widow, dated 2 May 1920, thanking her for a copy of *Last Poems*, of which 'Out in the Dark' is the last poem. See M. Millgate and K. Wilson, eds, *The Collected Letters of Thomas Hardy, Volume Eight, Further Letters 1861–1927* (Oxford: Clarendon Press, 2012), 179.

Both these poems articulate a new concern for the optical vulnerability induced by electric lighting. Neither poem, however, considers the interior reflected in the uncurtained window. When the light is switched on, not only does the outside become invisible, but the window becomes a mirror and the domestic space is at once doubled in size. A man within who looks on such a glass has no choice but to stay his eye. Curtains not only ensure privacy; they also spare us from passing our evenings against a mirror. Glass can either effect metonymies between its two sides or, by staying the eye and denying that it has another side, yield metaphors of reflection. Reflection is necessarily and simultaneously both metaphor and metonymy: the image must be in contiguity with what causes it to be a likeness; the likeness must be in contiguity with what produces it. Reflection is thus irresistible to poets and artists of ludic, enigmatic, or aporetic tendency.

Window and Mirror: The Gradual and the Dual

Few writers have been more ludically disposed than Vladimir Nabokov, who clearly had a good look at these two poems.[19] The 999-line poem 'Pale Fire', with which *Pale Fire* opens, opens thus:

> I was the shadow of the waxwing slain
> By the false azure in the windowpane;
> I was the smudge of ashen fluff – and I
> Lived on, flew on, in the reflected sky.
> And from the inside, too, I'd duplicate
> Myself, my lamp, an apple on a plate:
> Uncurtaining the night, I'd let dark glass
> Hang all the furniture above the grass,
> And how delightful when a fall of snow

19 Nabokov frequently alludes to Hardy's poetry; Edward Thomas had been a close friend of Robert Frost, a type of John Shade in *Pale Fire* [1962].

> Covered my glimpse of lawn and reached up so
> As to make chair and bed exactly stand
> Upon that snow, out in that crystal land!

The bird – a waxwing, suggesting Icarus – does not see the glass of the window, either because it is coated with a non-reflective substance (as developed during the Second World War), or because it reflects all too vividly the sky to which the bird would take its passage. Inspired by Alice's passing through the looking-glass, the bird, not unlike George Herbert, has followed its eye right through the glass and into the heaven it had not actually espied but had confused with its double; the waxwing flies on, though only in the poetic conceit of the false azure in the reflected sky.[20]

Poets have long figured themselves as birds inspired to sing, as skylark, nightingale or thrush, all virtually disembodied; Shelley's skylark is addressed 'Blithe spirit!' By heavy contrast is the embodied poet at home, at his desk and subject to physical frailties. This poet (named Shade) trades in duplication. It is the peculiar property of a poetic song-bird not to be constrained by bodily form, but to carry on through to the other side of glass. On the other hand, or side, the embodied poet finds in glass either an enigmatic limit or a duplicating surface. By 'uncurtaining the night' Shade doubles his interior world so that 'Myself, my lamp, an apple on a plate' are all visible in reflection. This doubling is itself doubled when the snow falls; apart from the reflection of himself and his interior world, he can now also see what lies metonymically beyond the window. And Nabokov (or his Shade) thinks of snow not only as a 'sheet of glistening white'; he reckons it to have a certain depth. With luck such a depth might correspond to the difference in height between the ground outside and the floor within, which would be raised above ground level. This is the difference of a front step or two, a difference which can be plausibly evened out by a New England snowfall. Where the furniture had been hanging above the

20 For a calculation of the number of birds killed annually by flying into windows, generally reckoned at a hundred million in the UK, and up to a billion in the US, see Charlotte McDonald, 'How many birds are killed by windows?' One would like to know more about the history of adhesive stickers of bird silhouettes, and of their efficacy in discouraging birds from flying into glass.

grass, now the snow, as though purposefully, with a design, 'reached up so/As to make chair and bed exactly stand/Upon that snow, out in that crystal land!'

This is the reconciliation of glass, a willed resolution of the enigma: window or mirror? No longer posing for us an optical choice between transparency and reflection, nor a figurative alternative between metaphor and metonymy, glass is now figured in both its aspects (and, note, seen in neither), brightly. Not only is the interior reflected out there, but we see the furniture standing exactly and precisely on the snow. In this consummation of glass we may figure the optical sublime: then shall I see even as also I am seen.

Like a reflected image, the sublime cannot be retained, repeated, or duplicated; it can be recorded but not represented, which is why a representation of the sublime must invoke the loss of what inspired it. 'Retake' is a cinematic term for a form of duplicating, in effort though not in effect. As we have seen, mirrors take no pictorial hostages, not even in the glass of *Pale Fire*, unless elsewise through ekphrasis. The optical sublime can be retaken only as loss, whose rewording may reward us with the poetic sublime:

> Retake the falling snow: each drifting flake
> Shapeless and slow, unsteady and opaque,
> A dull dark white against the day's pale white
> And abstract larches in the neutral light.
> And then the gradual and dual blue
> As night unites the viewer and the view ...[21]

A retake duplicates in time what has here already been duplicated in space. Night unites the viewer and the view, just as 'star and I and wind and deer/ Are in the dark together'. When the light is on and the glass is clear the optical comes into play and, as St Paul well knew, optics do not unite: they divide. To see is to constitute subject and object. The window defines this rule of optics; the mirror defies it. The envelope words, 'the gradual and dual blue' – *dual* lurking within *gradual* – enact what the window does when, the light switched on, it becomes a mirror: 'dual' is *literally* a synecdoche

21 Vladimir Nabokov, *Pale Fire* (New York: Putnam, 1962), Canto One, lines 1–18, 33.

of 'gradual', and thus a lexical metonym. In their senses, however, the two words are sharply contrasted. For *gradual* is the way of contiguity and metonymy, graded, by degrees – the only way for light or temperature to alter, until the modernity of glass – whereas *dual* is the breaking from oneness into two-ness, comparison, rivalry, the way of metaphor.

The enigma of glass may not be entirely resolved by 'Pale Fire', but St Paul would surely admire the attempt: this is seeing through glass to good purpose.

> How weak and little is the light,
> All the universe of sight,
> Love and delight,
> Before the might,
> If you love it not, of night.

To which Nabokov seems to respond by enfolding 'night' within 'unite': 'Night unites the viewer and the view'. What properly unites the viewer and the view is, of course, the last passing through, the final rite of passage. Our thinking about light can be traced back to its divine making: *fiat lux*. In the enigma of glass, figured in poetry, we have seen those optical gradations and divisions which, as metaphor and metonymy, make consciousness possible. And mortal consciousness ends when the viewer is united with the view. Writing twenty-two years after Herbert's 'Elixir' was published, and seventeen years after Descartes' *Dioptrique*, Henry Vaughan in 1655 tells of the telescope ('my perspective') through which he looks at the hill he longs to reach. The world outside is figured as passage to the world beyond, and the hill as life's goal and end. Mist darkens the view; as in St Paul the enigmatic obscurity of the glass suggests, and might even promise, something through there which does not merely correspond to what's here, so Vaughan's telescope brings the unattainable within optic reach:

> Either disperse these mists, which blot and fill
> My perspective (still) as they pass,
> Or else remove me hence unto that hill,
> Where I shall need no glass.

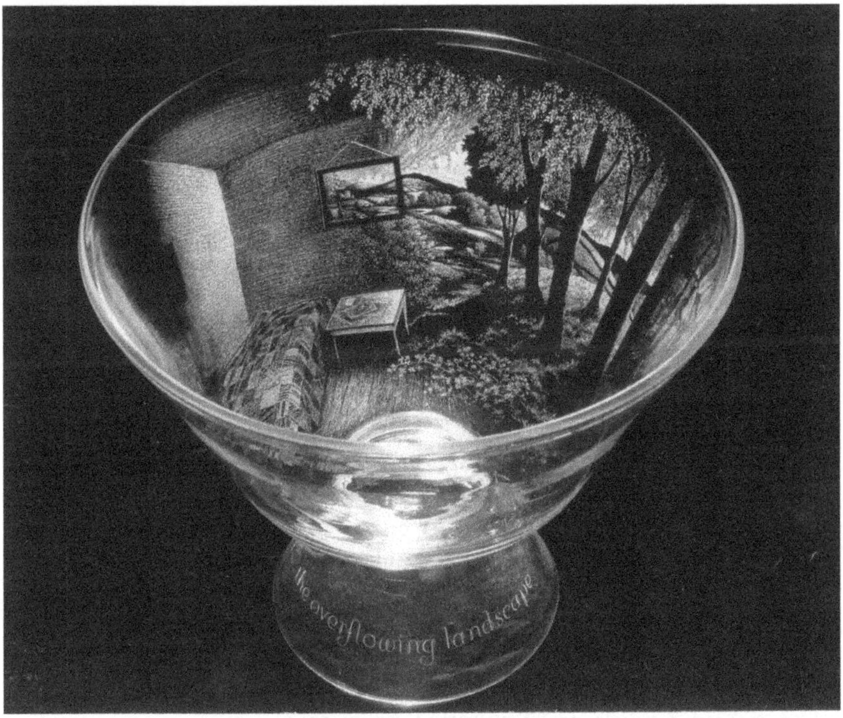

Fig. 1.1: Laurence Whistler, *The Overflowing Landscape* (1974).
Credit: The Estate of Laurence Whistler.

Though not mentioned in this chapter, this engraved glass bowl is chosen as an illustration to its argument; it forms a visual and quasi-tactile analogy to those window-mirrors in poems by Edward Thomas, Thomas Hardy and Vladimir Nabokov. The engraver – Sir Laurence Whistler (1912–2000) – explains: 'To the left, the interior of a country bedroom [...] All this is engraved inside the bowl. But the landscape has flowed out from behind the frame to form scenery [...] This is on the outside of the glass. Tree trunks gather to form the right-hand side of the room, and some of the boughs dip into it (engraved inside the glass – like the brambles extending across the floor).' Laurence Whistler, The Image on the Glass (London: John Murray, 1975), 60 (note to Plate 64).

Bibliography

Armstrong, Isobel, *Victorian Glassworlds: Glass Culture and the Imagination 1830–1880* (Oxford: Oxford University Press, 2008)

Brontë, Charlotte, *Jane Eyre* [1847].

Carroll, Lewis, *Through the Looking-Glass* [1871].

Cowper, William, *The Task* [1785] (London: Scolar Press, 1973).

Drayton, Richard, *Nature's Government: Science, British Imperialism and the Improvement of the World* (New Haven, CT: Yale University Press, 2000).

Hardy, Thomas, *Complete Poems: Variorum Edition*, ed. J. Gibson (London: Macmillan, 1979).

Herbert, George, *The Temple* [1633].

Hopkins, Gerard Manley, *The Poetical Works of Gerard Manley Hopkins*, ed. N. H. MacKenzie (Oxford: Clarendon Press, 1990).

Lock, Charles, 'Debts and Displacements: on Metaphor and Metonymy', *Acta Linguistica Hafniensia* (C. A. Reitzel, Copenhagen: Roman Jakobson special issue), Vol. 29 (1997), 321–37.

McDonald, Charlotte, 'How many birds are killed by windows?' BBC News online, 4 May 2013 <http://www.bbc.co.uk/news/magazine-22395664> accessed 26 May 2013.

Nabokov, Vladimir, *Pale Fire* (New York: Putnam, 1962).

Paterson, Allan, *The Gardens at Kew* (London: Francis Lincoln, 2008).

Prendergast, Mark, *Mirror/Mirror: A History of the Human Love Affair with Reflection* (New York: Basic Books, 2003).

Sebald, W. G., *A Place in the Country*, trans. Jo Catling (London: Hamish Hamilton, 2013).

Shakespeare, William, *Hamlet* [1623].

Strong's Exhaustive Concordance of the Bible Online: <http://www.biblestudytools.com/concordances/strongs-exhaustive-concordance/> accessed 2 June 2014.

Thomas, Edward, *Poems and Last Poems*, ed. Edna Longley (London: Collins, 1973).

Vaughan, Henry, *Silex Scintillans* [1655].

SLAVKO KACUNKO

2 Mirroring the Invisible

In what follows, I will summarise some of my observations relating to the cultural history of the mirror as a medium and material in art and science. I claim that mirrors play an important role in comprehending both the 'visible' and 'invisible' while helping us to understand the close relationship between 'observing' and 'measuring' within scientific and artistic practice. As a medial and material precondition for both 'vision' (the natural aspect of the visible) and 'visuality' (its cultural aspect), mirrors produce at the same time blind spots of both 'vision' and 'visuality' that require a research focus towards the very boundaries of visual cultural studies. This article demonstrates such a research interest by addressing the complementary relation between mirrors and images in the first section, followed by a short survey of mirror-mediated scientific extensions of the human field of vision in the second section. The third section discusses some prominent examples and concepts relating to modern architecture and contemporary cultural practices (including surveillance and popular film), thus reflecting some of the impact of mirror-mediated (in)visibility on modern culture more generally.

Mirror and Image

As a surface that has the ability to reflect incoming light rays, the mirror's distinct qualities have always inspired study within the humanities, where it has been traditionally comprehended either as a medium of self-knowledge, or, alternatively, as a void in the apprehension of the world. Instead of either of these approaches, I have been looking at some differences that might make other differences, such as the complementary relationship between mirror and image. The first difference between a painted picture or photograph, for example, and a mirror reflection, is that the surface of a painting has to be as visible as possible, i.e., it has to be kept rather dull in the sense of *not* reflecting (one only has to think of the problems that can arise when viewing pictures protected by untreated glass). The surface of the mirror, however, must be as invisible, or glossy, as possible, if it is to perform its basic function of reflecting light. The consequence is plain: the closer a surface is to the conditions of a perfect mirror, the more it loses its appearance as a surface. In fact, this 'ideal' invisibility of the medium affects all the media, but when it comes to the relationship between the mirror and image, this property is crucial.

The second constant of the mirror-image relationship represents the kinaesthetic component of perception and of our mirror-experience. From this we learn about the problematic visibility as well as visuality of mirrors: they are both heterotopic and heterochronic entities, something that apparently slides between 'image' and 'reality'. In recent years, much has been written about what has become known as 'iconic difference';[1] the difference between image and reality as conveyed by the mirror that I have described as a 'speculative' difference.[2] The third difference between a reflection or mirroring and an image is directly linked to the second: it is the fact that the mirror by definition does not maintain, save, or store the objects reflected on its surface, but transmits them from A to B and so forth. Conversely, and obviously, with the help of mirror-installations of any kind, light can be directed, guided and controlled in a sense, but on the other hand, the light itself cannot be stored in any way. So, in contrast to a storing medium such as an image, text, or numbers, the mirror must be understood as a medium of transmission. As a medium and as material (and not just as a motive, metaphor and model in the arts and sciences), it gradually entered into the optical-catoptrical, mechanical and other devices or philosophical toys of the nineteenth century, such as the *phenakistoscope* and *praxinoscope*, among others. Seen in technical terms, we could also deduce the genealogy of the first audio-visual medium, that is to say,

1 Gottfried Boehm, ed., *Was ist ein Bild?* (Munich: Fink, 1994).

2 Slavko Kacunko, *Spiegel. Medium. Kunst: Zur Geschichte des Spiegels im Zeitalter des Bildes* (Paderborn: Fink, 2010).

video and of electronic real-time transmission from a natural-analogue counterpart, from the phenomenology of the mirror. And if we go on to explore the no man's land between the respective media of transmission and storage, we may well find ourselves in the field of visual or other feedback systems, negotiated both in cybernetic and biological contexts.

The traditional leading metaphors – of vision, light and mirror – must therefore also be regarded as media. In the same way that light serves as the necessary prerequisite or medium of seeing, the mirror serves as a medium of light by directing it or intensifying it. We may say that if the sentence is the logical form of reality, then the mirror is the aesthetic form of the visual, of virtuality. Thereby, too, reflection and reflectivity in their non-metaphorical, catoptric senses should be comprehended as a fourth cultural technique alongside words, images and numbers. I will return to this later.

I began my inquiry on mirrors as media of art and culture by paraphrasing Mark Pendergrast and stating that the discovery of the mirror not only brought humankind closer to itself, but also propelled it farther into the infinity of the universe than has any other medium.[3] The human love-affair with reflection has definitely also been a narcissistic one, but my focus remains on the fact that it has always been platonic: untouchable, serving not least as a medium for reaching out to the invisible on both the micro and the macro levels.

The Extension of Light and Mirror Spectra

In the eyes of many, the practical use of so-called virtual, augmented, or mixed realities (among others) in the art and science of the twentieth century was a sign of a mechanisation of perception.[4] Given their various

3 Mark Pendergast, *Mirror/Mirror: A History of the Human Love Affair with Reflection* (New York: Basic Books, 2003).

4 Hartmut Böhme, 'Das Licht als Medium der Kunst: über Erfahrungsarmut und ästhetisches Gegenlicht in der technischen Zivilisation', *Paragrana: Internationale Zeitschrift für historische Anthropologie* 5 (1996), 111–37.

media properties, mirrors play a major role here: they transfer light, bend it and break it up, draw, colour, and not least intensify it, amplifying it. As the physicist Georg Christoph Lichtenberg (1742–99) pointed out, wherever light comes, it always comes together with reflection, inflexion, refraction and colouration.[5] This is why a mirror has to be understood on its phenomenal level as the meta-medium of both vision and visuality. But all these features as mentioned above are not necessarily special properties of our watching or seeing. That is, they are *not* primarily intersubjective; as a matter of fact, they represent an *interobjective* side of reflection. Therefore, we regard mirroring or reflection as an important cultural technique that can be judged by its ubiquitous presence in all areas of our lives in a large variety of mirror applications: take plain wardrobe and bathroom mirrors, convex shaving mirrors, the rear and side mirrors of vehicles, concave traffic mirrors at exits, turnoffs and street intersections, the hyperbolic-concave mirrors that serve as basic components of mirror telescopes, the parabolic mirrors used for solar thermal systems, the mirrors used in medical diagnosis, and so on. All of these mirrors transform not only our vision of the world, but the world itself, including ourselves.

Our understanding of such concepts and phenomena also implies precise knowledge about the capabilities and functions of so-called semi-transparent mirrors as prerequisites of artistic and architectural work with transparency and opacity. Already our intuitive reflection – that we are basically able to look only from the darker to the lighter side of a surface – is a part of that knowledge. To its main parameters belong the strength and the angle of incidental light rays, the thickness of the deposited reflective layer, and not least, the nature of the material (glass, metal and plastic). Many of these issues can be determined, calculated and applied experimentally and practically without any special knowledge, but they still belong to the preconditions for trans-disciplinary negotiation of the invisible. Additionally, there is an increasing knowledge and awareness of phenomena which can only indirectly be made visible with optical media – those which operate

5 Georg Christoph Lichtenberg, *Schriften und Briefe. Sudelbücher II* (Munich: Hanser 1975), 468.

beyond the reflection, diffraction, refraction and coloration of light: we are talking here about the phenomena of the invisible.

The point about visible light is that it extends between violet and red, which obviously covers only very tiny ranges of the electromagnetic spectrum, from 400 to 700 nanometres width. The short wavelengths of ultraviolet, X-rays and gamma rays have a much higher frequency than those of the long wavelengths of infrared, microwaves and radio waves. Radio waves were discovered by Heinrich Hertz in the late nineteenth century (1857–94), as part of his research on the dissemination of Maxwell's electromagnetic waves, and he also supplied the evidence that they behave similarly to those of visible light. It became clear that radio waves – because of their great length – do not need highly polished mirrors in order to be sent away, reflected and, therefore, visually perceived. On the other side of the electromagnetic wave spectrum, Wilhelm Conrad Röntgen (1845–1923) discovered the rays named after him, also called X-rays: these are even shorter than those of ultraviolet light, which make them even stronger or more assertive, and therefore even able, as it were, to penetrate through the mirror, the reflective surface.

Thus it became clear that mirrors reflect most, but not all, wavelengths of the electromagnetic spectrum. The reason that we as humans have at our disposal only this narrow window of both vision and visuality lies in turn in the fact that the earth's atmosphere blocks most neighbouring wavelengths. The only alternative to enable our human eye to see further would be to widen the size of our eyes to the size of a satellite dish, and to focus their corneas (their mirrors, so to speak) on the long wavelengths of radio waves, which are able to penetrate the atmosphere. So, size matters here quite objectively.

Scientists later found that heat in the form of infrared radiation is also another form of light, only with a longer wavelength. It appeared that all light represents one or another form of energy, which in most cases can be reflected or broken. Subsequently Max Planck and Albert Einstein and after them Niels Bohr (1885–1962), succeeded in demonstrating the line spectra of hydrogen (H) by using this, the simplest atom. Combining classical physics with quantum physics, Bohr ultimately delivered the model that explains how vision and reflection work. The investigations of the nineteenth century, in particular the physiological investigations of Hermann von Helmholtz (1821–94), were thus brought to a new level, and subjective vision could be drawn on the foil of visuality and inter-objectivity. According to Niels Bohr, light, with its specific wavelength/energy, strikes a specific receptor on the retina and is absorbed, while the electrons 'ignite' the neuronal 'firing' and the chemical reactions between neurons, with the result that their 'records' in certain spots or areas of the brain are registered as specific colours.

In turn, reflection itself, which is usually interpreted as a 'ricocheting' of the light on the polished surfaces, was explained more precisely by the interaction of photons with the loose electrons in the metal, because the photons are actually absorbed and then reradiated.[6] Although the reflection laws as seminal physical laws still generally work, it should be added that the individual photon absorption effects a slight difference between the incoming and reflecting angles because some of them (these particles of light) stay simply absorbed (at about 9 per cent silver). Since the quality of the mirroring/reflection obviously depends also on the conductivity of the material used, we still use silver for mirroring because of its high precision or 'hit rate' linked to the incoming and outcoming light rays. The essence of the mirrors we use, one could say, is therefore often the silver itself, since it is considered the lightest (whitest) substance in nature.[7]

Since this chapter intends to cover primarily the material and media aspects of the use and (cultural) production of invisibility and opacity, in what follows I should add a few hard and transparent facts linked to the production and manufacturing of glass, as well as to its cultural import in our times.[8] Like the process of its manufacture, the consistency of glass is far

6 Pendergast, *Mirror/Mirror*, 203.

7 The uncorroded surfaces of silver have the highest light-reflective properties of all metals. The freshly deposited silver reflects over 99.5 per cent of the visible light. Compare Pendergast, *Mirror/Mirror*, 204. Pendergast refers among others to Richard P. Feynman, *QED: The Strange Theory of Light and Matter* (New York: Princeton Science Library, 1985).

8 I have to skip an exciting field of mirror telescopes and their development thanks to research in quantum mechanics and spectral-analysis, which again lead the radio- and

from simple. Although glass is stiff and stable, the distribution of molecules in its inner structure follows the disordered, apparently random principle of liquids. It was not until the 1930s that the refraction of X-rays by simple glass revealed this general disorder. Molten glass contains silicon and oxygen atoms, all of which are so loosely distributed that the glass appears transparent. This disorder appears during the melting process, and before the atoms unite to the parent molecular patterns again during the cooling, all movement ceases in a 'frozen' state of apparent 'molecular chaos'.[9] It is this molecular, structural looseness that gives glass its enormous malleability and flexibility. But the molecular structure of glass is still a huge scientific challenge. It seems that the glass industry in particular has supplied the major impetus for glass research over the past 600 years. Glass's paradoxical nature as a solid liquid arises from the absence of a clearly identifiable crystalline structure that yet keeps its unique fragility, which no other solid material has. The molecular chaos of glass has its limits at the subatomic level, however, in a not yet decoded form: experiments with X-rays have revealed certain neutron scattering patterns on glass, but its structure is still a matter needing fundamental research, for, as Peter Krause of the Research Department of the Schott glassworks in Mainz concludes, 'with all the molecules and all the possibilities of their movement and interconnection and so on, even the largest computers are too small for the study of the structure of the glass [...] we do not do such studies here, although it is a good field for the universities.'[10] Certainly, this competence should be shared between the diverse natural sciences and the humanities. But not only the general, interdisciplinary, and as yet unresolved questions from the realm of so called 'basic research' in physics, chemistry, or material science make the relationship between mirrors and invisibility still appealing to

---

neutrinotelescopy and, finally, gravitations-waves-telescopy. The width and depth of this research and its practical applications have been indicated elsewhere. For telescopes, see Geoff Andersen, *The Telescope. Its History, Technology, and Future* (Princeton, NJ: Princeton University Press, 2007).

9 William S. Ellis, *Glass: From the First Mirror to Fiber Optics, the Story of the Substance that Changed the World* (New York: Avon Books, 1998), 6–7.

10 Ellis, *Glass*, 78.

us: the extensions of our knowledge about the light and mirror spectra, as briefly summarised in this second section of my paper, have subsequently also shown their immediate impact on various practical fields. The following section will therefore refer to some prominent examples and concepts of modern and recent architecture in order to reflect the impact of mirror-mediated (in-)visibility on modern culture in general.

Liquid Mirrors: Art and Commerce, Nature and Architecture

The mass production of mirrors has promoted cultural changes which found their prominent expression in the United States as early as the 1920s. The new consumer and youth culture, with its focus on visual appearance and not least on sex as a commodity, has been promoted mainly by improving the cultural techniques of (self-)observation, themselves based on the mirror and reflection. Consumer paradises like New York's Fifth Avenue, and its counterparts in Paris or Berlin, already known as 'cities of light',[11] provided the best lit background for the theatre of the city. Also, as early as 1895, King Gillette implicitly enhanced the boom in the production of shaving-mirrors through the invention of the modern double-edged razor. This again influenced the immensely changed appearance of men for the next century. An increased tendency for art and commerce, design and consumer culture, to blend together, became visible, particularly from the 'roaring Twenties' onward. The phenomenon of mirror-glazed arcades in the Paris of the nineteenth century, as described by Walter Benjamin and others, has become paradigmatic. An observer writing in the early 1930s noted: 'Not until the last few decades [...] had there been any appreciable advance in the production of reflecting surfaces [...]. The art of manufacturing mirrors, once as closely guarded as an alchemist's secret, is today a

11 Pendergast, *Mirror/Mirror*, 251.

science of quantity as well as quality production.'[12] The British glassmaker Pilkington revolutionised glass production in 1959 with a process in which the flow of glass was enabled to float on molten tin, thanks to the fact that glass has a higher melting point than tin. Gradually, the glass was cooled and hardened off, so that it then could be cut and stacked in large discs.[13] The first mirror glass building was realised, however, by Kinney Glass, a small glass company. It was completed in 1962: the Bell Labs in Holmdel, New Jersey. The mirror effect was owed to the electrolytic deposition of the reflective metals on the glass in a vacuum chamber.[14]

As is generally known, glazed doors and windows, with their reflective surfaces, have always been a challenge to perception and a notorious problem for painters. That challenge was compounded when glazing came to be spread over entire façades in the form of modernist curtain walls. Seen genealogically, it was a matter of creating fitting accommodation for the new and highly specialised textile factories (in England since 1790), banks, and insurance companies – buildings whose main purpose became to generate trust through a good image, which it was only possible to create from scratch. It is no exaggeration to speak of a strategic myth of transparency in this context, where the transparent, semi-transparent, and reflective properties of the material are used as a protective shield for the hidden processes behind: where everything is apparently transparent, there is no actual transparency, no place for choice or chance.

The accompanying ideology of the equality of opportunities for consumption thus became a relative banality, re-reflecting on our post-postmodern level what Ernst Bloch (1885–1977) called *The Principle of Hope*. In his eponymous major work (1954–9), he dedicated one chapter to buildings intended to represent a better world, 'architectural utopias'.[15] Architecture

12 Pendergast, *Mirror/Mirror*, 247, cited from William Lawrence Bottomley, *Mirrors in Interior Architecture* [1932].

13 Pendergast, *Mirror/Mirror*, 261.

14 Pamela Heyne, *Mirror by Design: Using Reflection to Transform Space* (New York: John Wiley & Sons, 1996), 37.

15 'Bauten, die eine bessere Welt abbilden, architektonische Utopien'. See this chapter in Ernst Bloch, *Werkausgabe: Band 5: Das Prinzip Hoffnung* (Frankfurt am Main: Suhrkamp 1985).

in general was described in that work as nothing but the production of a human home. However, this was not a reflection of the real environment.[16] Bloch saw in architecture by its very nature 'the expectation of the future, a utopia, the hope for change and improvement of living conditions'.[17] In this context, it is no surprise that, at the same time, ambassadors of the Congrès Internationaux d'Architecture Moderne (CIAM), such as Bauhaus founder Walter Gropius (1883–1969), enforced an architectural theory without historical references after Second World War. Gropius' own much earlier project; a *Bauhaus Building* (1927/8) in Dessau was regarded by the architectural historian H. R. Hitchcock as the first significant example of executed modern architecture.[18] In the studio-block, the possibilities of the transparency of glass had been exploited on a large scale for the first time.

Fitting to a certain extent to the CIAM programme, the American skyscrapers of the time have followed the short(ened) form, 'light, air and sun'. In this process, the glass has become the basic material by default. Between 1945 and 1975, this functionalism has been implemented and extended by the famous design programme according to which form has to follow function. At the same time, research into the other, so-called 'biological' materials has initiated, opened, and confirmed the growing importance of mirrored surfaces. Some authors have concluded that in the 1970s and 1980s, the transparency of glass architecture from the 1950s and 1960s became its apparent opposite – total mirroring. But no matter what our impression today might be, we can see that that this possible shift from transparency to mirroring was not just a product of aesthetic or institutional mimicry of the 'big-city-mirror'. We can see similar or identical functions of mirrors at work since the late seventeenth century, as part of a major cultural turn in Europe. With respect to architectural development both before, and especially after, Versailles and its famous

16 The Swiss architect and architectural historian Adolf Max Vogt has expressed this in Edward Lucie-Smith and A. M. Vogt, *Kunst der Gegenwart*, Vol. 13 (Frankfurt/Berlin/Vienna: Propyläen Kunstgeschichte, 1985), 101.

17 Lucie-Smith and Vogt, *Kunst der Gegenwart*, 101.

18 Henry-Russell Hitchcock, *Die Architektur des 19. und 20. Jahrhunderts* [1958] (Munich: Aries, 1994).

Galerie des Glaces, this might dialectically be referred to as the 'mirroring of the architecture' through the 'architecturalising of the mirror's scale'.[19] Now, appearing on an even larger urban scale, the mirrored glass buildings of the 1980s have popped up in the middle of the energy crisis, with their multifaceted functions. They serve to protect against UV radiation while providing visual interaction with the environment even when situation within allegedly 'unspoilt' natural settings, and where the peaceful coexistence of nature and architecture is an explicit goal.[20] No matter how they appear to us today, one can hardly deny their projected awareness of environmental responsibility as a contribution to humanity as a whole. One might talk about a second coming of the 'Prinzip Hoffnung', following Bloch's coinage of the late 1950s.

It is important to note in this context the process of our ambivalent perception of the phenomenon of glass, as a transparent, yet reflective medium. The possibilities for switching between the two modes by manipulating the interior lighting are practically endless. A similar feature can be added when one considers that smooth mirror glass surfaces may suggest both a visual continuity and autonomy. For example, the apparent structure of the mirrored office building in England (1975)[21] transforms it 'in the dark almost into its own inner light x-ray-image'.[22] On the other hand, during the day, it asserts its major aesthetic potential mainly through the reflection of its surface. In the *Tower of Winds* (1986) in Yokohama, Toyo Ito added yet another, kinaesthetic element: the 21m high ventilation tower of an underground shopping centre owes its media impact especially to the use of highly reflective perforated aluminium material that coats the aboveground oval cylinder. While the aluminium plates act as a mirror during the day, the supporting structure behind can be seen between them after sunset, reacting visibly to the wind. The mirror, hence also often called the

19 Kacunko, *Spiegel. Medium. Kunst*, 647.

20 Regarding the urban space, the famous and most-quoted example is probably Hans Holleins *Haas-Haus* in Vienna, 1987–90.

21 Foster Associates, *Office House Faber & Dumas*, Ipswich, England 1975–9.

22 Norbert Messler, 'Architektur und Spiegel', in *Spiegelbilder* (Berlin Kunstverein Hannover/W. Lehmbruck-Museum Duisburg/Haus am Waldsee Berlin, 1982), 206.

'chameleon of architecture',[23] appears in numerous projects in connection with reflecting façades, which deserve a separate volume or research network to represent them fully. However, the quadruple mutual impacts of vision, visuality, invisibility and opacity can be traced as continuous phenomena introducing other important issues related to media-supported transparent and mirrored architectural surfaces.

With advances in media technology and the increasing shift of all activities to the internet, so-called virtual architecture was developed, with the aim of taking over essential functions of traditional architecture. Here, forms are meant to occur at the interface of architecture and media, this applying also to the metaphor of the 'architecture of cyberspace'.[24] Its influence on the physical buildings of the real environment is reflected in the form of computer-generated buildings, or *blobs*. The development of virtual and 'liquid architecture',[25] however, took place mainly in the field of artistic (media-) installations, as seen for example in the work of the group *Asymptote*.[26] The architect and artist Marcos Novak, who styles himself a 'trans architect', belongs to the representatives and supporters of this self-appointed virtual architecture of invisible, flexible and especially liquid forms. The terms 'liquid' or 'fluid' in such architecture refers to what happens when computer generated ideas are blended with the real environment – smooth transitions between time and space concepts, with a minimum of rational limitations. The deconstructionist architecture of Frank O. Gehry and others are cases in point.[27]

In a more recent essay, artist and designer Joachim Sauter described the façade as 'a media skin of architecture' and made an attempt to summarise the *status quo* systematically as well as genealogically. Based on the four

23 Heyne, *Mirror by Design*, 1.

24 Marcos Novak, 'Liquid Architectures in Cyberspace', in Michael Benedikt, ed., *Cyberspace: First Steps* (Cambridge, MA: MIT Press, 1991), 254.

25 Novak, *Liquid Architectures*.

26 <http://www.asymptote.net/accessed> 17 October 2013.

27 As a matter of fact, the XXIII World Congress of the UIA (International Union of Architects) from 2008 has borrowed its theme – a Transmitting Architecture from one essay of Marcos Novak which dates back to 1995.

qualities of a digital computer (the capacity for interaction, multimediality, connectivity and generativity) Sauter described three developmental factors that led from screen applications and interactive installations and spaces to 'interactive architecture'.[28] In his view, it is only for economic reasons that the latter is limited today to the media-based design of the façade. Sauter sees its urban potential in furthering extensive identification of residents with their architectural habitats. He envisages controlled light projections on walls, projections, or LED screens as an 'adequate narrative', citing the pioneering example of a 'media façade', Ito's *Tower of Winds* in Yokohama.

Here one might speak about a 'third incarnation' of *The Principle of Hope* à la Bloch, following those of the late 1950s and the 1980s, if recent claims are to be taken seriously. In other words, the critical questions of (self-)reflection (and monitoring), as well as an acute awareness of the transparency, remain, as the CIAM conferences (1928–59) has only too clearly shown. Evidently the potential of media-mirrored, semi-reflective, as well as transparent façades is still far from exhausted, either in their commercial and political applications (advertising, propaganda) or in their artistic forms. That potential applies also to the initiative of *Media Architecture Group*,[29] with current projects such as the *Media Façades Festival Berlin* and *Media Architecture* in London, with its dialogue and cooperation with industry.

The fact that media technology is aging much faster than material architecture draws our attention on the one hand to new material developments, such as the surface-based adaptive and bio-luminescence screen films. On the other hand, architecture itself is aging faster than the laws of physics, not least in its bringing the laws of reflection to the fore (as shown above), while stimulating both further research into, and the use of, mirrors, in urban and rural contexts. This brings me to my conclusion.

28 Joachim Sauter, 'Das vierte Format: Die Fassade als mediale Haut der Architektur', in Monika Fleischmann and Wolfgang Strauss, eds, *Digitale Transformationen. Medienkunst als Schnittstelle von Kunst, Wissenschaft, Wirtschaft und Gesellschaft* (Heidelberg: whois verlags- & vertriebsgesellschaft, 2004).

29 <http://www.mediafacades.eu/2008/institutions/mag> accessed 17 October 2013.

Especially within the humanities, research dedicated to the cultural techniques of (self)observation offers a necessary supplement to research within the natural sciences. Interdisciplinary initiatives (such as the research network that has generated this volume) reflect these needs, and make them increasingly transparent for further disciplines to come.

Since the first massive public use of stealth technology during the initial Gulf War in 1991, we have witnessed growing interest in the phenomenon of invisibility. We can identify the same tendency towards invisibility in the military context today, especially when engineers all around the world compete for the patent rights for *real cloaking devices* and active camouflage suits. One could call them 'closed-circuit-invisible-making suits', because they are sometimes tailored from hundreds of tiny video screens (for the front), directly connected with the same, huge, number of chip video cameras (for the backs of their wearers). They seem to be counted among the creative and technological highlights of our time. One recent example from popular culture may illustrate the comedy and the tragedy of this trend. A scene from the Hollywood blockbuster *Mission Impossible IV: Ghost Protocol* (launched in December 2011 and directed by Brad Bird) confirmed this now decade-long continuing trend, which has its origins in the Cold War. Ethan Hunt (played by Tom Cruise) is able to stalk a guard in the security wing of the Kremlin archives by hiding behind an obscuring 'invisible-making-panel' – a portable device with eye-tracking controlled video camera projection modules and the projection showing to the person in front of it only the empty room behind the beholder of the panel.

In such contexts the supposed boundary between the technologies of attack and defence is taken in a subtle way to absurdity: only the invisible seems incomprehensible, and only the incomprehensible seems able to remain beyond control, holding an apparently unique subversive potential. Step by step, not unlike in the hiding-game of Ethan Hunt and his highly symbolic invisible approaching of an archive of the Other, the media art studies which we are representing are closing the vicious or dialectic circle between the immediacy of image and the image of immediacy. Some of the most important strategies of media artists and activists of the past two decades and of today have been explorations in this direction. This was at least the major trend of the 1990s, with its focus on invisible, natural, transparent, or intuitive interfaces. Recent interface-focused research in Denmark, Germany and in Austria shows that interest in the ubiquity of digital technology born out of such military rationale still attracts the attention of research programmes.[30] What I am referring to here is a dialectics of the actuality of history and the historical dimension of the here and now.

Such historicising is, as far as I can see, nothing other than a denial of the idea of inevitability. An understanding of the historical dimension of surveillance cultures should, however, contribute not only to the critical understanding of their ethical and political implications, but also to the awareness of their causes and genealogies, in order to help us develop together appropriate responses in the future. Applied to the principal issues and the current state of visual studies, these questions must be extended to include the critical questioning of visuality (the cultural aspect of vision) and our fixation on images, through the investigation of their theoretical and phenomenological frameworks. In other words, we need to investigate, in particular, mirrors in their complementary relation to images (as addressed at the beginning of this article) and to frames (as their *conditio sine qua non*).[31] Only then will we be able to grasp the movements between our metaphors of time and of space. And only thus will we become able to open a truly transdisciplinary perspective onto the unsolved disputes between the humanities and natural sciences, a perspective related not least to the apparently invisible phenomena of art and culture.

30 See Søren Bro Pold and Christian Ulrik Andersen, *Interface Criticism. Aesthetics Beyond the Buttons* (Aarhus: Aarhus Universitetsforlag, 2011); Søren Bro Pold, and Lone Koefoed Hansen, *Interface: Digital Kunst & Kultur* (Aarhus: Aarhus Universitetsforlag, 2006); Christa Sommerer, Laurent Mignonneau, and Laurent Dorothée King, eds, *Interface Cultures. Artistic Aspects of Interaction* (Bielefeld: Transcript, 2008); Christa Sommerer, Laurent Mignonneau, and Lakhmi C. Jain, eds, *The Art and Science of Interface and Interaction Design*, Vol. 1 (Vienna: Springer, 2008).

31 <http://www.framings.org/> accessed 17 October 2013.

Bibliography

Andersen, Geoff, *The Telescope. Its History, Technology, and Future* (Princeton, NJ: Princeton University Press, 2007).

Bloch, Ernst, *Werkausgabe: Band 5: Das Prinzip Hoffnung* (Frankfurt am Main: Suhrkamp 1985).

Boehm, Gottfried, ed., *Was ist ein Bild?* (Munich: Fink, 1994).

Böhme, Hartmut, 'Das Licht als Medium der Kunst: über Erfahrungsarmut und ästhetisches Gegenlicht in der technischen Zivilisation', in *Paragrana. Internationale Zeitschrift für historische Anthropologie* 5 (Berlin: Akademie Verlag, 1996).

Ellis, William S., *Glass: From the First Mirror to Fiber Optics, the Story of the Substance that Changed the World* (New York: Avon Books, 1998).

Feynman, Richard P., *QED: The Strange Theory of Light and Matter* (New York: Princeton Science Library, 1985).

Heyne, Pamela, *Mirror by Design: Using Reflection to Transform Space* (New York: John Wiley & Sons, 1996).

Hitchcock, Henry-Russell, *Die Architektur des 19. und 20. Jahrhunderts* [1958] (Munich: Aries, 1994).

Kacunko, Slavko, *Spiegel. Medium. Kunst. Zur Geschichte des Spiegels im Zeitalter des Bildes* (Paderborn: Fink, 2010). [Further bibliography to the different aspects of the mirror studies may be found here].

Lichtenberg, Georg Christoph, *Schriften und Briefe. Sudelbücher II* (Munich: Hanser 1975).

Lucie-Smith, Edward, and A. M. Vogt, *Kunst der Gegenwart* (Frankfurt/Berlin/Vienna: Propyläen Kunstgeschichte, 1985).

Messler, Norbert, 'Architektur und Spiegel', in *Spiegelbilder* (Berlin: Kunstverein Hannover/W. Lehmbruck-Museum Duisburg/Haus am Waldsee Berlin, 1982).

Novak, Marcos, 'Liquid Architectures in Cyberspace', in Michael Benedikt, ed., *Cyberspace: First Steps* (Cambridge, MA: MIT Press, 1991).

Pendergast, Mark, *Mirror/Mirror: A History of the Human Love Affair with Reflection* (New York: Basic Books, 2003).

Pold, Søren Bro, and Christian Ulrik Andersen, *Interface Criticism. Aesthetics Beyond the Buttons* (Aarhus: Aarhus Universitetsforlag, 2011).

Pold, Søren Bro, and Lone Koefoed Hansen, *Interface: Digital Kunst & Kultur* (Aarhus: Aarhus Universitetsforlag, 2006).

Sauter, Joachim, 'Das vierte Format: Die Fassade als mediale Haut der Architektur', in Monika Fleischmann and Wolfgang Strauss, eds, *Digitale Transformationen.*

Medienkunst als Schnittstelle von Kunst, Wissenschaft, Wirtschaft und Gesellschaft (Heidelberg: whois verlags- & vertriebsgesellschaft, 2004).

Sommerer, Christa, Laurent Mignonneau, and Laurent Dorothée King, eds, *Interface Cultures. Artistic Aspects of Interaction* (Bielefeld: Transcript, 2008).

Sommerer, Christa, Laurent Mignonneau, and Jain Lakhmi C., eds, *The Art and Science of Interface and Interaction Design* (Vienna: Springer, 2008).

MECHTILD WIDRICH

3 'I'll Be Your Mirror': Transparency, Voyeurism and Glass Architecture

> What is there of glass in your work? [...] How does one talk about it? In optical terms or in tactile terms? Regarding tactility, it would be good if [...] you would speak to our friends of the erotic tricks, of the calls to desire, do I dare say, of the sex appeal of the architectural forms of which you think, with which you work, for which you give yourself up.
>
> —JACQUES DERRIDA, letter to Peter Eisenman, 1990[1]

Around the time Derrida wrote his open letter to Eisenman, the glass surface typical of modernist architecture, with its claims to visibility and clarity, was once again under scrutiny. At the turn of the 1990s, glass was critically discussed as offering a game of confusing semi-transparencies, suggesting exclusion, control, framing and uncanny night visions, rather than light, clarity and democratic models of transparency – whether in work or in private life.

Theorists such as Anthony Vidler, José Quetglas, Rosemarie Haag Bletter, Joan Ockman and Stanislaus von Moos (building on doubts first expressed by Colin Rowe) based their reconsideration of the nature of glass as directly transparent, and thus as moral metaphor, on its reflective effect, its ambiguity in blending reflection, and on the opportunity for looking through the glass as a physical substance. In other words, they interpreted physical effects psychologically, and, finally, politically. In this discourse, it

1 Jacques Derrida, 'A *letter* to Peter Eisenman', *Assemblage: A Critical Journal of Architecture and Design* (12 August 1990), 6–12.

seems that glass is almost intrinsically liable to disappoint as a metaphor: for it is a substance that transmits visibility while barring passage, a transparency that turns into obstruction.[2] This suggestion, however, should give hope to the modernists: for the illusion and disorientation of glass would hardly be possible without its clarifying effect. Mirroring does not just hide, it also exposes. Contemporary artists have taken up the ambiguity of glass as transparent and reflective in order to inquire into the position of subjects in public: presenting and representing in an environment that is itself both seen and reflected. Their positions illuminate the debate around transparency in public building and public life, and can help us understand the issues at stake for a reading from the point of view of spectators in public space, whether these spectators are theorists or otherwise. In this chapter, I will focus on two projects that lie at the intersection of art and architecture, one by Austrian performance artist VALIE EXPORT, the other by Italian installation artist Monica Bonvicini, in order to explore how glass is used in a contemporary urban context to bring into focus the

2 The metaphor goes back to Rousseau, who uses the glass heart and the idea of transparency to indicate his vision of a just society without misunderstandings. Rousseau: 'His heart, transparent as a crystal, can hide nothing of what happens within it. Every mood it feels is transmitted to his eyes and his face.' *Dialogues*, in Roger D. Masters, and Christopher Kelly, eds, *The Collected Writings of Rousseau* (Hanover, NH: University Press of New England, 1990). Most important on Rousseau is Jean Starobinsky; on transparency, see Anthony Vidler, *The Architectural Uncanny. Essays in the Modern Unhomely* (Cambridge, MA: The MIT Press, 1992); Jose Quetglas, 'Perdida de la sintesis: el Pabellon de Mies', *Carrer de la Ciutat* 11 (April 1980), reprinted as 'Loss of Synthesis. Mies's Pavilion', in Michael Hays, ed., *Architecture Theory Since 1968* (Cambridge, MA: The MIT Press, 1998), 382–91. 'Toward a Theory of Normative Architecture', in Steven Harris and Deborah Berke, eds, *Architecture of the Everyday* (New York: Princeton Architectural Press, 1997), 122–52; Stanislaus von Moos, '"Glanzblitz!" Über Architektur, Transparenz und Multimedialität', in Monika Wagner and Dietmar Rübel, eds, *Material in Kunst und Alltag* (Berlin: Akademie Verlag, 2002), 47–63; Rosemarie Haag Bletter, 'The Interpretation of the Glass Dream – Expressionist Architecture and the History of the Crystal Metaphor', *The Journal of the Society of Architectural Historians* 40/1 (1981), 20–43. For a different critique of modernist glass façades, see also Richard Sennett, *The Fall of Public Man* (Cambridge: Cambridge University Press, 1974).

position of subjects in public space: glass as presenting and representing in an environment that is itself both seen and reflected.

Reviving Modernist Transparency

The Bauhaus, of course, had been the most prominent promoter of the glass surface as model for a new society – the thrill of which might have also been inherent in the ever-faster technological development of the curtain wall. One could even go further and accuse Modernism of a 'myth of transparency', as Anthony Vidler terms it: 'transparency of the self to nature, of the self to the other, of all selves to society.'[3] Even after the Second World War, its promises remained central in Germany. One example is the architecture of the constitutional court in Karlsruhe. From the point of view of the mid-1960s Federal Republic of Germany, this building tries hard, through an iconography of humbleness paired with transparency, to show that in the new Germany laws are made in a democratic, visible manner – in direct contrast to National Socialist judicial secrecy and absolutism.[4] Obviously, glass cannot hold so much weight.

Are such ambitions compatible with recent practice? Let us consider VALIE EXPORT's *Transparent Cube*, built in Vienna between 1999 and 2001. It consists of glass panels in a steel frame, set under the tracks of Otto Wagner's Wiener Stadtbahn, now part of the Viennese subway system (1894–1901).[5] EXPORT's first large-scale architectural work, it was

3 Vidler, *The Architectural Uncanny*, 217.

4 See the detailed description, 'Bundesverfassungsgericht in Karlsruhe', *Bauwelt* 1969, 48 (1714–22). This and other projects were discussed in the seminar I co-taught with Martino Stierli at ETH in the fall semester of 2011. Stierli, as well as the students in the seminar, helped me understand the discourse and shape my concerns with knowledge, insights, and questions.

5 See Magistrat der Stadt Wien, ed., *Der transparente Raum* (Vienna: MA 57 – Frauenförderung und Koordinierung von Frauenangelegenheiten, 2000).

initiated as part of a project for urban development funded by the European Union. The neighbourhood on the so-called belt or *Gürtel*, a circular road around the city, was then, and to a certain extent remains, despite sporadic gentrification, marked by heavy traffic, low property values, and (mostly legal) prostitution.[6] EXPORT, born in 1940, is internationally known for her explicitly feminist performances in public spaces, particularly *Touch Cinema* of 1968, in which she mounted a stage-like theatre apparatus around her breasts and invited the street public to visit her 'real chick flick'.[7] Many of her works are investigations of the relation between the built environment and female experience, between what is visible and the social threads of power that the visible environment only partially reveals. Voyeurism, hidden desires and the way architecture and social behaviour reflect each other are important concerns for EXPORT, who inhabits a theoretical tradition in which the feminist critique of power coexists with phenomenological inquiry into perception. There is certainly continuity here in the choice of glass, and the expanded idea of the screen as an intersection of the private self and its representation – a trope that became prominent *after* EXPORT's early work, in feminist literature of the seventies, particularly in what may be called the Lacanian turn in Anglophone film studies in the wake of the work of Laura Mulvey.[8] Yet the transparent cube is a departure insofar as EXPORT seems no longer interested in upsetting the assumed force of the male gaze hitting the objectified female, as is the point of *Touch Cinema*, where the male visitor is put on the spot.[9]

6 The European Union project *Gürtel Plus* was soon merged with the initiative *URBAN*. The architect who oversaw the entire operation was Silja Tillner. She approached EXPORT for the realisation of the cube. Madeleine Petrovic, *Der Wiener Gürtel Wiederentdeckung einer Prachtstraße* (Vienna, 2009), 89–103.

7 EXPORT's German is 'echter Frauenfilm', a wordplay lost in the bland English 'real women's film'. The connotation is emotional weepies of the Douglas Sirk variety; German versions at the time were humourless. 'Frauenfilm' did also come to mean 'feminist movie', but because of artists like EXPORT, not before her.

8 Laura Mulvey, 'Visual Pleasure and Narrative Cinema', *Screen* 16/3 (Autumn 1975), 6–18.

9 I discuss EXPORT's oeuvre in depth in my book *Performative Monuments* (Manchester: Manchester University Press, 2014).

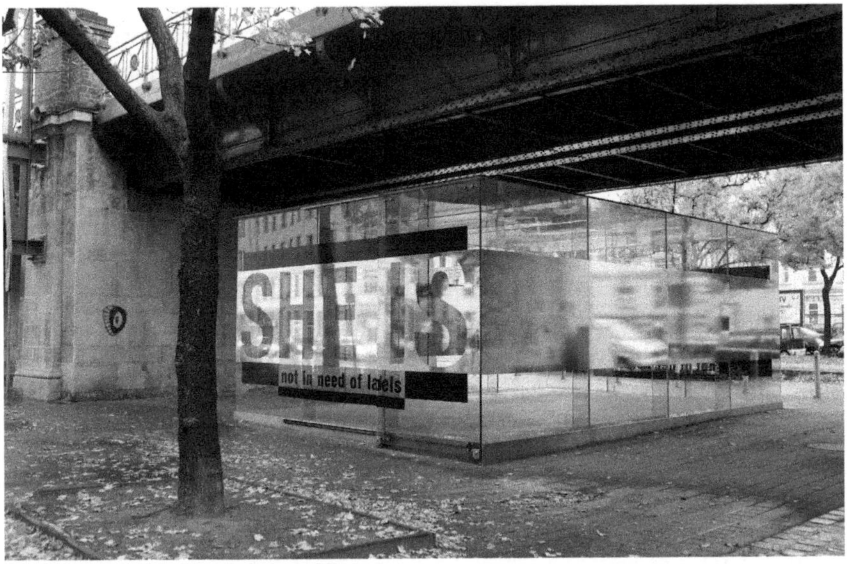

Fig. 3.1: VALIE EXPORT, Silja Tillner. *Transparent Cube*, Vienna.
Credit: Zobl/Schneider.

Let us look briefly at how the cube functions, or is meant to function. Intended as a space for exhibitions and events, predominantly but not exclusively for women, the idea is straightforward: seeing active female cultural producers inside the cube should offset the dynamic of the active male client selecting subservient paid female companions outside it. EXPORT wants to make women visible here as autonomous and self-determined, and by extension – that is, through the glass – in the urban environment as well. The cube is thus both contemporary social architecture – one almost wants to say behavioural architecture – and a monument to gendered urban experience.[10] The cube itself, fitted into the industrial architecture of the train

10 EXPORT's related *Allentsteig Memorial* (1998) in rural Austria, dedicated to the population deported by the National Socialists to make room for a military base, is also made of glass, and intervenes forcefully into space: called *Landschaftsmesser (Landscape-knife)*, the glass object protrudes into a river. See Rudi Palla, ed., *Erinnerungsstätte Allentsteig – eine Dokumentation* (Vienna: Triton, 1999), and my

tracks above, melds the motif of abiding with that of movement: two sides of the cube can be opened to 'make [...] the glass-body into a passage.'[11] All interaction in and around the transparent cube is supposed to become a public act, both in the present, as affirmation of powerful female action, or at least just of the interaction of the sexes, and as intrusion into the past – into the fabric of the city and the inequality that persists in its built environment.

There is another analogy with EXPORT's early work here, which only partially corresponds with the psychoanalytic theory that she seems to have anticipated. The idea of removing physical barriers to what is available psychically, such as the woman's body in *Touch Cinema*, is supposed to upset domination and to have a broad liberating effect: recall the so-called 'real chick flick'. In the *Transparent Cube*, this is done by literally opening the glass storefronts, so that they no longer allow outsiders to *look without touching*, but permit movement in and out of the space. EXPORT, the 1970s feminist, thus envisions visitors being able to write themselves into public memory via the flattening of inner and outer space.[12] Yet EXPORT's architecture does not fully disappear behind its empowered users: its formal rhetoric is full of authority; the modernist authority of clean lines, clearly visible interiors, and, an important corollary of these qualities, a kind of courageous interior activity that requires no architectural cover. In taking over these modernist claims, familiar from Mies van der Rohe's public buildings and villas, EXPORT delegates the performance of social conditions to the visitors of the cube. In a way, the visitors are made to play a pantomime, much like that described by Manfredo Tafuri for the inhabitants of van der Rohe's houses and offices.[13]

But beside this insistent and not wholly innocent transparency, EXPORT's cube also aims at a mirror effect: for she wants the activity inside to have consequences, its mirror image so to speak, projected onto the fabric of the city, particularly on the environs around Wagner's Stadtbahn.

---

unpublished manuscript 'Delegate Architecture' (lecture held at the University of Florida, Gainesville in February 2013).

11 VALIE EXPORT, 'Der Transparente Raum', in *Der Transparente Raum*, 138.

12 Richard Sennett discusses 'isolation in the midst of visibility' in the glass architecture of the international style in *The Fall of Public Man*, 13.

13 Manfredo Taffuri, 'Il teatro come città virtuale. Da Appia al Totaltheater', *Lotus* 17 (December 1977), 30–53.

The city is supposed to increasingly resemble the cube in its equitable transparency. The choice of material makes EXPORT's motives blatant, but I am not sure it accomplishes them. In particular, we may wonder whether glass makes possible an extension of female autonomy into the supposedly male-dominated space outside. The act of 'making seen' immediately raises problems, however, for the glass cube can easily be read as a showcase, with all the objectifying qualities of one. This criticism is valid, I believe, since, in trying to upset patriarchal domination, EXPORT cannot just make glass mean what she wants – she is forced to work with the effects it already has in public space. There is thus a strange utopian ascription to the material glass in EXPORT's approach, which leads us right to the heart of the political and moral debate about glass architecture.

Walter Benjamin, writing in 1929, declared that '[t]o live in a glass house is a revolutionary virtue par excellence. It is also an intoxication, a moral exhibitionism, that we badly need. Discretion concerning one's own existence, once an aristocratic virtue, has become more and more an affair of petty-bourgeois parvenus.'[14] I have to wonder if Benjamin is not more perceptive here than his politics are, for his approving phrase 'a moral exhibitionism that we badly need' can of course be made to retort on the glass house. Benjamin's text also points to the other political aspect of glass architecture: even at the beginning of the twentieth century, as can be seen in the expressionist strands of Paul Scheerbart's and Bruno Taut's early work, glass carried with it a mystical ideal of redemption. Anthony Vidler, in his postmodern defence of *The Architectural Uncanny*, sums up Modernist hopes thus: 'Transparency, it was thought, would eradicate the domain of myth, suspicion, tyranny, and, above all, the irrational.'[15] Against these hopes, Vidler emphasises the uncanny features of transparency, pointing to glass as a material physically disconnecting inside and outside, the unsettling effects of glare and reflectance that change with the outside

14 Walter Benjamin, 'Surrealism: The Last Snapshot of the European Intelligentsia', in Michael W. Jennings, Howard Eiland, Gary Smith, eds, *Walter Benjamin: Selected Writings, 1927–30* (Vol. 2, Pt.1) (Cambridge, MA: Harvard University Press, 1999), 209. The context is a passage of rather extravagant praise of André Breton's *Nadja*. Cf. Vidler, *The Architectural Uncanny*, 218.

15 Vidler, *The Architectural Uncanny*, 168.

conditions (day/night, bright light/clouds), and the mirroring effect of glass, with its sudden estrangement.[16] Vidler's criticism seems pertinent: there is no reason to think that transparency equals enlightenment. But his positive point seems an odd inversion of the modernist faith: purely physical phenomena of occlusion supposedly signal psychic and political problems, and an architecture consciously opaque and transparent at the same time (he mentions Rem Koolhaas) is proposed as the right and proper visual expression of the complexity of contemporary social relations.[17]

So the question remains whether or not there is a way to criticise the modernist fixation on transparency without falling oneself into an utopianism of obscurity. Jeff Wall, in a reading of Dan Graham's *Alterations to a Suburban House* (I will come back to this work later) famously discussed Philip Johnson's 1949 *Glass House* and Mies van der Rohe's 1950 *Farnsworth House*, Illinois, as sites of 'excessive openness', whose 'control of nature' forbids the introduction of mirrors.[18] There are no mirrors in these houses apart from in the bathrooms, according to Wall, because they would disturb the play of reflection and opacity of the glass façades. In this playful architectural setting, the inhabitant of the house is master, and outside space is his dominion too. Yet the modernist embargo on mirrors is in vain. Night turns the power play on its head, for we can no longer see out and thus control nature outside. In Wall's evocative prose, the house becomes a grave in which vampires lurk, caught in the reflections and mirroring games of the now-impenetrable glass wall. The complexity of seeing in these glass cubes, which Wall relates to traditions such as the Belvedere palaces of the nobility, is achieved primarily through the choice of material. For Wall, the modernist

16 Vidler, *The Architectural Uncanny*, 216–25.

17 One should probably bear in mind here Colin Rowe and Robert Slutzky, who argue for a ('phenomenal') transparency, favouring overlap and complexity over modernist ('literal') transparency. Colin Rowe and Robert Slutzky, 'Transparency. Literal and Phenomenal', *Perspecta* 8 (1963), 45–54.

18 Jeff Wall, 'Dan Graham's Kammerspiel' [1985], in Miriam Katzeff, Thomas Lawson, and Susan Morgan, eds, *Real Life Magazine: Selected Writings and Projects, 1979–94* (New York: Primary Information, 2006), 194–217; cf. Beatriz Colomina, 'Double exposure: Alteration to a suburban house' [2001], in Alex Kitnick, ed., *Dan Graham* (Cambridge, MA: MIT Press/October Files, 2011), 163–71.

dream of rationality *and* control may have been doomed from the start, but it is the task of politically engaged art and architecture of our present time to question this ideology; to replace the false clarity of transparent glass with the clear disorientation, so to speak, of a system of mirrors. In this rather bleak perspective, Graham's glass house, which strips a suburban interior of its privacy through the provision of a massive glass wall, is no solution, but a laying bare of the problem, at best a therapeutic airing of the wound.

How does EXPORT's cube stand in relation to these issues of control, vision, gaze and the uncanny? Does she embrace modernist openness for a feminist cause, and does this project run aground on its opacity? EXPORT's cube fails on the quite modernist understanding of transparency as a directness of social relations on a par with unobstructed viewing. It is not the case that EXPORT's cube is problematic because it generates ghostly reflections and occlusions, but rather because it places its ostensibly challenging content in a fishbowl, where, potentially, at any given point, and from any given perspective, nothing is hidden.

Cracking Transparency

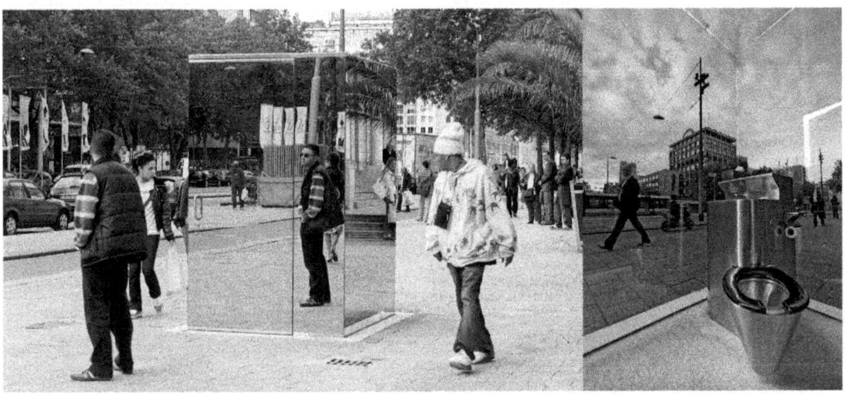

Fig. 3.2: Monica Bonvicini, *Don't Miss A Sec'*, 2004, Exhibition View: PUBLIC (in front of Rotterdam City Hall) IBC Rotterdam/Sculpture International. Credit: Jannes Linders © Monica Bonvicini, VG Bild-Kunst, Bonn.

Another cube, Monica Bonvicini's *Don't Miss A Sec'* of 2004, is a sculpture enclosing a functioning public toilet, which was part of several exhibitions in Zurich, Cologne, and elsewhere. Consisting of two glass panels, which have a semi-transparent mirror effect, this technical specificity allowed the users inside to look out onto the busy street. The presumed power of surveillance, potentially letting the person inside watch without being seen, is upset by the disconcerting fact that one sees all this while using the toilet, in the awkward position of doubting one's own invisibility from the other side. In a way, this is the ultimate Bellevue in Johnson's sense, but also a high-tech update of the humble variants on Jeremy Bentham's Panopticon found in clinics and police stations. Complete vision backfires; it disrupts the sense of security in such an intimate place. This feeling of vulnerability for the privileged viewer is of course enforced by the mirrored façade, which invites passers-by to examine their own reflections. The mechanisms of visibility and the uncanny are shown in this work to be less ghostly and irrational than Vidler's focus on E. T. A. Hoffmann would lead one to believe: the constant potential entanglement of private and public inherent in modernist glass architecture is what causes discomfort, and is here played out fully in the choice of mirror glass. Despite or even because of this banality, Bonvicini's staging of the loss of privacy in public space is ironic and aggressive: visitors had to, as the artist phrased it, 'defy their own embarrassment'.[19] While the notion of being watched, brought on by being able to watch, is threatening for the person inside, it is not at all clear that the object is perceived as a threat by spectators on the street. The box is treated as a solid object, and the passers-by reproduced in Bonvicini's catalogues appear not to know whether someone is inside, or even that someone *could be* inside. In a way, the threat to them is only legible to someone who has projected him or herself into the situation of the toilet-user. From the outside, the cube is a minimalist object, taking up space, making spectators walk around it and adapt their passage consciously to its forms. As such, it resembles the minimalism that occupied

19 *BBC World News*, online version, 3 December 2003 <http://news.bbc.co.uk/2/hi/entertainment/3257370.stm> accessed 17 October 2013.

galleries in the 1960s – Bonvicini is theatrical in just the way Michael Fried found minimalism to be, provoking visitors to walk around the object and take up an attitude to it, instead of being able to contemplate its physical presence without thinking of their bodies.[20] *Don't Miss A Sec'* is basically a comment on many of Dan Graham's pavilions and on the idea of transparency in modernism – 'quite cynical,' Bonvicini recently noted, an interesting coupling, because, of course, Graham is a critic of modernism.[21] Yet this lumping together of modernism and Dan Graham, however cynical it may be, should make us pause: is minimalism, with its insistence on lived experience and the body, really the opposite of modernist clarity? Fried and the artists he criticised certainly thought so, but perhaps the contrast is overdrawn. After all, the mirrored surface of the cube helps it blend into the environment and become less of an obstacle; the supposed impetus to focus on one's own body is to a large extent a product of the neutrality of the object itself. Bonvicini's cube seems ordinary from the outside, but also unthreatening, in contrast to the simultaneously claustrophobic and exposed effect inside. This makes for an interesting twist of preconceived notions of the public and the private spheres: the public sphere becomes the safe one, while the private is attacked optically by the offer of an outside view. Implicit knowledge, more than any profound psychic mechanism, is responsible for this. It is a fact of normal perception that we are perceived as well as perceiving. To be an unperceived perceiver in an everyday setting makes one feel like a ghost, with or without Jeff Wall's pop vampirism.

The context-dependence of discomfort that attends Bonvicini's sculpture emerges clearly if we compare it to apparently more intimidating scenarios. We might encounter such a mirror in a police interrogation room. But while here we would at least suspect that we are being watched, the effect of being on the other side, with no motive to investigate anyone, leaves one unsure of one's own invisibility, which is after all assured by

20 Michael Fried, 'Art and Objecthood' [1967] in *Essays and Reviews* (Chicago, London: Chicago University Press, 1998), 148–72.

21 Massimiliano Gioni and Monica Bonvicini, 'Destroy She Says', *Flash Art* 257 (April 2007) <http://www.flashartonline.com/interno.php?pagina=articolo_det&id_art=32&det=ok&title=MONICA-BONVICINI> accessed 17 October 2013.

the exterior view of the mirror surface which precedes entering. This is reinforced by the panoramic effect of the urban architecture as seen from the toilet, overlaid with one's own faint mirror image inside the bathroom.

Of course one could interpret Bonvicini's juxtaposition of Graham and modernism not in terms of modernist art, but of modernist architecture as it entered the urban mainstream. Mirrored glass, orthodox in what may be called advanced sculpture since the 1960s, has become as much a part of the corporate skyline as the curtain wall. And so, apart from a minimalist tradition of objects in space and their interaction with environment and audience, Bonvicini plays on the mirror façades of public architecture. Architectural historian Joan Ockman has analysed the hegemony of the international style in the postwar United States, under the title 'Toward a Normative Architecture', as a historical development from the radical Bauhaus years under Gropius, van der Rohe and Moholy-Nagy, towards a triumphant American style that was exported back to Europe. In this transnational transfer, Ockman argues, it became non-political, non-critical and impersonal, affirming Cold War politics.[22] The glass façade is the major player in this story, representing technological skill and a shift from democratic aspirations to an architecture of domination. Seemingly neutral in its cube-like openness, without ornament and without obvious signifiers of hierarchies, this neutrality is a capitalist success story – reflection but no access, visual or otherwise, while inside, the boss in his corner office can look on the street without looming over it.

Bonvicini has taken up the ideology of the modernist glass façade in another project she developed for Zurich. Expressly citing Gordon

22 Joan Ockman, 'Toward a Theory of Normative Architecture', in Steven Harris and Deborah Berke, eds, *Architecture of the Everyday* (New York: Princeton Architectural Press, 1997). See also Reinhold Martin, *The Organizational Complex: Architecture, Media, and Corporate Space* (Cambridge, MA: MIT Press, 2003). Most pertinent for my text is Martin's recent book, *Utopia's Ghost: Architecture and Postmodernism, Again* (Minneapolis: University of Minnesota Press, 2010), where, criticising and generalising from the equations of mirrors and capitalist spectacle in David Harvey and Frederic Jameson, Martin defines the mirror as 'a feedback loop', 106. Martin sees the mirror as 'the paradigmatic object ... of postmodern architecture', 123.

Matta-Clark's *Window Blow Out* action of 1976, Bonvicini's *Façade* was intended as an intervention on an existing glass façade. The glass panels of a business office built in the early 1990s should have been replaced by carefully shattered glass panels, evoking both Matta-Clark's action, in which the artist shot into the windows of a building at Cornell University, and its referents, urban poverty and violence. Bonvicini's shattered glass can be read as an attack on the capitalist take-over of the glass façade, but also, as she herself says, a return to the 'startling crystal' of Bruno Taut, with its utopian aspirations, located in the apparent coming together of the natural and the manufactured in crystalline architecture.[23] Here, the sublime effect is achieved by a parallel between nature and industry, but violence is at issue as well. Bonvicini later proposed an alternative version, also in Zurich, in a glass pavilion that at first sight resembles EXPORT's in Vienna. However, in contrast, it presents itself as a dystopian place of danger rather than protection, inaccessible, lit at night with bright neon light. Mirroring our fears of property devaluation, rioting and gang violence, the project at the same time elevates the damaged skin of modernism to artistic craft. Or it should have: the project proved impossible to execute, on technical and logistic grounds.

Is there anything that we can conclude from these glass cubes, other than that we should be as suspicious of totalising narratives about glass and mirrors as about anything else? I think that, with caution, we can say more. It is true that in public space, the functions of glass and mirrors cannot easily be predicted in advance. Depending on lighting and the physical properties of mirroring or transparency, their social effects of stimulating curiosity or discomfiture are highly user and context dependent. Functions and expectations intertwine in what we see and what we expect, and ultimately, being able to see ourselves projected on buildings and our environment both gives us the power to perceive what is behind and around us (including other persons in public space), but also a sense that vision is

23 Monica Bonvicini, 'Projekt für Zürich', project paper for Kunst Öffentlichkeit Zürich, 2005. I would like to thank Christoph Schenker, head of the Art Public Zurich projects, for discussing the piece with me.

blocked from us – we cannot see ahead, despite utopian promises to the contrary, both modern and postmodern. In any case, given recent interest in the emotional, imaginative and playful dimensions of the production of knowledge, it seems we cannot accept postmodern approaches to glass as obstruction without at the same time giving qualified assent to classic modernist theories of glass as medium of (self)clarification.

In conclusion, I want to examine a recent suggestion by Reinhold Martin, that to criticise the ubiquity of mirrors in corporate architecture, we should not be seduced by a rhetoric of disappearance, mimesis, or dematerialisation that comes with the modernist 'look into the mirror', but 'learn first to look *at* the mirror.'[24] Martin hopes, perhaps a bit romantically, that this might allow us to find the reality beyond 'postmodernity's self-reflexive feedback loops.' Yet in a sense, if we abandon a rhetoric pitting modernism against postmodernism, it will seem that artists have been concerned with this look *at* the mirror for some time. Take one of the most prominent artists investigating the mirror effect at the intersection of art and architecture, Dan Graham, in the aforementioned *Alteration to a Suburban House* (1978). The model shows a typical US-suburban ranch house. The façade has been removed and replaced by a glass plate. In the middle of the house, a mirror plane divides the building, reflecting the living room onto the street, while the more private parts of the house (bedrooms, bathrooms) are hidden behind. It is tempting to read this as an indictment of modernism; but it is just as clearly an indictment of American suburban building, which is its opposite. How to understand transparency in Graham? The artist had worked with mirrors in many of his canonical performances of the 1970s, *Performance, Audience, Mirror* (1975) in particular: Graham discussed the actions of the audience he saw in the mirror, sometimes facing these persons, sometimes facing the mirror that reflected them. The audience, at least in its physical presence within the confines of the performance (sometimes optimistically glossed as its 'collaboration') is made part of the piece, and the mirror is the 'medium' that throws doubt on the assurance of pure presence possessed exclusively

24 Martin, *Utopia's Ghost*, 114.

by the artist, or any certainty that we might have about our relationship to one another and our environment. But does it make any difference whether Graham faced his spectators or their reflections, watching him in the mirror? In a context of one-way surveillance, where of the two parties facing one another, only one is aware of the other, a mirror makes all the difference. In Graham's case, with the audience following him *and* the mirror, this is not so clear – even though his point at the time might have been to 'reflect' on the difference between the two. He addressed the *same* audience in both cases.

For a feminist endeavour, this aspect of the mirror – its parity, symmetry and potential identity between viewer and viewed – is particularly interesting. Take Adrian Piper's *Food for the Spirit*, in which she photographed herself in a mirror while fasting, purportedly in response to Kant's *Critique of Pure Reason*, an investigation of the limits of the self and the world. It is expressly part of Piper's feminist, philosophically inclined performance that the image of herself nude, photographed in the mirror, that results, is not a product of narcissistic or commercial exploitation. Does the mirror make a difference to this turning around of perception? Some questions would need further exploration: how does the private mirror differ from the glass wall? How exactly does reflection question our sense of perception, and, in particular for public space, engage us in a game of confusing reflections that suggest control, framing, but also a blending into our environment, including the supra-vision of the world behind us? In what sense is gender an issue in this relationship? I close, as I began, with Derrida: how do we speak about glass in 'technical or material terms' and at the same time 'in terms of transparency and immediacy, of love or of police, of the border that is perhaps erased between the public and the private, etc.?'[25] There are, indeed, what he terms 'calls for desire', but in as much as we will react as individual subjects, engendered and shaped by our own experiences, the results will not be easily anticipated by capitalists and technocrats, and neither can they easily be predicted by artists, architects, and theorists.

25 Derrida, *Assemblage*, 9.

Bibliography

Benjamin, Walter, 'Surrealism: The Last Snapshot of the European Intelligentsia', in Michael W. Jennings, Howard Eiland and Gary Smith, eds, *Walter Benjamin: Selected Writings, 1927–1930* (Cambridge, MA: Harvard University Press, 1999), 209.

Bonvicini, Monica, 'Projekt für Zürich', project paper for Kunst Öffentlichkeit Zürich, 2005.

Colomina, Beatriz, 'Double exposure: Alteration to a suburban house' [2001] in Alex Kitnick, ed., *Dan Graham* (Cambridge, MA: MIT Press/October Files, 2011), 163–71.

Derrida, Jacques, 'A letter to Peter Eisenman', *Assemblage: A Critical Journal of Architecture and Design* (12 August 1990), 6–12.

Fried, Michael, 'Art and Objecthood' [1967], in *Essays and Reviews* (Chicago, London: Chicago University Press, 1998).

Gioni, Massimiliano, and Monica Bonvicini, 'Destroy She Says', *Flash Art* 257 (April 2007) <http://www.flashartonline.com/interno.php?pagina=articolo_det&id_art=32&det=ok&title=MONICA-BONVICINI>

Haag Bletter, Rosemarie, 'The Interpretation of the Glass Dream – Expressionist Architecture and the History of the Crystal Metaphor', *The Journal of the Society of Architectural Historians* 40/1 (1981), 20–43.

Magistrat der Stadt Wien, ed., *Der transparente Raum* (Vienna: MA 57 – Frauenförderung und Koordinierung von Frauenangelegenheiten, 2000).

Martin, Reinhold, *The Organizational Complex: Architecture, Media, and Corporate Space* (Cambridge, MA: MIT Press, 2003).

——, *Utopia's Ghost: Architecture and Postmodernism, Again* (Minneapolis: University of Minnesota Press, 2010).

Masters, Roger D., and Christopher Kelly, eds, The Collected Writings of Rousseau (Hanover, NH: University Press of New England, 1990).

Mulvey, Laura, 'Visual Pleasure and Narrative Cinema', *Screen* 16/3 (Autumn 1975), 6–18.

Ockman, Joan, 'Toward a Theory of Normative Architecture', in Steven Harris and Deborah Berke, eds, *Architecture of the Everyday* (New York: Princeton Architectural Press, 1997).

Palla, Rudi, ed., *Erinnerungsstätte Allentsteig – eine Dokumentation* (Vienna: Triton, 1999).

Petrovic, Madeleine, *Der Wiener Gürtel Wiederentdeckung einer Prachtstraße* (Vienna, 2009), 89–103.

Quetglas, Jose, 'Perdida de la sintesis: el Pabellon de Mies', *Carrer de la Ciutat* 11 (April 1980), reprinted as 'Loss of Synthesis. Mies's Pavilion', in Hays, Michael, ed., *Architecture Theory Since 1968* (Cambridge, MA: The MIT Press, 1998), 382–91.

——, 'Toward a Theory of Normative Architecture', in Steven Harris and Deborah Berke, eds, *Architecture of the Everyday* (New York: Princeton Architectural Press, 1997), 122–52.

Rowe, Colin, and Robert Slutzky, 'Transparency. Literal and Phenomenal', *Perspecta* 8 (1963), 45–54.

Sennett, Richard, *The Fall of Public Man* (Cambridge: Cambridge University Press, 1974).

Taffuri, Manfredo, 'Il teatro come città virtuale. Da Appia al Totaltheater', *Lotus* 17 (December 1977), 30–53.

Vidler, Anthony, *The Architectural Uncanny. Essays in the Modern Unhomely* (Cambridge, MA: The MIT Press: 1992).

Von Moos, Stanislaus, '"Glanzblitz!" Über Architektur, Transparenz und Multimedialität', in Monika Wagner and Dietmar Rübel, eds, *Material in Kunst und Alltag* (Berlin: Akademie Verlag, 2002), 47–63.

Wall, Jeff, 'Dan Graham's Kammerspiel' [1985], in Miriam Katzeff, Thomas Lawson and Susan Morgan, eds, *Real Life Magazine: Selected Writings and Projects, 1979–94* (New York: Primary Information, 2006), 194–217.

Widrich, Mechtild, *Performative Monuments* (Manchester: Manchester University Press, 2014).

LORENS HOLM

4 Transparency: Effable and Ineffable

> Then a boundless depth opens up, effaces the walls, drives away contingent presences, *accomplishes the miracle of ineffable space*.
>
> —LE CORBUSIER, introduction to *New World of Space* (1948)

> Where would I go, if I could go, who would I be, if I could be, what would I say, if I had a voice, who says this, saying it's me?
>
> —SAMUEL BECKETT, *Texts for Nothing IV* (1951/1966), opening lines

Space is not a bad starting point for a discussion of what is visible and invisible in contemporary culture, because like our subjectivity, which we bring to every encounter – even to encounters with our self (I am thinking here of Beckett) – it is everywhere and nowhere all around us. Like our subjectivity, we see through space to reach things, and if it were not for its seeming invisibility, intangibility and nothingness, nothing would have an appearance. If space or subjectivity were to thicken, become material, or be mistaken for material, nothing would have an appearance. We do not image it,[1] and yet it seems to be the precondition for imaging everything else. The rationality and materiality of architecture (probably its two bugbears) make the elusive status of space and its spurious logic all the more problematic.

1 I use 'image' as a verb, instead of 'see' or 'visualise', in order to underscore the intersubjective condition of perception: the fact that in order to communicate what you see or visualise to yourself or to others, you have to either describe it (a mental image) or draw it (a visual image). I return to this point in the concluding paragraph to the section 'Space and the Projective Subject', below.

And let us be clear: by 'space', we do not mean space metaphorically speaking, or 'personal space', which isn't space at all, but body heat. We mean space literally, the space that architecture makes, the space between things.

Space and the self seem to be always already fading away. If I look really hard, all I see are the surfaces that shape space. Space, with its essential emptiness, seems a disappearing act, which we can only, disappointingly, measure.[2] And the harder I focus on what's going on in my head, the more I feel other to myself.[3] Whenever I try to capture space and subjects in photographs, all I get are objects. Space is not constituted by the walls, floors, ceilings, hats on tables, fish on worktops ..., arranged *in* space (think of Le Corbusier's photographs of his purist interiors), but by the perspectival organisation of these elements *on* the photograph around the vanishing point, the way they seem to get farther from the viewing subject or its surrogate, the camera, by getting smaller. This portrait of space is not an image, but the organisation of the image for the subject. Likewise, the subject – its desire, knowledge, power – is precisely what is not captured in the portrait, no matter how many accessories it may be portrayed with. A portrait is just a talking head, a façade, meat with make-up. If there is an appearance of the subject to itself, to others, that appearance is elsewhere.

There have been architectural forays into the invisible, but most are about the attenuation of material, not space, which is, if anything, marked by the absence of material.[4] Ives Klein proposed an air architecture.[5] He

2 This insistence on the invisibility we call space is what Heidegger alluded to with his empty jug, and what Lacan alluded to when he writes in *Seminar 7, The Ethics of Psychoanalysis* that architecture like painting is organised around emptiness. Cf. Heidegger's paper, 'The Thing', in *Poetry Language Thought*, trans. Albert Hofstadter (New York: Harper, 1971), 163ff. The emptiness of the jug is a precondition for engagement with it. Jacques Lacan, *The Seminar of Jacques Lacan, Book VII: The Ethics of Psychoanalysis 1959–60* (New York: Norton 1992), 136.

3 William James, who invented the term 'stream of consciousness', notes this phenomenon of self-scrutiny and relates it to psychosis. Cf. *Principles of Psychology* (London: Macmillan, 1890), the chapters 'The Consciousness of Self' and 'The Stream of Thought'.

4 See the bibliography (below) for a sampling of papers on the transparency of material in architecture.

5 See the catalogue, *Invisible* (London: Hayward, 2012), 33.

worked on an air roof (tested in the kitchen sink) that would protect its residents from the weather by air pressure. It uses air pressure to make walls, but space is not air. Air thresholds are used in cold storage systems, sometimes with clear plastic flaps. Diller + Scofidio's *Blur Building* is a spray mist that conceals the grid of pipes that emits it.[6] We could add the wall that the mime makes by miming, which is a special case of invisibility, because it is not about attenuating a material that is real, but imagining one that is not.[7]

It might be more promising to locate the invisible in the relation between subject and space. The invisible is a property of a relation, not of things: something in the relation renders space – if not invisible – at least unseen. Walter Benjamin argued that we receive architecture in a state of distraction: architecture is the backdrop material that no one sees; nowhere is this more evident than when someone walks the street speaking on their mobile. Things are invisible because we blank them, a form of repression in the visual register. According to Lacan, there is always a blind spot in the centre of vision. This is the condition of the neurotic, to be positioned before his/her objects, but not see them; it is the opposite with psychotics. In his seminal paper, 'Mimicry and Legendary Psychasthenia', Roger Caillois notes that his distressed patients can see their objects, but cannot locate themselves. They are too disorganised to see from a position.[8] This is a breakdown in the pact between subject and space: the subject is supposed to coalesce to a point of thought and action; space is supposed to radiate from that point – it makes sense to subjects because it triangulates.

6 Swiss Expo 2002, Lake Neuchatel (Yverdon-les-Bains, Switzerland).

7 The mime sees something that others do not. In the sense that it is for him/her only, it is imaginary. The opposite of the mime's wall are experiments in digital architecture which aim for maximum not minimum visuality, but are otherwise immaterial.

8 First published *Minatoure 7* (Skira, Paris 1935) republished in English in October 31 (Cambridge, MA: MIT Press, 1984). Caillois documents symptoms of a form of psychical collapse of identity that he called *legendary psychasthenia*. He reports patients who claimed they could not locate themselves in the space they were in. Or who felt invaded by space, as if space failed to localise and individuate them. For Walter Benjamin, see 'The Work of Art in the Age of Mechanical Reproduction' [1936], *Illuminations* (London: Fontana, 1973).

In their elegant and influential paper 'Transparency Literal and Phenomenal' (1963), Colin Rowe and Robert Slutzky nominate transparency as the principle signifier of modernism and modern architecture. It is one of the most eloquent forays by the discipline of architecture into the question of space and its visibilities. It may seem irksome to continue to associate space and subjectivity, yet it seems they always are associated. In 'Transparency Literal and Phenomenal', the question of the subject seems to shadow its authors' every move.

This chapter explores Rowe's and Slutzky's articulation of modern space, and the challenges to it. It is part of an ongoing project about how architecture constructs subjectivity. In a nutshell, the subject's functions – its desire, identity, knowledge and power – map onto space. By subjectivity, I do not mean sense of self. Most selves have a pretty nebulous sense of self. I mean above all, the function of *I* in discourse. Psychoanalysis has mined culture and experience in order to build a picture of the I, its functions and articulations, which is both theoretic and empirical. We will call this I/eye, the projective subject.[9]

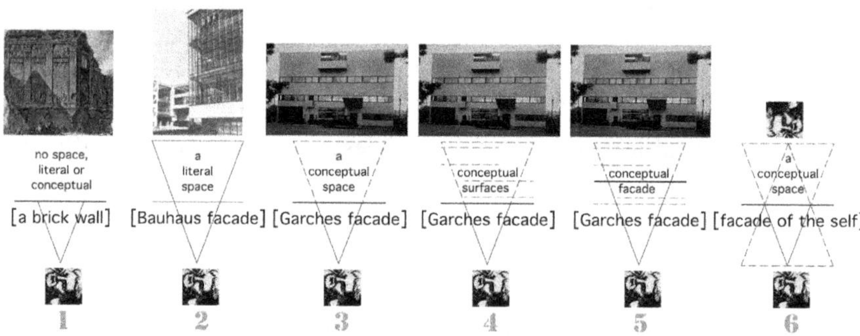

Fig. 4.1: Space and the projective subject: the subject …
1. views an opaque plane surface like the side of a brick tomb from which the travertine cladding has been stripped.

9 J. Laplanche and J-B. Pontalis, *The Language of Psycho-Analysis* (London: Hogarth Press and the Institute of Psycho-Analysis, 1973) for a discussion of projection in Freudian psychoanalysis.

2. views a transparent plane surface like the glass Bauhaus façade or the picture plane of an illusionistic painting.
3. views a phenomenally transparent plane surface, like the façade of Garches or a cubist painting.
4. views the façade of Garches, showing the plan organised as a series of transparent planes …
5. … in which the picture plane is displaced from façade to interior.
6. views the phenomenally transparent surface that I project, upon which the subject projects a depth of intention, desire, etc. This, according to Lacan, is the space of the self.[10]
Credit: Lorens Holm.

Space and the Projective Subject

According to Rowe and Slutzky, there are two forms of transparency in modern art and architecture: the literal, which is 'a property of materials', and the phenomenal, which is an implied transparency where there is none, the effect of 'a form of organisation'.[11] They manifest in the different attitudes to glass. The authors compare the glass curtain wall of the Bauhaus by Gropius (2) and the façade of *Villa Stein* at Garches by Le Corbusier (3). Gropius was interested in diagonal views of the corner, which display the transparent properties of glass to their best advantage. Le Corbusier was interested in the taut 'planar qualities of glass',[12] the frontal view, and the Leger-like composition of strip windows, balconies, and other elements, which undermine simple figure/ground oppositions. In plan, Le Corbusier aligned columns and walls to imply a layering of shallow stratified spaces that crosscut the deep space running back from the façade (4); rather the way the jars and bowls in the cubist still life are organised by dense

10 I have borrowed Lacan's diagram of the visual field, published in his *The Four Fundamental Concepts of Psychoanalysis* (New York: Norton, 1981), 106.

11 Rowe, Colin and Robert Slutzky, 'Transparency: Literal and Phenomenal' in Rowe, *Mathematics of the Ideal Villa and other essays* (Cambridge MA: MIT Press, 1976), 161.

12 Ibid., 167.

gridding and diagonals which seem to impart to them a dual allegiance, to the picture plane and to the shallow space sponsored by it. The phenomenal transparency of *Villa Stein* depends upon the simultaneous reading of overlapping spaces and spatial figures: 'one space which is explicit and another which is implied',[13] 'a real and deep space and an ideal and shallow one'.[14] 'Space becomes constructed' from particular 'locations'.[15] It is clear where Rowe's and Slutzky's sympathies lie: the unambiguous exercises in transparent planes and objects in deep space by Moholy-Nagy (bad); 'the Cubist "discovery" of shallow space',[16] the multiple readings of space and object, figure and ground, frontality and rotation, explored by Cézanne, Léger, and Juan Gris (good).

Rowe and Slutzky discern two types of phenomenal transparency:

1. The reading of shallow space into an opaque plane, the façade. Derrida would have called it a reading event. Freud, projection.
2. The simultaneous perception of a deep space (the view) crosscut by the reading of a shallow stratified space. They 'interpenetrate without optical destruction of each other'.[17]

Rowe's and Slutzky's argument plots a familiar narrative arc that moves from paintings (Juan Gris) to façades (Garches) to interiors. We assume they begin with painting because it is easier to articulate first in painting what they want finally to say about architecture. A multi-layered narrative goes from literal to phenomenal/implied, real to ideal, material to conceptual, and most critically, from surface to space. The authors appeal to an implicit spatial logic that goes through the plane surface to space, a logic we call projective. For Rowe and Slutzky, space is always the projection of a surface by a subject. Space seems never to be here and material;

13 Ibid., 171.
14 Ibid., 174.
15 Ibid., 175.
16 Ibid., 170.
17 Ibid., 161, 168.

it is always out there and conceptual, ideal, symbolic. The purpose of this chapter is to make this projective logic explicit.

Despite their interest in destabilising simple figure/ground oppositions, Rowe and Slutzky continue to think within the paradigm of the projective subject. Their primal scene: the visitor to the Bauhaus stands before its workshop wing, looking through the glass to the interior. This relationship was codified by Brunelleschi (fifteenth century) with the demonstration of perspective. He asked the good citizens of Florence to view the Baptistery through a perspective painting of the Baptistery, so that their view and his picture coincided.[18] The viewer of the perspective painting gazes through it the way s/he gazes through a window (Alberti's metaphor, he was thinking of fresco), to an imagined depth beyond. Rowe and Slutzky assume a similar spatial scenario comprised of a viewing subject – defined by the single (although not necessarily stationary) point of projection – standing before a plane surface (painting, glass curtain wall). The surface screens an interior that is accessed by an inquisitive gaze. Perspective was invented by Cartesian man, for whom two things are always before his eyes: an image and an idea. This scenario has been the spatial template for all viewing, modernist or otherwise, at least since the Renaissance. Panofsky called it symbolic form.[19]

With phenomenal transparency, the question of the subject becomes inescapable. It is no longer possible to fob transparency off on materials. Unlike the Bauhaus, Garches is only transparent for a projective subject. This is nowhere clearer than in its monumental headwall, into whose opacity we are asked to read a shallow stratified depth. The plan diagrams and axonometric

18 Cf. Lorens Holm, *Brunelleschi, Lacan Le Corbusier: Architecture, Space, and the Construction of Subjectivity* (London: Routledge, 2010), 77–130.

19 Erwin Panofsky, *Perspective as Symbolic Form* [1927] (New York: Zone Books, 1991). Panofsky attributes 'symbolic form' to the Kant scholar Ernst Cassirer, *The Philosophy of Symbolic Forms* in 3 volumes (Oxford University Press 1953, 1955, 1957) although he does not reference Cassirer's text. See Panofsky pp. 40–1, 'But if perspective is not a factor of value, it is surely a factor of style. Indeed, it may even be characterised as (to extend Ernst Cassirer's felicitous term to the history of art) one of those "symbolic forms" in which "spiritual meaning is attached to a concrete, material sign and intrinsically given to this sign"'.

drawings that Rowe and Slutzky publish of Le Corbusier's League of Nations project confirm it. They ask us to stand before it in our minds' eye, to see the depth in it that they see (it has the form of an expanding view sectioned by a sequence of parallel picture planes, Alberti's pyramid of vision).

Both forms of transparency imply the integrity and continuity of a positioned subject. Projection is not merely an architectural supplement to subjectivity; it is constitutive. Rowe and Slutzky ask us to do with the façade of *Villa Stein* at Garches what we do all the time with the face, that other literally opaque but phenomenally transparent surface we encounter in every mirror, and in every other person's face (6). I am a subject for myself because you attribute subjectivity to me. I stand before you, you hear my voice, you follow my eyes; and upon the great surface of my façade (that image I project), you project an almost infinite phenomenal depth of intention, thought, love, doubt, fear of dying. This projective subject has at least three characteristics. It is positioned (in space) as a single point of thought and action. It projects (makes space). And, at least for the purposes of projection, what it projects onto functions for it as a screen.

We usually expect to encounter the screen as a façade, and in any case, as material.[20] But we read the phenomenal screen into space wherever we look. Garches restages this act by displacing the screen that first appears as a façade where it is a form of material into the plan where it reappears as a form of organisation (5). The screen that is first materialised as the façade of *Villa Stein* at Garches is then reinstated as a trace in the plan. Garches restages the symbolic conditions for viewing, which we experience as the transparency of space. This is an example of the power of architecture to show us what we already knew about space and ourselves. The affinity of Le Corbusier's work to photography is often remarked. It is now clear why.

20 Hence Rowe and Slutzky's façade studies in 'Transparency: Literal and Phenomenal Part 2' in *Perspecta 13/14* (1971) 'But some of these suppositions are of so tendentious ... a nature that in the present article it is proposed to consign them to temporary oblivion, and to concentrate ... not on the three dimensional or spatial aspects of phenomenal transparency, but ... upon its two dimensional manifestations – upon phenomenal transparency as pattern [i.e. façades].', 288. This paper appears to backpedal to a conventional position about façades from a more radical one about space.

It is not merely that the work is photogenic, that it solicits, as it were, the camera's surrogate look. It also re-stages the symbolic support of image production, which makes visual experience possible.

The screen undergoes two displacements in Rowe's and Slutzky's account of phenomenal transparency: it is repositioned in the space and it becomes conceptual. This displacement is reflected in every perspective diagram. As a diagram for vision (which it purports to be) as opposed to simply an instruction about how to make realistic pictures, it depends upon a series of equivalences. The image is always depicted in two places: in the eye of the viewer (retina or mind's eye) and on a screen in the space s/he views, where it is always disappearing into the space itself.

When their argument shifts from the façades to space, the road gets rocky. The complexity here – unacknowledged by the authors – has to do with the fact that space, strictly speaking, is neither literally nor phenomenally transparent, only picture planes and façades are. Space does not have material properties because it is not exactly a material (hence not literally transparent); and yet it does not seem to require a great deal of cognition to look through it (hence it is not phenomenally transparent). Space is rather a precondition for transparency: its projective geometry defines the transparency of the picture plane. Things have an appearance to the subject because they are projected as an image upon the picture plane to the subject. For the subject, vision is about having perceptions, or in the terms of this chapter, images. The world is filled with light, but light is just light; the visibility of the world depends upon the fact that images are projected upon screens.[21] Space, or at least visual space, supports images because it is everywhere marked by the geometric trace of the transparent screen, and some architectures, like Garches, make us aware of it. It is on account of this symbolic apparatus, that we attribute invisibility to space. Invisibility is an attribute of space not because we blank it, or because it is ultra-transparent, but because it constitutes the symbolic, geometric ground for images. Henceforth, we will designate as invisible the space that

21 Lacan argued this point in *The Four Fundamental Concepts of Psychoanalysis*, cf. the chapter 'The Line and Light', 91ff.

supports the screen of the viewing subject. Although Rowe and Slutzky do not make this claim, their argument entails it.

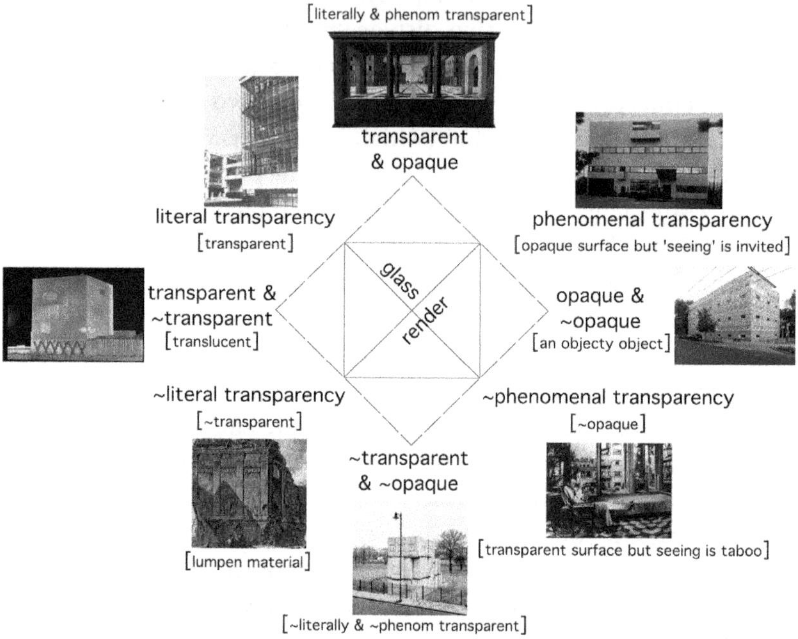

Fig. 4.2: Klein Square 1, working through literal and phenomenal transparency: classifying objects. Credit: Lorens Holm.

Klein Square 1

We can map Rowe's and Slutzky's argument onto the Klein square, which Rosalind Krauss introduced to the humanities in her paper 'Sculpture in the Expanded Field'.[22] This gives us a typology of architectural objects and

22 Rosalind Krauss, 'Sculpture in the Expanded Field', *October 8* (Spring 1979), 30–44.

viewing conditions (Fig. 4.2). In order to map the argument, we have to invoke the look or gaze of the viewer. This is a typology of relations between object and subject, not simply a typology of objects and their material properties. In the Klein square you place the two opposing terms of an argument on the top two corners of the square, and their negations on the bottom two. The top terms, usually a term and its other, are supplied by the argument and are taken as given, but their negations are often subject to dispute. A first pass would place literal and phenomenal transparency as opposing terms, with non-literal and non-phenomenal transparency below. The not-literally transparent could be a number of things that are simply not transparent (there are a number of ways of negating it), but we shall go for the obvious option of the opaque, represented by a tomb of lumpen masonry stripped of its travertine cladding. For the first term and its negation, there is a fit between the material properties of the object, and its visual possibilities: if the Bauhaus is transparent and you can see inside, the tomb is opaque and you cannot see inside.

If the façade of *Villa Stein* at Garches is phenomenally transparent, an example of the not-phenomenally transparent is the courtyard elevations of Manhattan apartment buildings. Although the windows are as transparent as the Bauhaus façade, there is an injunction against looking that disrupts the gaze and makes viewing difficult, which amounts to a kind of phenomenal opacity. Despite their close proximity, people tend not to stare into each other's windows, at least not obviously. Edward Hopper knew this. This social contract is broken by Jimmy Stewart's photographer in Hitchcock's *Rear Window* (1954); it is this breaking of the taboo against looking as much as the malevolence of the occupant (Raymond Burr) across the courtyard that spells trouble for Stewart, and casts a pall of unease over the movie.[23] With the term and its negation, there is a non-fit between material and seeing: Garches is opaque but you can 'see'; Rear Window is transparent but you 'can't'.[24]

23 This phenomenal opacity is signified by Jimmy Stewart's typical position in the film. He is always between two picture planes (camera and window) and always in profile, never looking out.

24 Note also that there is an equivalence of terms along the diagonal axes of the Klein square: the Bauhaus and the apartment building are transparent, and the façade of

There is a second tier to the diagram. The perspective painting is literally and phenomenally transparent because we pretend to be able to look through it as if it were a window. Rachel Whiteread's *House* (1993) is neither literally nor phenomenally transparent. Like the tomb, it is as opaque as a solid lump; additionally, it seems to repel the gaze, which is probably why it was so unpopular with the neighbours: the curtained windows of most houses invite looking, even, as in the case of the Manhattan apartment, it is forbidden. Koolhaas' translucent National Library project (1989) is transparent and not transparent at the same time. Vidler argues that the sense of the emergence of objects out of the depth of the block produces anxiety.[25] The tattooed surface of Herzog & de Meuron's Eberswalde Library (1996) seems to be phenomenally and not phenomenally transparent (i.e., opaque and not opaque) at the same time. Its image surface offers the promise – unfulfilled – of looking in, without relinquishing its opacity.

Fig. 4.3 (opposite): The Square positions figure, ground, not-figure and not-ground. Figure and ground correlate with object and space. Rowe and Slutzky's thesis about literal and phenomenal transparency lies on the axis of representation, which is marked by the pairs figure ground (literal) and not-figure not-ground (phenomenal transparency). This is the axis that defines the projective subject and the normative projective logic of space, represented by (top to bottom) a perspective diagram, the Bauhaus and Villa Stein. The axis of the real – marked by the pair figure not-figure and ground not-ground – is more difficult to talk about, and impossible to image, because it defies the logic of non-contradiction. Like that which is real, it makes no sense, it just is. If we feel compelled to fill this senseless void, to give it value, we might, in a gesture as speculative as it is desperate, use this axis to position Kant's things-in-themselves, and Le Corbusier's espace indicible.

Garches and the tomb are opaque. To fully map Rowe and Slutzky's argument, we would probably have to include a second Klein Square that mapped literal and phenomenal opacity with Garches and *Rear Window* in these positions respectively.

25 See Anthony Vidler, 'Transparency' in *The Architectural Uncanny: Essays in the Modern Unhomely* (Cambridge, MA: MIT Press, 1992).

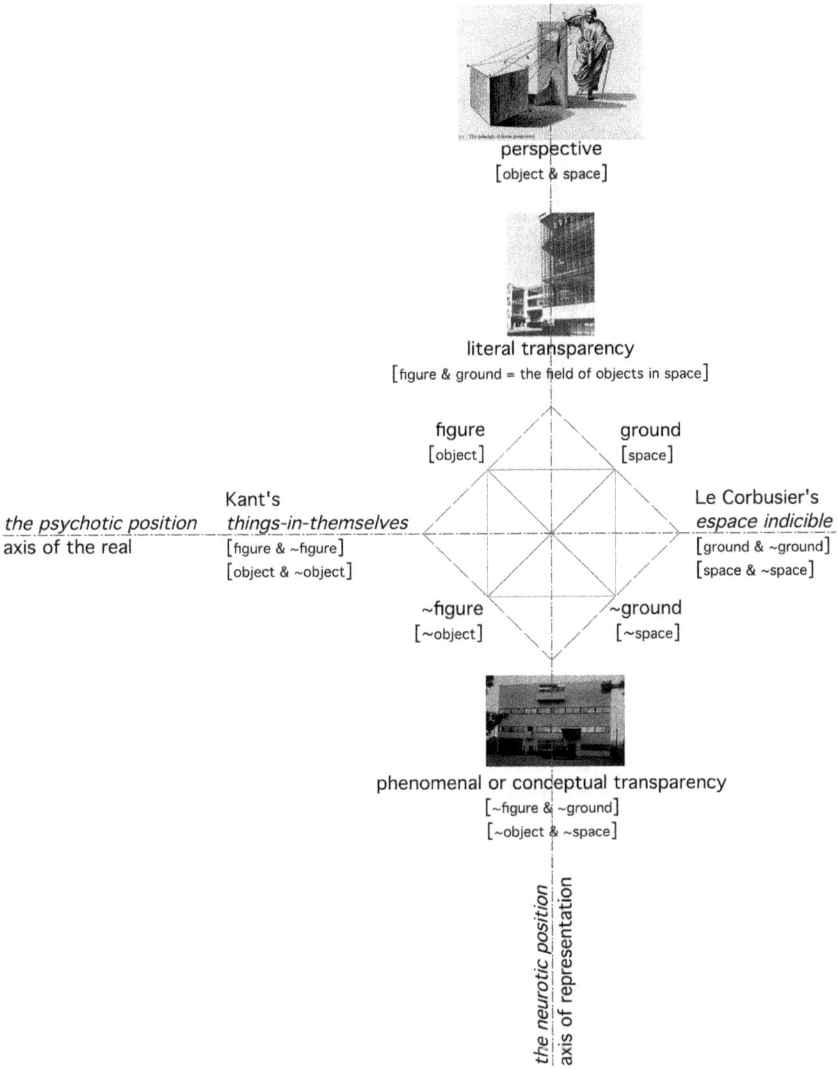

Fig. 4.3: Klein Square 2, working through figure and ground: classifying subjects and spaces. Credit: Lorens Holm.

Klein Square 2

At this point we need to focus more closely on space. Rowe and Slutzky describe the phenomenal transparency of the Garches interior as a shift from the conventional figure/ground binary of the classical plan and perspective, in which there is no ambiguity between what is object and what is space, to the not-figure/not-ground binary of the purist villa plan and cubist painting, in which there is the simultaneous reading of multiple spatial figures. We can begin a new Klein square (Fig. 4.3) with figure and ground, the clear articulation of which underlies the representational possibilities of literal transparency, and which define material reality. We locate their negations, ~figure and ~ground, on the lower two corners. In a binary figure/ground spatial logic, the ~figure is tantamount to a ground (space), hence a seeming equivalence of terms along the diagonal axes; but free from that logic, a ~figure could be anything, space or otherwise, that is simply not a figure to a ground. Similarly for the ~ground, it is simply whatever does not play the role of ground to a figure. Depending upon the context, these terms could be satisfied by concepts, screens, fluids or clouds, the *Blur Building*, spittle, or subjects (is *I* a figure? a ground?). Literal transparency lies between the top two terms, figure & ground, which includes figures in their grounds, objects in their space. It is exemplified by the Bauhaus elevation and illusionistic painting. Phenomenal transparency lies between the bottom terms, as it is a spatial position defined by ~figure & ~ground. Here, figure and ground are always in flux, a condition exemplified by cubist painting, the façade and plan of Garches, which are organised in such a way that no part is ever unambiguously figure to another part's ground.

These two spatial positions, the literally and phenomenally transparent, define the space we call 'invisible' because it is the support for projection. I call this axis *representation* not only because – as we have seen – it relates to a form of space that is closely aligned with projection and perspective, but more importantly because it is space, in so far as we are able to represent it to ourselves and to others, by means of words, drawings and architecture, and has thereby been brought into discourse and made part of our world.

There is another more difficult axis marked by the positions figure & ~figure, and ground & ~ground, which forces us into the bastard logic of direct contradiction. These positions are difficult to characterise in anything but negative terms. Figure/~figure would be things that cannot be represented, objects that are not individuated by space. Kant's *things-in-themselves* are what exist before the forms of experience (what Kant called *intuition*) are imposed upon them. He understood that space and time were not objects of experience, but rather the *a priori* forms of intuition that precede experience and make it possible. We would not understand the world as a distribution of objects and a succession of events if we did not already organise the world in space and time. *Things-in-themselves* mark this *a priori* condition in advance of representation. Piranesi may have glimpsed this impossible world when he drew the classical tombs on *Via Appia Antica*, stripped of the cladding by which architecture represents itself, as formless lumps of masonry.[26]

Ground/~ground would be an unstable space that does not support representation. It is space, but it cannot individuate objects from one another or, more to the point, objects from subjects. It is approximated by Le Corbusier's ineffable/unsayable space. In 'Ineffable Space' (1948), Le Corbusier described an ecstatic space of kinetic, radiant, and acoustic energy.[27] The space of modernism has begun to thicken and flow. Elsewhere

26 Immanuel Kant, *Critique of Pure Reason*, trans. Norman Kemp Smith (London: Macmillan, 1929). Cf. 'Transcendental Doctrine of Elements, First Part: Transcendental Aesthetic, Section 1: Space', 67–74 and 'Section 2: Time', 74–91, in which he argues that space and time are forms of intuition, and not objects of intuition, and defines the *thing-in-itself* as an *a priori* object of which space and time are not properties. 'Space is not an empirical concept which has been derived from outer experiences.', 68. 'Space is a necessary *a priori* representation.', 68. 'Space does not represent any property of things in themselves, nor does it represent them in their relation to one another.', 71. 'Space is nothing but the form or all appearances of outer sense.', 71. 'Time is not an empirical concept that has been derived from any experience.', 74. 'Time is a necessary representation that underlies all intuitions.', 74–5, and so on …

27 Le Corbusier, '*L'Espace Indicible*', in *L'Architecture d'Aujourd'hui*, Paris, January 1946, 9–10, published in English as 'Ineffable Space' in *New World of Space* (New York: Reynal & Hitchcock, 1948).

I have argued that this 'boundless depth' that 'drives away contingent presences' is not about a synthesis of the arts – as most Le Corbusier scholars would have it – but about a non-projective space that does not locate a viewing subject. A boundless depth would be a space unbounded by the vanishing point that terminates every view. Walls would no longer converge as they recede from the viewer. If this space does not terminate as views, it also does not emanate from anywhere either. A boundless depth would be a space that cannot be put in relation to a viewing subject, an I/eye. Like Caillois's suffering psychastheniacs, if Le Corbusier is in this space, he is in it without position, and without any of the localising attributes that we expect of spatial subjects. It is difficult to call it visual space, at least as we know it, as it seems to lack the capacity to support the viewing I/eye's visual images (projection through a plane, either literally or phenomenally), which is the precondition of the visual.[28]

We call this axis *real* because whatever is on it is not representable by us to ourselves or to others.[29] In this sense it is beyond what we can symbolise or imagine. Its possibility does not suggest that representation is falsification, indeed the association of transparency with representation suggests the opposite, but simply to acknowledge that we throw the net of the symbol – the concept and the image – over all our forms, by necessity, in order to bring them into discourse. This is also the axis of creation, from which something new and unknown emerges, from a nowhere about which we cannot speak. The creator (author artist architect) is in the position of having to draw forth something that is not yet known and not yet named,

28 See my 'Psychosis and the ineffable space of modernism', *The Journal of Architecture* 18/3 (2013). As hallucinogenic as it may seem, Le Corbusier's ineffable space is closer to reality, for space is not really organised for the subject or its desire, not for me not for you. Walls do not really converge and objects do not really get smaller as they get farther away from us. And it really is full of energy and motion.

29 I make covert reference to Lacan's three orders of experience here: the real, the symbolic, and the imaginary. The symbolic and imaginary encompass all that can be thought or perceived (the imaginary relates to sensory images, i.e., perception). The real is what escapes. For succinct expositions, see the entries on the Real, Symbolic, and Imaginary in Dylan Evans, *An Introductory Dictionary of Lacanian Psycho-Analysis* (New York: Routledge, 1996).

shaped and materialised, but whose immeasurable distance pulls at his/her desire and whose imminent proximity clouds him/her with anxiety. Something emerges out of nothing to become, by the arduous work of representation, figure or ground, object or space. We receive our symbols from others, and rarely do we have to confront the horror of something new – creation in the sense of coming from this nothing. Arguably, the invisibility of space, in which we stand before the transparent screen looking into infinite depth the way the frontier legionnaire stands at the parapet, is a defense against the anxiety of that possibility: Look! Nothing there![30]

Conclusion: The Invisible Trace of the Transparent

The aim of this critique of Rowe and Slutzky has been to argue that for them, space is the projection of a plane surface, and – more critically – that this conception of space has been a general condition of subjectivity since the Renaissance. Although they put their fingers on the spatial effects of the most radical form of modernism, the geometric template for the modern subject they invoke was first demonstrated by Brunelleschi, and subsequently symbolised and given a geometric notation by Alberti

30 We can assign subject positions to these two axes based on the two clinical categories in psychoanalytic thought. If transparency literal or phenomenal marks what we could call the neurotic position of normal space, in which there are rules for the production of images, and hence good images and bad ones, we call ineffable space the psychotic position because it is marked by the lack of the law of perspective. The symbolic form of perspective, which binds the subject to its spatial reality, seems not to work. Here, there is no getting it right or wrong, only the continual rearrangement of space and our relation to it. This disengagement of the symbolic order is the hallmark of psychosis. The symbolic order does not work for the psychotic; it is – in the terminology of Lacan in *The Psychoses* (1956) – *foreclosed* to him/her. This disengagement of the symbolic order puts the psychotic in direct relation to the real.

in the first half of the fifteenth century.[31] Their work is an example of how space and the subject are symbolised together through architecture. Architecture is a symptom of the unconscious structure of the spatial self. For architecture, there is one form, the projective form, that links space and subject in a single structure. Rowe's and Slutzky's work on modernism suggests that not a lot has changed since the Renaissance. The frontality of cubist painting is a symptom of the projective subject. The invisibility of space and its correlative, the transparency of the picture plane, are symptoms of it. There have been challenges, like Le Corbusier's conception of ineffable space, Beckett's conception of the *Unnamable* I, or Kant's *thing-in-itself*, but these seem to have been reabsorbed into the spatial cannon from which they attempted to emerge, having never gained an independent existence.

The conception of space that Rowe and Slutzky describe involves a certain form of transparency, which can either be literal or phenomenal depending upon whether the plane surface is transparent or opaque. Their thesis is not only about plane surfaces, but about space, and it is when they move from façades to plans that their argument becomes complex. By analogy from plane surfaces, they argue that in the case of phenomenally transparent space, spatial figures interpenetrate without destroying each other. Their example is a deep space running diagonally through a series of shallow spaces, which they discern in cubist still life and in Le Corbusier's purist villas.

This chapter argues that Rowe's and Slutzky's shallow stratified space is a general condition of visual space. Garches is a special case only because it makes manifest a general condition that is usually latent in other architectures. Visual space is everywhere marked by the trace of the picture plane.

31 Whether Brunelleschi's demonstration of perspective is a discovery or an invention is debated by historians, including Gombrich, Panofsky, and Damisch, and it depends upon whether you regard perspective as a natural form (Gombrich) or a symbolic one (Panofsky). The argument in this paper assumes that perspective is a symbolic form. For a discussion, see Hubert Damisch, *The Origin of Perspective* (Cambridge, MA: MIT Press, 1994) and Lorens Holm, *Brunelleschi Lacan Le Corbusier: Architecture, Space, and the Construction of Subjectivity* (London: Routledge, 2010).

Planes can be transparent or not, but space cannot, itself, be transparent, because it is the precondition for transparency. The invisible geometry of projection, which includes transparent plane surfaces and projective subjects, defines the visibility of the world and makes visibility possible. The invisibility of space is a precondition for the transparency of the image surface, without which, nothing would be visible. Space is invisible because it is everywhere marked by the trace of the picture plane.[32]

Rowe's and Slutzky's insight was to discern within such a literal spatial practice as architecture, the moment architecture lifts itself to the level of the concept, when it ceases to be material and begins to speak. This is the moment it becomes symptomatic of our condition as subjects. In order for something to be brought into the human world of discourse, we must find the language with which to name it and share it with others, as Hannah Arendt argued in *The Human Condition* (1958). For Rowe and Slutzky, the surface is the signifier under which space is summoned into discourse. Real space, whatever that may be, slippery and unknown (Vidler would say *dark*, Le Corbusier *indicible*) because otherwise inaccessible, lies beneath it. Although architecture is not exactly a language, it is the symbolic form by which we communicate spatial experience to ourselves and to others.

We have traced the consequences of the literal and phenomenal through two Klein diagrams. The first traced different viewing conditions of the architectural object, which expanded Rowe's and Slutzky's original classification for transparency. The second diagram mapped the difference between visual space (the space of representation) and its other, a space whose opacity does not support representation, or in which representation is problematic. This axis is defined by subjects and objects that cannot be represented because they cannot be brought into discourse. It is beyond the scope of this chapter to explore the spatial possibilities of Le Corbusier's

32 Rowe and Slutzky conflate the transparency of the plane with the invisibility of space because they are interested in phenomena. At the level of how space seems to the subject, which is the level of consciousness, transparency and invisibility make little difference. I have shifted the terms of the argument from phenomena to concept (i.e. the symbolic) because I am interested in the invisible logic underlying visual space.

indicible space, or Beckett's *Unnamable* I, but I have put them out there as beacons indicating what lies beyond the horizons of the internal space of the subject and the external space of the world.

If there is something ineffable about transparency, it is precisely at that moment when we realise, in our architectural reveries, that the subject and its space coincide. It is to this coincidence between the subject and space – the realisation that they are planar, that they align, superimpose, are transparent to each other – that we attribute the invisibility of the subject and space. In their different media, Le Corbusier and Beckett tarry with breaking the couple between the subject and its space: Le Corbusier touches the limits of space, Beckett the limits of the I. In so doing they arrive at an opacity that marks the limits of experience. With his earlier work – Garches, League of Nations, the purist villas – Le Corbusier did the opposite, he showed us how the subject and space are coupled, how they are planar, transparent and coincident. This coincidence is not literal: there is no screen in me or in my room. Nor is it phenomenal: neither I nor my room are opaque. This transparency is ineffable, unsayable, unseeable, because it is an effect of the couple that has to precede the saying and the seeing, to make them possible.

Bibliography

Alberti, Leon Battista, *On Painting*, trans. John R. Spencer (New Haven, CT: Yale University Press, 1966); first published as *Della Pittura* [1435/36].

Alvarez, Al, ed., *The New Poetry: an anthology selected and introduced by A. Alvarez* (Harmondsworth: Penguin, 1962) [in which he discusses a form of crumbling and materialising subjectivity].

Arendt, Hannah, *The Human Condition* (Chicago: University of Chicago Press, 1958).

Barrie, Andrew, 'New Transparency, Kengo Kuma', *Architecture New Zealand* 3 (2007).

Beckett, Samuel, *Texts for Nothing IV* (London, 1951/1966).

——, *The Unnamable* [1952/59] in *Molloy; Malone Dies; The Unnamable* (London, 1966) [see the opening lines, 'Where now? Who now? When now? Unquestioning. I, say I'. See also the BBC production of Beckett's *Not I* (1973)].

Benjamin, Walter, 'The work of art in the age of mechanical reproduction' [1936], *Illuminations* (London: Fontana, 1973).

Blau, Eve, 'Transparency and the Irreconcilable Contradictions of Modernity', *Praxis: journal of writing + building* 9 (2007) [transparency and objective and subjective modes of cognition].

Bletter, Rosemarie Haag, 'Mies and Dark Transparency', *AV monographs* 92 (2001), 58–73.

——, 'Opaque Transparency', *Oppositions 13* (1978), 121–30 [Bletter questions the methodology used by Rowe and Slutzky in their 'Transparency' essays].

Caillois, Roger, 'Mimicry and legendary psychasthenia', *October 31*, trans. Roger Sheply (MIT Press, Winter 1984); first published in *Minatoure 7* [Paris 1935].

Carpenter, James, 'La Transparence Entre Mémoire Et Rêve/Transparency between Memory and Dream', *Architecture d'aujourd'hui* 342 (2002), 100–3. [Critical review of work by Richard Meier and Murphy Jahn].

Damisch, Hubert, *The Origin of Perspective* (Cambridge, MA: MIT Press, 1994).

Evans, Dylan, *An Introductory Dictionary of Lacanian Psycho-Analysis* (New York, Routledge, 1996) [see the entries on the Real, Symbolic, and Imaginary].

Freud, Sigmund, 'The Loss of Reality in Neurosis and Psychosis' [1924], in *The Standard Edition volume XIX*, 181–87.

——, 'Negation' [1925] in A. Richards and J. Strachey, eds, *Sigmund Freud: on Metapsychology: The Theory of Psychoanalysis* (London: Penguin, 1991), 437–42.

——, 'Neurosis and Psychosis' [1924/1923], in James Strachey, ed., *The Standard Edition of the Complete Psychological Works of Sigmund Freud* volume *XIX (1923–25) The Ego and the Id and other works* (London: The Hogarth Press and the Institute of Psycho-Analysis), 147–53.

——, 'Psychoanalytic Notes on an Autobiographical Account of a Case of Paranoia (Dementia Paranoides)' [1911] in A. Richards, ed., *Sigmund Freud 9: Case Histories II: 'Rat Man', Schreber, 'Wolf Man', Female Homosexuality* (London: Penguin Books, 1981).

Giedion, Sigfried, *The Eternal Present: The Beginnings of Architecture: A Contribution on Constancy and Change* (London: Oxford University Press, 1964). [Cf. the discussion of the three space conceptions].

——, 'Transparency: Primitive and Modern', *Art news* 51 (1952), 47–50.

Gombrich, Ernest H., *Art and Illusion: A Study in the Psychology of Pictorial Representation* (Princeton, NJ: Princeton University Press, 1960). [Gombrich takes issue with Panofsky's thesis that perspective is the symbolisation of space and argues that it is a natural way of seeing space].

Graham, Dan and Pietro Valle, 'Pietro Valle – Dan Graham: Transparency – Reflection Interview', *Lotus International* 125 (2005), 42–53.

Gregory, Jane, 'I can See Right through You', *RSA journal* 149/3 (2002), 8–9.

Hays, Michael K., *Sanctuaries: The Last Works of John Hejduk* (New York: Whitney Museum and Harry Abrams, 2002) [including a discussion of Le Corbusier's 'inexpressible space' and opacity and transparency].

Heidegger, Martin, 'The Thing', *Poetry Language Thought*, trans. Albert Hofstadter (New York, Harper, 1971). [The emptiness of the jug is a precondition for engagement with it].

Herzog & de Meuron, *Eberswalde Technical School Library* (Eberswalde: 1994/99).

Hitchcock, Alfred, *Rear Window* (Paramount Pictures, 1954). Starring Raymond Burr, Grace Kelly, and James Stewart.

Holm, Lorens, *Brunelleschi Lacan Le Corbusier: Architecture, Space, and the Construction of Subjectivity* (London: Routledge 2010).

——, 'Psychosis and the ineffable space of modernism', *The Journal of Architecture* 18/3.

James, William, *Principles of Psychology* (London: Macmillan, 1890). [The chapters 'The Consciousness of Self' and 'The Stream of Thought'. James invented the term 'stream of consciousness', and relates the phenomena of extreme self-scrutiny to psychosis].

Jarosinski, Eric, 'Architectural Symbolism and the Rhetoric of Transparency: A Berlin Ghost Story', *Journal of Urban History* 29/1 (2002), 62–77.

Jones, Peter, 'Building the Empire of the Gaze: The Modern Movement and the Surveillance Society', *Architectural Theory Review* 4/2 (1999), 1–14. [Discussion of Michel Foucault's surveillance society, the Modern Movement, Le Corbusier's Villa Savoye].

Kant, Immanuel, *Critique of Pure Reason*, trans. Norman Kemp Smith (London: Macmillan, 1929). [Cf. 'Transcendental Doctrine of Elements, First Part: Transcendental Aesthetic, Section 1: Space', 67–74 and 'Section 2: Time', 74–91 in which he determines that space and time are forms of intuition, and defines the *thing-in-itself* as an *a priori* object of which space and time are not properties].

Kepes, Gyorgy, *The Language of Vision* (Chicago: Paul Theobald & Co, 1944).

Koolhaas, Rem, *Très Grande Bibliothèque* (Paris, 1989).

Krauss, Rosalind, 'Sculpture in the Expanded Field', *October* 8, 33–44 [from whence a worked example of the Klein diagram.] Reprinted in Krauss, *The Originality of the Avant-Garde and other Modernist Myths* (MIT Press, 1985).

Lacan, Jacques, *The Four Fundamental Concepts of Psychoanalysis*, trans. Alan Sheridan (New York: Norton, 1981). [See the section, 'Of the gaze as *objet petit a*', 67–119, in which Lacan discusses projection and the gaze].

——, 'On a Question Prior to any Possible Treatment of Psychosis' [1958] in *Ecrits: the first complete edition in English*, trans. Bruce Fink (New York: Norton, 2006), 445–88.

——, *The Seminar of Jacques Lacan, Book III: The Psychoses 1955–56* (New York: Norton, 1993).
——, *The Seminar of Jacques Lacan, Book VII: The Ethics of Psychoanalysis 1959–60*, trans. Dennis Porter (New York: Norton 1992), 136. ['... architecture like painting is organised around emptiness ...'].
Laplanche, J. and J-B. Pontalis, *The Language of Psycho-Analysis* (London: Hogarth Press and the Institute of Psycho-Analysis 1973).
Le Corbusier, 'Ineffable space', in *New World of Space* (New York & Boston, Reynal & Hitchcock and the Institute for Contemporary Art, 1948).
Leatherbarrow, David, 'Opacity', *AA Files 32* (1996), 49–64.
Lerida, Javier Mozas, 'Transparency & Modernity', *A + U 7* (1996), 4–17. [Review of work by Pei, Herzog & de Meuron, Koolhaas].
Mallinson, Helen, 'Architecture Taken Seriously – Questioning the Ideology of Transparency: Zumthor's Hairy Paradise Serpentine Pavilion 2011', *Arq: Architectural Research Quarterly* 15/4 (2011), 304–8.
Mertins, Detlef, 'Transparencies Yet to Come: Sigfried Giedion and Adolf Behne', *A + U: Architecture and Urbanism* 10 (1997), 17.
——, 'Transparency: Autonomy & Relationality', *AA Files* 32 (1996), 3–11. [A re-evaluation of Rowe and Slutzky's 1963 essay 'Transparency: literal and phenomenal'].
Moholy-Nagy, Laslo, *Vision in Motion* (Chicago: Paul Theobald & Co, 1965). [With sections on the writings of the Psychotic, Freud, James Joyce, Finnegan's Wake, referenced by Rowe and Slutzky].
Panofsky, Erwin, *Perspective as Symbolic Form*, trans. Christopher S. Wood (New York: Zone Books, 1991).
Pieters, Dominique, 'Transparency and Translucence Illuminated', *Architect* 33 (2002), 34–9.
Rowe, Colin and Robert Slutzky, 'Transparency: Literal and Phenomenal', *Perspecta: the Yale Architectural Journal* 8 (1963), 45–54. Reprinted in Rowe, *Mathematics of the Ideal Villa and other essays* (Cambridge, MA: MIT Press, 1976).
——, 'Transparency: Literal and Phenomenal Part 2', *Perspecta: the Yale Architectural Journal* 13/14 (1971), 287–301.
Rugoff, Ralph, 'How to look at invisible art', *Invisible: Art about the Unseen, 1957–2012* (London: Hayward 2012). Catalogue to the exhibition *Invisible* at the Hayward.
Slessor, Catherine, 'Nothing there: The Art and Science of Transparency', *Architectural Review* 217 (2005), 39.
Slutzky, Robert, 'Rereading Transparency', *Daidalos* (Sept 1989), 106–9.
Somol, Robert, 'Oublier Rowe', *Formwork: Colin Rowe, Any* 7/8 (1994), 8–15.
Vidler, Anthony, 'Transparency', in *The Architectural Uncanny: Essays in the Modern Unhomely* (Cambridge, MA: MIT Press, 1992).

——, 'Transparency, Literal and Phenomenal', *Journal of Architectural Education* 56/4 (2003), 6–7.

Weinstock, Michael, 'Transparency and the Performance of Building Skins', *Architectural Design* 72/5 (2002), 120–123. [Current engineering and Mies' dream of seamless glass walls].

Whiteread, Rachel, *House* (London, 1993).

Themed issue on transparency, *Architectural Review* 203 (1998).

Themed issue on transparency, *Journal of Architectural Education* 56/4 (2003).

PART II

Urban Topography, Void and Display

zURBS
Prelude II

In Chloe, a great city, the people who move through the streets are all strangers. At each encounter, they imagine a thousand things about one another; meetings which could take place between them, conversations, surprises, caresses, bites. But no one greets anyone; eyes look for a second, then dart away, seeking other eyes, never stopping.

—ITALO CALVINO, *Invisible Cities*

There is such a thing as a distribution of the sensible: an underlying structure that is hardly visible in urban space, but that nevertheless, according to the French philosopher Jacques Rancière, determines what is possible, acceptable, and even perceptible in a certain place. This structure shapes the spatial forms that social phenomena and material things take on, and it influences all the different realities, possibilities, images, meanings, futures, perceptions, experiences, connections, forms, patterns, relations and structures that these spatial forms consist in. In short, the distribution of the sensible shapes and controls our spatial realities.

Space, then, can be seen as the precondition for re-imagination: encounters that could take you on a carousel of fantasies. Disagreements that could escalate into love affairs. Your envious car glancing at a bike while impatiently waiting for green light. The intimate experience of holding hands with a stranger during a thunderstorm. The joy of sitting in a café without buying anything before eating your breakfast at a roundabout. Sudden doubt about democratic decision making when sitting in a packed bus at 7 am in the morning. The instant urge to pick little yellow flowers from your neighbour's balcony. The stroll after midnight along the echo of other people's dreams ...

How can we re-imagine spatial realities in order to critically explore the invisible distribution of the sensible?

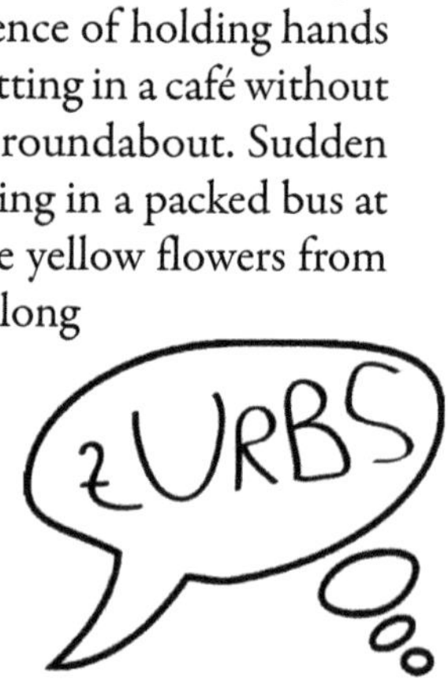

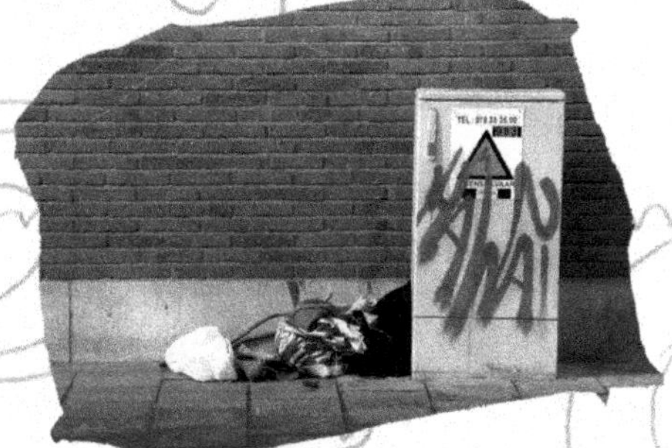

- smell of freshly baked bread
- the smell of death water
- loud foreign music coming from cars with many people in it
- 'singing' conversations
- certain houses tell what's for dinner
- mixture of sounds & smells from all sort of transpost

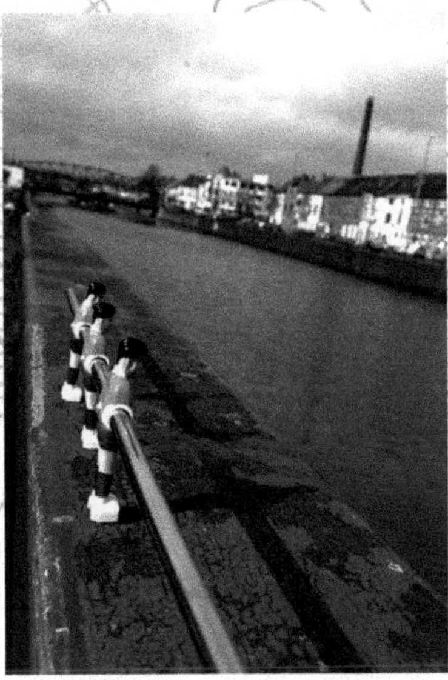

AT EACH ENCOUNTER THEY IMAGINE A THOUSAND THINGS ABOUT ONE ANOTHER

BERND NICOLAI

5 Mendelsohn and Libeskind: A Hidden History – Jewish Identity, the Void, Architectural Metaphors and Traces through Twentieth-Century Berlin

For the negotiation of (in)visiblities in twentieth-century cityscapes, no other European city than Berlin offers such a wide range of different historical and cultural layers, trapped links and crossroads, as well as real excavation sites. Berlin itself stands for an immense commemorative ensemble, emblematic of the fundamental disruptions of modernity in the last century.[1]

Two striking artistic projects of the 1990s reveal the dimensions of the visible and invisible, as well as those of memory and oblivion, as essential for our understanding of contemporary Berlin. They address Berlin's most tragic history, that is, the Nazi dictatorship, based on racist and anti-Semitic principles that precipitated the Second Word War and the Shoah, and finally the physical destruction of Berlin's urban fabric. These projects are Shimon Attie's 1991 installation, *Mulack Street 37*, a projection of Jewish remembrance that deals with the gap between the visible and the invisible, even more relevant after reunification in 1990,[2] and the social

1 Neil Leach, 'Erasing the traces, the 'denazification' of post-revolutionary Berlin and Bukarest', in Neil Leach ed., *The Hieroglyphics of Space, Reading and Experiencing the Modern Metropolis* (London: Routledge 2002), 80–91.

2 Ziva Amishai-Maisels, 'Hunting the empty space', in Steve Feinstein, eds, *Absence/presence: Essays and Reflections on the Artistic Memory of the Holocaust* (Syracuse, NY: Syracuse Univ. Press, 2005), 123–50, here 135. Jean Dethier and Alain Guilheux, eds, *La Ville, art et architecture en Europe 1870–1993* (Paris: Editions Centre Pompidou 1994), 384.

sculpture of Renata Stih and Frieder Schnock, *Orte des Erinnerns/Places of Remembrance: A Memorial for Jews Living in Berlin from 1933 to 1945*, assembled in the Schöneberg district, called the Bavarian Neighbourhood, in Berlin 1992/93 (Fig. 5.1). This project visualises the banality and brutality of exclusionary, racist legislation that expelled Jews from the public space, causing segregation, deportation, and finally physical extinction, represented artistically by duplex signs that play with advertising emblems related to citations of Nazi laws on the reverse side.[3]

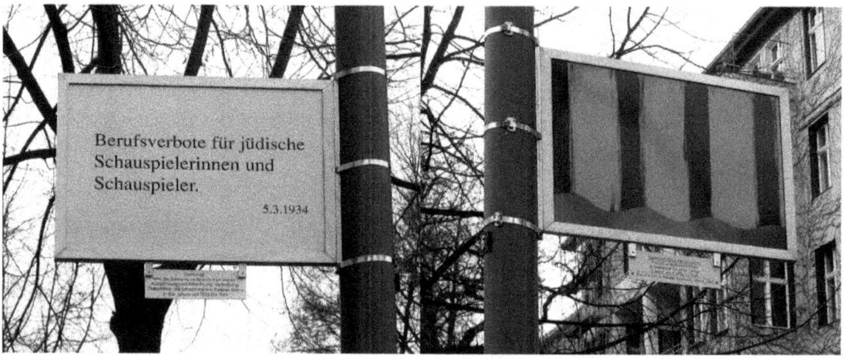

Fig. 5.1: Renata Stih and Frieder Schnock, *Orte des Erinnerns/ Places of Remembrance: A Memorial for Jews Living in Berlin from 1933 to 1945*, Berlin-Schöneberg, Bayerischer Platz 1993/1994. Credit: Stih and Schnock, Berlin/VG BildKunst, Bonn/Berlin/ARS, New York City.

But besides this well-known layer of history connected with Nazi totalitarianism and war, and post-war urban destruction, Berlin also is lacking visible evidence which would link it up with earlier historic epochs, such as

3 James Edward Young, *At Memory's Edge: After-Images of the Holocaust in Contemporary Art and Architecture* (New Haven, London: Yale University Press 2000), 123; James Edward Young, 'Memory and Counter-Memory', *Harvard Design Magazine* 9/Fall (1999), 23–35; in particular Renta Stih, Frieder Schnock, *Arbeitsbuch für ein Denkmal in Berlin. Orte des Erinnerns im Bayerischen Viertel – Ausgrenzung und Entrechtung, Vertreibung, Deportation und Ermordung von Berliner Juden in den Jahren 1933 bis 1945* (Berlin: Gatza, 1995).

the Baroque and the nineteenth century. This is so, because Berlin became known as a city of rising modernism around 1900, a city 'always to become and never to be', as Karl Scheffler claimed in his famous book *Berlin, a City's Fate* in 1910.[4]

Both the imagined or remembered, as well as the real metropolis of Berlin, form a sort of systematic archive that, 'between tradition and oblivion', reveals, according to Foucault, 'the rules of a practice that enables statements both to survive and to undergo regular modification. It's the general system of formation and transformation of statements'.[5] One of the most striking examples of this statement can be seen in Christian Boltanski's extraordinary conceptual work *The Missing House*, which reveals the ambiguous character of references to the past by displaying plaques on bleak walls, remains of a ruined now missing house, in the style of death notices inscriptions on headstones.[6] Who knows what happened to the individuals represented by the names. Did they die during air strikes, were they deported to concentrations camps, or did they simply move or pass away? Both the void and the plaques give place for reflection and imagination, without revealing the concrete historic context, and in this ambiguity lies the outstanding quality of Boltanski's conceptual art. Yet, Boltanski also conceptualised a counter-project based on concrete historic facts concerning the 'missing house' at another place by creating what he calls *The Museum*, a permanent exhibition displaying official files and private documents in an open-air showcase. Here, another dimension has been opened, since the word 'museum' refers to the former function of the area close to the Lehrter Station where in the annual exhibition the Great

4 Karl Scheffler, *Berlin, Ein Stadtschicksal* (Berlin-Westend: Reiss 1910), 265. Cf. Alan Balfour, *The Politics of Order, 1737–1989* (New York: Rizzoli, 1990).

5 Michael Foucault, *The Archaeology of Knowledge* (London, New York: Routledge, 1989), 146.

6 Abigail Solomon-Godeau, 'Mourning or Melancholia. Christian Boltanski's Missing House', *Oxford Art Journal* 21/2 (1998), 3–20. Werner Herzogenrath, ed., *Die Endlichkeit der Freiheit* (Berlin, 1990); Michael Glasmeier, *Christian Boltanski, Christiane Büchner, Andreas Fischer, The Missing House, The Museum* (Berlin: DAAD, 1992). See also Dora Osborne's contribution to this volume.

Berlin art show took place, a site where, for example, El Lissitzky exhibited his famous 'Proun Room' in 1922.[7]

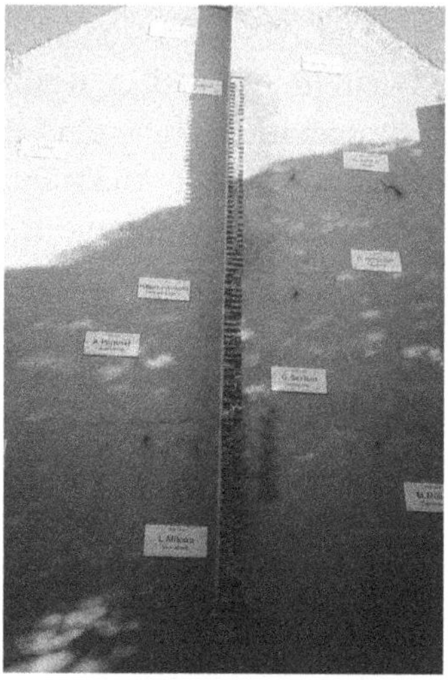

Fig. 5.2: Christian Boltanski with Christiane Büchner and Andreas Fischer, *The Missing House*, Grosse Hamburger Strasse 15/16, Berlin, 1990. Credit: Bernd Nicolai.

Berlin is certainly 'most closely linked with the recent surge of memory culture', as Uta Staiger and Henriette Steiner have recently observed.[8] But Berlin is also a place where one has to decode and re-contextualise the visible and the invisible layers of the urban fabric. Memory is closely linked with spatiality, and – according to Aleida and Jan Assmann – it has also become one of the new paradigms of cultural studies. However, in another sense spatiality and memory are related in the context of post-structuralist

7 Éva Forgács, 'Definitive Space, The many utopias of El Lissitzky's Proun Room', in Nancy Perloff and Brian Reed, eds, *Situating El Lissitzky: Vitebsk, Berlin, Moscow* (Los Angeles: Getty Trust, 2003), 47–75, here 48; the exhibition ground is described in *Berlin und seine Bauten*, Vol. 2 (Berlin: Ernst & Sohn, 1896), 241–4.

8 Uta Staiger, Henriette Steiner, ed., 'Introduction', *Memory Culture and Contemporary City Building Sites* (New York: Macmillan, 2009), 1.

interpretation. Here, memory is highlighted metaphorically through absence and emptiness, and architectonically through voids as non-spaces, places out of time, and through commercialisation, yielding numerous modes of perception, from the sublime delightful horror, caused by fear and anxiety, to simple contemplation.[9]

Erich Mendelsohn (1887–1953) and Daniel Libeskind (1946–) constitute two case studies we could choose for thinking about modernism, memory and void. They represent two diametrically opposed architectural positions of modernism and postmodernism. In cultural terms, Mendelsohn and Libeskind are separated through painful disruptions, and the overcoming of the modernist paradigm of the twentieth century. Mendelsohn was one of the most successful modernist Jewish architects of the 1920s and early 1930s, based on the clarity and unambiguousness of his projects, as well on the (later fragile) security of his living arrangements, something that Libeskind, although he was born in 1946 as Jew in Poland, could not enjoy. Whereas for Libeskind the process of memory is definitely inscribed in the cityscape and architecture, rendering the invisible obvious, Mendelsohn took qualities such as anticipation, progress and dynamism as principles of his modernist architecture as it developed between 1919 and 1933.[10] This future-oriented, progressive dimension changed entirely after Hitler came to power, and Mendelsohn immediately left Germany forever. He subsequently chose a more self-reflective approach combined with a prophetical political analysis, to which we shall return later. While Mendelsohn's intention was to shape the surface of a dynamically changing world without being superficial, Libeskind's work is based on a strong

9 Daniel Libeskind, 'Global Building Sites between Past and Future', in Uta Staiger, Henriette Steiner and Andrew Webber, eds, *Memory Culture and Contemporary City Building Sites* (New York, Basingstoke: Palgrave Macmillan, 2009), 69–84.

10 Erich Mendelsohn, 'International Agreement in New Architectural Thought', lecture given in Amsterdam in 1923, in Oskar Beyer, ed., *Eric Mendelsohn, Letters of an Architect* (London, New York: Abelard-Shulman 1967), 61; in contrast the programmatic statement Daniel Libeskind, 'Between the Lines, Jewish Museum Berlin', in Connie Wolf, ed., *Daniel Libeskind and the Contemporaray Jewish Museum: New Jewish Architecture from Berlin to san Francisco* (New York: Rizzoli 2008), 63.

conceptual approach and an architectural play with the relation between depth and surfacing.

Despite their differences, Mendelsohn and Libeskind are connected through the metaphysical dimension of architecture. Further, both are rooted in an ideal sense in Jewishness, although Jewish identity more generally was completely reconstituted after the Holocaust and the foundation of the state of Israel in 1948.[11] Mendelsohn had to face the failure of Jewish assimilation in German society, while Libeskind, aware of his family's annihilation, came to Berlin, the site of a nearly completely annihilated Jewish culture. Mendelsohn, through displacement, as it were, transformed from a Berliner into a Jew, while Libeskind, as a Jew, became a Berliner. Both were affected by the myth of Berlin as a metropolis, but we are talking here about two entirely different cities, connected only through the fragile tracks of memories and traces in the cityscape.

Perhaps Mendelsohn would have supported Libeskind's attempt to entangle Jewish history with Berlin's history, and the creation of a commemorative site in the Berlin Jewish Museum. Libeskind plotted a matrix on the city map of Berlin as an intellectual approach to the problem of highlighting the visible, revealing the invisible, and eventually connecting visible and invisible sites and layers: 'At the same time that there was this actual visible site,' Libeskind has claimed:

> I felt that there was an invisible matrix of connections, a connection of relationships between figures of Germans and Jews. Even though the competition was held before the Wall fell, I felt that the one binding feature which crossed East and West was the relationship of Germans to Jews. Certain people, workers, writers, composers, artists, scientists and poets formed the link between Jewish tradition and German culture. I found this connection and I plotted an irrational matrix, which would yield reference to the emblematics of a compressed and distorted star: the yellow star that was so frequently worn on this very site. This is the first aspect of the project.[12]

11 Robert S. Wistrich, *Laboratory for World Destruction: Germans and Jews in Central Europe* (Lincoln: University of Nebraska Press, 2007), cf. David Weinberg, 'Between America and Israel: The Quest for a Distinct European Jewish Identity in the Post-War Era', *Jewish Culture and History* 5/1 (2002), 91–120.

12 Daniel Libeskind, *Counter Design* (New York: Rizzoli, 1991), 86.

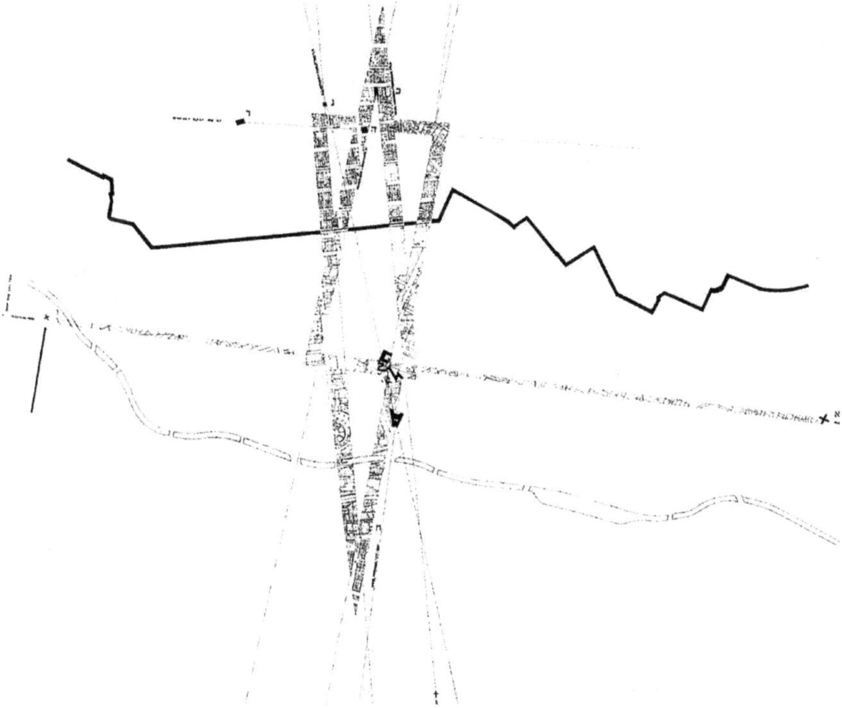

Fig. 5.3: Daniel Libeskind, Matrix of the star: urban conception for the Jewish Museum Berlin 1989.
Credit: Studio Libeskind.

This thoroughly personally determined matrix puts the star on the Baroque grid of the Friedrichstadt city extension, and connects, at central points, the locations of the writer and jurist E. T. A. Hoffmann, the poet Heinrich Heine, the founder of the most important Enlightenment salon in Berlin, Rahel Varnhagen, and buildings such as the *Kollegienhaus* (later *Kammergericht* and *Berlin Museum*), the Libeskind building itself, Mendelsohn's metal worker's trade union building, and southward as an imaginary axis, the tombs of Rahel Varnhagen and her husband. A slightly shifted east-west axis, centred on the Jewish Museum, connects the Berlin studio of Mies van der Rohe, Am Karlsbad, which was celebrated in Libeskind's own IBA project *Berlin City Edge* in 1985, and the domicile of Paul Celan in Kreuzberg. On a general level Libeskind also refers to Benjamin, by depicting traces and points on sites according to Benjamin's observation that 'Dwelling means leaving traces.'[13] In a Benjaminian sense, present-day Berlin is a city of the unconscious, where a vast stratification of historic layers indirectly forms the life and culture of contemporary Berlin. It is also the city of Benjamin's *Berlin Childhood*, whose sites can both be depicted and undergo reconfiguration.

To understand this matrix, we must decipher some of the layers underneath it. It was around thirty years ago that the International Building Exhibition Berlin in 1984 (IBA) rediscovered the former West Berlin parts of this area, close to the wall, as new dwelling sites. This process began with some striking buildings by Rob Krier and Hans Kollhoff and Arthur A. Ovaska in the Ritter- and Lindenstrasse. It was broken up because of the special conditions of an isolated West Berlin urban culture. What Rob Krier and the chief planner Paul Joseph Kleihues were going to restore by reconstruction, in a postmodern understanding of the term, was no less than a reconstruction of a holistic cityscape,[14] based on a proper plan, as shown in Kleihues's IBA plan, but one that ignored all breaks and the traces of the postwar divided city. During the 1980s, all traces and effects of destruction and erasure of the Baroque urban fabric of Berlin were still perceptible. In this context, Libeskind's concept focused on the museum as transitory commemorative site to connect the past, present and future: 'Precisely because Berlin became the central point of annihilation of the European Jews, it became the centre of devastation par excellence and became the centre of the transformation of our world into what it is today.'[15]

From the very beginning, the Jewish Museum had a quasi-archaeological dimension because, as Libeskind stated, 'it is based on the invisible figures whose traces originated the geometry of the building. The soil, where

13 Walter Benjamin, *Berlin Childhood around 1900* (Cambridge, MA: Belknap Press, 2006), 17.

14 Paul Joself Kleihues and Hans Klotz, eds, *International Building Exhibition Berlin 1987: Examples for a New Architecture* (London: Academy, 1986).

15 Ibid., 88.

the building is standing, is not only the visible one of Kreuzberg, but also the invisible one, located below and above.'[16] The Friedrichstadt as city space contains different layers, not only of buildings and town planning conceptions now fragmented or entirely vanished, but also of planned projects and even utopias. Further, it contains the immaterial history of thoughts, processes and results represented by such sites as the Enlightenment Salon of Rahel Varnhagen, the coffeeshop Lutter & Wegener, frequented by the intellectuals of the *Vormärz*, or Schinkel's famous neo-classical *Prince Albrecht Palais*, later used as SS-Reichssicherheitshauptamt (Reich Main Security Office) as headquarters of the Holocaust.[17]

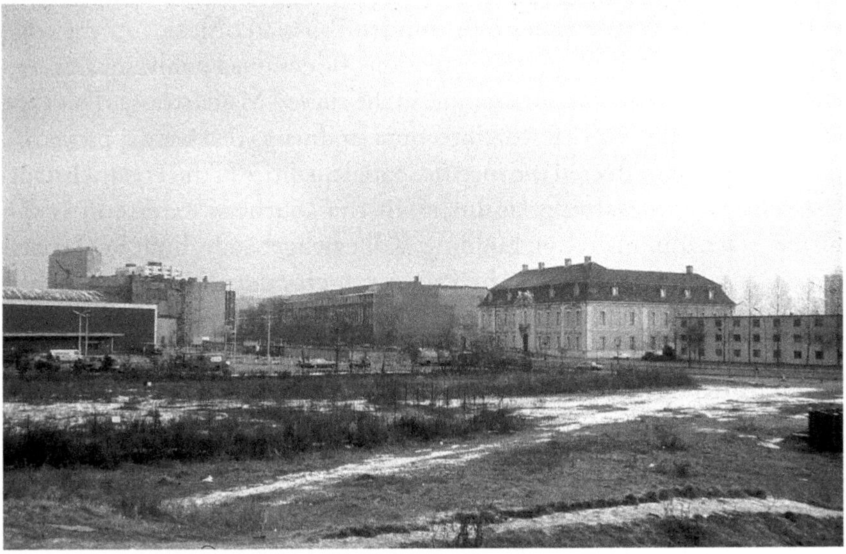

Fig. 5.4: Berlin-Kreuzberg, Berlin Museum and its environment, 1981. Credit: Bernd Nicolai.

16 Schneider, 17.

17 Hans Wilderotter, *Alltag der Macht, Berlin Wilhelmstrasse* (Berlin: Jovis, 1998), cf. *Topography of Terror. Gestapo, SS and Reich Security Main Office on Wilhelm- and Prinz-Albrecht-Straße. A Documentation* (Berlin: Stiftung Topographie des Terrors, 2010), 126–45.

The second extension of the Friedrichstadt represents the real matrix as a remarkably rational city-grid, according to the principles of an enlightened Prussian absolutism, shaped with representative entrance squares such as the Quarré, Octogon and the Rondell. Southwards it forms a triangle with its peak in the Rondell (Mehringplatz), where the main streets, the noble Wilhelmstrasse, the central axis of Friedrichstrasse and, as eastern edge, Lindenstrasse, converge.[18] Aside from the Wilhelmstrasse Palais, dwelling houses were based on type-buildings designed by the military engineer and architect Philipp Gerlach. With one exception, these disappeared as early as the early twentieth century, and for many years at checkpoint Charlie a painted cross-section scheme referred to these Baroque dwellings. But Gerlach was by no means a single-minded Prussian officer.[19] At the edge between the first and second city extensions, he designed public squares centred on church buildings, for example in the curved Mauerstrasse. This type of layout, together with a few architectural landmarks that were approved by the King himself, affected the specific spatial qualities of the Friedrichstadt.

The only remaining landmark in the southern extension is the former state administration building, Kollegiengebäude, built by Gerlach 1734–5, which later became the Prussian high-court (Kammergericht), with E. T. A. Hoffman presiding as judge there in the 1820s. After its destruction through aerial bombing and its reconstruction in 1970 it became the Berlin Museum. This became the nucleus for the actual Jewish Museum, which as a Jüdische Abteilung (Jewish Department) was conceived as the former city historical museum's annexe. Libeskind was scared by the idea of an annexe that took its name of 'Jewish Department' from a Nazi term; the Jewish Department was part of the SS main security office founded by Reinhard Heydrich, the so-called 'architect of the Holocaust'.[20] He turned

18 A short overlook Wolfgang Schäche, 'Die Friedrichstadt in Berlin-Mitte, Geschichte, Bestand, Planung', *Berlin Jahrbuch* 2 (1993/94), 62–69.

19 For a limited analysis of Gerlach's contribution and the Friedrichstadt extension, cf. Hermann Heckmann, *Baumeister des Barock und Rokoko, Brandenburg, Preussen* (Berlin: Verlag für Bauwesen, 1999), 266–71.

20 Daniel Libeskind with Sarah Crichton, *Breaking Ground, adventures in life and architecture* (New York: Riverhead Book, 2004) (German edition Cologne: Kiepenheuer & Witsch, 2004, 95–6).

this concept on its head by projecting a vast space as a Jewish Museum of its own, where the old Berlin Museum featured as an annexe. At least one detail highlights this changed conception: the new museum entrance. The connection between the two buildings was not designed as a bridge, as in the other competition entries, but rather as an 'underground bridge', because, according to Libeskind, throughout its history Berlin had lost touch with the ideals of the Enlightenment, represented for him by the former Kollegienhaus. The absence of enlightenment, like a horizontal void, was finally expressed through a quasi-submerged non-entrance to the new museum.

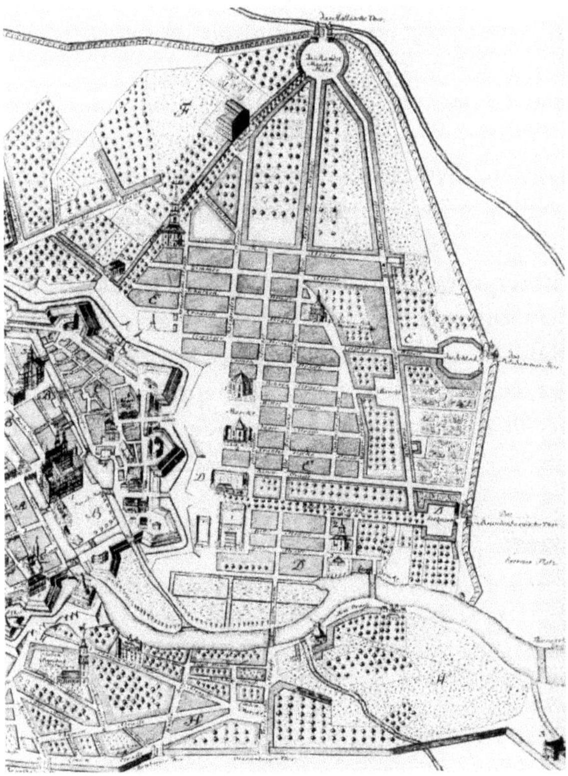

Fig. 5.5: Second Friedrichstadt extension by Philip Gerlach, 'Grund-Riss', plan by Johann Friedrich Walther (Waltherplan), 1737; plan is oriented south. Credit: Berlin: Landesarchiv.

In his matrix, with reference to Mies van der Rohe's studio Am Karlsbad, Libeskind also addressed the modernist Berlin of the 1920s and early 1930s, a dynamic city, and one that in the eyes of some commentators was the most advanced city in the world. In 1931 Amedée Ozenfant interpreted Berlin's dynamism optimistically, stating that 'Paul Morand describes Berlin as a failed New York. Who knows if in twenty years time New York will be seen as a failed Berlin!'[21] As we now know, things turned out somewhat differently. In his 1986 competition entry, *Haus am Checkpoint Charlie*, executed until 1990, Rem Koolhaas highlighted the failed utopianism of Berlin's modernism, and advocated a new modernism on the 'tabula rasa' of the Friedrichstadt. Shown from a bird's eye view, the Friedrichstadt grid assembles the major projects of an unbuilt modernist Berlin, including Koolhaas' project as its terminus.[22]

Mies van der Rohe, one of modernism's points of reference as early as 1921, designed the first unbuilt landmark with the famous Friedrichstrasse crystal skyscraper, followed by the central business district project of Ludwig Hilberseimer in 1928. Hilberseimer contrasted the new urban fabric, displayed in a straight row system according to the principles of light and air, with the Baroque fabric, but also suggested 'a hidden affinity between historical and modernist topography of power.'[23] Hilberseimer further projected a high-rise scheme at Blücherplatz as a metropolitan counterpart to the Baroque Rondell square. After the Depression in 1929, such projects remained unbuilt and at the same time modernist concepts and buildings faced criticism because of their formalism and authoritarian character. Not

21 Quoted after Iain Boyd Whyte, 'National Socialism and Modernism', in Dawn Ades, Tim Benton, David Elliott and Iain Boyd Whyte, eds, *Art and Power, London, Europe under the Dictators 1930–45* (London: Hayward Gallery 1995), 258.

22 Rem Koolhaas, 'Shipwrecked', in Jennifer Sigler, ed., *Small, Medium, Large, Extra-Large, Office of Metropolitan Architecture, Rem Koolhaas, Bruce Mau* (New York: The Monacelli Press, 1995), 254–69; cf. Paul Josef Kleihues and Hans Klotz, eds, *International Building Exhibition Berlin 1987, Examples for a New Architecture* (London: Academy 1986), 154–7.

23 Sabine Hake, *Topographies of Class. Modern Architecture and Mass Society in Weimar Berlin* (Ann Arbor: University of Michigan, 2008), 126.

incidentally, the 1930 German edition of Aldous Huxley's *Brave New World* was set in Berlin, where all power to manipulate information regarding a new genetically modified society was situated in high-rise towers of the Kochstrasse, in the middle of Friedrichstadt.[24]

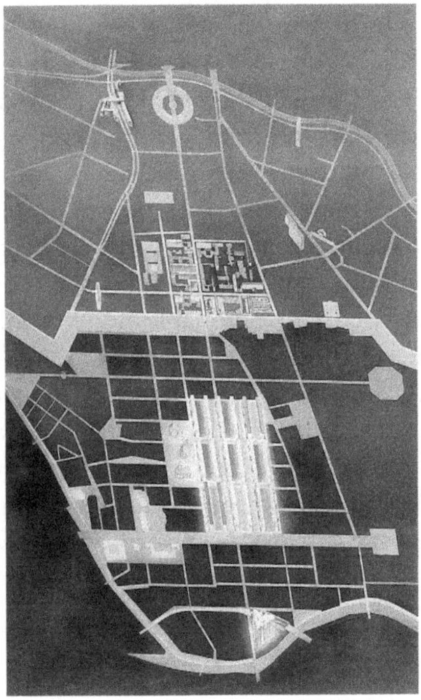

Fig. 5.6: Rem Koolhaas, House at Checkpoint Charlie (Shipwrecked), 1986, rendering of the Friedrichstadt; plan is oriented south.
Source: Paul Josef Kleihues and Hans Klotz, eds, *International Building Exhibition Berlin 1987, Examples for a New Architecture* (London: Academy, 1986), p. 155.
Credit: DAM (German Architecture Museum, Frankfurt).

24 Hilberseimer's project is discussed by Christine Mengin, 'L'architettura della Großstadt', *Rassegna* 27 (1986) (Ludwig Hilberseimer 1886–1967), 42–5; Aldous Huxley, *Brave New World*, trans. Herberth E. Herlitschka in German with the title: *Welt – wohin?* (Leipzig: Insel, 1932); since 1953 *Schöne neue Welt* (Frankfurt: Fischer 1953), revised translation (Frankfurt: Fischer 1981), 75.

Besides its real fabric, the imagined and utopian architecture of Berlin emphasises its character as shelter and archive of a modernist metropolis, a dimension of desire that became part of both Libeskind's and Koolhaas' conceptions. Mendelsohn's project, the *Metal Workers Union Building*, planned in 1929 and executed in the Depression years until 1931, is represented at the top of Koolhaas's architectural vision of Berlin, as well as in Libeskind's matrix. Together with his own villa, *Rupenhorn*, built around the same time in 1930/31 on the shores of the river Havel, where wealthy Berliners had their homes, the *Metal Workers Union Building* is Mendelsohn's only structure in Berlin to survive war, demolition, reconstruction, and ignorant practices of restoration, more or less in its original state. Koolhaas' rendering sets Mendelsohn's project as a counterpart to Mies' crystal skyscraper. It is a sober modern building, typical of Mendelsohn's new 'steep' style from 1928 onwards that avoided any fashionable modernism. In the second project, we find a dominant, concave, central part of the solitaire building that corresponds with the projecting convex entrance pavilion of the ground floor, and forms the peak of the building's triangular layout.[25] In the first project, the trade union administration building was only one aspect of the project; the other, larger project was the adjoining publishing house and printing plant of the left wing Socialdemocratic *Vorwärts* newspaper.

25 The second project, together with Rudolf W. Reichel's winning project, was first published in *Wasmuths Monatshefte für Baukunst und Städtebau* 14 (1930), 467; cf. Bruno Zevi and Erich Mendelsohn, *The Complete Works* (Basel, Boston, Berlin: Birkhäuser, 1999), 178–83; Regina Stephan, '"Wir glauben an Berlin", Das Metalarbeiterhaus, das Columbushaus und andere Geschäftshäuser in Berlin', in Regina Stephan, ed., *Erich Mendelsohn, Architekt 1887–1953, Gebaute Welten* (Ostfildern-Ruit: Hatje, 1998) (engl. edition New York: Monacelli Press, 1999), 144–65, here 146–51.

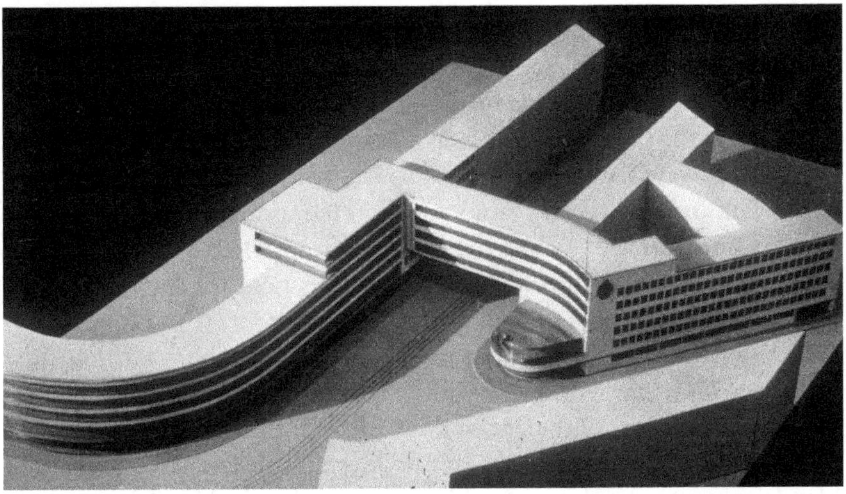

Fig. 5.7: Erich Mendelsohn, Metallworker Union Building and Vorwärts Administration Building project, model-photo 1929.
Photo: Bruno Zevi, *Erich Mendelsohn, Complete Works* (Basel, Boston: Birkhäuser, 1999), p. 223.
Credit: Berlin SMB, Kunstbibliothek.

The whole was a complex structure with an urban impact, creating a new street and connecting both buildings by a cantilevered four-storey high bridge building that formed a unit with the central part of the trade union administration. In retrospect, from his American exile, Mendelsohn explained in 1948:

> In the meantime, the horizontals of my early sketches and buildings were running round the world. They reached their maximum in the 'Town Planning Scheme' of 1929 with the Weimar Republic's printing press to the left and the metalworkers' union administration building to the right – knitted well together architectonically but not politically! When the Union's building is built, the connecting bridge was vanished and the building's face is substantially 'lifted'.[26]

26 Erich Mendelsohn, 'My own contribution to contemporary architecture, Los Angeles 1948', in Oskar Beyer, ed., *Eric Mendelsohn, Letters of an Architect* (London, New York: Abelard-Schuman, 1967), 169.

Mendelsohn's first project very clearly represented an architectural conception within the modern city based on 'natural order and mutual consent', as Balfour has explained.[27] He further sees Mendelsohn's later Berlin buildings, such as the *Columbus House*, as an expression of a specifically Jewish approach towards architecture and space, according to the arguments established in Bruno Zevi's famous essay 'Hebraism and the Concept of Space, Time in Arts'.[28] While the Greek concept of art – understood in Zevi's sense – searches for ideality and timelessness, for the Jew, 'man is defined in the dynamics of daily living.'[29]

'A new rhythm', as Mendelsohn claimed in *Dynamic and Function* as early as 1923, 'has seized the world a new movement [...]. The man of our day, out of the excitement of daily life, can find compensation only in unrestrained horizontality.'[30] But besides this questionable relation of Mendelsohn's modernism to Jewish Culture –whereby Mendelsohn chose a sober, nearly static articulation of his *Columbus House* in this massive ten storey building, with a slight elegant curve towards the boulevard leading to the *Brandenburg Gate* – it is obvious that Mendelsohn was part of, or even a leader of, the organic branch of modernism that defined the city anew. Reorganising the modern city also meant making some surgical interventions in the old urban fabric by opening up new streets. Mendelsohn's union building project had this dimension, comparable to the famous street opening project through the gardens of the ministries by Hans Scharoun, Peter Behrens and others, intended to link the Friedrichstadt with the western districts.[31] All of this took place under the auspices of Martin Wagner, city-planner and 'conductor of the metropolis' in Berlin from 1926 to 1933, with its focal points of Potsdamer and Alexanderplatz. Like Wagner, Mendelsohn was part of the famous *Chain* (Ring) association. Other members, such

27 Balfour, *The Politics of Order*, 114.

28 Bruno Zevi, 'Hebraism and the concept of space-time in art', in Andrea Oppenheimer Dean, ed., *Bruno Zevi on Modern Architecture* (New York: Rizzoli, 1983), 165.

29 Balfour, *The Politics of Order*, 115.

30 Mendelsohn, 'International Agreement in New Architectural Thought'.

31 Anne Leutloff, *Turmhaus, Großhaus, Wolkenschaber: Eine Studie zu Berliner Hochhausentwürfen der 1920er Jahre* (Kiel: Ludwig 2011), 246–50.

as Wassili and Hans Luckhardt, not only made the famous design for the Alexanderplatz competition, referring to Mendelsohn's 'horizontals', but also for the Potsdamer Platz, with a central tower house flanked by the Columbus House and its newly invented replica on the other side of the square. Mendelsohn himself designed other proposals for this incarnation of the modern city square.[32]

In the metalworkers' union building, together with the *Columbus House*, Mendelsohn, despite his soberness, celebrated reinforced concrete-crystal architecture as avant-gardist for the last time in Germany. It marks not only a break in his own œuvre, but represents the change in avant-garde style, especially in public buildings, around 1930.

After the Nazis gained power, Friedrich Paulsen, editor of the influential *Wasmuth's Monatshefte*, called for a representative soberness, a 'severe soberness'.[33] Interestingly, Ernst Sagebiel, Mendelsohn's chief co-worker, who supervised the Union Building as well as the Columbus House, joined the Nazis and became chief architect of Hermann Göring in the newly founded Ministry of the Air Force. When Sagebiel constructed the new ministry complex at Wilhelmstrasse between 1934 and 1936, he made the first large-scale building of the Third Reich, designed in 'severe soberness' for a totalitarian state. Indeed, this style arose earlier, as a new conception for large-scale public buildings in the Weimar Republic, in the competitions of the court of justice extension and the famous Reichsbank competition before 1933, but Sagebiel transformed it into a rational monumentalism with political implications that became characteristic of the first phase of Nazi dictatorship until 1938.[34]

32 Bernd Nicolai, 'The Symphony of the Metropolis: Berlin as Newlin in the Twentieth Century', in Thomas Deckker, ed., *Twentieth Century Cities Revisited* (London: Spon Press, 2000), 9–26.

33 Friedrich Paulsen, 'Urteile über Bauten', *Wasmuths Monatshefte für Baukunst und Städtebau* 18 (1934), 391–2, 443–4; cf. Bernd Nicolai, *Moderne und Exil, deutschsprachige Architekten in der Türkei 1925 bis 1955* (Berlin: Verlag für Bauwesen, 1998), 114–5.

34 Andrea Meseke, 'Zur Spezifik der Repräsentationsarchitektur im Nationalsozialismus', in Thorsten Scheer, Josef Paul Kleihues et al., eds, *Stadt der Architektur, Architektur*

Mendelsohn, however, being clear-sighted about the changing political conditions, left Berlin in February 1933 due to the Nazi attacks on liberal, and especially Jewish, artists, architects and intellectuals. After a short stopover in Amsterdam with Wijdeveld, with whom he planned to establish the European Mediterranean Academy in Cavalière, near St Tropez, he settled in London. The Mediterranean Academy, a supra-international enterprise, was conceived as an 'international work community',[35] a mixture of an alternative Bauhaus and Frank Lloyd Wright's Taliesin workshop. Finally, however, he decided to set up a new studio with Serge Chermayeff in London. His interest in the Academy project diminished, and after a fire burned the entire building site to the ground, he concentrated on new tasks in England and Palestine. Nonetheless, Mendelsohn took the Mediterranean as a catalyst for transforming his own modern architecture into a new archetypical, quasi-natural order, 'After a long walk,' he claimed, 'architecture has got back to the elements of space, i.e. cubic shape, to elements that include Mediterranean history as its very own possession.'[36] The *Weitzman House* in Rehovoth in the British Mandate is one result of this change in conception.

Mendelsohn's emigration and exile entailed two principal points: first, self-reflection and a sort of self-referential architecture;[37] second, a new form of contemporary architecture, based on archetypes and the search

---

der Stadt, Berlin 1900–2000 (Berlin: Nicolai 2000), 187–99, esp. 189–91. Engl. edition *City of Architecture of the City: Berlin 1900–2000* (Berlin: Nicolai 2000), cf. recently Elke Dittrich and Ernst Sagebiel, *Leben und Werk (1892–1970)* (Berlin: Lukas 2005), 71–8.

35 Theodor Wijdeveld, *Eine Internationale Arbeitsgemeinschaft*, Santpoort 1931, with the famous cover image.

36 Erich Mendelsohn, 'Das Mittelmeer und die neue Architektur' (1932) in Ita Heinze-Greenberg and Regina Stephan, eds, *Erich Mendelsohn, Gedankenwelten* (Ostfildern-Ruit 2000), 124 (translation by the author).

37 Cf. Bernd Nicolai, 'Exil-Akkulturation-Kulturtransfer: Prolegomena zu einer Professionsgeschichte der deutschsprachigen Architekten in der Emigration 1930 – 60', in Bernd Nicolai, ed., *Architektur und Exil, Kulturtransfer und architektonische Emigration, 1930 bis 1950* (Trier: Porta Alba 2003) 5–13; Bernd Nicolai, 'The Different Exile, Architectural Exile and the Spirit of California', in Jacek Purchla

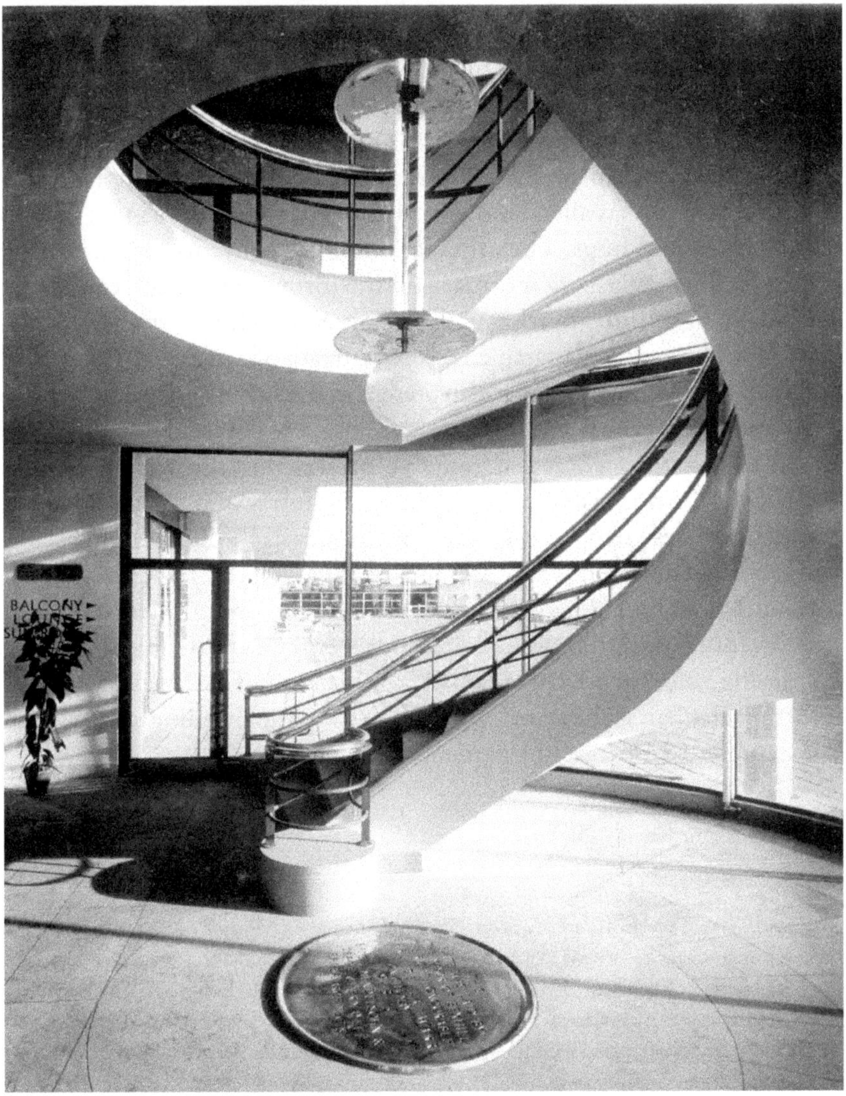

Fig. 5.8: Erich Mendelsohn, De-La-Warr-Pavilion, 1934–1936, Bexhill-on-Sea, Essex, UK, sea-side oriented staircase.
Credit: Postcard collection owned by the author.

for a new synthesis of modernism that Mendelsohn claimed as a synthesis of Orient and Occident, and which emerged through *Mediterranée*.[38] The first aspect is represented in the famous *De La Warr Pavilion* in Bexhill-on-Sea, in the south of England. It was not only an outstanding pioneer building of a newly formed English modern architecture,[39] but a form of self-reassurance in an alien land. Bexhill cites Mendelsohn's most important German buildings. The articulation of the convention hall wing is related to the Königsberg mortuary on the former Jewish cemetery. The landside wing with its overhanging elegant glass cylinder stairs cites the marvellous Schocken department store staircase of Stuttgart. The Berlin Metalworker Union building is also present in the shape of spiral staircase, a manifestation of transparency and spatial elegance. This staircase also made its way to Palestine, where it became a central part of the Weizmann villa in Rehovoth, a new *Rupenhorn*, 'a house absolutely of our time',[40] which Mendelsohn designed for the leader of the Jewish World Congress, later first President of Israel. 'There are climatic, topographic, but even cultural reasons that let him (Mendelsohn) come back to classical-Mediterranean and Levantine tradition,' as his wife Louise explained.[41] Cubic shape and interfering volumes are characteristic of this kind of east-west synthesis. A further element is the transformation of the patio dwelling type with an inner courtyard, open to the garden.

---

and Wolf Tegethoff, ed., *Nation, Style, Modernism* (Munich: Zentralinstitut für Kunstgeschichte, 2006) 285–305, esp. 293–300.

38 Ita Heinze-Greenberg, 'Erich Mendelsohn's Mediterranean Longings. The European Mediterranean Academy and beyond in Palestine', in Jean-Franois Lejeune, and Michelangelo Sabatino, ed., *Modern Architecture and the Mediterranean* (London: Routledge, 2010), 174–91.

39 Alastair Fairley, *De la Warr Pavilion, the modernist masterpiece* (London: Merell 2006).

40 Ita Heinze-Mühleib, *Erich Mendelsohn. Bauten und Projekte in Palästina (1934–41)* (Munich: Scaneg, 1986), 112.

41 Louise Mendelsohn, *My life in a changing world, unpublished memoirs* (San Francisco: Ms Kunstbibliothek SMB, Berlin), 641, qouted after Heinze-Greenberg, Ita, '"Ich bin ein freier Bauer?"', 251.

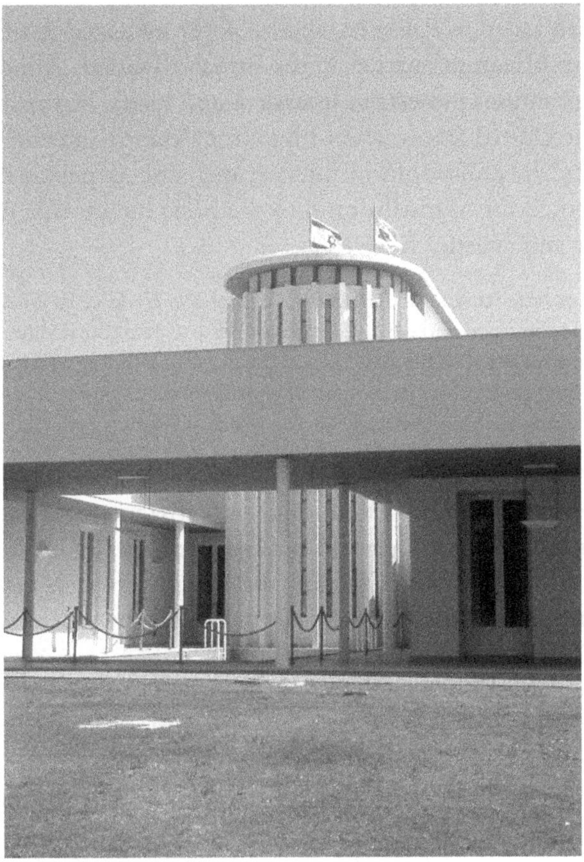

Fig. 5.9: Mendelsohn, Villa Weizmann, Rehovoth/Israel, 1934–1936, inner courtyard with staircase tower.
Credit: Bernd Nicolai.

Julius Posener, as member of the left wing Tel Aviv *Chug* (Chain), opposed this inherent traditionalism when he criticised his former master in 1938: 'With such misunderstandings (of a synthesis) we are confronted also in detail, where the modern architect tries to build in a broader sense traditional. [...] What we believe is that all search [...] for a synthesis remain inconsistent.'[42] Mendelsohn's

42 Julius Posener, 'Traditionelles und modernes Bauen in Palästina', *Das Werk* 25 (1938), 257–71, quotation 269 (translation by the author); Alona Nitzan-Shiftan, 'Contested

new approach failed in Palestine, and he never managed to obtain a chief position in architectural matters in the British Mandate. Although he was engaged with various projects in Jerusalem and Haifa, he finally emigrated in 1941 to the United States, where his journey 'came to an end'.[43]

Memory, the philosophy of absence, and issues of personal breaks and friction, merged for Mendelsohn into the basic humanistic principles of architecture and artistic creativity:

> Where use, structure and architectural expression coalesce to an organic whole, where scientific facts and creative vision combine to an unbreakable pattern – there is art, the great art of architecture, where the finished building strikes you as a flower which didn't exist before in the garden of architecture, where the author's original mind is clearly visible – there and there alone is a creative personality; there a great architect has left his imprint for everybody to see.[44]

For Mendelsohn, who had lived long years in an insecure state despite his professional success, and who became after 1933 a modern nomad, searching for his place in a changing world that shifted its centre of gravity from Europe towards America, it was important to leave his mark as gifted architect.

In a comparison of Mendelsohn's and Libeskind's architectural conceptions, we could say that for Mendelsohn, a building was definitely an 'exclamation mark', while for Libeskind it is first of all 'question marks'. In his acceptance speech for the German Architecture Prize in 1999 Libeskind emphasised that '[a] building can be experienced as an unfinished journey. It can awaken our desires, propose imaginary conclusions. It is not about form, image or text, but about the experience, which is not to be simulated. A building can awaken us to the fact that it has never been anything more than a huge question mark.'[45]

Zionism-Alternative Modernism: Erich Mendelsohn and the Tel Aviv Chug in Mandate Palestine', *Architectural History* 39 (1996), 147–80.

43 Cf. Nicolai, 'Exil-Akkulturation-Kulturtransfer, Prolegomena zu einer Professionsgeschichte der deutschsprachigen Architekten in der Emigration 1930–60'.

44 Beyer, 'International Agreement in New Architectural Thought', 172.

45 German Architecture Prize Speech. Speech given by Daniel Libeskind on the occasion of being awarded the German Architecture Prize for the Jewish Museum, Berlin, 1999.

As early as his 1987 project *Berlin City Edge* he linked different aspects, like breaking convention, floating architecture, and eventually the historic dimension of the site. Its title *Counter Design* referred to Soviet constructivism.[46] Libeskind combined admiration for Soviet avant-garde art with a commemoration of the dwelling of one of the masters of classical modern architecture, Mies van der Rohe. The antagonism between classical architecture and avant-garde is annihilated with reference to Leonardo da Vinci. *Berlin City Edge* can be seen as a model for what was enlarged and much more contextualised in the project for the Jewish Museum.

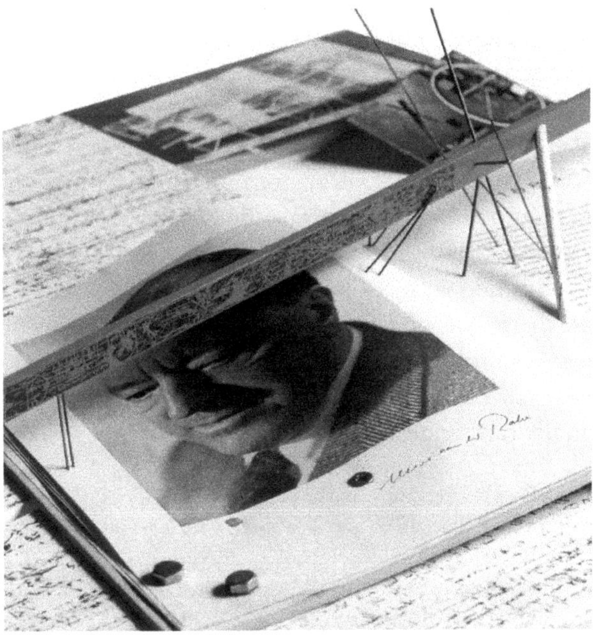

Fig. 5.10: Daniel Libeskind, *Nowhere is a center*, memorial for Mies van der Rohe, Project: *Berlin City Edge*, 1987.
Credit: Studio Libeskind.

The dichotomy between the classical and the avant-garde was already being discussed under the changing conditions of avant-garde modernity in

46 Libeskind, *Counter Design*, 63–83.

the 1930s. Not only Mendelsohn but also Bruno Taut claimed in his book *Lessons on Architecture*, written in exile in Istanbul 1937, that 'a building could at the same time be modern and traditional,' if it comprises all elements of traditional knowledge and sense for contemporaneity.[47] Libeskind some 60 years later also comes back to this phenomenon, and describes the Jewish Museum as a paradox: 'This museum is basically a building without archetype, but it is not an avant-garde architecture, after all a traditional work of architecture.'[48] Like Mendelsohn and Taut, Libeskind's interest in such statements was to be noticed as a timeless architect.

The sublime character of the Jewish Museum is striking if we notice our emotional perception of this spatial arrangement of open spaces and voids. When asked about the problems of constructing such a meaningful building, Libeskind answered in awareness of his normative power: 'Of course it is precarious and therefore I had to make it.' For Libeskind, in this and other museum projects, architecture becomes another form of collective memory, besides text and image, as a complex structure of commemoration.

This is combined with a soberness that provokes a sculptural, nearly archetypal aesthetic. It is no wonder that the building was most celebrated when it stood as a building shell, an empty space without any function, a modern memorial. This architecture interferes with the cityscape, with its users, and finally raises questions:

> Architecture is a direct response to the permanent questions posed to human beings by the evolution of space in society – a space which seems to be autonomous, yet seeks a profound and ethical discourse. Architecture is generated, sustained and propelled into the future by dreams and aspirations; by awakenings and realisations; by the visible and the invisible.[49]

47 Bruno Taut, *Architekturlehre. Arch + Zeitschrift für Architektur und Städtebau 194* (2009).

48 Daniel Libeskind, *Jüdisches Museum Berlin* (Dresden: Verlag der Kunst 2000), 30.

49 Hong Wee, *Between, Beside, and Beyond*, 245.

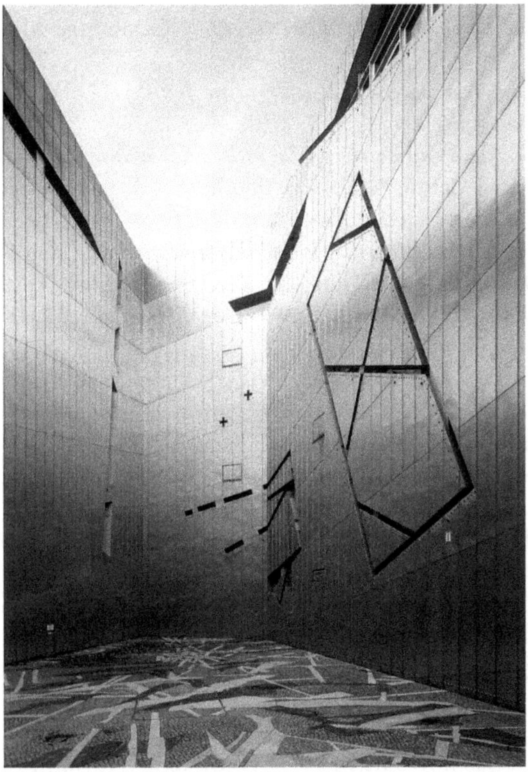

Fig. 5.11: Daniel Liberskind, Jewish Museum Berlin, Paul Celan Court. Credit: DAM, Frankfurt.

Bibliography

Amishai-Maisels, Ziva, 'Hunting the empty space', in Steve Feinstein, ed., *Absence/presence: Essays and Reflections on the Artistic Memory of the Holocaust* (Syracuse, NY: Syracuse University Press, 2005), 123–50.

Architekten Verein zu Berlin, eds, *Berlin und seine Bauten*, Vol. 2 (Berlin: Ernst & Sohn, 1896).

Balfour, Alan, *The Politics of Order, 1737–1989* (New York: Rizzoli, 1990).

Benjamin, Walter, *Berlin Childhood Around 1900* (Cambridge, MA: Belknap Press, 2006).

Beyer, Oskar, ed., *Eric Mendelsohn, Letters of an Architect* (London, New York: Abelard-Shulman, 1967).

Dethier, Jean, and Alain Guilheux, eds, *La Ville, art et architecture en Europe 1870–1993* (Paris: Editions Centre Pompidou, 1994).

Dittrich, Elke and Ernst Sagebiel, *Leben und Werk (1892–1970)* (Berlin: Lukas, 2005).

Fairley, Alastair, *De la Warr Pavilion. The Modernist Masterpiece* (London: Merell, 2006).

Forgács, Éva, 'Definitive Space. The Many Utopias of El Lissitzky's Proun Room', in Nancy Perloff and Brian Reed, eds, *Situating El Lissitzky: Vitebsk, Berlin, Moscow* (Los Angeles: Getty Trust, 2003), 47–75.

Foucault, Michael, *The Archaeology of Knowledge* (London, New York: Routledge, 1989).

Hake, Sabine, *Topographies of Class. Modern Architecture and Mass Society in Weimar Berlin* (Ann Arbor: University of Michigan, 2008).

Heckmann, Hermann, *Baumeister des Barock und Rokoko, Brandenburg, Preussen* (Berlin: Verlag für Bauwesen, 1999).

Heinze-Mühleib, Ita, *Erich Mendelsohn. Bauten und Projekte in Palästina (1934–41)* (Munich: Scaneg, 1986).

Heinze-Greenberg, Ita, 'Erich Mendelsohn's Mediterranean Longings. The European Mediterranean Academy and beyond in Palestine', in Jean-Franois Lejeune and Michelangelo Sabatino, eds, *Modern architecture and the Mediterranean* (London: Routledge, 2010), 174–91.

——, '"Ich bin ein freier Bauer". Bauten in Palästina 1934–41', in Regina Stephan, ed., *Erich Mendelsohn. Architect 1887–1953. Gebaute Welten, Arbeiten für Europa, Palästina und Amerika* (Ostfildern-Ruit: Hatje, 1998), 240–87.

Heinze-Greenberg, Ita, and Regina Stephan, eds, *Luise und Erich Mendelsohn: eine Partnerschaft für die Kunst* (Ostfildern: Hatje-Cantz, 2004).

Herzogenrath, Wener, ed., *Die Endlichkeit der Freiheit* (Berlin 1990); Michael Glasmeier, *Christian Boltanski, Christiane Büchner, Andreas Fischer, The Missing House, The Museum* (Berlin: DAAD, 1992).

Hong Wee, Michael Lee, ed., *Between, Beside, and Beyond, Daniel Libeskind's Reflections and Key Works 1989–2014* (Singapore: Keppel Land Limited, 2007).

Huxley, Aldous, *Brave New World*, trans. Herberth E. Herlitschka in German with the title: *Welt – wohin?* (Leipzig: Insel, 1932); since 1953 *Schöne neue Welt* (Frankfurt: Fischer, 1953), revised translation (Frankfurt: Fischer, 1981).

Kleihues, Paul Joseph, and Heinrich Klotz, eds, *International Building Exhibition Berlin 1987: Examples for a New Architecture* (London: Academy, 1986).

Koolhaas, Rem, 'Shipwrecked', in Jennifer Sigler, ed., *Small, Medium, Large, Extra-Large, Office of Metropolitan Architecture, Rem Koolhaas, Bruce Mau* (New York: The Monacelli Press, 1995), 254–69.

Leach, Neil, 'Erasing the traces, the "denazification" of post-revolutionary Berlin and Bukarest' in Neil Leach, ed., *The Hieroglyphics of Space, Reading and Experiencing the Modern Metropolis* (London: Routledge, 2002), 80–91.

Leutloff, Anne, *Turmhaus, Großhaus, Wolkenschaber: Eine Studie zu Berliner Hochhausentwürfen der 1920er Jahre* (Kiel: Ludwig, 2011).

Libeskind, Daniel, 'Between the Lines, Jewish Museum Berlin', in Connie Wolf, ed., *Daniel Libeskind and the Contemporaray Jewish Museum: New Jewish Architecture from Berlin to San Francisco* (New York: Rizzoli, 2008).

——, *Counter Design* (New York: Rizzoli, 1991).

——, 'Global Building Sites between Past and Future', in Uta Staiger and Henriette Steiner, *Memory Culture and Contemporary City Building Sites* (New York: Macmillan, 2009), 69–84.

——, *Jüdisches Museum Berlin* (Dresden: Verlag der Kunst, 2000).

——, with Sarah Crichton, *Breaking Ground, adventures in life and architecture* (New York: Riverhead Book, 2004).

Mendelsohn, Erich, 'International Agreement in New Architectural Thought' [1923], in Oskar Beyer, ed., *Eric Mendelsohn, Letters of an Architect* (London, New York: Abelard-Schuman, 1967).

——, 'Das Mittelmeer und die neue Architektur' (1932) in Ita Heinze-Greenberg and Regina Stephan, eds, *Erich Mendelsohn, Gedankenwelten* (Ostfildern-Ruit, 2000).

——, 'My own contribution to contemporary architecture, Los Angeles 1948', in Oskar Beyer, ed., *Eric Mendelsohn, Letters of an Architect* (London, New York: Abelard-Schuman, 1967).

Mengin, Christine, 'L'architettura della Großstadt', *Rassegna* 27 (1986), 42–5.

Meseke, Andrea, 'Zur Spezifik der Repräsentationsarchitektur im Nationalsozialismus', in Thorsten Scheer, Josef Paul Kleihues et al., eds, *Stadt der Architektur, Architektur der Stadt, Berlin 1900–2000* (Berlin: Nicolai, 2000), 187–99.

Nicolai, Bernd, 'The different Exile, Architectural Exile and the Spirit of California', in Jacek Purchla and Wolf Tegethoff, ed., *Nation, Style, Modernism* (Munich: Zentralinstitut für Kunstgeschichte, 2006) 285–305.

——, 'Exil-Akkulturation-Kulturtransfer, Prolegomena zu einer Professionsgeschichte der deutschsprachigen Architekten in der Emigration 1930–60', in Bernd Nicolai, ed., *Architektur und Exil, Kulturtransfer und architektonische Emigration, 1930 bis 1950* (Trier: Porta Alba, 2003) 5–13.

——, *Moderne und Exil, deutschsprachige Architekten in der Türkei 1925 bis 1955* (Berlin: Verlag für Bauwesen, 1998).

——, 'The Symphony of the Metropolis: Berlin as Newlin in the Twentieth Century', in Thomas Deckker, ed., *Twentieth Century Cities Revisited* (London: Spon Press, 2000), 9–26.

Nitzan-Shiftan, Alona, 'Contested Zionism-Alternative Modernism: Erich Mendelsohn and the Tel Aviv Chug in Mandate Palestine', *Architectural History* 39 (1996), 147–80.

Paulsen, Friedrich, 'Urteile über Bauten', *Wasmuths Monatshefte für Baukunst und Städtebau* 18 (1934), 391–2, 443–4.

Posener, Julius, 'Traditionelles und modernes Bauen in Palästina', *Das Werk* 25 (1938), 257–71.

Schäche, Wolfgang, 'Die Friedrichstadt in Berlin-Mitte, Geschichte, Bestand, Planung', *Berlin Jahrbuch* 2 (1993/94), 62–9.

Scheffler, Karl, *Berlin, Ein Stadtschicksal* (Berlin-Westend: Reiss, 1910).

Solomon-Godeau, Abigail, 'Mourning or Melancholia. Christian Boltanski's Missing House', *Oxford Art Journal* 21/2 (1998), 3–20.

Staiger, Uta, Henriette Steiner and Andrew Webber, eds, *Memory Culture and Contemporary City Building Sites* (New York, Basingstoke: Palgrave Macmillan, 2009), 69–84.

Stephan, Regina, '"Wir glauben an Berlin", Das Metalarbeiterhaus, das Columbushaus und andere Geschäftshäuser in Berlin', in Regina Stephan, ed., *Erich Mendelsohn, Architekt 1887–1953, Gebaute Welten* (Ostfildern-Ruit: Hatje, 1998), 146–51.

Taut, Bruno, *Architekturlehre* (*Arch +194 Zeitschrift für Architektur und Städtebau*, 2009) ed. Manfred Speidel, originally published in Turkish as *Mirmarî Bilgisi* (Istanbul: Güzel San'atlar Akademisi, 1938).

Weinberg, David 'Between America and Israel: The Quest for a Distinct European Jewish Identity in the Post-War Era', *Jewish Culture and History* 5/1 (2002), 91–120.

Whyte, Iain Boyd, 'National Socialism and Modernism', in Dawn Ades, Tim Benton, David Elliott and Iain Boyd Whyte, eds, *Art and Power, London, Europe under the Dictators 1930–45* (London: Hayward Gallery, 1995).

Wilderotter, Hans, *Alltag der Macht, Berlin Wilhelmstrasse* (Berlin: Jovis, 1998), cf. *Topography of Terror. Gestapo, SS and Reich Security Main Office on Wilhelm- and Prinz-Albrecht-Straße. A Documentation* (Berlin: Stiftung Topographie des Terrors, 2010), 126–45.

Wistrich, Robert S., *Laboratory for World Destruction: Germans and Jews in Central Europe* (Lincoln: University of Nebraska Press, 2007).

Young, James Edward, 'Memory and Counter-Memory', *Harvard Design Magazine* 9/Fall (1999), 23–35.

——, *At Memory's Edge: After-Images of the Holocaust in Contemporary Art and Architecture* (New Haven, London: Yale University Press, 2000).

Zevi, Bruno, 'Hebraism and the concept of space-time in art', in Andrea Oppenheimer Dean, ed., *Bruno Zevi on Modern Architecture* (New York: Rizzoli, 1983).

Zevi, Bruno, and Erich Mendelsohn, *The Complete Works* (Basel, Boston, Berlin: Birkhäuser, 1999), 178–83.

HENRIK REEH

6 Urban Bottles and Green Glass: Display and Transparencies in Post-Industrial Tuborg

Diversified Visualities

Since the late twentieth century, European industrial areas with harbour facilities have frequently been converted into urban settings in which glass is a major architectural component. Incorporated into the façades of both dwellings and office buildings, glass is often closely connected to positive commercial and lifestyle-related narratives, which focus on the extensive view of the sea, canals, or other aquatic surfaces. Yet glass may also inspire narratives of surveillance that affect the mental and the social spirit of such places, and contradict certain desires for the unmediated urban presence of human beings. After all, glass participates in a new urban or suburban culture, where life is increasingly protected, insulated, or at least mediated by the glass surfaces of houses as well as automobiles. While urban spaces in such coastal or harbour areas are sometimes designed with great care, they are also strikingly vacant, devoid of human bodies, and even hostile to civic encounters. At least, this is the impression frequently reported from a wealthy redeveloped area on the coast just outside Copenhagen – an area whose modes of display and diverse forms of transparency we will explore in the following pages on post-industrial Tuborg.

For more than a century, Denmark's world-famous Tuborg beer was brewed at a heterogeneous industrial site named 'Tuborg', situated on the threshold between the Danish capital, Copenhagen, and the wealthy suburbs up the coast of Øresund. Since the 1980s, brewing activities have been transferred to efficient factories in the provinces, while the forty hectares of industrial land and harbour facilities are being converted into an urban zone for upscale housing and corporate headquarters, supported by a few educational or cultural institutions, a shopping centre and a marina. In this way, the transformation of Tuborg into 'Tuborg Harbour' shares generic traits, but also certain problems, with post-industrial conversions throughout Europe as industrial enclaves tend to become urban or suburban ones. On the other hand, each place adopts specific forms that may be decisive for the long-term development of its urban-cultural potentials.

At Tuborg, the transition that is currently underway implies a diversified redefinition of display and transparencies all along the borderline between the city and the site, as well as inside the area between the private interiors on the one hand, and the publicly accessible exteriors on the other. Tuborg's long history as a beer brewing and industrial harbour site, closed to the public, did not prepare the ground for the development of a lively urban area, although Copenhagen and dense suburban districts are right next door. Moreover, the accelerated urbanisation of Tuborg has been based, primarily, on traditional building types such as apartment dwellings and corporate offices, thus favouring distinctly residential or professional functions. Despite the luxurious marina and its extensive boardwalks, civic areas and practices have hardly been considered in this new urban district; instead of public playgrounds or bathing facilities, there are numerous warning signs indicating that areas are private and access is prohibited.

In the present chapter, the negotiation of urban visibilities inside the Tuborg setting is traced by means of *bottles* and *glass*, two motifs (or analytical 'dispositifs')[1] that may allow us to identify the ways in which visual attention and hierarchies are established. Echoing the iconic Tuborg beer bottle, a series of monumental architectures actually represent bottles and elaborate on the cultural heritage of the place. Such examples of deliberate *display* are explored in five variations on bottles. On the other hand, glass provides a decisive medium for visual practices throughout Tuborg. Uniting and separating, glass involves external observers and local inhabitants, passing customers and permanent employees. Moreover, glass surfaces promote a wide range of *transparencies* (in the plural). Constituting limits

1 'Dispositif' is a concept developed by French philosopher Michel Foucault in his studies of particular articulations between power, technology and subjectivity. See for instance Michel Foucault, *Dits et écrits*, Vol. II (Paris: Gallimard, 1994), 299–300.

and enabling transitions between inside and outside, glass allows complex patterns of contemplative and distracted gazes to evolve. Selected aspects of those relations are treated in four variations on glass.

By delving into sensory perceptions and photographic images, this chapter presents a series of kaleidoscopic observations on Tuborg's monumental bottles and architectural glass surfaces.[2] The actual succession of notes reflects the labyrinthine itinerary of a pedestrian visitor with his camera, thus representing the experience of an outside observer who explores the new urban zone along its public paths and roads, pavements and boardwalks. Addressing urban landmarks, residential architecture and corporate headquarters as well as the marina and its canals, the labyrinthine walk detects and deciphers the urban-cultural reality from below. Focusing on the results of intentional display (bottles) and on subtle degrees of transparency (glass), the following pages signal a variety of urban potentials that may after all be germinating in this area.

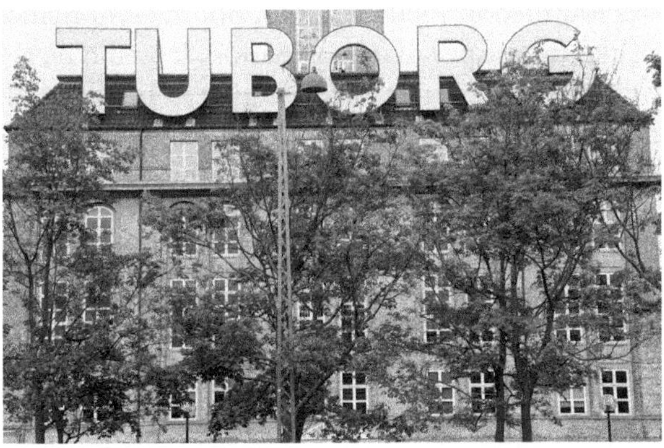

Fig. 6.1: The Tuborg Sign. Are the Tuborg Breweries still running? No, but the Tuborg sign is branding the area. Credit: Henrik Reeh, 2011.

2 This study elaborates on empirical materials discussed in Henrik Reeh, 'Tuborg *en passant*: Urbane forvandlingsbilleder', in Ning de Coninck-Smith and Harriet Tranum-Jensen, eds, *2900 Hellerup – Set i Bakspejlet* (Charlottenlund: Strandbergs Forlag, 2011), 84–103 and 143–44, in which further references may be found, as well as a series of thirty-seven colour photographs by the author.

Variation on Bottles: Tuborg – a Beer and an Urban Threshold

An appropriate drink to accompany a traditional Danish lunch is the so-called 'Grøn Tuborg' – 'Green Tuborg' – which has for a long time been the emblematic beer of the Danish middle classes. When preparing smoked herring with chives, sliced onions and radishes, with, of course, an egg yolk on top and rye bread underneath, one should not forget the Tuborg, without which the dish would not be quite complete. A solid brand in many contexts, Green Tuborg basically owes its commercial identity to the green label on the front of the bottle, a label listing information such as 'Green Tuborg Lager'/'Brewed since 1880'/'Purveyor to the Royal Danish Court' but also: 'Founded in Hellerup'.[3]

We might ask why it is so important that Tuborg – the company, not the beer – was founded in Hellerup, a toponomy synonymous with the Danish upper class in the popular imagination. It would be more accurate to say that the Tuborg Breweries were founded at Tuborg itself, a location up the coast of Øresund, just outside the city boundary of Copenhagen. Named after the 1690-owner of a restaurant along the dusty road, Tuborg, in 1873, entered the name of the 'Tuborg Factories' company, the diverse activities of which were united by a harbour which, albeit altered, is still there. Whereas the beer itself is yellowish, the glass bottle of a Green Tuborg was originally dark green, and is today olive-green, in order to protect the content against ultraviolet rays of light. Since the Breweries' foundation, the green colour of label and bottle has remained essential to the corporate identity of the Tuborg Breweries; accordingly, the tall gables of the modernist corporate headquarters of the mid-1960s were glazed green.[4] One may have observed this humorous sign when driving up the coast, past the

3 Translated from the Danish text of a Grøn Tuborg label by the author.

4 For an illustrated historical account of the first hundred years of the Tuborg Breweries, see Birgit Nüchel Thomsen, *Tuborg, 1873–13. maj 1973: Tuborg og Bryggeriindustrien under Skiftende Markedsvilkår 1873–1973* (Hellerup: Tuborgs Bryggerier, 1973).

pell-mell industrial site of Tuborg which was a kind of pause between the urban fabric of Copenhagen and the mixed typologies of villas and apartments in the socially privileged suburbs.

Today, most of industrial Tuborg is gone, but not all. On a former factory façade, huge illuminated letters reading TUBORG are visible from afar, as if the breweries were still active. In addition, selected buildings have been preserved and stand out as modernised remains from the history of architecture, including Art Nouveau. But the millions of glass bottles which were stacked everywhere behind the wire fences of the breweries themselves or around Tuborg's own glass factory are now absent. Nonetheless, both glass and bottles still play prominent roles in recently urbanised Tuborg.

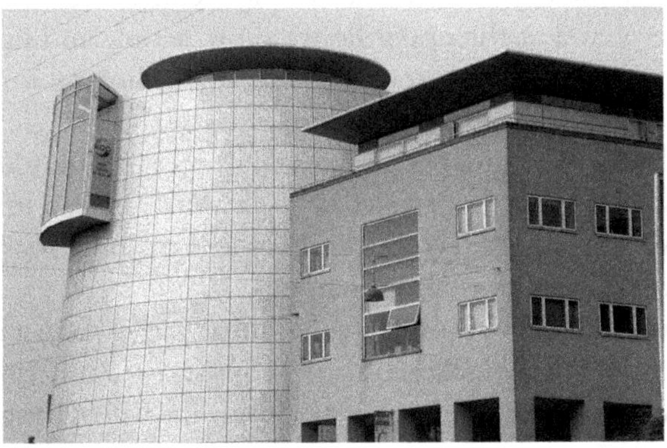

Fig. 6.2: The Tuborg Rotunda, aka the Thermos, by architect Henning Larsen. Credit: Henrik Reeh, 2011.

Variation on Bottles: The Urban Thermos – From Beer to Coffee

To be sure, beer is no longer the lunchtime drink of choice on weekdays. The neoliberal work ethic is incompatible with alcoholic drinks being consumed during business hours, the exit of which was followed by that of cigarettes.

So far, however, nobody has seriously questioned the continuous consumption of coffee in most offices, since coffee keeps employees going and prevents them from falling asleep at meetings or in front of computers. Given this change in habits from beer to coffee, it is an amusing fact that the new Tuborg rotunda, designed as a first urban-architectural monument in 1994 by Danish architect Henning Larsen, has been nicknamed 'the thermos' or 'the coffeepot'. It certainly resembles one, as it emerges by the side of the slightly turning road, just before the urban section of Hellerup, and the socio-cultural context in which it is embedded now has more to do with coffee than with beer.

With its oblique exterior walls, this rotunda, covered by perforated metal plates, is not a cylinder, but a truncated cone. A few glass openings at ground level and at the upper floors allow people and light to enter. The rotunda contributes to transforming the industrial no-man's land into an urban fabric. With the erection of Larsen's light grey and brick-clad ensembles of apartments, shops and offices in the mid-1990s, the former brownfield area first started to look a little like an urban setting, in which five-storey architectural volumes and a mix of social functions enable employees and consumers to mingle.

Architecturally, the rotunda is a sculpture rather than a building for commercial use; its sole practical function consists in conducting customers towards a supermarket at the back. Once inside the hall of the rotunda, you should take your time and contemplate the tall interior, which continues uninterruptedly for about four storeys. Despite its role as a passageway, the rotunda forms a poetic space, inviting the visitor to explore the vertical magic of the room. Carved into the white walls, a spiral staircase allows you to climb the inside of this apparently empty building which, nonetheless, contains a two-storey space on top, arrived at by means of this staircase.

At the opening of the rotunda in 1996, a Thai restaurant was located at the summit. Some years ago, a real-estate agent had taken over. More recently, the space upstairs was empty and for rent. Standing at the top of the narrow staircase, one hardly imagines the impressive view from the top floors. While the façade of the thermos is opaque and metallic, glass takes over and offers a panorama of the entire area and the sea nearby. So far, however, the basis for a successful business inside this urban landmark is missing.

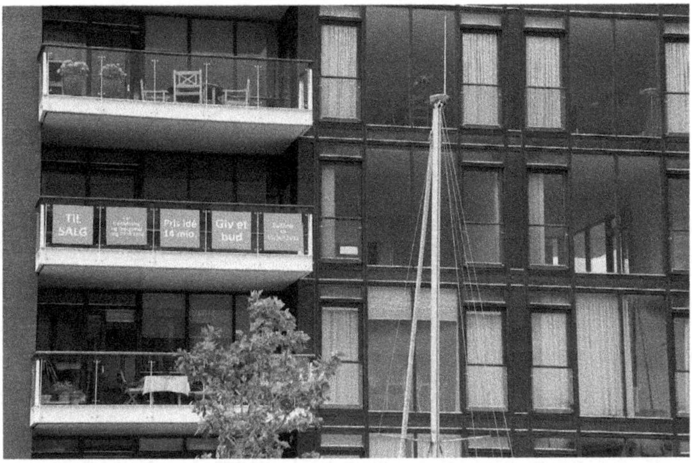

Fig. 6.3: A nearly transparent apartment, by Vilhelm Lauritzen Architects, for sale by auction. Credit: Henrik Reeh, 2011.

Variation on Glass: Apartments with a View

Glass was essential to the production of beer and soda bottles at Tuborg. But as a construction material, glass played a minor role in the industrial buildings of the site. It was not until the local bottle factory and the breweries disappeared that glass became a pervasive component in the new architectures of Tuborg, residential and corporate alike. The most comprehensive use of glass is found in residential architecture. Here, the modernist ideal of windows offering a contemplative view of nature still makes sense, aesthetically and commercially. While water surfaces are visible from any apartment, the glass employed is apparently colourless and highly transparent. Designed by well-known Danish architects, none of the apartment blocks are built with glass walls only, but they all contain large glass surfaces, which favour views from within towards the architectural and natural surroundings.

Perhaps surprisingly, glass was employed more extensively in the early stages of Tuborg's new residential architecture. Built around 2000, the first apartments (design: Vilhelm Lauritzen Architects) might look organic and traditional thanks to their supportive brick walls, and their door and window frames of precious wood. But these apartments have modernist glass walls from floor to ceiling in all rooms, be they living and dining rooms, or bedrooms or kitchens. Even the collective staircases have glass walls, as do the large balconies. The following wave of apartments (design: Arkitema Architects) appear light and transparent, due to their white exteriors with metallic grey window frames, as well as to their location next to the sea in a dune-like landscape. But the use of glass for the exterior walls is less extensive; individual rooms and kitchens have medium-sized windows only, which leave room for privacy and storage.

The limitation of glass surfaces continues in the third generation of Tuborg's recent residential architecture (design: Dissing & Weitling Architects, founded by two former collaborators of modernist master Arne Jacobsen). These apartment blocks have neither glass balconies nor transparent staircases. Instead, opaque white façades of bricks and concrete refer to a general Bauhaus-idiom, but particularly to Arne Jacobsen's white Bella Vista housing estate from the mid-1930s, five kilometres up the coast. Yet, despite the obvious quotation from Jacobsen's curved balconies, which promoted a view of the sea while securing the visual privacy of each apartment, the Tuborg version appears less sophisticated in housing blocks, which are taller, and look massive and serial compared to Bella Vista.

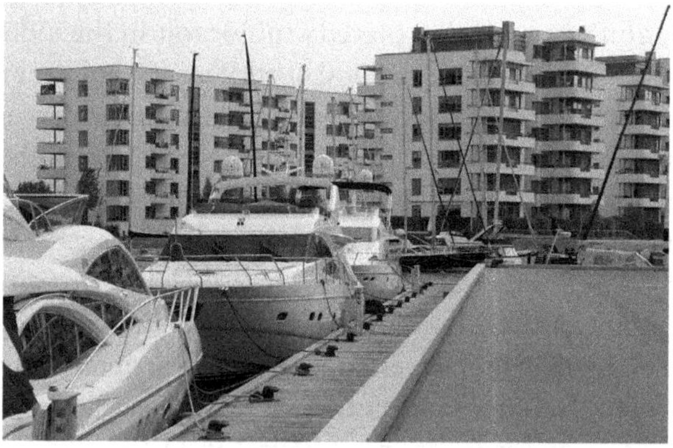

Fig. 6.4: Third-stage, limited transparency, by Dissing & Weitling Architects – rewriting Arne Jacobsen's Bella Vista housing estate for the twenty-first century. Credit: Henrik Reeh, 2011

Variation on Glass: Transparency and Visibilities

Dwellings with glass façades remain a modernist dream, but the accompanying narratives of health and nature, technology and progress, do not fully apply to the lifeworld realities of the twenty-first century. Nevertheless, all the recent Tuborg apartment blocks deploy an extensive use of glass – a material that privileges the inhabitant's distracted or contemplative view from inside, but which also promotes a visual reciprocity between indoors and outdoors. Large surfaces of glass in apartment buildings may thus participate in a culture of exhibition and surveillance.

Still, if glass surfaces in private dwellings inevitably enhance the relationship between elements of interior privacy and exterior publicity, it would be naive to accept the widespread hypothesis according to which glass automatically provides full transparency from the outside towards the interiors.[5] Indeed, exhibitionism and narcissism are favoured by lifestyle magazines and 'social media' such as Facebook, but practices of secrecy and opacity remain structurally powerful within postmodern subjectivities. Curtains and blinds of all sorts limit the uninhibited entry of light, and reject foreign gazes. And glass itself is far from generating absolute transparency. While glass has often been promoted as a medium that could bring bourgeois interiority to an end,[6] lifeworld realities – visual and cultural – of housing areas prove more complex.

The inhabitants of the expensive apartments at Tuborg certainly furnish their rooms according to their own preferences, some deliberately exhibiting their wealth and tastes to the outside. Although the huge glass surfaces actually allow private signs and objects to appear to the attentive gaze of passing urbanites, most passers-by are on their way somewhere else,

5 In a Danish context, this simplistic argument – nearly a phantasm? – was often used with reference to Bjarke Ingels and Julien de Smedt's so-called *VM Houses* in Ørestad from the early 2000s.

6 The crisis of subjectivity after the horrors of the First World War challenged the traditional ideals of privacy and authenticity. See Walter Benjamin's essay from the mid-1930s, 'Erfahrung und Armut' in his *Gesammelte Schriften*, Vol. II (Frankfurt am Main: Suhrkamp Verlag, 1980).

and have neither the curiosity nor the courage to stop and watch whatever may be visible inside particular apartments.[7] And seeing inside is not that easy. In order to look inside, the external observer's angle of vision should, first of all, be quite frontal, and distance helps circumvent the reflective qualities of glass. Otherwise glass soon turns into a mirror reflecting the surroundings or, as in the case of open environments such as Tuborg, the sky.

Secondly, in order to ensure effective visibility, there should be light behind a glass pane. One large window will not suffice if the room behind is deep and dark. Indeed, quite a few Tuborg apartments have rooms and terraces with several glass walls. Echoing major modernist buildings such as Philip Johnson's Glass House in Connecticut (which was supplemented by an opaque stone house for sleeping in), the multiple glass walls in certain Tuborg apartments promote a higher degree of transparency than do most architectures with large windows.

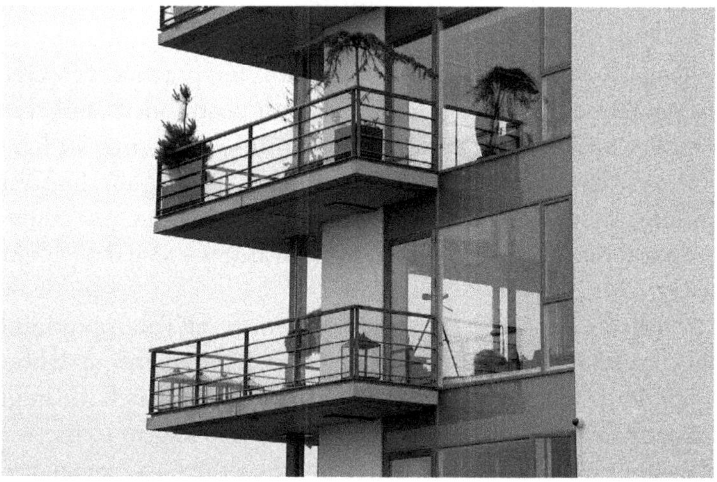

Fig. 6.5: Exhibiting transparency: Overlooking the sea.
Apartments by Arkitema Architects.
Credit: Henrik Reeh, 2011.

7 On the perception of architecture between contemplation and distraction, between optics and tactics, see Henrik Reeh, 'Blik i brug – Walter Benjamin og Erfaringens Arkitektur', in Carsten Thau, ed., *Filosofi & Arkitektur i det 20. Århundrede* (Copenhagen: Kunstakademiets Arkitektskole, 2006), 83–124.

In urban reality, however, the passer-by seldom gains insight into the precise order of things and signs. Even at Tuborg, the visibility of interiors from the outside is most striking when apartments are empty. The consequence of this is paradoxical: either private furnishings obstruct the outsider's vision, or, in the case of vacant apartments, there will be nothing to see but the rooms themselves. Extensive transparency may thus reveal a void and an absence of life – an experience prefigured by the scarcity of human beings visible inside apartments or on balconies.

Finally, one should be aware of the fact that huge glass surfaces are not themselves fully transparent. The human eye may barely notice this feature in passing, but systematic observation of photographs reveals how glass is not as colourless as we expect it to be. When two layers of glass are superimposed onto one another, a green tint becomes visible. One clearly sees it where one glass side of a balcony is doubled either by a window behind it, or by a second side of the same balcony; all of a sudden a greenish colour invades the expected transparency and reduces it. Such shades of green are undeniably there in staircases, whose window panes seem to have a special coating. As soon as one starts looking, one realises the extent to which apparently colourless glass turns greenish, as if the colour green were an intrinsic property of the material itself.

Indeed, the tint observed is not necessarily due to coating or colouring (as in the cases of sunglasses, or car windows that make the world appear darker). The green aspect is automatically there in the soda-lime glass of windowpanes; chemically speaking, the green tint results from iron oxides present in the glass material itself. Tuborg's most recent apartments have no large windows from floor to ceiling and, therefore, do not reveal the interior volumes to the gaze of people passing. Yet certain windows join at corners, and thus, discreetly, display a green tint as part of the mediation operated by glass between private and public. In everyday life, the underground presence of green in colourless glass becomes visible if one casts a lateral glance at a thick glass plate of, say, a sofa table: the very glass that seems colourless from above suddenly takes on a green depth which grows increasingly opaque as your eye approaches the horizontal level of the table.[8]

8 Photographs of glass-piles, 'Glasplatten', taken by German photographer Willy Zielke around 1930, allow us to make a similar observation: colourless glass takes on both

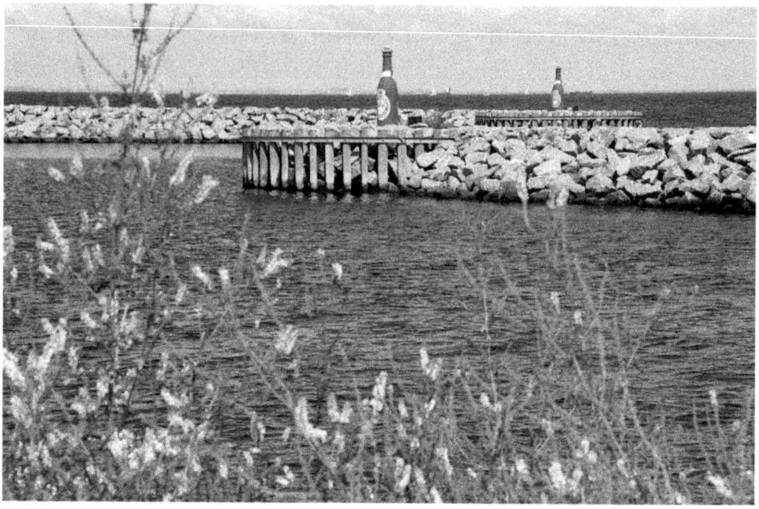

Fig. 6.6: Remains from old Tuborg: Red and green light towers from the industrial harbour – at the entry of the new suburban marina.
Credit: Henrik Reeh, 2011.

Variation on Bottles: Red and Green – From Harbour to Marina

Despite the demise of local breweries and glassworks, monumental beer bottles remain part of the new cityscape, and attract the attention of visitors and residents. At the end of a public path along the sea and the exclusive apartments, two oversized replicas of a green and a red Tuborg bottle, respectively, show up. They serve as light towers at the seaward entrance of Tuborg's harbour. They did so for decades when the harbour was still used for shipping beer or receiving coal, as well as when it hosted ferry

colour and shade and even become opaque when observed from certain angles. See photographs in *Traverses* 46 (1989), especially front page and p. 89.

boats bringing people, trucks and cars from Copenhagen to Landskrona in Sweden, or vice versa. Despite the fact that the lager beer Rød Tuborg – Red Tuborg – has little commercial importance, the structural opposition between red and green is fundamental in the world of sailing. Accordingly, the two huge bottles with red and green lights at their caps continue to help sailors find their way into the local harbour.

'Tuborg Harbour': it would be more precise to talk of a marina, as all functions and categories other than leisure and leisure boats have now disappeared. Since the first urban master plan of 1989, the extension of canals into brownfield Tuborg has remained a strategic feature for the development of the entire quarter. In Tuborg, dwellings and corporate headquarters are located inside a framework of marina piers. The inhabitants of apartments are entitled to rent an aquatic parking lot for their pleasure boats, whether with sails or with a motor, just below their balconies. In addition, the Royal Danish Yacht Club and its restaurant – open to the public – are housed in an extravagant piece of architecture, centrally located in the harbour. To a certain extent, the public realm has been taken over by the basins and the canals of the marina.

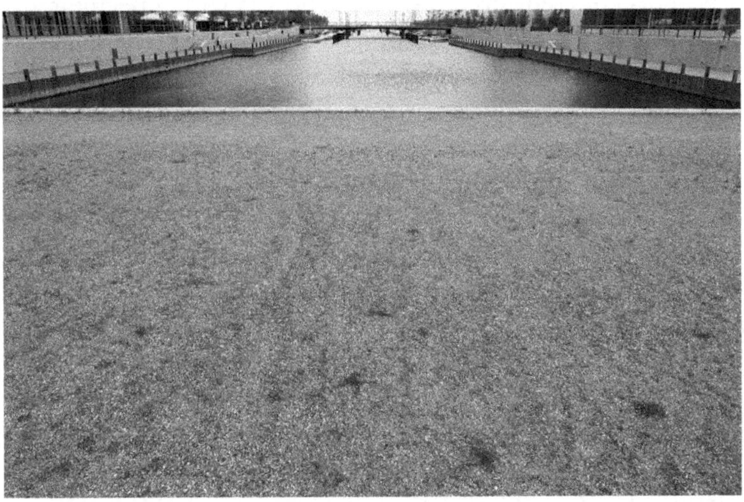

Fig. 6.7: Public space at 14:22:50 on June 21, the longest day of the year. Credit: Henrik Reeh, 2011.

Variation on Bottles: White Yachts, Blue Waters – But No Benches on the Boardwalk

For the general image of the Tuborg area, the presence of yachts and huge motor boats is a powerful signal. With their connotations of luxury, the white boats on the intensely dark blue water provide attractive imagery for the real-estate market. If apartments and offices do not have a direct view onto the sea (Øresund), many of them provide a view (or glimpses) of the central harbour and its side canals. A brief but perspectival view of a long and wide harbour canal is also enjoyed by passengers in cars and buses on their way from the suburbs to the centre of Copenhagen. Where they used to pass the fenced and confusing industrial landscape of Tuborg, they are now invited to notice a large canal with a shopping centre on one side and a couple of eccentric corporate headquarters on the other.

Tuborg's harbour areas display an extensive network of meticulously designed boardwalks, at various levels and for pedestrian movements of all sorts. This coherent urban design contrasts with a peculiar absence of human beings throughout the day. To be sure, there are no benches or other furniture that would allow people to take a rest during their promenade. Instead, there are numerous signs informing them that green spaces are private property, and that parking requires a special licence, just as it is strictly illegal to ride a skateboard on piers or sidewalks. Nevertheless, one should not be paranoid; this is no gated community in the common sense of the word. The local property owners, many of whom are retired and wealthy, simply imagine public life to be as peaceful and pleasant as their own private lives inside condominiums overlooking the harbour or the sea.

The tendency to name the area 'Tuborg Harbour' (and not simply 'Tuborg') contributes to an aquatic branding of the place. What used to be a brownfield is slowly becoming part of the surrounding city. Still, the inhabitants of Tuborg Harbour prefer not be invaded by urban crowds capable of disturbing the peace and quiet of a community dressed up in white and blue, and obeying the signals of red and green.

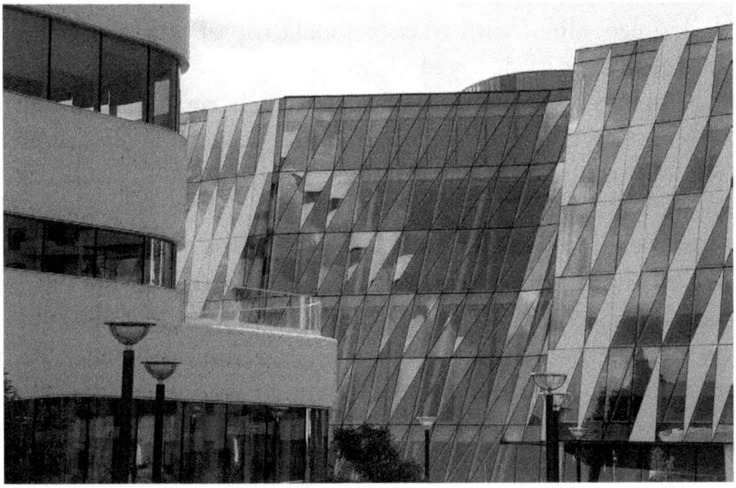

Fig. 6.8: Anybody home? Headquarters of Saxo Bank, by 3XN Architects. Credit: Henrik Reeh, 2011.

Variation on Glass: Reflections in Green with Still Life

While some of the apartments in this urban enclave seem to cultivate a desire for complete transparency between outside and inside,[9] none of the numerous corporate headquarters in the area engenders this illusion. Indeed, they have glass all over. Though sometimes framed or complemented by granite and travertine, glass remains the common denominator of huge architectural volumes, whose outer surfaces are haunted by darkness and quasi-opacity.

If there is no doubt that this glass is tinted, it is hard to determine the exact colour of façades and windows. Most of the time the windowpanes

9 See Sigfried Giedion, *Building in France, Building in Iron, Building in Ferro-Concrete* (Santa Monica: The Getty Center for Arts and the Humanities, 1995) [German original 1928].

look dark green, albeit with an occasional drop of blue. On other occasions, the glass appears nearly black-green, or grey-dark green. One single building employs a mirroring glass that clearly reflects the environment and the sky, but this is an exception from the rule; in general, glass surfaces are opaque – non-transparent – and vaguely reflective.

It is difficult to discern human beings behind those glass screens – that is, if actual people are there at all. Surprisingly few silhouettes are visible at desks or behind computers. Even conference rooms seem to be empty. Although summer is approaching, one might expect employees to be present, by mid afternoon, inside offices and atria, but they remain invisible. Instead, slicing machines and canteen tools of a corporate headquarters suddenly form a contemporary still life. Flooded by sunlight and therefore visible, a vacant triangular meeting room with expensive furniture and a screen on the wall similarly exhibits a stage-set of privileged working conditions.

The opacity of corporate glass architecture may reflect twin intentions; to reduce indoor temperatures and to be able to work without too many curious eyes looking in. Given the role of transparency and immateriality in the discourses on glass architecture, it is striking, however, that dark glass is so dominant in the corporate headquarters. Apart from a few recent buildings, designed by signature-architects, most of the headquarters rely on their imposing physical volume to provide an architectural image of the company. In general, these buildings seem to ignore the history of glass architecture as practiced by international architectural avant-gardes, such as expressionism or modernism, of the early and late twentieth century.[10]

From an urban-architectural viewpoint, a positive exception is provided by Henning Larsen's Coca Cola headquarters, which has its own public square in direction of the city. Making an exchange possible between inside and outside via shops on the ground floor, this building also constitutes one half of an architectural gate inviting the bustling city to enter the invisible parts of Tuborg behind. This architectural volume clearly communicates with the neighbouring building stock of historical Tuborg, yet without giving up a contemporary architectural language. Larsen's

10 Claude Massu, 'Le verre ou la clarté absente'.

architecture has external blinds of burnt clay, but underneath one discovers the well-known greenish glass employed in the other corporate headquarters. Despite the need for cooling as well as privacy, it is tempting to interpret the pervasive use of green glass as a tribute – albeit involuntary – to Green Tuborg, which powered the economy and iconicity of the Tuborg Breweries from the nineteenth century onward.

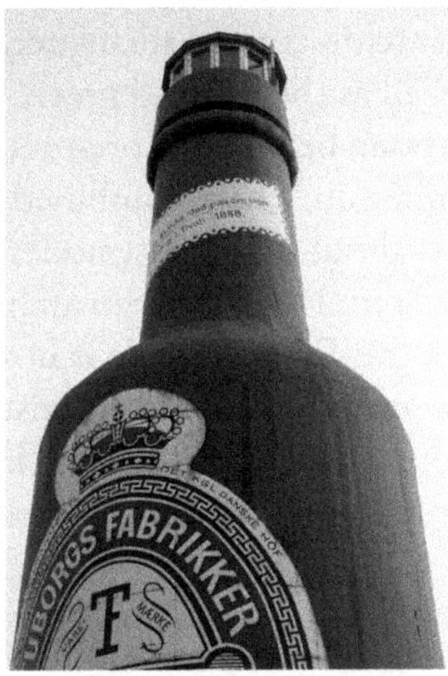

Fig. 6.9: The grand Tuborg Bottle of 1888: providing a panoramic view of the Tuborg area in the early twenty-first century. Credit: Henrik Reeh, 2011.

Variation on Bottles: A Green Urban Icon

One year before the achievement of the Eiffel Tower at the Paris World Exposition of 1889, a Danish tower, measuring twenty-six metres, was erected at the Nordic Exhibition in Copenhagen. This tower represented a green Tuborg beer bottle, just one twelfth the size of the Eiffel Tower, but nonetheless a sign of modernity, and equipped with an elevator. Later, this Tuborg Bottle became the urban landmark of the brewery district. In the midst of a heterogeneous area, one's distracted gaze could hold on to the Tuborg Bottle while one was passing the breweries and smelling their fermenting barley.

The green Tuborg Bottle survived the end of local beer brewing, and from behind a gas station in the last authentic and messy corner of the former industrial zone it still attracts the gaze of passsers-by. Now as then, the Tuborg Bottle is an example of commercial display in an urban context, although its precise iconic form did not reflect the structural abstraction of engineering and modern architecture as adequately as did the Eiffel Tower. The Tuborg Bottle, as well as the red and green Tuborg light towers on the piers of the local harbour, belong to a pre-modern order of simulacra, that of *contrefaçon* or imitation,[11] here combined with magnification. In certain ways, Tuborg was ahead of the postmodern aesthetics outlined in *Learning from Las Vegas* (1972) by American architect Robert Venturi.[12]

In functional terms, the Tuborg Bottle is now a ruin, insofar as neither the elevator nor the panoramic platform exists. One has to climb the entirely darkened interior on a spiralling wooden ladder, which terminates at an indoor platform with room for only three people.

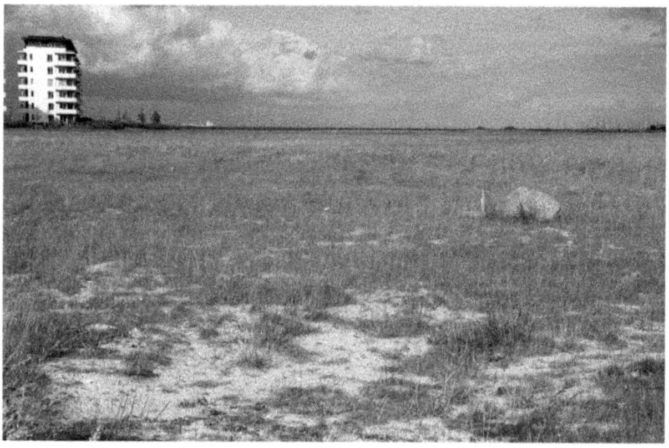

Fig. 6.10: An urban desert: Barely five years after the demolition of Tuborg's bottling halls, an urban desert to become a public salt meadow. Credit: Henrik Reeh, 2011.

11 Jean Baudrillard, *L'échange symbolique et la mort* (Paris: Gallimard, 1976), 75–84.

12 Robert Venturi, Denise Scott Brown, Steven Izenour, *Learning from Las Vegas* (Cambridge, MA: The MIT Press, 1977 [1972]).

Variation on Glass: A Panorama of Urban Times

Recalling the importance of panoramic vision in the nineteenth century, windows at the cap of the Tuborg Bottle provide a 360-degree panorama of Copenhagen, Hellerup and distant suburbs. Villas, former working class dwellings and industrial buildings merge in an image rendering metropolitan reality strangely disordered and provincial from this viewpoint, which is neither fully above nor simply identical to that of ordinary human beings moving at street level.

Since the height of the Tuborg Bottle corresponds to that of the seven-storey headquarters across the street, most of the new infrastructures and architecture in Tuborg Harbour are hidden. Still, the immediate surroundings may be explored by the elevated gaze one has in the Bottle. At the end of the boulevard heading towards the sea, a large natural area appears as a reddish moor in the midst of the cityscape. The common conviction that this moor has been there for a long time is fallacious; until the late 2000s, Tuborg's gigantic bottling halls occupied this land. Thus, a few years are all it takes to make industrial culture disappear and, in reverse, to call forth a landscape that appears natural but in reality is left-over, a remnant reflecting the end of industrialism.

This urban desert awaits future interventions. According to a revised master plan, the dwellings to be built differ from the oblong blocks dominating the residential architecture of Tuborg so far. Instead, taller and denser ensembles will be constructed next to the water, conserving the inner parts of the plot as a salt meadow, which will become Tuborg's first public park. Is another strategy for display and transparency about to break through?

Exit: Perspectives for the City

Focusing on the visuality linked to the motifs of bottles and glass, the preceding observations of this chapter mimic a labyrinthine walk through the newly urbanised Tuborg site. This itinerary takes us from the urban landmark of the 'thermos' rotunda by Henning Larsen, via the magnified Tuborg bottles – green and red – used for light towers at the harbour entry, all the way to the 26-metre Tuborg Bottle that remains an icon of the strangely hidden Tuborg area in privileged Hellerup. The three bottles, spanning 1888 and 1996, illustrate the extent to which Tuborg as a company knew how to display large scale urban objects as a promotion of its brand, both within beer brewing and, now, urban redevelopment.

Like the genuine Tuborg bottles for beer and soda, of which millions were visible in the days of brewing, the three mega-bottles en route all contain glass elements, in particular at their caps, where glass is a medium for panoramic vision or circular light emission. Further, it seems as if the loss of Tuborg's beer and soda glass bottles is compensated for by the omnipresence of glass in recent architectures. Similarly, the extensive use of colourless glass in the luxurious apartments recalls the transparent soda bottles of the past. Yet a green tint appears within the glass of windows, walls, doors and balconies. Do such appearances of green suggest that certain elements of non-transparency survive, and may challenge the narratives of unlimited visibility on which the boosted real-estate values rely?

Employing even more glass than did apartment blocks, the architecture of corporate headquarters appears dark green, and indirectly pays tribute to the tradition of Green Tuborg and green beer bottles. Within the building type of headquarters, transparency is limited, as if something inside the glass houses should be protected – as the beer of Green Tuborg is protected in a glass bottle.[13]

These encounters with bottles and glass surfaces signal policies of display and varieties of transparency. In this way, the experience of new Tuborg may contribute to a future dialogue with larger spheres of metropolitan culture.

13 Glass with a green tint (as used in new automobiles) is frequently used for windows in contemporary apartment buildings. From such apartments, the outside world may appear as seen through sunglasses.

Bibliography

Baudrillard, Jean, *L'échange symbolique et la mort* (Paris: Gallimard, 1976), 75–84.

Benjamin, Walter, 'Erfahrung und Armut', in *Gesammelte Schriften*, Vol. II (Frankfurt am Main: Suhrkamp Verlag, 1980).

Giedion, Sigfried, *Building in France, Building in Iron, Building in Ferro-Concrete* (Santa Monica: The Getty Center for Arts and the Humanities, 1995). [German original 1928].

Massu, Claude, 'Le verre ou la clarté absente', *Traverses* 46 (1989), 42–59.

Reeh, Henrik, 'Tuborg *en passant*: Urbane Forvandlingsbilleder', in Ning de Coninck-Smith and Harriet Tranum-Jensen, eds, *2900 Hellerup – set i bakspejlet* (Charlottenlund: Strandbergs Forlag, 2011).

Thomsen, Birgit Nüchel, *Tuborg, 1873–13. maj 1973: Tuborg og bryggeriindustrien under skiftende markedsvilkår 1873–1973* (Hellerup: Tuborgs Bryggerier, 1973).

Venturi, Robert, Denise Scott Brown and Steven Izenour, *Learning from Las Vegas* [1972] (Cambridge, MA: The MIT Press, 1977).

MARK VACHER

7 Spaces of Difference, Different Spaces: A Study of Urban Transformations in an Old Paint Factory

One day in 2010 two friends who shared a history as squatters and underground cultural activists were taking a walk in the industrial area of Amager. During the walk, the two friends, Christian Fumz and Jesper Koefoed-Melson, discovered a site kept in a state of hibernation. What they found was an old abandoned paint factory at Prags Boulevard 43 (henceforth PB43), which used to belong to the company Sadolin and Holmblad and is now owned by AkzoNobel; they imagined how the place had the potential to become something other than a fenced off, abandoned factory. In order to realise the potential of the abandoned site, they decided to form the organisation Givrum.nu, which aims at putting empty buildings into use by negotiating low rents for artist and providers of underground cultural activities.[1] They made a proposal to the owners, AkzoNobel: if the latter would agree to receive no rent for the site, Givrum.nu would pay the annual property tax and organise a revitalisation, which they managed to convince AkzoNobel would increase the economic value of the place, and brand the company as a socially responsible corporation rather than a polluting industry. AkzoNobel agreed to sign a two-year contract putting Givrum.nu in charge of their vacant premises at Prags Boulevard 43.

This chapter explores the dynamics at play in an urban transformation. Through the mentioned example of the transformation of an old industrial factory in eastern Copenhagen into a centre for cultural events, I intend to illustrate how not only different notions of space but also different invisibilities are produced. My argument is theoretically informed by the French philosopher Henri Lefebvre's approach to space as a product of human conception,

1 <http://givrum.nu/om/> accessed 17 October 2013.

perception and bodily activity.[2] Hence, space is understood as the outcome of, as much as the premise for, any physical appearance. In the following, 'The Factory' and 'PB43' will be explored as two different spatial manifestations, with an added third dimension, which I will refer to as 'The Void'.

This gives rise to the following question: what constitutes a spatial manifestation? According to Lefebvre, 'space is always, now and formerly, a *present* space, given as an immediate whole, complete with its associations and connections in their actuality. Thus production process and product present themselves as two inseparable aspects, not as two separable ideas.'[3] As I will demonstrate, the timeline of the types of spatial manifestations that can be found at this place as it develops from being a production plant that is subsequently vacated before it is re-occupied by urban activists can be denoted by the terms 'The Factory', 'The Void' and 'PB43'. These constitute three different examples of such presence, appearing as complete wholes of production processes and products. At the factory, the space-producing processes and products are related to varnish and paint as commodities, at the void they are related to absence and evasion, while space at PB43, to a large extent, is related to art and unleashing artistic potentials.

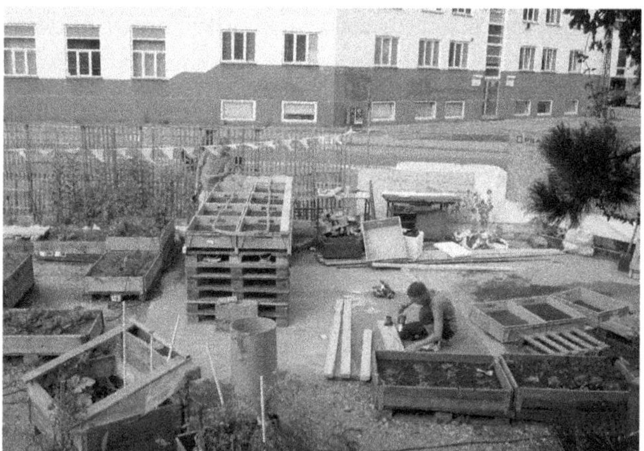

Fig. 7.1: PB43. Credit: Mark Vacher.

2 Henri Lefebvre, *The Production of Space* (Oxford: Blackwell, 1991 [1974]), 22.
3 Lefebvre, *The Production of Space*, 37.

Unpacking Lefebvre

Before moving into an analysis of the specific manifestations, it is necessary to make a detour in order to render Lefebvre's notion of space analytically operational. To state that space is inseparable from production, that it is a matter of presence, and that it constitutes an immediate whole, calls for elaboration regarding the relationship between space, process, and product. By introducing concepts developed by Charles Sanders Peirce and Jacques Derrida, I will establish a way to analyse space as an entity, but without falling into the trap of confusing it with location or place, which in this case is not only the same for the three different manifestations, but also fails to account for the transformative dynamics at play.

Although, according to Lefebvre, process and product present inseparable aspects of spatial manifestations, their stated inseparableness is not always clear. In the cases of The Factory and PB43, space is a product of the production of exchangeable products (varnish and paint in the factory and cultural events and crafts made by the various designers and artists working at PB43). Due to their exchangeable nature and related qualities, these tangible products are, unlike space, not only detachable from location and process of production, they also have the potential to become travelling signs, in the sense that they can refer to something they are not. As signs, the paint, like the pieces of art, refer to – but are not identical to – the process of production. As Lefebvre states, they 'supply clues to and testimony about, this productive process – a process which subsumes signifying processes without being reducible to them'.[4]

When charged with semiotic reference, products express the ability to articulate absence of, or distance from, whatever they refer to. That is, a can of paint can refer to a production site and a production process that may be located far away. The factory might not even exist anymore, or its spatial constitution might have changed dramatically. Likewise, the painter, the sculptor, or the choreographer behind a piece of art might be deceased, or the many hours of practicing might have taken place elsewhere. In this

4 Ibid.

way, the location and process of production becomes a distant referent rather than the incarnated presence described by Lefebvre. It becomes an origin, a point of departure, a destination, a part rather than 'an immediate whole'[5] – in short, it becomes a place. In other words, when we think and speak of The Factory or PB43 as a location, we tend not to describe space or spatial qualities, but places. A place is somewhere we go to or come from, something we take, somewhere we think, talk, dream and sing about. It is, according to the French philosopher Michel de Certeau, 'an instantaneous configuration of positions [...] [which] implies an indication of stability'.[6]

What this shows is that space presents a double challenge. All products are clues and testimonies to the existence of space, but when such clues and testimonies are read as signs, they transform space into place. Unlike space, places are semiotically potent. According to Peirce, semiotic capacity presupposes the co-presence of three qualities: iconic presence (its ability to distinguishably stand out from its surroundings); indexical ability to point/refer to something or someone beyond the iconic presence (its ability to stand for something else); and attachment of symbolic meaning (that the sign reader knows that the iconic presence indexically stands for something else).[7] Space does not possess these qualities. It cannot be represented. No can of paint, manual labour, works of art or artist can provide an iconic substitution, indexically stand for, or relate to space. Nor can it be symbolically loaded, since it lacks an iconic body for knowledge to be attached to it.

This does not change the fact that space is produced and should be regarded as a product,[8] nor does it mean that it lacks significance or that it should be considered unimportant. While place appears as an object of

5 Ibid.

6 Michel de Certeau, *The Practice of Everyday Life* (Berkeley: University of California Press, 1984), 117.

7 Charles Sanders Peirce, *Semiotik og Pragmatisme* (Copenhagen: Nordisk Forlag A/S, 1994 [1902, 1903]), 100. Milton Singer, *Man's Glassy Essence* (Bloomington: Indiana University Press, 1984), 60.

8 Lefebvre, *The Production of Space*, 26.

attention (whatever takes place and whatever it substitutes), space is what installs and facilitates an 'in-between'. It is that which separates the object of attention from its audience, and the sign from whatever it refers to. In this sense, all signs are spatial, insofar as they signify, on the basis of the distance between sign and referent. However, this distance, whether it is temporal, spatial or both, cannot be articulated, but only experienced, as difference[9] between signs and places and other signs and places.[10] Space is an absent/distance-making presence which is produced when a product is assembled, carved out, or mixed together. It is produced when ingredients are brought together, processed, or when products leave production sites. As a product, or to put it differently, an outcome, space is always temporal, but unlike places that have their moments in time, space is never historical. Lacking semiotic qualities, it is unable to take on the manifestation of itself as an event but, nevertheless, the difference between here and there always implies a differentiation, which is played out between now and then.

Space constitutes a connection, a relationship between the different, which can be stretched and contracted, but can also be extended and expire. As a consequence, space can be lost as well as produced. Loss of space happens when the ability to install and handle difference is limited. At a factory where access to resources is being reduced and/or demand for products is decreasing, space produced by producing whatever commodities the factory produces is also decreasing. When resources cease to be transformed into products, then space also ceases to be produced. This may be due to reduced access and limited exchange, or occur if difference becomes irrelevant. In other words, space is only produced where and when difference matters. If and when difference matters in different ways, then, as Lefebvre argues, we are also dealing with different kinds

9 By deliberately misspelling difference in his lecture *La differance* the French philosopher Jacques Derrida addresses the ever present difference at play in all semiotic systems. Jacques Derrida, *Difference* (Frederiksberg: DET lille Forlag, 2002 [1972]).

10 Derrida, *Difference*, 54. Jacques Derrida, *Om Grammatologi* (Copenhagen: Arena, 1970 [1967]), 113. Mark Vacher, *Urban Transit* (Copenhagen: Københavns Universitet. PhD-række, vol. 34, 2005), 110.

of space.[11] Therefore, he states, space is always related to a specific mode of production.[12] This matters for my chapter because the difference that matters at a factory that produces paint and varnish for sale on a market differs from the differences mattering in relation to an abandoned ruin or a centre for cultural activities.[13]

This does not necessarily mean that different modes of production are unrelated. What matters and how difference is installed and handled is always a matter of struggle and often a matter of competition, negotiation and cunning. Modes of production grow from prior modes of production, which they replace in order to enable their own production.[14] In the present case, this can be seen in the importance of fencing. At all three manifestations of the production of space, locks and fences are used to protect and prevent other modes of production from interfering with or getting in the way of the present one. What such measures indicate is that the production of space implies an unfolding of power relations. Depending on agency, skills, traditions and force, differences can be handled in different ways, and hence produce different kinds of space. The different productions of space may take place at the same location and maybe even at the same time, so long as they do not collide, but if they do, one must incorporate, expel, or redefine the other in order to continue its production. An example could be a stain of paint in an abandoned paint factory. As a matter of difference, it no longer relates to the production of paint. No resources are brought together, merged into products, or distributed. Nevertheless, this stain can still be involved in different productions of space. In being present as a sign, it can refer to something

11 Lefebvre, *The Production of Space*, 52.

12 Ibid., 31.

13 This implies not only three different productions of space, but even a fourth one, being the analytical distinction made in the present analysis between the three different versions of the same location. This fourth production of space will not be discussed further in the present work but nevertheless underlines the point made by Lefebvre that every mode of production, and every production process, including academia, is space producing. Lefebvre, *The Production of Space*, 31.

14 Ibid., 34, 47.

lost. Displaying the qualities of a sign, it indicates absence or distance, and becomes a reference to 'there' and 'then' when the factory was a production site for paint and varnish. As such, the stain supports a new production of presence, not of paint, but of whatever differences matter in a nostalgic relation to 'here' and 'now'. According to the American sociologist Sharon Zukin, signs of an industrial past have become a major asset in the gentrification processes turning decaying urban areas into revitalised neighborhoods highly valued for their authenticity.[15] In such cases, the production of an authentic presence requires the permanent presence of references to the past.

The stain of paint may be valued for producing the abandoned factory as an authentic place, but when transforming parts of the factory at PB43 into an exhibition hall, stains of paint came to make an important space producing difference in an entirely different way. The process of producing paint and varnish includes handling very toxic ingredients. When spilled, paint in various stages of production becomes a highly polluting remnant, which has to be removed if the location is to be used for art exhibitions. In this case, the past mode of production is still present to the extent that it gets in the way of a new one. It took months of hard, manual, difference-making labour in an unhealthy environment to pave the way for a new mode of production by domesticating the colliding reminiscences of an old one. Today there are still stains of paint and other semiotic references to a memorable past, but despite its presence, this past no longer gets in the way of the space producing present – it has been, quite literally, domesticated. On the contrary, it supports the present by hinting at authenticity, originality and production – not of paint itself, but of paintings and other artworks.

Having 'unpacked' Lefebvre's notion of space in order to operate it analytically, I will now examine its unfolding at the Sadolin & Holmblad production site, which until 2006 hosted the production of paint and varnish.

15 Sharon Zukin, *Naked City – The Death and Life of Authentic Urban Places* (New York: Oxford University Press, 2010).

Production of Space at the Factory

As a consequence of the invention of the wood preservative Pinotex in the 1950s, the already well-established producer of paint and varnish Sadolin & Holmblad decided to expand their production by constructing a new factory at Prags Boulevard on the island of Amager south of Copenhagen. The market for paint and varnish like Pinotex can thus be seen as indicative of a lucrative difference between market demands and the ability to meet these in a profitable way.

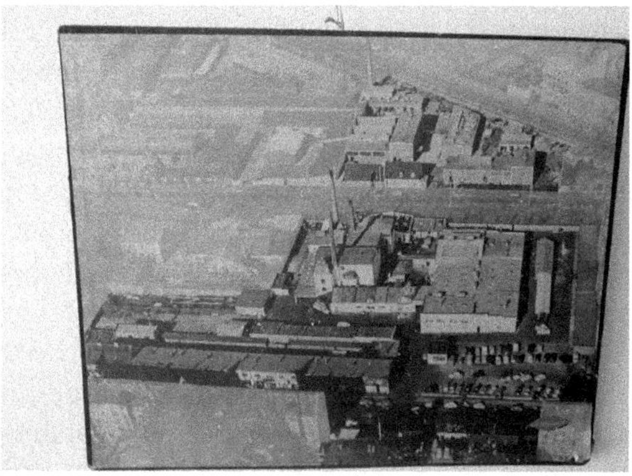

Fig. 7.2: The factory.
Credit: Mark Vacher.

According to the ideas of anthropologist David Graeber, this detected difference constitutes a central value in relation to the physical presence of the factory. Value, he argues, can be defined as 'the way actors represent the importance of their own actions to themselves as part of some larger whole'.[16] The discovery and wish to exploit this difference not only initiated

16 David Graeber, 'Value: anthropological theories of value', in James G. Carrier, ed., *A Handbook of Economic Anthropology* (Cheltenham: Edward Elgar Publishing Inc., 2005), 451.

the construction of the factory, but remained a space-making precondition through its existence as such. It was in relation to the difference at play that the factory was constructed, its functionality defined, and its potentials were measured. The same goes for the activities taking place at the factory. Like buildings and equipment, social relationships were invested in and established in order to make profit. Ingredients were mixed and merged in containers and shipped off by employees. These employees were summoned through an exchange of labour for wages, and motivated to cooperate in accordance with the overall aim of the factory. Production processes, work shifts, hierarchies, lunch breaks, salaries, safety regulations, storage, removal of refuse, notions of order and disorder were all distinctions that matter, organising actions around the central value. As a result, a particular kind of space was produced. Measuring, mixing, directing, processing, packing, storing, distributing, cleaning, maintaining and taking a rest produced particular spatial differences between 'here' and 'there' and 'now' and 'then' which made the factory work, produce goods and perform as a factory.

Despite being the dominant value, making profit was not the only space-making difference at play at the factory. In their book on the Danish shipyard B&W, ethnologists Torkil Adsersen and Niels Jul Nielsen account for a large number of more or less informal activities performed by employees at a large industrial production site. Extra pauses, use of facilities for purposes other than producing the intended commodity, and petty theft, were also activities that could take place and produce space at a factory like the one at Prags Boulevard.[17] Such alternative uses were to a large extent counterproductive, and their acceptance dependent on the power relations between employers and employees. If possible, activities obstructing or in opposition to the intended production were sanctioned. Fences and locks would keep unwanted visitors out of the production site and prevent theft and unauthorised use; rules and regulations would regulate the employ-

17 Torkil Adsersen and Niels Jul Nielsen, *Sjak, Mestre og Skibsbyggeri – Arbejdsliv og Dagligdag på B&W 1945–1996* (Copenhagen: Arbejdermuseet, Danmarks Tekniske Museum, Handels- og Søfartsmuseet, Københavns Bymuseum, Nationalmuseet, Copenhagen, 2005).

ees' behaviour, as would the threat of getting fired. Nevertheless, these counterproductive activities and their space-making differentiations can be seen as being dependent on the difference articulated and valued as a demand for paint and varnish. Without the overall purpose of producing commodities for a market, there would have been no mattering differences to make theft and unauthorised use tempting activities.

The sum total of these many differences constituted the space produced at and around the place, which I am referring to as 'The Factory'.[18] It was the nature and effect of these differences to make the factory appear busy, effective, productive, and valuable to its various stakeholders. Constructing the factory made a difference, going to work made a difference, producing paint and varnish made a difference, and so did the less legitimate practices taking place. It was the presence of all these space producing differences that made the factory appear as a physical gestalt, or as Lefebvre describes it, 'an immediate whole, complete with its associations and connections in their actuality'.[19]

The Void

That the factory was 'an immediate whole' became clear in 2006, when production at Prags Boulevard was shut down. Over the years, market conditions had changed, and the factory could no longer make the required difference in relation to producing paint and varnish. As a consequence, the owners AkzoNobel moved production to a more efficient production site in Sweden.[20] Due to many years of production involving toxic ingredients,

18 The list of differences can never be exhaustive. As pointed out by Peirce, the meaning of difference (the symbolic aspect) depends on the individual to whom something or someone makes/articulates a difference. Charles Sanders Peirce, *Semiotik og pragmatisme*, 122. Milton Singer, *Man's Glassy Essence*, 60.

19 Lefebvre, *The Production of Space*, 37.

20 In 1987 Sadolin & Holmblad was bought by the Swedish company Nobel which in 1994 merged with the Dutch company Akzo.

the site had become contaminated, and along with the fact that large-scale industry in Denmark was becoming less profitable compared to that of other countries, to invest in the necessary decontamination of the site before putting it up for sale would have made it too expensive to dispose of. Consequently, AkzoNobel decided not sell off the closed factory. Instead, it was sealed off, and maintenance kept at a minimum.

When the factory ceased to produce paint and varnish, it ceased to produce industrial space, but also to present the framework for a large number of other related differences. Employees were laid off or offered jobs elsewhere and social relations ended. Power, heat, and water supplies were shut down in order to reduce the cost of owning a complex of empty buildings. Valuable equipment and ingredients in stock were sold or taken to places where they could make a profitable difference. No longer able to make a difference in relation to an overall value, the factory, as a totality of space-producing differences, became obsolete and began to fall apart as an 'immediate whole'.[21] Apart from the basic maintenance that prevented the buildings from collapsing and the yard form getting covered with litter and weeds, nothing took place.

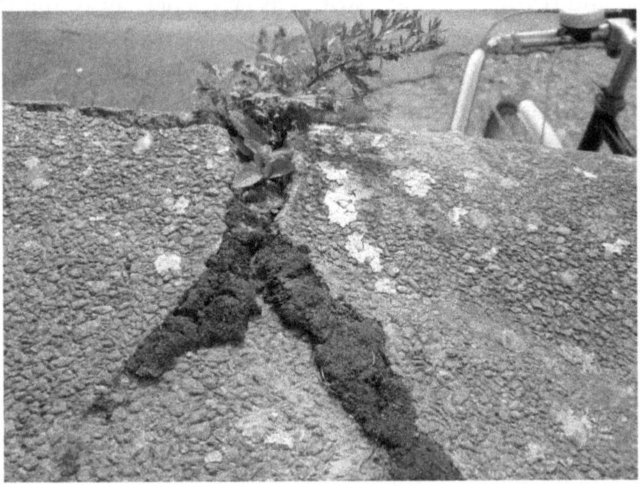

Fig. 7.3: Crack in the concrete. Credit: Mark Vacher.

21 Lefebvre, *The Production of Space*, 37.

The fact that nothing took place might lead us to the assumption that no space was being produced. To a certain extent this is true in relation to an industrial space where no industrial activities take place. However, when a production has ended, it still involves a number of differentiating activities. As already noted, employees were told not to show up, power, water and heat were turned off, equipment and stock were removed. In this process, a different kind of space was being produced – a space of evasion and dismantlement.

To some, it became the place where there was no longer work and production, which included an element of sadness, because it also meant the end of an opportunity for making a living. To others, the abandoned factory became testament to a certain past, when Denmark, Copenhagen, Amager, and Prags Boulevard were, respectively, an industrial country, capital, area, and place. As such, the abandoned factory became what geographer Tim Edensor defines as an *excessive space*[22] where the past – often in an invasive way – is communicated to the present. In this way, he argues, even as 'memory continually adapts to changing contexts, so decaying buildings extinguish and reveal successive stories as layers peel away and things fall out from their hiding places'.[23]

Although Edensor refers to excessive space, following Lefebvre, both ways of perceiving the abandoned factory relate to it as a *place*. The site becomes a reference to a past, something it no longer is. This does not mean that space is absent; on the contrary, what the semiotic nature of the abandoned factory indicates is that along with its iconic presence (the seen and perceived), a symbolic installation of mattering difference, and an indexical pointing towards a distant past, immediately and presently produce an installation of space between a semiotic 'now' and a semiotic 'then'.

As in the case of the factory, it is the *difference*, the produced space, which flavours and articulates the value of the place. Although the place

22 Tim Edensor, 'The ghost of industrial ruins: ordering and disordering memory in excessive space', *Environment and Planning D: Society and Space* 23 (2005), 829.

23 Tim Edensor, 'The ghost of industrial ruins', 834.

described by Edensor is nostalgic, the experience of nostalgia is not that of the past, but always a phenomenon of presence. In the case of nostalgia, what is present is an experience of absence. In other words, the space produced at the abandoned factory, which makes it appear 'as an immediate whole, complete with its associations and connections in their actuality',[24] is the presence of absence. Absence is present in the decaying buildings, in the broken windows, the damaged plastering. It is present in the empty production halls, the water pipes without water, the electrical wiring without voltage, and the staff room without employees.

Because absence itself is difference, when nothing happens, nothing becomes something. Tiles and windows break, plastering falls off, weed grows in the yard, and unwanted objects and visitors arrive causing damage and decay, creating more absence with their presence.

For the nostalgically minded, the presence of absence is an experience of relating the present to the past ('now' to 'then'), but to the owners of the abandoned factory, the accumulating presence of absence constitutes a differentiation of another sort. As mentioned above, the abandoned factory was too contaminated to be sold without economic loss. In this way it still represented a value to AkzoNobel. To paraphrase Graeber, keeping the site was regarded as an important action in relation to a wider whole.[25] However, although keeping it was considered a better investment than selling it off, the site still represented an expense due to the annual property tax paid to the Danish state. Furthermore, future developments within real estate could potentially increase the value of the site, which made keeping and maintaining it a rational investment. As a consequence, efforts were made to reduce the presence of absence. Doors and windows were locked and fences were repaired to prevent unauthorised use. In this way, the space produced by the process of nothing becoming something was countered by the owner's attempt to prevent absence from taking over the place. In their doing so, a particular kind of space was being produced. Actions were taken to prevent further accumulation of absence by fencing off, repairing,

24 Lefebvre, *The Production of Space*, 37.

25 David Graeber, 'Value: anthropological theories of value', 451.

and cleaning up. Nothing was actively kept in a state of being nothing. In this way, space was actively produced through maintenance because space, like time, is money.

PB43

On Friday 19 September 2010, Christian Fumz and Jesper Koefoed-Melson summoned friends and like-minded people to a meeting regarding the former paint factory. Their idea was to divide the premises into many small leases in order to attract a wide variety of activities and to keep the rent as low as possible. The meeting was well attended, and the opportunity to rent anything from a tiny office to a large yard convinced architects, freelance philosophers, artists, carpenters, bike repairers, game developers, gallery owners, and event makers that PB43 could become an attractive setting for their individual activities. Some of the larger production halls were divided into smaller workshops, making room for even more small enterprises. In 2011 more than twenty-two workshops and offices were active at PB43, and many of these were organised as joint leases, making the total number of paying users much higher than the actual number of leases.[26] Apart from the urban garden 'Prags Have', most activities were financed by the users themselves.

As an abandoned factory, the overall production of space at PB43 was related to an increasing presence of absence, linking the site to an increasingly distant past. What has changed at PB43 is the nature of difference and the way it matters. As I have outlined, the difference experienced by Givrum.nu is that of a potential future. As presence, the experience of difference calls for actions, which have resulted in a radical transformation of the place. Firstly, dividing the site into many small leases has

26 Steen Andersen and Marie Toft-Jensen, *Byen bliver til* (Copenhagen: Forlaget PB43, 2012).

produced room for many different potential futures to be realised in many ways, at different speeds, and by many different people. In this way, PB43 differs from the factory in which production processes were strictly coordinated and the outcome directed specifically towards a market. At PB43 the products produced in many of the small workshops are also intended for a market, but unlike the factory, the overall existence of PB43 does not depend on the ability to produce or sell products to customers but rather to generate incoming rent paid by workshop leasers. To many of the lessees, the opportunity and space to express oneself artistically weighs if not more than, then at least as much as, the making of profit. In this way, the future of PB43 depends more on experienced quality of the activities related to the specific site than the profit made from the outcome of them.

The strategy of dividing major space producing differences into smaller ones takes other shapes and reaches further than the appearance of small workshops, galleries, and offices. In the case of the garden, it has been a way to handle the polluted soil. Instead of sowing and planting directly in the ground, the garden has been arranged in many little boxes placed on movable pallets. In doing so a mattering difference between the polluted soil and the garden has been initiated, making it possible to allow a large number of space making activities that were not possible before. These take the shape of events that create a difference between sowing and harvesting, weeding, watering, cooking food, gathering people for common dining on Wednesdays etc. In this way, new space, which differs from e.g. Edensor's nostalgia, flavours and informs the participants' experience of PB43.

The installation of a garden in (on) a polluted former industrial production site has had a high semiotic significance resulting in public awareness of the place. It stands out (as an icon) from its surroundings, it (indexically) indicates local engagement and use, and it is valued (symbolically) as being creative and innovative to such an extent that it has received a public award.

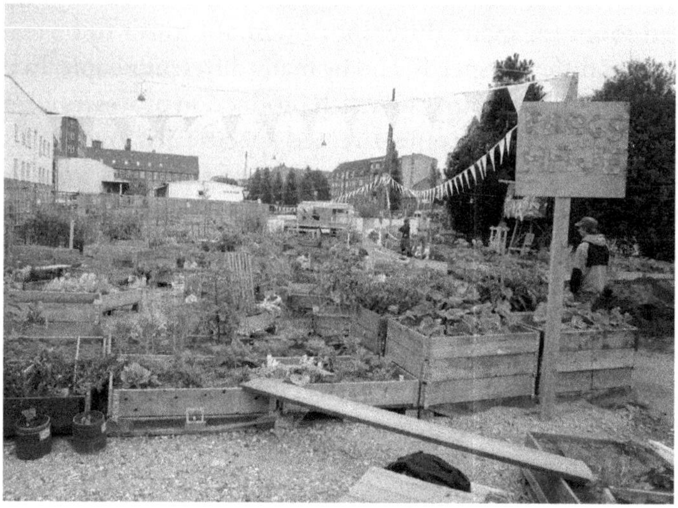

Fig. 7.4: Prags Have.
Credit: Mark Vacher.

The possibility of seeing in PB43 a potential future has set off a new mode of production, resulting in a new kind of space. Dividing the totality of the abandoned factory into a totality of small entities has not only produced space for a variety of potential futures, but has also put them within reach. As small challenges, the present gap between 'now' and a future 'then' can be bridged through space-making activities like scraping off toxic paint, filling clean soil into boxes, and separating workshops by dividing large production halls (and thereby lowering the individual rent). In this way, the mattering difference has been circumvented, transforming from a matter of present absence into a matter of absent presence. Formerly a place where people do not work anymore, PB43 has become a place where people imagine working in the future: it has changed from a site where there is no water or power *anymore* to one where there is no water or power *yet*. Since 2011, water and electricity have returned, and so have new facilities, such as the internet. In the future, the aim is to host concerts and conferences along with the ongoing activities, and in order to ensure this, projectors, sound equipment, safe storage facilities, forms of insurance as well as different authorisations have to make their way to PB43.

Bridging 'here' and 'now' with the future definitely makes PB43 'a present space, given as an immediate whole, complete with its associations and connections in their actuality'.[27] However, there is still an overall mattering difference to take into account. The contract with AkzoNobel has to be renegotiated on a regular basis. In 2012 it was prolonged until 2016. After that, it is hoped enough money will be made from the activities to buy the premises from the present owners. If not, the future of PB43 will remain a matter of difference to AkzoNobel.

Conclusion

Inspired by Lefebvre's understanding of space, I have explored the dynamics at play in urban transformations. I have done so through the analysis of an old factory. I have shown how space is produced as difference, from difference, in ongoing processes. Despite its differentiating and transformative nature (changing 'there' and 'then' to 'here' and 'now'), space also connects, in that space ties things that are different together in mattering (valued) relationships. Thus, space is produced whenever differences are articulated, discovered and handled.

By taking this approach to space and transformations, a wide range of relevant questions have been raised and laid open for further analysis and discussion. What are the rationales and economies behind spatial manifestations? What are the shaping dynamics that unfold in production or the hibernation of a place? What happens when nothing happens? What inclusive and excluding parameters are at issue or in play? What are the formal as well as informal power structures? What does it take to make or define a difference, and who is empowered to do so? And finally, what does it take to qualify as a friend or likeminded person; to be invited for meetings that set space-making differences?

27 Lefebvre, *The Production of Space*, 37.

The answers to these questions are complex and point in many different (and potentially space producing) directions, but, nevertheless, they are crucial to consider if we want to ensure that our cities develop and transform along democratic lines. At PB43, fences and locks still play an important part in producing and protecting spatial differences. A central difference is that between locals. During the day, gates and doors are opened to locals, who are invited to work and play in the garden. At night-time they are closed to prevent locals from invading and vandalising the area. Despite their differences, something all of the spatial totalities discussed in this paper have in common is that in order to benefit from their valuable differences, one has to be able move through a fence.

Bibliography

Andersen, Torkil, and Niels Jul Nielsen, *Sjak, Mestre og Skibsbyggeri – Arbejdsliv og Dagligdag på B&W 1945–1996* (Copenhagen: Arbejdermuseet, Danmarks Tekniske Museum, Handels- og Søfartsmuseet, Københavns Bymuseum, Nationalmuseet, Copenhagen, 2005).

Andersen, Steen, and Marie Toft-Jensen, *Byen bliver til* (Copenhagen: Forlaget PB43, 2012).

De Certeau, Michel, *The Practice of Everyday Life* (Berkeley: University of California Press, 1984).

Derrida, Jacques, *Difference* [1972] (Frederiksberg: DET lille Forlag, 2002).

——, *Om Grammatologi* [1967] (Copenhagen: Arena, 1970).

Edensor, Tim, 'The Ghost of Industrial Ruins: Ordering and Disordering Memory in Excessive Space', *Environment and Planning D: Society and Space* 23 (2005), 829–49.

Graeber, David, 'Value: anthropological theories of value', in James G. Carrier, ed., *A Handbook of Economic Anthropology* (Cheltenham: Edward Elgar Publishing Inc., 2005) 439–54.

Lefebvre, Henri, *The Production of Space* [1974] (Oxford: Blackwell, 1991).

Peirce, Charles Sanders, *Semiotik og pragmatisme* [1902, 1903] (Copenhagen: Nordisk Forlag A/S, 1994).

Singer, Milton, *Man's Glassy Essence* (Bloomington: Indiana University Press, 1984).

Vacher, Mark, *Urban Transit* (Copenhagen: Københavns Universitet. Phd-række, vol. 34, 2005).

Zukin, Sharon, *Naked City – The death and life of authentic urban places* (New York: Oxford University Press, 2010).

DORA OSBORNE

8 Negotiating (In)Visibilities in German Memory Culture

In recent decades, Germany has been characterised by a so-called *Erinnerungskultur*, or memory culture, which remembers and commemorates in particular its National Socialist past.[1] Evidence of this is visible in the high-profile cultural and geographical landmarks of the capital Berlin, such as Daniel Libeskind's Jewish Museum and the Memorial to the Murdered Jews of Europe. Yet even such initially prominent and controversial memorial projects have come to occupy a more established and thus less conspicuous place in the city. The position of memorials between visibility and invisibility is nothing new – as Musil famously remarked, there is nothing so inconspicuous as a monument – but (in)visibility is a particular feature of Germany's recent memory culture and the memorials that have been made in this context.[2] Indeed, the play between visibility and invisibility underpinned the so-called countermonuments of the 1980s and 1990s, which quite literally undid the form of conventional memorials. Artists like Horst Hoheisel and Jochen Gerz sought provocative alternatives in order to show how grand, imposing structures were not appropriate to the commemoration of the Holocaust, and to challenge how communities engaged with the legacy of National Socialism. For his *2146 Stones – Monument against Racism* (1993), Gerz removed cobbles from the castle square in Saarbrücken and inscribed on their bases the names of Germany's

1 For an account of the shifts in and problems associated with this German culture of memory, see Aleida Assmann, *Das neue Unbehagen an der Erinnerungskultur. Eine Intervention* (Munich: Beck, 2013).

2 Robert Musil, 'Denkmale', *Nachlaß zu Lebzeiten*, in Adolf Frisé, ed., *Gesammelte Werke* vol. 7 (Hamburg: Rowohlt, 1978), 506–9, 506.

Jewish cemeteries in use before the Second World War. Since this act was carried out at night and the stones replaced with their new inscriptions face down, its provocative force lay not in the memorial's visibility, but in its temporary disruption of public space. As James E. Young notes, the power of such memorials is found in their potential 'not to console but to provoke; [...] not to accept graciously the burden of memory but to throw it back at the town's feet'.[3] But even whilst countermonuments have proved 'insistent, importunate and intrusive',[4] they have nevertheless become a publically accepted part of Germany's memorial landscape – Gerz's illegal intervention was approved and retrospectively commissioned by the regional parliament and the castle square renamed 'Platz des *Unsichtbaren* Mahnmals' [Square of the *Invisible* Monument] (my emphasis). Moreover, as previously unacknowledged legacies of the Third Reich find forms of public commemoration, memorials might be considered a ubiquitous and thus unremarkable feature of the Berlin Republic.[5] We might say that, despite the disruptive potential of many memorial projects, the very fact of their integration makes them a part of the cityscape that no longer stands out.[6]

In what follows, I want to consider how the challenges of recent memory culture – negotiating between appropriate commemoration of, and the need to work through (in order to move beyond), a traumatic past – are reflected in the (in)visibility of the memorial form. I will discuss three memorial projects which, initiated more than two decades ago; have lost their initial provocative force and are now challenged by their increasing

3 James E. Young, *The Texture of Memory: Holocaust Memorials and Meaning* (Yale: Yale University Press, 1993), 30.

4 Bill Niven and Chloe Paver, 'Introduction', Bill Niven and Chloe Paver, eds, *Memorialization in Germany since 1945* (Basingstoke: Palgrave Macmillan, 2010), 7.

5 For a survey of these diverse memorial initiatives, see Niven and Paver, eds, *Memorialization in Germany since 1945*.

6 Recent scholarship has shown how, as a form of urban memory, memorials are threatened by amnesia even as they seem to ward against this (see Andreas Huyssen, *Present Pasts: Urban Palimpsests and the Politics of Memory* (Stanford CA: Stanford University Press, 2003), 11–29; and Mark Crinson, 'Urban Memory – An Introduction', in Mark Crinson, ed., *Urban Memory: History and Amnesia in the Modern City* (London and New York: Routledge, 2005), 11–20).

invisibility. In the two-part installation *The Missing House* and *The Museum* (1990) French artist Christian Boltanski uses the site of a bombed-out Berlin residence and related documents to evoke the memory of those who disappeared in the war years; in Berlin's Bavarian Quarter, Renata Stih and Frieder Schnock's street sign series, *Orte des Erinnerns* (*Places of Remembrance*) (1993) documents the systematic exclusion of Jewish citizens in the Third Reich; and with his *Stolpersteine*, or stumbling stones – small brass plaques set in the pavement – the German artist Gunter Demnig commemorates those deported from their homes under National Socialism. Found in relatively inconspicuous locations, on the threshold between private and public spaces, these site-specific memorials provoke an 'unexpected encounter' with the past.[7] They also provide (either incidentally or intentionally) counterpoints to the high-profile controversy surrounding the plans for and construction of an official, centralised Holocaust memorial for Berlin – a monument so visible it can scarcely be avoided. Retrieving and making visible again forgotten traces of war, persecution, and deportation, these artists represent what Margaret Ewing describes as 'a strain of contemporary art practice devoted to historical recovery', made, we might add, via the archive.[8] Indeed, the idea of the archive as a site of deposit and preservation is pivotal to their engagement with traces of the past, but it also means their projects gesture towards renewed invisibility and oblivion, and the (in)visibility of their memorials can be understood in terms of the (in)visibility of the archive. It is in the act of withdrawing and concealing that the remnants of the past come to be housed in the archive. As Derrida argues, '[i]t is thus, in this *domiciliation*, this house arrest, that

7 Margaret Ewing, 'The Unexpected Encounter. Confronting Holocaust Memory in the Streets of Post-Wall Berlin', in Anne Teresa Demo and Bradford Vivian, eds, *Rhetoric, Remembrance, and Visual Form: Sighting Memory* (Routledge, 2012), 33–49.

8 Ewing, 'The Unexpected Encounter', 33. Before her analyses of the documentary elements of the memorial projects by Boltanski and Demnig, Ewing discusses Shimon Attie's *The Writing on the Wall* (1991–3), a series of photographic projections onto Berlin buildings, which also uses archive material, 35–8.

archives take place'.[9] The archive marks the passage between the private and the public, but this does not mean the visibility of the past, rather it exposes what remains as 'spectral *a priori*: neither present nor absent "in the flesh", neither visible nor invisible'.[10] In the case of the countermonument, Henry W. Pickford explains, the memorial is effectively displaced, even negated by the focus on 'historical research and documentation'.[11] Yet whilst archival research is fundamental to these projects, both the act of research and the documentary material retrieved are arguably displaced by the memorial that emerges as a consequence. Like the archives that inform them, the memorials by Boltanski, Stih and Schnock and Demnig are caught between presence and absence, visibility and invisibility, remembering and forgetting. They make visible once more traces housed in the archive, even functioning in turn as a sort of archive, yet in so doing, threaten to conceal these traces again.

The negotiation of (in)visibility in memorial projects does not simply mean privileging the visible over the invisible, however. Rather it concerns their critical, disruptive potential. This is easily lost as they gain public acceptance, but it is crucial if they are to provoke meaningful engagement with the legacy of Germany's violent past. Establishing a link to the past, the archive is pivotal to this negotiation. But it also threatens fixation on the material and documentary, on that which can be formalised and regulated as history, and thus consignment of the messier, uncontainable elements of the past to a space outside representation. As Jean-François Lyotard observes, in 'the anonymity of the archives', there is no space for the 'custom, or story, or rhythm' of memory.[12] According to performance theorist Rebecca Schneider, flesh is the 'blind spot' of the phallocentric, ocularcentric archive, which assumes that 'if it is not visible, or given to

9 Jacques Derrida, *Archive Fever: A Freudian Impression*, trans. Eric Prenowitz (Chicago: University of Chicago Press, 1996), 2–3.

10 Derrida, *Archive Fever*, 84.

11 Henry W. Pickford, 'Conflict and Commemoration: Two Berlin Memorials', *Modernism/Modernity* 12/1 (2005), 162.

12 Jean-François Lyotard, *The Inhuman. Reflections on Time*, trans. Geoffrey Bennington and Rachel Bowlby (Cambridge: Polity, 1993), 194.

documentation [...] or otherwise "houseable" [...] it is lost, disappeared'. But, she insists, flesh '*does* ghost bone' in the 'body-to-body-transmission' of the past, which counters the conventionally conceived archive.[13] Whilst the fact of historical violence might disrupt 'body-to-body transmission' in any literal sense, the movement of individuals and communities on and through memorial sites constitutes an important part of the relationship between past and present.[14] Thus, the crucial element of these works by Boltanski, Stih and Schnock and Demnig is the response they provoke in those who encounter them. Such effects are provisional and change over time, but they indicate the contemporary significance of memorials, memory culture, and Germany's shifting relationship to its recent past.

Christian Boltanski, *The Missing House* and *The Museum*

In 1990, following the unification of Germany, an art project was launched that was particularly motivated by questions of visibility and invisibility, and the ways in which Berlin was still marked by topographical, cultural and ideological difference.[15] Contributions to *Die Endlichkeit der Freiheit* [*The Finitude of Freedom*] were to link the city's two halves, showing how '[t]he visible becomes invisible, the hidden comes to light'.[16] And so the projects negotiated not only between East and West, but also between public and private, used and abandoned spaces. Christian Boltanski responded with a two-part piece, *The Missing House* on Große Hamburger Straße in the

13 Rebecca Schneider, *Performing Remains: Art and War in Times of Theatrical Reenactment* (Oxford and New York: Routledge, 2011), 100–2.

14 Young emphasises how 'we cannot separate the monument from its public life', *The Texture of Memory*, 13.

15 Heiner Müller, 'Berlin Twohearted City', in Wulf Herzogenrath, Joachim Sartorius and Christoph Tannert, eds, *Die Endlichkeit der Freiheit. Berlin 1990* (Berlin: Edition Hentrich, 1990), 9; my translation.

16 <http://www.cultd.net/endlichkeit/> accessed 1 November 2012.

East (part of the former Jewish district of the Scheunenviertel) and *The Museum* on a disused exhibition ground near the Lehrter station in the West. Whilst Boltanski's choice of locations reflects the broader focus of the initiative – the fall of the Berlin Wall and Germany's reunification – his piece ultimately returned to older traces of violence, almost but not quite invisible, either despite or because of reunification.

The Missing House is the better known half of Boltanski's contribution, and can still be seen by passers-by today. It uses the space left by a house bombed during the Second World War, a void in the heart of the street and city, and a sign perhaps of stalled redevelopment in the East, compared with swift reconstruction in the West. Boltanski first had his assistants research those living there during the war, then he made commemorative plaques with the names, period of occupancy and professions of various residents and affixed them to the firewalls of the adjoining houses.

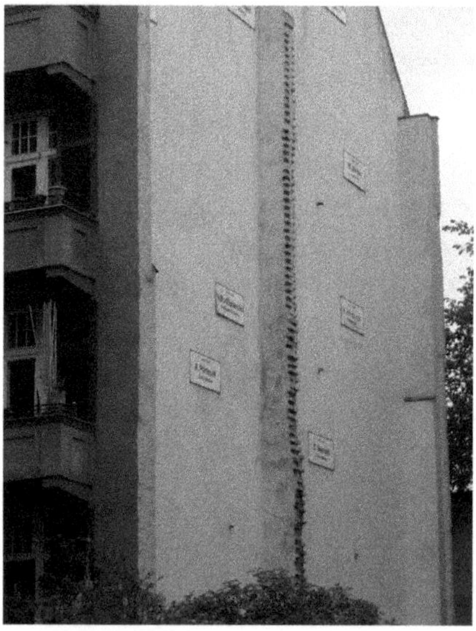

Fig. 8.1: Christian Boltanski, *The Missing House*, Große Hamburger Straße 15/16, Berlin. Credit: Dora Osborne.

The archival material brought to light showed that some residents of *The Missing House* were Jewish, thus putting Große Hamburger Straße back on the map as a centre of Jewish life in Berlin, perhaps reinscribing its former name 'Toleranzstraße' [Tolerance Street].[17] This material also formed the basis for the other part of Boltanski's installation. Like *The Missing House*, *The Museum* was an open-air installation and comprised ten glass vitrines set out in two rows, each displaying copies of the documents that went some way to describing the fates of the residents. These included property deeds, address books, postcards, photographs, accounts of bombings and documentation relating to deportation. Boltanski installed *The Museum* on a former nineteenth-century exhibition ground, which, in 1934, was converted into a national aviation museum, but also used for meetings of the Berlin NSDAP and eventually for the interrogation, torture and execution of prisoners.[18] It was bombed in 1943 and dismantled in 1951. The site is thus a palimpsest of Berlin history – cosmopolitanism, technological prowess and fascism. But now these traces are invisible: in the shadow of Berlin's new main station, the park lies abandoned, a staircase the only evidence of its former grandeur.

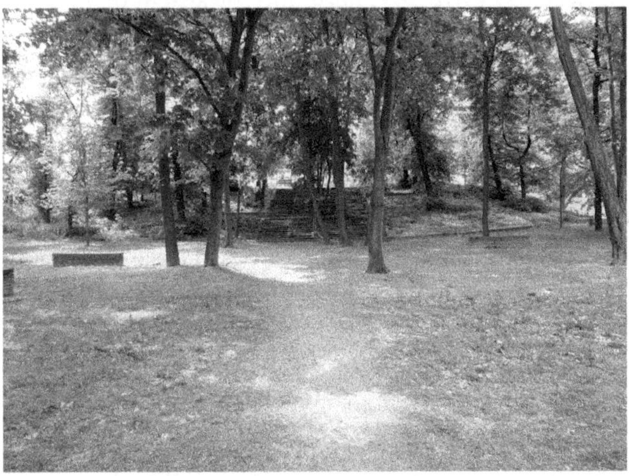

Fig. 8.2: ULAP-Gelände, park on the site of the former exhibition site between Invalidenstraße and Berlin's main station. Credit: Dora Osborne.

17 Wulf Herzogenrath, 'The Missing House', *Die Endlichkeit der Freiheit*, 84.

18 Benz, Wolfgang and Barbara Distel, eds, *Der Ort des Terrors. Geschichte der nationalsozialistischen Konzentrationslager*, vol. 2 (Munich: Beck, 2005), 63–5.

The two-part structure is fundamental to Boltanski's response: in a physical sense, it draws a line between the two halves of the city, whilst showing the still disjointed nature of its East-West topographies, and in a symbolic sense, it uses this physical divide to show the interdependent, but equally disjointed, relationship between domestic and archival spaces, between private lives and public history, and the relative (in)visibility of these spheres. As Aleida Assmann observes, the two parts show how 'memory is not possible without knowledge'.[19] But the division and non-coincidence of *The Missing House* and *The Museum* also makes apparent the difficulty of piecing together the details of lives shattered by war and persecution: we can see the place where these people once lived, but the details of who they were have been displaced to another site, made part of an archival order, available for viewing only temporarily, and in duplicate form.

As Margaret Ewing explains, Boltanski's use of the archive in this project (as in his other work) is also intended to expose 'its inherent limitations'.[20] Between *The Missing House* and the absent or 'missing' architecture of *The Museum*, Boltanski reveals a fundamental concern of memory culture: how can the traces of the past be accommodated in a way that ensures their visibility *and* their preservation? Until the artist's intervention on Große Hamburger Straße, there was no visible sign of the former residents. Any remaining traces could be found elsewhere, in the archive, but making them visible meant taking them out of the order that ensured their safekeeping. Moreover, by using *copies* of documents and protocols of interviews conducted as part of the project, Boltanski emphasised how the availability of these traces was contingent on his own intervention – an archive would never have permitted the unprotected display of original documents, and Boltanski also supplemented these sources with his own. So with both parts of his installation, Boltanksi showed how the city had failed both to accommodate *and* keep visible traces of its residents. This failure was underscored when, in this neglected no-man's land, *The Museum*

19 Aleida Assmann, *Cultural Memory and Western Civilization: Functions, Media, Archives* (Cambridge: Cambridge University Press, 2011), 364.

20 Ewing, 'The Unexpected Encounter', 43.

was vandalised after only a few weeks, and when *The Finitude of Freedom* finished later that year, dismantled.[21] In Boltanski's *Museum*, the vitrines were exposed to wilful destruction. This act of vandalism is particularly interesting because it suggests unease about confrontation with the past: *The Museum* was the more visible part of Boltanski's installation, and apparently the most provocative. Whilst it is unclear what motivated the damage, it seems the documentary evidence of persecution and deportation was an unwanted presence in this public space. In the recently reunified city, it was not possible to find a secure place for these traces outside the seclusion of the archive. *The Missing House*, meanwhile, is less conspicuous – it is possible to walk past without noticing it. In this sense, perhaps the former name 'Toleranzstraße' takes on a different meaning, suggesting how here there was greater tolerance for the less disruptive part of Boltanski's memorial.

The unforeseen damage to *The Museum* changes Boltanski's piece fundamentally. As John Czaplicka notes, without its archival counterpoint, *The Missing House* becomes more like 'the autonomous art object, for this evacuation of information is also an evacuation of history'.[22] Nonetheless, Czaplicka posits the remaining walls as a kind of 'archive' to be read by an 'informed beholder', but precisely this element is missing: Boltanski's project is, as Eric Santner calls it, an 'archive of absence', and in its dual structure, doubly so; that is, both a repository of absences and a now absent archive.[23] Moreover, the remaining installation is less provocative than its missing counterpart and has become integrated into Berlin's self-consciously memorialising cityscape; today *The Missing House* witnesses a steady stream of

21 Abigail Solomon-Godeau, 'Mourning or Melancholia: Christian Boltanski's "Missing House"', *Oxford Art Journal* 21/2 (1998), 7.

22 John Czaplicka, 'History, Aesthetics, and Contemporary Commemorative Practice in Berlin', *New German Critique* 65 (1995), 161.

23 Eric L. Santner, *On Creaturely Life: Rilke, Benjamin, Sebald* (Chicago: University of Chicago Press, 2006), 53. Andrew Webber posits Boltanski's *Archiv der deutschen Abgeordneten* (1999) in the basement of the Reichstag as a 'companion piece' to *The Missing House*, 'where the tightly spaced walls also display the emptiness of the archive' (Andrew Webber, *Berlin in the Twentieth Century: A Cultural Topography* (Cambridge: Cambridge University Press, 2008), 30).

tourists who pause to take photographs before moving on to the next location on their memory map. But the legibility of the signs is in fact limited by the gate blocking direct access to the firewalls: close to the synagogue and drawing the gaze of others, they must have some connection with Berlin's Jewish past, but this is increasingly a matter of supposition rather than informed understanding.

Stih and Schnock, *Places of Remembrance*

Those who encounter Stih and Schnock's memorial in Berlin's Bavarian Quarter, meanwhile, can be in no doubt as to its meaning. These signs, found on lampposts around the neighbourhood, show on one side simple pictures and on the other official regulations that clearly state the increasingly inhumane restrictions and prohibitions to which Jewish citizens were subject in the Third Reich. *Places of Remembrance* is a later phase of a memorial project which was initiated in the district of Schöneberg in 1983 and which recovered evidence of over 6,000 deportations from the area, known as 'Jewish Switzerland'. Despite other initiatives and exhibitions, it is the part which has gained and sustained greatest visibility.[24] Nevertheless, the extraordinary aspect of the memorial is tempered by its likeness to more ubiquitous urban signage: as Juliet Koss puts it, 'the signs flirt with camouflage, fading into their environment and reappearing with unexpected force'.[25]

24 Margit Sinka has shown how fundamental this bigger project is to an understanding of Stih and Schnock's project (Margit Sinka, 'The "Different" Holocaust Memorial in Berlin's *Bayerisches Viertel*: Personal and Collective Remembrance Thematizing Perpetrator/Victim Relationships', in Laurel Cohen-Pfister and Dagmar Wienröder-Skinner, eds, *Victims and Perpetrators: 1933–45. (Re)Presenting the Past in Post-Unification Culture* (Berlin: DeGruyter 2006), 197–221.

25 Juliet Koss, 'Coming to Terms with the Present', *Grey Room* 16 (2004), 117.

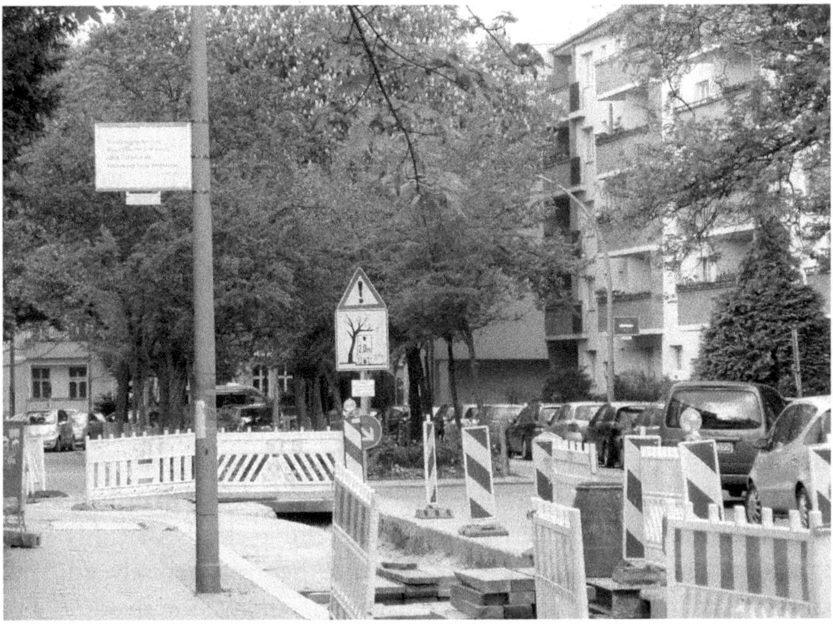

Fig. 8.3: Urban signs amongst two signs from *Places of Remembrance* by Renate Stih and Frieder Schnock, Bavarian Quarter, Berlin.
Credit: Dora Osborne with kind permission of the artists.

Drawing on the extensive documentary research of the neighbourhood and its Jewish residents undertaken as part of the Schöneberg project, Stih and Schnock 'retrieve history' via the archive, presenting these traces of the Nazi past 'in a way that would encourage passersby to take notice and confront the past in the present'.[26] But like Boltanski, Stih and Schnock also draw on the archive in order to call into question any claim to comprehensive documentation: one of their signs shows an image of an ordinary box file and on its reverse the regulation 'Akten, deren Gegenstand anti-jüdische Tätigkeiten sind, sind zu vernichten' (Files documenting anti-Jewish activities are to be destroyed). Exposing these 'anti-democratic goals [...] pursued

26 Karen E. Till, *The New Berlin. Memory, Politics, Place* (Minneapolis and London: University of Minnesota Press, 2005), 158.

under the cloak of legality',[27] Stih and Schnock also confront us with the unreliability of the archive. Moreover, they suggest how serious the implications of such archival duplicity are for our understanding of the past: following persecution, deportation and annihilation, the only traces of the neighbourhood's former Jewish residents are predominantly those that have been displaced to the archive. The artists also deviate from their own model, including on a few signs extracts from eye-witness accounts instead of anti-Semitic regulations. These contrast with the prescriptions of Nazi law and give momentary glimpses of experience recorded and preserved in less official mode. Ultimately, however, the network of signs, like Boltanski's *Missing House*, is now an accepted and integrated part of Berlin's memorial landscape, which has all but lost its disruptive potential. When the signs first appeared, they sparked reactions from alarmed passers-by who thought they were signs of resurgent anti-Semitism. In order to allay such fears, extra notices were attached, explaining clearly that this was a memorial. These 'meta-signs' made clear that the signs themselves did not speak the law, but merely cited it in the name of commemorative art.[28] The signs are thus read as examples of memory culture, their historical, juridical function displaced, if not obscured by a cultural-aesthetic one.

Gunter Demnig, *Stolpersteine*

The historical significance of both the Bayerisches Viertel and 15/16 Große Hamburger Straße is underscored, although not necessarily explained, through the presence of small brass plaques in the pavements, instantly recognisable as *Stolpersteine*, or stumbling stones. Together with thousands of similar stones found across Europe, they form part of a 'decentralized

27 Pickford, 'Conflict and Commemoration', 167.

28 Pickford 'Conflict and Commemoration', 166; Pickford notes that the signs' text 'does not denote nor name, but rather *cites*', 165 (emphasis in the original).

memorial' by the German artist Gunter Demnig.[29] Demnig laid his first *Stolpersteine* in Berlin in 1996 as part of the project *Künstler forschen nach Auschwitz* [*Artists research Auschwitz* (where 'nach' implies both searching for and in the wake of)]. Artists were to engage with the difficulties of remembering and representing the Holocaust, producing work that would also respond to the fierce debates surrounding the planned Holocaust memorial.[30] Demnig researched the fate of residents who had been deported during the Third Reich, then engraved brass plaques with the basic data of name, date of birth and, where known, date and place of death, and laid these in front of their homes. Political, conceptual and using an element of performance, Demnig's original idea, like other countermonumental art, challenged mainstream, state-endorsed memorials. Setting a few stones in the pavement without permission from the authorities, Demnig was making a clandestine intervention in municipal space, and retracing forgotten lives, unsettling the contemporary urban topography.

Since its modest, localised beginnings, the initiative has grown beyond expectation, with over 45,000 stones laid in over 1000 towns across Europe.[31] Demnig has been praised (and honoured) for creating a memorial that subverts conventional modes of commemoration, dispersing public attention away from single sites. As the artist says, you don't *have* to visit a museum, but people can't help stumbling across his stones.[32] Demnig's site-specific memorial aims to return the names of the victims to the last place of voluntary residence, an act of restitution performed with the words 'hier wohnte …' [… lived here]. The stones are located in a physical sense on the threshold between private and public spaces, but also in a metaphorical sense, between the homes of deportees and the archives that hold the last

29 See Michael Imort, 'Stumbling Blocks: A Decentralized Memorial to Holocaust Victims', *Memorialization in Germany since 1945*, 233–42.

30 <http://www.germangalleries.com/NGBK/Bakunin-ein_Denkmal.html> accessed 15 November 2012.

31 The development of Demnig's project is nicely documented in Dörte Franke's film *Stolperstein* (Hanfgarn & Ufer, 2008). See also Dora Osborne, 'Mal d'archive: On the Growth of Gunter Demnig's *Stolperstein*-Project', *Paragraph* 37/3 (2014), 372–86.

32 Anne Goebel, 'Neue Diskussion über die "Stolpersteine"', *Süddeutsche Zeitung* (17 May 2010).

information about their fate. Indeed, each stone requires archival research in order to bring hidden traces to light. This was undertaken initially by the artist and often by relatives, but increasingly local communities also uncover the traces of vanished residents. Of course, this poses questions about who is commemorated and who is not, and the motivation for those with no personal connection to victims to become involved in researching selected biographies. Thus Demnig's project adopts a precarious position between municipal monument and personal memorial, and between a desire for visibility and invisibility.

As well as its supporters, Demnig's project has many dissenters: notoriously, Munich's local council has refused to allow the stones in municipal spaces, and particularly in former East Germany, stones have been vandalised, even removed. In 2012 protesters covered *Stolpersteine* in Wismar with steel plates inscribed with the names of Wehrmacht soldiers, and on the anniversary of the November Pogrom that year, right-wing extremists were suspected of forcefully removing eleven *Stolpersteine* from the pavements of Greifswald.[33] Such acts suggest a similarly destructive impulse to that shown towards Boltanski's *Museum*, underscoring how making the traces housed in archives visible also makes them vulnerable. But beyond these isolated incidents, the stones have found acceptance in the wider community (an appeal in Greifswald quickly raised six times more than was needed to replace the vandalised stones).[34] As the name implies, *Stolpersteine* are supposed to stop us in our tracks, but Demnig's stones have also become part of the urban fabric, and thus rather unobtrusive. The stones are no longer laid illegally, but rather by appointment, and with written consent from local authorities, and since most people know what the stones represent in a broad sense, their potential to disrupt everyday

33 See <http://www.zeit.de/gesellschaft/zeitgeschehen/2012-11/stolpersteine-greifswald-geschaendet> and <http://ino.blogsport.de/2012/09/23/wismar-stolpersteine-mit-stahlplatten-ueberklebt/> accessed 30 November 2013.

34 <http://www.ndr.de/regional/mecklenburg-vorpommern/stolpersteine171.html> accessed 30 November 2013. According to a press spokesperson for Cologne, the project has won the acceptance on which it depends (Goebel, 'Neue Diskussion über die "Stolpersteine"').

life has diminished. Moreover, as the project has grown in popularity, the stones threaten to displace the individual victims they claim to commemorate. In other words, whilst the stones initially made visible those lives that had fallen into oblivion, as they become more ubiquitous, they are seen first and foremost as an example of Demnig's memorial. Despite Demnig's emphatic positioning of *Stolpersteine* outside museum spaces, they are increasingly found behind glass, that is, as exhibits. In Munich, where the stones are banned, supporters have organised exhibitions in order to make the project prominent in other ways and other places.[35] Whilst the Munich ban suggests that *Stolpersteine* still have the potential to provoke, such initiatives, which aim to counter objections, cast a particularly reverential light on the project, promoting it as an integral but ultimately inoffensive part of Germany's contemporary memory culture. Such exhibitions are also troubling because they use the names and identities of deportees to showcase Demnig's project. When *Stolpersteine* are put on display, this questions who or what is being commemorated: the stones, the victims, or the artist's idea? When in 2010 Demnig was invited to display *Stolpersteine* in the German pavilion of the Expo in Shanghai, his stones became visual artefacts in an ultimately nationalistic exhibition.[36] But what is it that is perceived here as typically or even exemplarily 'German'? Demnig's art, *Stolpersteine* as memorial, or the way in which Germans have engaged with the legacy of fascism? And above all, who decides which names will be put on display, and on what grounds?

A *Stolperstein*, dedicated to Herbert Budzislawski, is to be found outside Boltanski's *Missing House*. It also suggests an exhibit, seen not only (or no longer) as a provocation, but as evidence of a phenomenon. Indeed, this juxtaposition questions what is visible here. It seems that these two different projects shape Berlin's memorial landscape by supplementing each other: the work of the French Jewish artist stands alongside that of the German; the

35 <http://alt.stolpersteine-muenchen.de/Archiv/docu.htm> accessed 15 November 2012.

36 The invitation was announced on the 'Stolpersteine' website but has since been removed <http://www.stolpersteine.com/DE/chronik.html> accessed 19 October 2011.

vertical memorial stands next to the horizontal; and Boltanski's use of a now exposed residence borders Demnig's use of the liminal space between private and public. Found in such close proximity, they seem, in combination, to heighten the visibility of the lives commemorated. But their juxtaposition in fact produces obscurity, emphasising the invisibility of the absent community. At first glance, it appears Demnig's *Stolperstein* is dedicated to the same H. Budzislawski commemorated on one of Boltanski's plaques, and that the information provided by Boltanski is supplemented by Demnig's later intervention: according to Boltanski's sign, H. Budzislawski lived at 15/16 Große Hamburger Straße between 1933 and 1942, and Demnig's stone tells us Herbert Budzislawski was executed at Berlin-Plötzensee in 1943. But the two plaques actually commemorate two people: H. Budzislawski was a *female* poultry seller (Geflügelhändler*in*); unlike her son, Hedwig was not executed at Plötzensee, but deported, probably to Riga.[37] The two memorials set out some coordinates, but the use of such minimal data threatens to reduce two biographies to one. Herbert Budzislawski was executed for his involvement with the Herbert Baum resistance movement, but as a Jewish Communist who had same-sex relationships, he was a Nazi target on several levels.[38] Yet even as Budzislawski is commemorated, the contours of his identity are flattened out and his name becomes barely distinguishable from that of his mother. Neither plaque makes details visible. Rather, flush against their respective vertical and horizontal planes, they make the lives they commemorate seem relatively inconspicuous.

To conclude, I would like to turn to a different project also made on Germany's streets, but shown in gallery spaces. This project equally negotiates the (in)visibility of memory and the archive, but retains more disruptive potential than either Boltanski's or Demnig's site-specific memorials. Following an encounter with a Berlin street sign that read 'Jüdenstraße' or 'Jews' Street', the American-born artist Susan Hiller researched, indexed,

37 Regina Scheer, *Im Schatten der Sterne. Eine jüdische Widerstandsgruppe* (Berlin: Aufbau, 2004), 197–202.

38 <http://www.hirschfeld.in-berlin.de/frame.html?http://www.hirschfeld.in-berlin.de/gedenken/herbert_budzislawski.html> accessed 17 May 2013; Scheer, *Im Schatten der Sterne*, 197.

and archived all 303 streets in Germany that still carry the word Jew in their name. The resulting *J Street Project* (2002–5) comprised a video, a series of photographs, and a book. As Mark Godfrey notes, whilst Hiller provided an apparently complete archive, her project was haunted by the loss of the Jewish communities it retraced.[39] The artist explains:

> Ghosts are invisible to most people but visible to a few. […] These street names are ghosts of the past, haunting the present. […] Although the name was clearly meant as a respectful commemoration, […] it seemed to me there was a strange ambiguity in retaining or restoring the name of a street commemorating people who had been exterminated within living memory.[40]

Revealing the 'existing archive, which lies hidden in the folds of the German landscape', Hiller shows the country's complex, palimpsestic history in relation to Jewish presence and absence.[41] Indeed, these street signs are both burdened with, and evacuated of, historical significance. Surrounded by other, mundane urban signs, the 'J-Street' signifier is not always apparent, and its meaning is a matter of speculation.

Although absence seems to dominate the *J-Street Project*, it does not focus only on ghosts. Whilst many of the places are seemingly devoid of human presence, this is often intimated though signs of recent traffic – human, animal, commercial, vehicular. Hiller could have framed her shots to focus on the street sign alone, but often she includes indications of life in the various communities – residential streets with open windows, a door left ajar, washing on the line, a car with its headlights on. And people are in fact visible in almost sixty of three hundred and three photographs. Notably, Hiller captures them in motion, making the movement of bodies through the frame a recurring feature of her still images. Consequently the

39 Mark Godfrey, *Abstraction and the Holocaust* (New Haven and London: Yale University Press, 2007), 265.

40 Susan Hiller, 'Introduction', *The J Street Project* (Compton Verney and Berlin: Compton Verney/DAAD, 2005), 6.

41 Uriel Orlow, 'Latent Archives, Roving Lens', in Jane Connarty and Josephine Lanyon, eds, *Ghosting: The Role of the Archive within Contemporary Artists' Film and Video* (Bristol: Picture this Moving Image, 2006), 41.

majority of these figures are slightly blurred, caught with legs raised, just leaving or entering the frame; they are walking along streets, shopping, riding bicycles, driving municipal or agricultural vehicles. The movement of bodies across the frame is also integral to her film, where sporadic traffic contrasts with long periods of stasis. Thus, as well as revealing absence, Hiller's project captures life, and these mundane snapshots in fact disrupt any reverent contemplation of these scenes as memorials to vanished communities. Hiller resists the stasis and smooth surfaces of integrated installations like those by Boltanski, Stih and Schnock, and Demnig, instead layering her images with the signs of life and death across history, with the human traffic that constitutes and changes communities, and which cannot be easily arrested. For instance, Hiller captures evidence of contemporary migrant or ethnic communities, causing the street signs to reverberate with new significance where these people are present, though often still socially invisible, in Germany's towns and cities. These figures do not clarify the meaning of the 'J-Street' signs, rather they complicate our understanding of Germany's past and present. But precisely by agitating her images with movement in and across communities, Hiller shows Germany's relationship to both its past and present, with all its contradictions and instabilities. In this sense, Hiller confronts us with the 'flesh', that which resists accommodation in the archive, but which constitutes and carries collective memory.[42] Whereas the site-specific projects discussed above have become integrated almost seamlessly into the everyday urban fabric, Hiller's exhibition pieces provide a more challenging encounter with contemporary Germany: small but disruptive details, such as the everyday movement of bodies, represent what cannot be integrated into neat municipal histories accommodated in the archives; it persists as a reminder of all that is unresolved and contested about Germany's past and its contemporary identity.

Of course, as a gallery piece, Hiller's work is seen by fewer people than site-specific memorials. But it offers a particularly revealing image of contemporary Germany in relation to its recent past. As such, it might be seen as another kind of memorial project, and as part of Germany's memory

42 Schneider, *Performing Remains*, 100–2.

culture in all its controversy and contradiction. The recent proliferation of such projects means they do not stand alone, rather, like *The Missing House* and Demnig's *Stolperstein*, they overlap. This does not guarantee prominence, however. Caught between visibility and invisibility, between public and private spaces, these installations gesture instead towards the importance of reading the traces of the past carefully, and as part of a more extensive narrative, one that cannot be confined to the archives, but which spills out onto the streets and into communities. In this sense, site-specific memorials are most interesting for the responses they elicit: the damage done to Boltanski's *Museum* shows resistance to seeing the traces of the past in public spaces, whereas the integration of *The Missing House* into Berlin's tourist trail results in an essentially standard response, where tourists pause to photograph the plaques before moving on. Stih and Schnock's signs were intended to confront a contemporary audience with the same prohibitions imposed on Jewish citizens, but the addition of a reassuring 'meta-sign' to explain that these statements are mere citation causes the individual victims to recede and gives greatest visibility to the memorial itself. Demnig's *Stolpersteine* retain the potential to provoke, as seen in Munich and the isolated instances of vandalism, but the increasing focus on the project and its supporters reduces the visibility of those named on the stones. As James Young explains, the sometimes hostile response to Jochen and Esther Gerz's 1986 *Monument Against Fascism* in the German town of Harburg was an inherent part of this countermemorial, one which betrayed 'not only the Germans' secret desire that all these monuments just disappear, but also the urge to strike back at such memory'.[43] In the case of the memorials discussed here, initial provocation gives way to acceptance, a response which may signal tolerance and a shift away from this 'secret desire' for disappearance, on the one hand, but on the other, suggests that such memorial projects are seen as unremarkable, an inherent, tolerated part of memory culture in the Berlin Republic. As memorials are increasingly accepted as part of Germany's self-consciously memorialising topography, the visibility of the events or lives they commemorate perhaps diminishes;

43 Young, *Texture of Memory*, 34.

these details risk being obscured by the more readily understood shorthand of the memorial itself.

Acknowledgement

I am grateful to the Leverhulme Trust for supporting the research that led to this paper.

Bibliography

Assmann, Aleida, *Cultural Memory and Western Civilization: Functions, Media, Archives* (Cambridge and New York: Cambridge University Press, 2011).

——, *Das neue Unbehagen an der Erinnerungskultur. Eine Intervention* (Munich: Beck, 2013).

Benz, Wolfgang, and Barbara Distel, eds, *Der Ort des Terrors. Geschichte der nationalsozialistischen Konzentrationslager* (Munich: Beck, 2005).

Cordes, Gesche-M., *Stolperstein und Angehörige* (Herzogenrath: Murken-Altrogge, 2012).

Crinson, Mark, ed., *Urban Memory: History and Amnesia in the Modern City* (London and New York: Routledge, 2005).

Czaplicka, John, 'History, Aesthetics, and Contemporary Commemorative Practice in Berlin', *New German Critique* 65 (1995), 155–87.

Derrida, Jacques, *Archive Fever: A Freudian Impression*, trans. Eric Prenowitz (Chicago: University of Chicago Press, 1996).

Ewing, Margaret, 'The Unexpected Encounter. Confronting Holocaust Memory in the Streets of Post-Wall Berlin', in Anne Teresa Demo and Bradford Vivian, eds, *Rhetoric, Remembrance, and Visual Form: Sighting Memory* (London: Routledge, 2012), 33–49.

Franke, Dörte (dir.), *Stolperstein* (Berlin: Hanfgarn & Ufer, 2008).

Gay, Caroline, 'Remembering for the Future, Engaging with the Present: National Memory Management and the Dialectic of Normality in the "Berlin Republic"', in

William Niven and James Jordan, eds, *Politics and Culture in Twentieth-Century Germany* (Rochester, NY: Camden House, 2003), 201–26.

Godfrey, Mark, *Abstraction and the Holocaust* (New Haven and London: Yale University Press, 2007).

Goebel, Anne, 'Neue Diskussion über die "Stolpersteine"', *Süddeutsche Zeitung* (17 May 2010).

Herzogenrath, Wulf, Joachim Sartorius and Christoph Tannert, eds, *Die Endlichkeit der Freiheit. Berlin 1990* (Berlin: Edition Hentrich, 1990).

Hiller, Susan, *The J Street Project* (Compton Verney and Berlin: Compton Verney/DAAD, 2005).

Huyssen, Andreas, *Present Pasts: Urban Palimpsests and the Politics of Memory* (Stanford, CA: Stanford University Press, 2003).

Imort, Michael, 'Stumbling Blocks: A Decentralized Memorial to Holocaust Victims', in Bill Niven and Chloe Paver, eds, *Memorialization in Germany since 1945* (Basingstoke: Palgrave Macmillan, 2010), 233–42.

Koss, Juliet, 'Coming to Terms with the Present', *Grey Room* 16 (2004), 116–31.

Lyotard, Jean-François, *The Inhuman. Reflections on Time*, trans. Geoffrey Bennington and Rachel Bowlby (Cambridge: Polity, 1993).

Musil, Robert, 'Denkmale', *Nachlaß zu Lebzeiten, Gesammelte Werke*, ed. Adolf Frisé (Hamburg: Rowohlt, 1978), 506–09.

Niven, Bill, and Chloe Paver, eds, *Memorialization in Germany since 1945* (Basingstoke: Palgrave Macmillan, 2010).

Orlow, Uriel, 'Latent Archives, Roving Lens', in Jane Connarty and Josephine Lanyon, eds, *Ghosting: The Role of the Archive within Contemporary Artists' Film and Video* (Bristol: Picture this Moving Image, 2006), 34–47.

Osborne, Dora, 'Mal d'archive: On the Growth of Gunter Demnig's *Stolperstein*-Project', *Paragraph*, 37/3, 372–86.

Pickford, Henry W., 'Conflict and Commemoration: Two Berlin Memorials', *Modernism/Modernity* 12/1 (2005), 133–73.

Santner, Eric L., *On Creaturely Life: Rilke, Benjamin, Sebald* (Chicago: University of Chicago Press, 2006).

Scheer, Regina, *Im Schatten der Sterne. Eine jüdische Widerstandsgruppe* (Berlin: Aufbau, 2004).

Schimmeck, Tom, 'Volkszorn in der Jüdenstraße', *Die Zeit* (14 November 2002).

Schneider, Rebecca, *Performing Remains: Art and War in Times of Theatrical Reenactment* (Oxford and New York: Routledge, 2011).

Schuhen, Sarah, 'Die Stolpersteine rücken vor', <http://www.merkur-online.de/lokales/regionen/stolpersteine-ruecken-348091.html> accessed 15 November 2012.

Sinka, Margit, 'The "Different" Holocaust Memorial in Berlin's *Bayerisches Viertel*: Personal and Collective Remembrance Thematizing Perpetrator/Victim Relationships', in Laurel Cohen-Pfister and Dagmar Wienröder-Skinner, eds, *Victims and Perpetrators: 1933–45. (Re)Presenting the Past in Post-Unification Culture* (Berlin: DeGruyter, 2006), 197–221.

Solomon-Godeau, Abigail, 'Mourning or Melancholia: Christian Boltanski's "Missing House"', *Oxford Art Journal* 21/2 (1998), 3–20.

Staiger, Uta, Henriette Steiner and Andrew Webber, eds, *Memory Culture and the Contemporary City. Building Sites* (Basingstoke: Palgrave Macmillan, 2009).

Steffen, Tilman and dapd, 'Unbekannte reißen in Greifswald sämtliche Stolpersteine aus', *Die Zeit*, 9 November 2012 <http://www.zeit.de/gesellschaft/zeitgeschehen/2012-11/stolpersteine-greifswald-geschaendet> accessed 30 November 2013.

Till, Karen E., *The New Berlin. Memory, Politics, Place* (Minneapolis and London: University of Minnesota Press, 2005).

Webber, Andrew, *Berlin in the Twentieth Century: A Cultural Topography* (Cambridge: Cambridge University Press, 2008).

Young, James E., *The Texture of Memory: Holocaust Memorials and Meaning* (Yale: Yale University Press, 1993).

Websites

Cultd.net <http://www.cultd.net/endlichkeit/> accessed 1 November 2012.

German Galleries <http://www.germangalleries.com/NGBK/Bakunin-ein_Denkmal.html> accessed 15 November 2012.

Lindenstrasse.de <http://www.lindenstrasse.de/Information/Panorama/_2011/Ausstellung_JuedischesMuseumMuenchen.jsp> accessed 20 November 2011.

Magnus Hirschfeld Gesellschaft <http://www.hirschfeld.in-berlin.de/frame.html?http://www.hirschfeld.in-berlin.de/gedenken/herbert_budzislawski.html> accessed 17 May 2013.

Ndr.de <http://www.ndr.de/regional/mecklenburg-vorpommern/stolpersteine171.html> accessed 30 November 2013.

Stolpersteine München <http://alt.stolpersteine-muenchen.de/Archiv/docu.htm> accessed 15 November 2012.

Stolpersteine.eu <http://www.stolpersteine.com/DE/chronik.html> accessed 19 October 2011.

PART III

Surfaces, Secrets and Interior Spaces

THE CITY DOES NOT TELL OF

zURBS
Prelude III

I could tell you how many steps make up the streets rising like stairways [...] but I already know this would be the same as telling you nothing. The city does not consist of this, but of relationships between the measurements of its space and the events of its past: [...] A description of Zaira as it is today should contain all Zaira's past. The city, however, does not tell its past, but contains it like the lines of a hand.

—ITALO CALVINO, *Invisible Cities*

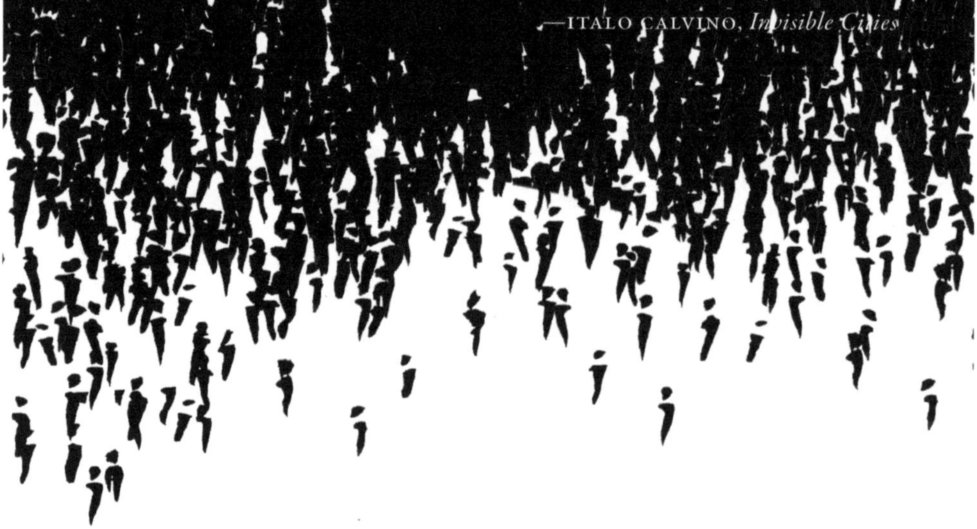

Life is spatial as much as it is temporal. Since ancient times people have linked their identites and histories with physical shapes. The creation of places, buildings and roads reaffirms identity in the present, and passes it on to the future.

Space then, is loaded with traces of the past: the manifestation of a solution for a problem that is long gone. A message that has lost its meaning. A street that leads nowhere, somewhere there used to be something – or where there was something that was supposed to come, but never did. An old man sitting at the end of a bench. A bench long enough for himself and his three friends. Now there's only him. A footstep in the tarmac that collects the leaves of last autumn. The empty show window of a vegetarian butcher. Rusty train tracks telling stories of dirty hands and hard-working men. A climbing wall that allows you to shake hands with Jesus in a former church ...

What traces of the past can help you shape ideas of possible futures?

ITS PAST BUT CONTAINS IT LIKE THE LINES OF A HAND

Contemporary cities are places of memory, since they contain traces of the past while producing memory for future generations. Thus, space should not be reduced to a static representation of one fixed meaning and reality that ignores its temporality. This would restrict our imagination of time to one singular (hi)story, and the possibility of multiple narratives and the openness of space would be lost. This brings to the fore an underlying disturbance not only of our notions of the past, but also of our imagination of the future.

Space can help us keep the future open by facilitating multiplicities. Imagine then, that by tracing the many different pasts of a city, whether in abandoned factories, cracks in the asphalt, graffiti on fences, reflections in windows or litter in the streets, you could shape ideas of possible futures.

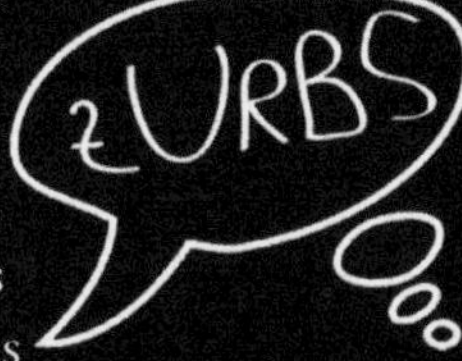

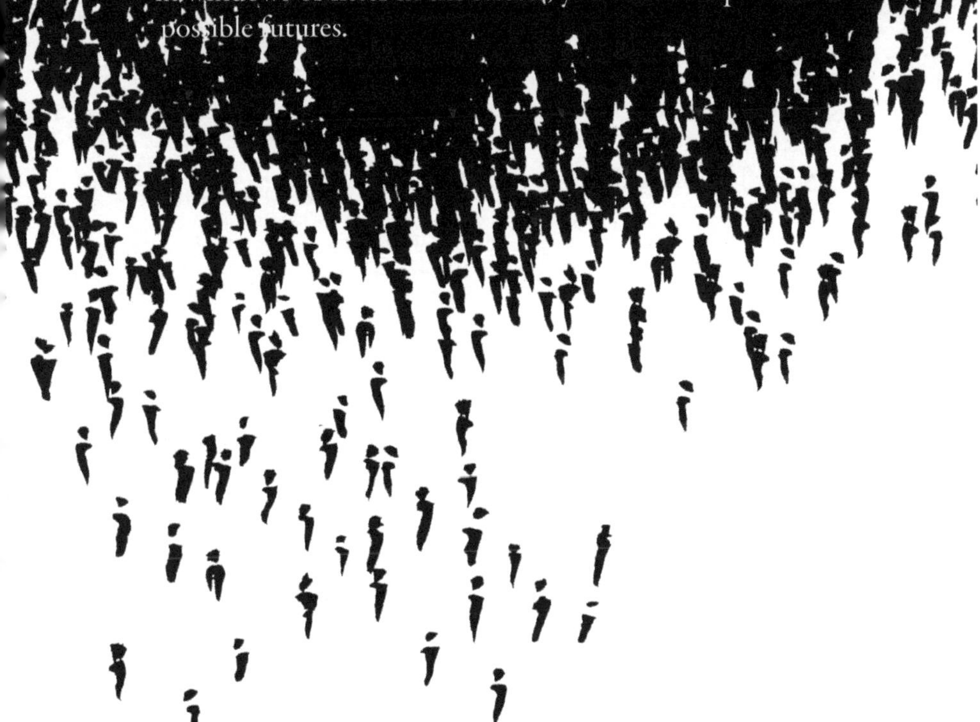

JANE RENDELL

9 Surface Encounters: On Being Centred, Decentred and Recentred by the Works of Do-Ho Suh[1]

If criticism can be defined as providing a commentary (for some a judgement, for others a discriminating point of view, for others yet, a response or perhaps even a point of departure) on a cultural work – art, literature, film and architecture – then criticism always has 'an other' in mind. The key task of criticism might be considered then as providing an answer to the question: how does one make a relationship with another? In thinking about the position of the other in criticism and psychoanalysis, the work of psychoanalyst Jean Laplanche is illuminating.

For Laplanche, the message imparted to the subject by the other (for Laplanche the 'mother' or 'concrete other') is an enigma both to the receiver but also to the sender of the message: he says these 'messages are enigmatic because [...] [they] are strange to themselves.'[2] This first inscription, according to Laplanche, does not require a translation 'it is a pure and simple

1 I was invited to give a gallery talk about the exhibition, Do-Ho Suh (23 April – 26 May 2002) Serpentine Gallery, London and this text derives from my script for the guided tour. *Do-Ho Suh*, curated by Lisa G. Corrin and Mary Shirley, debuted at the Serpentine Gallery, London, 2002, and travelled to the Seattle Art Museum and Seattle Asian Art Museum, Seattle, 2002. The text was published in Jane Rendell, *Site-Writing: The Architecture of Art Criticism* (London: IB Tauris, 2010), and the material in this chapter is taken from configuration 5 of that book. I would like to extend my thanks to IB Tauris for allowing this reproduction of the text, albeit in a new arrangement.

2 Cathy Caruth, 'An Interview with Jean Laplanche', © 2001 Cathy Caruth. See <http://www3.iath.virginia.edu/pmc/text-only/issue.101/11.2caruth.txt> accessed 3 May 2006.

implantation'.[3] These enigmatic messages are elements of perception, they do 'make a sign', but a sign whose signifier does not need to be transcribed, since it is already a 'signifier to', in other words this is a signifier *to someone* rather than a signifier *of something*.[4]

In Laplanche's view, some aspects of the adult's enigmatic message to the child are translated, while others are excluded and repressed, becoming unconscious.[5] In his account, repression – the negative side of the translation of the enigmatic message – produces dislocation:[6]

> For in between the primary intervention of the other and the creation of the other thing in me, there occurs a process called repression – an extremely complex process comprising at least two stages in mutual interaction, and leading to a veritable dislocation/reconfiguration of (explicit and implicit-enigmatic) experiential elements.[7]

For Laplanche, the result of this process of translation is that the ego and id are separated, the ego integrates that which can be translated, and that which cannot constitutes the id. During the process of repression, the initial Copernican relationship, where the centre of gravity is located in the other, radically alters to become a Ptolemic one, centered on the self. According to Laplanche, once the ego is constituted as an agency, the psychic system shuts in on itself, and the external otherness of *der Andere* (the other person) undergoes primary repression to become the internal otherness of *das Andere* (the other thing).[8]

In this chapter I explore how Laplanche's understanding of Copernican and Ptolemic movement allows us to consider how a critic's encounter

3 Jean Laplanche, 'A Short Treatise on the Unconscious' [1993], in John Fletcher, ed., *Essays on Otherness*, trans. Luke Thurston (London: Routledge, 1999), 97.

4 Ibid., 91, note 18.

5 Ibid., 97.

6 Ibid., 104.

7 Laplanche, 'The Unfinished Copernican Revolution', 71, note 37. Here the reader is referred to Jean Laplanche, *New Foundations for Psychoanalysis* [1987] trans. David Macey (Oxford: Basil Blackwell Ltd., 1989), 130–3.

8 Jean Laplanche, 'The Aims of the Psychoanalytic Process', trans. Joan Tambureno, *Journal of European Psychoanalysis* 5 Spring–Fall (1997), 75.

with a work of art operates through processes of centring, decentring and recentring. I suggest that such movements suspend what we might describe as judgement or discrimination in criticism, and instead, through what I call the practice of *site-writing*, trace and construct relations between sites – visible and invisible – connecting and disconnecting critics, works, artists, essays and readers. Site-writing is a way of configuring what happens when discussions concerning situatedness and site-specificity in art practice extend to involve the processes of writing criticism, so questioning the terms of reference that relate the critic to the work positioned 'under' critique, and proposing instead alternative positions.

Site-writing is a critical spatial practice[9] which emphasises the differing qualities of those sites of the critic's engagement with art – material, emotional, political and conceptual – including the artwork's construction, exhibition and documentation, as well as those remembered, dreamed and imagined by the artist, the critic, and other viewers and users of the work.[10] The intention is to focus on how spatial concepts may be embodied through encounters with artworks and reproduced in writings that respond to these experiences. This process is perhaps particularly pertinent when considered in connection to works, such as those of Do-Ho Suh, a Korean-born artist now based in New York, which explicitly examine issues around location and dislocation with regard to personal and cultural identity, memory and home. In what follows, I investigate how through encounters with surfaces in a number of works by Do-Ho Suh, this critic,

9 I first introduced the term 'critical spatial practice' in my article Jane Rendell, 'A Place Between Art, Architecture and Critical Theory', in *Proceedings to Place and Location* (Tallinn, Estonia: 2003), 221–33 and later consolidated and developed the concept in my book Jane Rendell, *Art and Architecture* (London: IB Tauris, 2006). Since that time, the same term has been taken up by individuals such as Judith Rugg in her seminars at the RIBA, London, from around 2008; Eyal Weisman to describe activities as part of the 'MA: Research Architecture' at Goldsmiths College of Art, London; and most recently by Marcus Miessen to identify the 'MA: Architecture and Critical Spatial Practice' launched in 2011 at the Städelschule, Frankfurt.

10 For a longer discussion where I conceptualise my practice of site-writing, see Rendell, *Site-Writing*, 1–20.

through centring, decentring and recentring devices, positions the work in relation to personal memories and situated experiences of her own.

In her essay for Do-Ho Suh's solo show at the Serpentine Gallery, London in 2002, art critic Miwon Kwon took issue with notions of authenticity that could be ascribed to the work, not just the 'original' Korean home that Suh's travelling piece *Seoul Home/L.A. Home/New York Home/ Baltimore Home/London Home/Seattle Home* (1999) duplicates, but the myth of the authenticity of mobility itself.[11] Although Kwon's critique of 'cosmopolitan homelessness' argues quite rightly that the movement experienced and described by the international art scene as a universal condition needs to be understood as a privilege enjoyed by very few, her own position in this context is not subject to address.

My own engagement with Suh's work (and Kwon's essay) took place just after I returned from a visit to Seoul.[12] In what follows I recount how my first-hand experience of South Korea operates to locate the work, to both centre and decentre it. I try to resist the use of autobiographical details of my visit to situate the work in relation to an image of an authentic Korea, nor do I argue that critics must experience the original cultures that artworks refer to and the actual sites in which they are located in order to understand the work. I do, however, seek to draw attention to the specificity of the particular sites through which we engage with works, in the case of my encounter with Suh's work –Seoul and London. I question why autobiographical and biographical details are assumed to operate as centring devices, and wonder instead whether they have the potential to decentre the critic's position with respect to the work, as well as the reader's relation to the critical essay.

11 Miwon Kwon, 'The Other Otherness: The Art of Do-Ho Suh', in *Do-Ho Suh* (London: Serpentine Gallery, 2002), 23. For an extended discussion of site-specificity and dislocation see Miwon Kwon, *One Place After Another: Site Specific Art and Locational Identity* (Cambridge, MA: The MIT Press, 2002).

12 I participated in an art and architecture workshop in Seoul, Korea organised by Junghee Lee in April 2002.

Biography as a Device that Centres, Decentres and Recentres

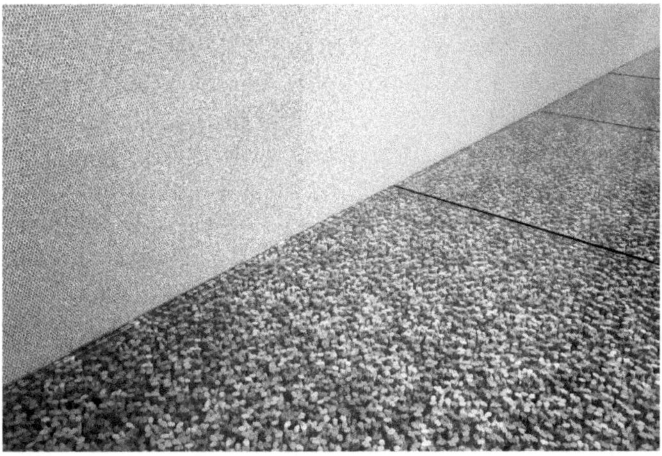

Fig. 9.1: Do-Ho Suh, *Who Am We?* (Multi) (2000) Serpentine Gallery, London, 2002. Four-colour offset wallpaper. Each sheet: 61 × 91.4 cm. And Do-Ho Suh, *Floor* (1997–2000) Serpentine Gallery, London, 2002. PVC figures, glass plates, phenolithic sheets, polyeruthane resin. Serpentine Gallery: 25 modules. Each module: 100 × 100 cm. Credit: Stephen White. Reproduced with kind permission of Serpentine Gallery.

On entering the first room of Suh's solo show at the Serpentine Gallery at first I am only aware of the presence of a glass floor, on which I have to step in order to continue my passage through the gallery. The walls seem to have nothing on them; they appear slightly coloured, but no more than off-white. Moving closer to inspect them more fully I discover that their surfaces are covered with thousands of tiny dots. Closer still I see that these dots are miniature faces in oval frames, all the same size, but each one different, a little like passport photographs in their ability to combine uniformity and variety.[13] *Walking onto and looking down at the floor more carefully, I find myself standing on millions of tiny pairs of hands, which on a more detailed examination I realise belong to figurines.*[14] *Unbending, the hands disappear; moving back,*

13 Do-Ho Suh, *Who Am We? (Multi)* (2000). The 37,000 images of faces are taken from high school yearbooks of Suh and his friends. For a critical commentary, see for example, Miwon Kwon, 'The Other Otherness', 9.

14 Do-Ho Suh, *Floor* (1997–2000). This work consists of 180,000 figures cast from six different moulds. The figures differ from those in *Doormat: Welcome (Amber)*

the faces become invisible again. But I am left with the feeling of being silently watched, and when I move again I do so extremely lightly.

Much of the critical conversation about Suh's work has focused on the relationship the work has to minimalism,[15] and the emphasis it places on the perception of an artwork as a public rather than an intimate experience. Kwon argues that Suh's work 'extends the lessons of minimalism' but also, by 'creating intimate relations with his viewer', makes '*anti*-minimalist moves'.[16] For Kwon, *Who Am We?* (2000) and *Floor* (1997–2000) at first decentre the viewer because s/he only discovers the work once s/he is within it. Kwon asserts that the revelation of the detail brings a privileged sense of knowledge gained and with this a feeling of recentring.[17]

However, I am not sure the viewing experience is constructed so sequentially – as decentring followed by recentring. The discovery of the hands in *Floor*, for example, positions the viewer in a powerful location, but the realisation that s/he is crushing those who continue to support him/her brings with it discomfort and confusion. Kwon recognises this double positioning, indeed she argues that it is intentional on the part of the artist, and in her view its clear legibility produces resolution and thus pleasure, not displeasure, for the viewer. She mistrusts pleasure, because it undermines the 'disturbing undercurrents' of other works by Suh, such as *Some/One* (2001), a majestic military robe constructed from thousands of

---

(2000) also exhibited at the Serpentine Gallery, and *Doormat: Welcome (Green)* (1998) described by Katie Clifford as less defined, apparently because Suh wanted them to appear as if they had been rubbed away by people stepping on them. See Katie Clifford, 'A Soldier's Story', *Art News* (January 2002), 104.

15 See for example Janet Kraynak, 'Travelling in Do-Ho Suh's World', in *La Biennale di Venezia/Korean Pavilion: Do-Ho Suh* (Seoul: The Korean Culture and Arts Foundation, 2001), 41–2.

16 Kwon, 'The Other Otherness', 12.

17 Ibid. In a similar vein, artist Tom Csaszar has commented that Suh's work often 'inverts or suspends expectations' but he does not argue that the inversion is then itself overturned. See Tom Csaszar, 'Social Structures and Shared Autobiographies: A Conversation with Do-Ho Suh', *Sculpture* 24/10 (2005), 34–41, 40.

army-style tags and *High School Uni-Form* (1996), a single entity composed of multiple empty uniforms.[18]

The view of the collective presented is ambivalent, but from whose perspective? It is not clear whether Suh's work asks the viewer to identify with the position of the worker represented, and their resistance and/or collusion with dominant power structures,[19] or whether he wishes the viewer to consider whether he, the artist, is critiquing disciplinary regimes of power or affirming that individuality must be subsumed for the common good. Certainly for the viewer, the links that he or she might presume this Korean-born artist is making between what Kwon calls the Eastern virtue of 'self-sacrifice in the name of a larger social or political entity' and the colonisation of subjects, raises questions concerning whether the discipline of order comes from outside or within. Kwon asks whether 'we' in contemporary society are the agents of our own oppression or liberation.[20] But to which 'we' is she referring?

Resisting the tendency to explain the ambivalence in Suh's work in relation to his biography, as she argues other critics have done,[21] Kwon chooses to produce a more historical interpretation, by exploring Michael Hardt's

18 Other critics have also drawn out the more threatening aspects of *Some/One* and *High School Uni-Form*. For example, Frances Richard connects *Some/One* with 'enigma and threat' and *High School Uni-Form* as well as *Who Am We?* with 'an oppressive sameness', in distinction to what she calls the 'collective strength' of *Floor*. See Frances Richard, 'The Art of Do-Ho Suh', *Art Forum* (January 2002), 117. *High School Uni-Form* has been described by Clifford as 'militaristic', a comment made in connection to an article in which she frames Suh's work in relation to his time in military service. See Clifford, 'A Soldier's Story', 104. Audrey Walon has stated that *Some/One* 'bring[s] out the military strength of the collective' in a more confrontational way than other pieces by Suh, an interpretation formulated in response to the installation of this work at the heart of the capitalist corporation Philip Morris. See Audrey Walen, 'Do-Ho Suh: Whitney Museum at Philip Morris', *Sculpture* 20/8 (October 2001), 72.

19 Glenn Harper asks whether the figures in the Suh's *Floor* are 'oppressed masses' or the 'workers who support the world'? See Glenn Harper, 'Do-Ho Suh: Lehmann Maupin', *Sculpture* 20/1 (January–February 2001), 62.

20 Kwon discusses all these ambiguities. See Kwon, 'The Other Otherness', 13.

21 Kwon refers particularly to Clifford, 'A Soldier's Story'. See Kwon, 'The Other Otherness', 13.

and Antonio Negri's theorisation of 'the new global order of Empire', and their concept of the 'multitude' rather than the 'people'.[22] This allows her to develop her argument concerning pieces such as *Floor* with a degree of loss rather than the satisfaction of fulfilment with which she, earlier in the essay, connects the work.[23]

That Suh was born and educated in Korea, and later moved to the United States to continue his studies as an artist, seems to me a historical as well as a biographical detail that helps to situate but does not necessarily explain or centre the ambivalence of the work.[24] To reject the biographical but retain the historical might well be the decision of a scholarly mode of art criticism, but does this then mean that all mention of Suh's life is to be eradicated from what is written about his work, even if his art emerges out of his personal mobility?

On my visit to Seoul I learnt that Confucianism dominates Korean culture. In this ethical system, originating in China, a particular set of rules, based on respect, age, status and gender govern the construction of social relations. To someone unfamiliar with this collective ethos the predetermined nature of relationships can appear rather oppressive, but perhaps no more so than global capitalism's myth of individual freedom. In Korean art practice there is a palpable tension between eastern and western values.

That Suh's father, Se-Ok Suh, is a well-known artist working in the traditional manner – ink on rice paper – and his mother, Min-Za Chung, is active in retaining Korean cultural heritage, are biographical details often referred to in discussions of Suh's work. At Seoul National University, where Suh first studied, with its focus on traditional painting and sculpture, I met Insu Choi, Professor of Sculpture.[25] Although Choi studied in Karlsruhe, Germany, in the early 1980s, for him the birth of modernism brought with

22 Kwon, 'The Other Otherness', 13 and 16. See also Michael Hardt and Antonio Negri, *Empire* (Cambridge, MA: Harvard University Press, 2000).

23 Kwon, 'The Other Otherness', 17.

24 Ibid., 13.

25 My understanding of Insu Choi's views come from a conversation with him where Junghee Lee acted as an informal translator. If there are any inaccuracies in my articulation of his position, they come from my own misunderstanding.

it the death of representative painting and figurative sculpture, and in his view such western traditions should not be forced on artists in Korea, but adopted through choice.[26] I also had many conversations with one of Suh's teachers, Yoon Young Seok, Professor at Kyungwon University. An artist who also trained in Germany, in Stuttgart, Soon occupies a very different position from Choi. He embraced his western education and is currently engaged in the making of what he calls 'conceptual objects' located within a contemporary context that acknowledges the position of Korea in relation to the west, and vice versa.[27] A large number of Korean artists have studied in Germany and the United States. Some have returned to Korea, but others, like Suh, have not. For many the frictions between freedom and individuality that arise out of this particular east/west dislocation are generative impulses in their practice.

Is this information gleaned from informal conversations over dinner and my reflections upon it too autobiographical for inclusion here? Are they only valid if they do not seek to explain or centre interpretations of the work? But whose biography precisely is the problem: the artist's or the critic's – Suh's, mine, or Kwon's own?

Kwon is now based in the United States, but she grew up in Seoul. I found this out by reading her earlier 1998 article on Suh's work, where she refers to her Korean childhood.[28] In a perceptive account of *Who Am We?* and *High School Uni-Form*, she eloquently describes how the 'destablizing conditions of cultural displacement', both chosen and forced, create a sense of longing connected with leaving. Here, it is out of biographical details that a complex understanding of cultural and historical context emerges,

26 Choi places a strong emphasis on taoist tradition and meditative practice in his own work. In the winter he draws lines on paper in response to the length of his breath and in the summer he rolls clay. For Choi, the hand is a tool, which in the act of shaping integrates spirit and matter. See for example, Insu Choi, Nigel Hall, Christain Herdeg and Paul Isenrath, *Beyond the Circle* (The Moran Museum of Art, 2000).

27 See for example Young Seok Yoon, *Temple of Time* (Seoul, Korea: TOTAL Museum of Contemporary Art, 1999). See also Young Seok Yoon's *Piggy Plantation* (2002) shown at PS1 and the Clock Tower Gallery, New York.

28 See Miwon Kwon, 'Uniform Appearance', *frieze* 38 (January–February 1998), 68–9.

which, far from explaining, produces an informed exposition, subtle yet precise, of the work's ambiguities.[29]

I wonder then whether the so-called vacancy or absence Kwon detects at the core of Suh's work comes less from Hardt's and Negri's political theory and more from a loss of her own. Is it fear of the charge of sentimentality or nostalgia that makes Kwon remove her own history as well as Suh's in her second account of his work? It is hard to know, yet the loss she finds via a more theoretical route paradoxically serves to recentre her in the role of art critic. Likewise the knowledge I gained in Seoul that provided me with a sense of anchorage in a foreign culture also serves to recentre my understanding of the decentring devices in Suh's work.

A Replica of a Replica of a Replica ...

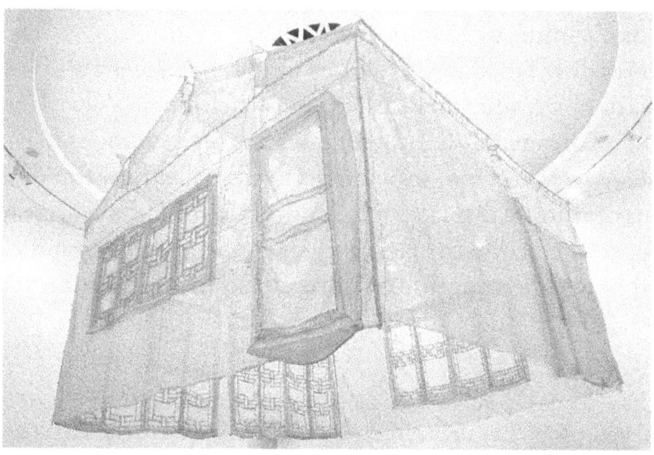

Fig. 9.2: *Seoul Home/L.A. Home/New York Home/Baltimore Home/London Home/ Seattle Home* (1999) Serpentine Gallery, London, 2002. Silk. 378.5 × 609.6 × 609.6 cm. The Museum of Contemporary Art, Los Angeles. Purchased with funds provided by an anonymous donor and a gift of the artist.
Credit: Stephen White. Reproduced with kind permission of Serpentine Gallery.

29 Ibid.

In 1999, when asked to exhibit at the Korean Cultural Centre in Los Angeles, Suh saw on display photographs of traditional nineteenth-century buildings in Korea. These images reminded him of his home in Seoul, based on parts of the Changdeokgung Palace.[30] For *Seoul Home/L.A. Home/New York Home/Baltimore Home/London Home/Seattle Home* (1999) Suh fabricated a replica of his home in green silk. Conceived originally as 'custom-made clothing for a room',[31] this work is a development of an earlier one, *Room 516/516–I/516–II* (1994) where Suh made a copy of his studio in muslin.[32]

Seoul Home/L.A. Home/New York Home/Baltimore Home/London Home/Seattle Home is a home that is portable and has travelled around the world. With each new show, the work adds to its title the name of the town in which it has been exhibited, clearly marking its growing itinerary as well as Suh's increasing international recognition.

Although generated through his interest in 'transportable site-specificity',[33] the physical substance of the work does not change; rather it transports the specific site of his Seoul home to each new location. The work is altered in the way it addresses each of its new sites or homes. In Los Angeles it was placed on top of a central staircase, and each viewer had to pass through the inside of the work before seeing it from the outside as an object in totality. In London, at the Serpentine Gallery, its floating position high up in the roof produced comparisons with air balloons or parachutes, which while also inaccessible differ from *Seoul Home/L.A. Home/New York Home/Baltimore Home/London Home/Seattle Home* in concealing rather than revealing their interiors when seen from below. The tension between stasis and change is highlighted in the work's title, where the repetition of the word home, accompanied by a different town in each pair of words, can be understood either to indicate the transformation of Suh's Seoul home into a new one in each new location, or that despite its changing geography, home continues to refer back to the same origin.

30 Lisa G. Corrin, 'The Perfect Home: A Conversation with Do-Ho Suh', *Do-Ho Suh* (London: Serpentine Gallery, 2002), 27.

31 Ibid., 27.

32 Ibid., 28.

33 Ibid., 27.

In Seoul I visited Changdeokgung Palace, and in so doing encountered aspects of Suh's home.[34] Changdeokgung Palace is a traditional Korean building constructed of wood and rice paper, waxed to keep out the rain. The use of paper reduces the emphasis on vision that comes with glass, but this architecture is not a sealed box: it is porous to the environment. From inside you can hear and smell what is outside. Suh has discussed how his motivation to make the work came from being disturbed at night in his flat in New York and remembering how peacefully he had slept in his childhood home.[35] A strange reversal, then, that the key characteristic of the architecture of his childhood home – its permeability to light, smell and sound – should be remembered as a protecting envelope.

As Kwon has noted, Suh's home is 'a replica of a replica of a replica'.[36] The artwork is a replica of a replica his father made of two nineteenth-century buildings – a library and master's house –from the palace complex. When some of these buildings were demolished to make way for new roads, Suh's father salvaged timbers to construct a house for his family, in which, as Suh describes, the original library became their family kitchen and dining room.[37] Interestingly it turns out that the library and master's house were themselves replicas.[38] Suh outlines how, in 1828, King Sunjo made copies of 'civilian-style houses' in order to experience the life of 'ordinary people'.[39] However, the term 'commoner' used by Kwon,[40] which mirrors Suh's use of the phrase 'ordinary people', and works to create an understanding of Korean royalty as wishing to learn from ordinary experience, is decentred by my reading of the guidebook to Changdeokgung Palace, which states

34 See for example, the photographs and short texts describing Yeon–Gyeongdang (House) including the Husband's Quarters, the Housewife's Quarters, the Inner Servants' Quarters and Seonhyangjae (Library) in Jong-Soon Yoon, *Changdeokgung (Palace)* (Seoul: Sung Min Publishing House, 2000), 46–51.

35 Corrin, 'The Perfect Home', 28.

36 Kwon, 'The Other Otherness', 25, note 19.

37 Clifford, 'A Soldier's Story', 105.

38 Kwon, 'The Other Otherness', 17.

39 Corrin, 'The Perfect Home', 29.

40 This is the term Kwon uses. See Kwon, 'The Other Otherness', 25, note 19.

that these houses belonged to members of the yangban class of intellectuals, who although not members of the royal family, were considered to be a 'largely hereditary aristocratic class based on scholarship and official position rather than wealth'.[41] This left me with unanswered questions concerning how the act of reproducing certain kinds of architecture could at the same time serve to reinforce a conceptual understanding of the work with respect to references to class distinctions in Korean history, while also to destabilise the viewer by suggesting that they imagine a site located physically distant from the work in the gallery.

Between the Outside of the Inside and the Inside of the Outside

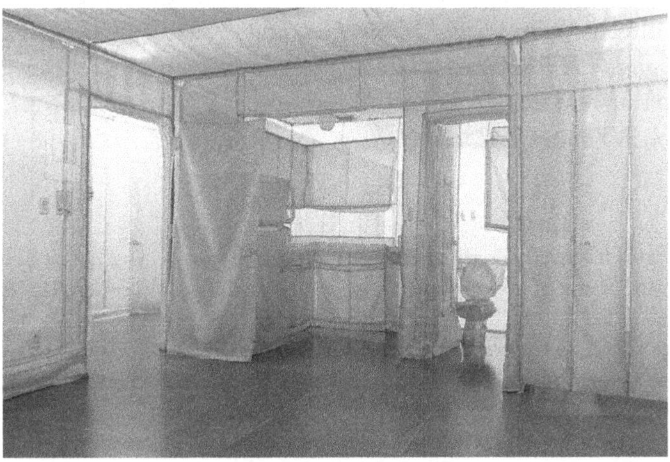

Fig. 9.3: Do-Ho Suh, *348 West 22nd Street, Apt. A, New York, NY 10011 at Rodin Gallery, Seoul/Toyko Opera City Art Gallery/Serpentine Gallery, London/Biennale of Sydney/Seattle Art Museum* (2000) Serpentine Gallery, London, 2002. Translucent nylon. 430 × 690 × 245 cm. Edition 2/3. Collection Ninah and Michael Lynne. Credit: Stephen White. Reproduced with kind permission of Serpentine Gallery.

41 Yoon, *Changdeokgung (Palace)*, 46.

For *My Home is Yours, Your Home is Mine* (2000) at the Rodin Gallery in Seoul, Suh made a companion piece to *Seoul Home/L.A. Home/New York Home/Baltimore Home/London Home/Seattle Home*, the first of what has become a collection of replicas of his home in New York; of the apartment itself, *348 West 22nd Street, Apt. A, New York, NY 10011 at Rodin Gallery, Seoul/Toyko Opera City Art Gallery/Serpentine Gallery, London/Biennale of Sydney/Seattle Art Museum* (2000) made in grey nylon,[42] and the corridor, *348 West 22nd Street, Apt. A, New York, NY 10011 at Rodin Gallery, Seoul/Toyko Opera City Art Gallery/Serpentine Gallery, London/Biennale of Sydney/Seattle Art Museum (Corridor)* (2001) fabricated in rose-pink nylon, added in subsequent exhibitions, such as the Serpentine Gallery, London in 2002.[43] When exhibited together these two works have also been titled first *Perfect Home I*,[44] and then, when accompanied by part of the staircase from Suh's apartment block formed of yellow nylon, *Perfect Home II*.[45]

At the Serpentine Gallery, Suh's two homes do not encounter one another directly. While *Seoul Home/L.A. Home/New York Home/Baltimore Home/London Home/Seattle Home* floats down from the ceiling, allowing us to look up and into its beautiful interior, *348 West 22nd Street, Apt. A, New York, NY 10011 at Rodin Gallery, Seoul/Toyko Opera City Art Gallery/*

42 The grey has been described as 'dust-coloured'. Richard, 'The Art of Do-Ho Suh', 116. And also as generic in contrast to the culturally specific 'celadon' green of *Seoul Home* …. See Kwon, 'The Other Otherness', 17.

43 Critics have drawn attention to the colouring of the work, some argue that it articulates the functional zoning of architectural design emphasised in the colour coding of drawings. See C. K. Ho, 'Do-Ho Suh: Lehmann Maupin Gallery', *Modern Painters* 16/3 (August 2003), 122. Others suggest the choice of colours is emotive, with the pink of the corridor considered to be indicative of the 'rose-tinted', 'idealised' and 'fantasised connection' between the different elements of the piece. See Richard, 'The Art of Do-Ho Suh', 116.

44 For example when installed in the Seattle Art Museum and Seattle Asian Art Museum, Seattle, 2002. See Anon., 'Do-Ho Suh: The Perfect Home', *Fiberarts* 29/3 (November–December 2002), 22–3.

45 For example when installed at the Lehmann Maupin Gallery, New York, 2003. See <http://www.lehmannmaupin.com/#/exhibitions/2003-05-30_do-ho-suh/> accessed 14 June 2008.

Serpentine Gallery, London/Biennale of Sydney/Seattle Art Museum is constructed upwards from the ground up like a tent, with slightly sagging sides. In tracing an interior architecture at a scale of 1:1 and exploring the experiential qualities of absence, Suh's work raises comparisons to Rachel Whiteread's *House* (1993), her concrete cast of the interior of a Victorian house in London's East End.[46] But while Whiteread's casts turn inside out, Suh's linings face inwards not outwards. His stitched lines are sewn twice, from inside and outside, suggesting the structures are reversible.[47] However, if inhabiting the work from the inside clothes the viewer in an absent architecture, occupying the work from the outside is to be faced by an impossible object, one that decentres rather than recentres the viewer.

> *On the outside, trying to imagine the absent architecture to which I am being referred I find myself located behind the interior paint finish of Suh's New York apartment, inside a solid brick wall or, depending on the construction technique, among the insulation, studwork and builder's rubbish commonly packed into the cavity. As I address the impossible position in which the work places me, I realise I am right between the outside of the inside wall of Suh's apartment and the inside of the outside wall of the Serpentine Gallery.*

This is precisely how the *at* in this work's title operates. The insertion of *at* – a preposition of address – points to the meeting point between the site *in* which the work is located and the site *to* which the work refers. *348 West 22nd Street, Apt. A, New York, NY 10011 at Rodin Gallery, Seoul/Toyko Opera City Art Gallery/Serpentine Gallery, London/Biennale of Sydney/Seattle Art Museum* addresses itself to each gallery it visits, this is quite unlike *Seoul Home/L.A. Home/New York Home/Baltimore Home/London Home/Seattle Home* where the city in which the gallery is located becomes an adjective used to describe home, and where each city home is added to an ever growing list, separated by a forward slash, indicating a clear distinction from its predecessor. The address or *at* in *348 West 22nd Street, Apt. A, New York, NY 10011 at Rodin Gallery, Seoul/Toyko Opera City Art Gallery/Serpentine Gallery, London/Biennale of Sydney/Seattle Art Museum*

46 See for example James Lingwood, ed., *Rachel Whiteread: House* (London: Phaidon Press, 1995).

47 Kwon, 'The Other Otherness', 25, note 20.

opens up a gap for the critic to occupy between the site in which the work is located and the site to which the work refers.

If Laplanche describes the 'signifer of' as 'a metapsychology of the trace or of representation' and a self-referential movement which 'remains irreducibly solipsistic',[48] and thus operational as a centring device, then the *at* in this work by Doho Suh might focus as well on the experience of Laplanche's concept of a 'signifier to', whose enigmatic message is decentring. This distinction between 'signifying of' and 'signifying to' is very important for Laplanche, as it allows him to account for meanings that are not already pre-contained in the signified and simply transmitted via the signifier to the addressee, but rather to conceptualise those meanings that might be enigmatic, in other words, not necessarily already known to the one who is addressed or the one who does the addressing, but produced through the act of addressing itself.

I argue that it is possible to consider the role of surface in *348 West 22nd Street, Apt. A, New York, NY 10011 at Rodin Gallery, Seoul/Toyko Opera City Art Gallery/Serpentine Gallery, London/Biennale of Sydney/Seattle Art Museum* as productive of this act of addressing: the surface of the work is not only capable of transmitting meanings *of 348 West 22nd Street, Apt. A, New York, NY 10011* but also *to* the Serpentine Gallery. These meanings *of* and *to* are created through points of address – *ats* – sites where the surfaces of the work and the gallery meet, and where subjects are produced in addressing and being addressed by these surface encounters.

Bibliography

Anon., 'Do-Ho Suh: The Perfect Home', *Fiberarts* 29/3 (November–December 2002), 22–3.

Caruth, Cathy, 'An Interview with Jean Laplanche', 2001 <http://www3.iath.virginia.edu/pmc/text-only/issue.101/11.2caruth.txt> accessed 3 May 2006.

48 Laplanche, 'Sublimation and/or Inspiration', 45.

Choi, Insu, Nigel Hall, Christain Herdeg and Paul Isenrath, *Beyond the Circle* (The Moran Museum of Art, 2000).
Clifford, Katie 'A Soldier's Story', *Art News* (January 2002), 102–5.
Corrin, Lisa G., 'The Perfect Home: A Conversation with Do-Ho Suh', *Do-Ho Suh* (London: Serpentine Gallery, 2002), 27–39.
Csaszar, Tom, 'Social Structures and Shared Autobiographies: A Conversation with Do-Ho Suh', *Sculpture* 24/10 (December 2005), 34–41.
Hardt, Michael and Antonio Negri, *Empire* (Cambridge, MA: Harvard University Press, 2000).
Harper, Glenn, 'Do-Ho Suh: Lehmann Maupin', *Sculpture* 20/1 (January–February 2001), 62–3.
Ho, C. K., 'Do-Ho Suh: Lehmann Maupin Gallery', *Modern Painters* 16/3 (August 2003), 122–3.
Kraynak, Janet, 'Travelling in Do-Ho Suh's World', *La Biennale di Venezia/Korean Pavilion: Do-Ho Suh* (Seoul: The Korean Culture and Arts Foundation, 2001), 41–2.
Kwon, Miwon, *One Place After Another: Site Specific Art and Locational Identity* (Cambridge, MA: The MIT Press, 2002).
——, 'The Other Otherness: The Art of Do-Ho Suh', *Do-Ho Suh* (London: Serpentine Gallery, 2002), 9–25.
——, 'Uniform Appearance', *Frieze* 38 (January–February 1998), 68–9.
Laplanche, Jean, 'The Aims of the Psychoanalytic Process', trans. Joan Tambureno, *Journal of European Psychoanalysis* 5 (Spring–Fall 1997), 69–79.
——, 'A Short Treatise on the Unconscious' [1993], *Essays on Otherness*, ed. John Fletcher, trans. Luke Thurston (London: Routledge, 1999), 84–116.
——, 'The Unfinished Copernican Revolution' [1992] *Essays on Otherness*, ed. John Fletcher, trans. Luke Thurston (London: Routledge, 1999), 52–83.
Lingwood, James, ed., *Rachel Whiteread: House* (London: Phaidon Press, 1995).
Rendell, Jane, *Art and Architecture* (London: IB Tauris, 2006).
——, 'A Place Between Art, Architecture and Critical Theory', *Proceedings to Place and Location* (Tallinn, Estonia: 2003), 221–33.
——, *Site-Writing: The Architecture of Art Criticism* (London: IB Tauris, 2010).
Richard, Frances, 'The Art of Do-Ho Suh', *Art Forum* (January 2002), 115–7.
Walen, Audrey, 'Do-Ho Suh: Whitney Museum at Philip Morris', *Sculpture* 20/8 (October 2001), 72–3.
Yoon, Jong-Soo, *Changdeokgung (Palace)* (Seoul: Sung Min Publishing House, 2000) 46–51.
Yoon, Young Seok, *Piggy Plantation* (2002) shown at PS1 and the Clock Tower Gallery, New York.
——, *Temple of Time* (Seoul: TOTAL Museum of Contemporary Art, 1999).

CLAUS BECH-DANIELSEN

10 The Secret Suburb: Second Lives in Second Homes

The ability to be 'invisible' seems to be an important quality in relation to a summerhouse. In fact, summerhouses can be said to be 'invisible' in a double sense. As I will explore in this chapter, summerhouses are neglected in planning and partly forgotten in Danish building regulations, at the same time as their owners like to see summerhouses as hidden places where they can live secret lives, hidden away from the modern world.

Let me start by looking at developments in early twentieth-century domestic architecture. Naturally, the home was the primary focus for the architects of modernism, because the home was considered to be the space in which crucial aspects of modern life develop and unfold. The leading architects of modernism therefore developed a number of homes that have become architectural landmarks of the time and a continuing source of inspiration for architects today. The best of these homes have the status of icons, representing modernist domestic architecture and the prevailing ideals for which it stood. These icons feature in almost all literature about domestic architecture in the first half of the twentieth century. I will now briefly describe four buildings, built in different decades, which are among the most important of these icons.

Villa Savoye, designed by Le Corbusier in 1928, is probably the most reproduced building in books about the domestic architecture from the 1920s. With its white walls and the almost ritual ascent through the house, from the small washbasin at the entrance to the sunbed on the roof terrace, the house symbolises the physical and mental cleansing process that was to take place in the modernist home.

Falling Water, designed by Frank Lloyd Wright in 1935, is probably the most pictured house in literature about housing architecture from the 1930s. *Falling Water* expresses a strong attachment to place, and as an example of Wright's organic architecture, it has often been said to provide a counter-image to the domestic architecture of European modernism.

Glass House was designed by Philip Johnson and built in 1949. The transparency of the glass and the close interplay between the building's interior and exterior have had an enormous influence on subsequent trends in domestic architecture. *Glass House* was built for Philip Johnson himself, and is often described as 'Philip Johnson's own home'.

Farnsworth House was designed by Ludwig Mies van der Rohe and built in 1951.[1] Industrial materials were used experimentally, and here, too, the transparency of the glass gives the building its special qualities. Today, the building serves as a place for visitors and its official website presents it as 'one of the most famous examples of modernist domestic architecture'.

Figs 10.1a–d: The four houses which represent icons of domestic architecture in four different decades. The four houses are consistently given prominent roles in the literature about domestic architecture in the first half of the twentieth century.

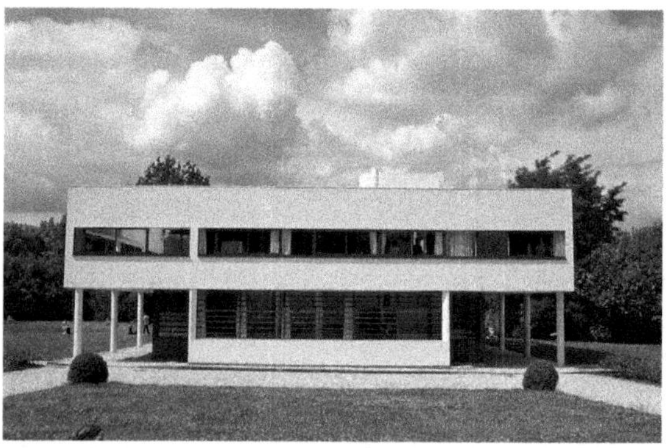

Fig. 10.1a: *Villa Savoye*.
Credit: Claus Bech-Danielsen.

1 Plans to build the house were underway for many years and, in reality, the designs inspired Johnson's *Glass House*, which was built two years earlier. According to Alice T. Friedman, Johnson curated an exhibition of Mies van der Rohes' work at the Museum of Modern Art in 1947, featuring a model of the *Farnsworth House*.

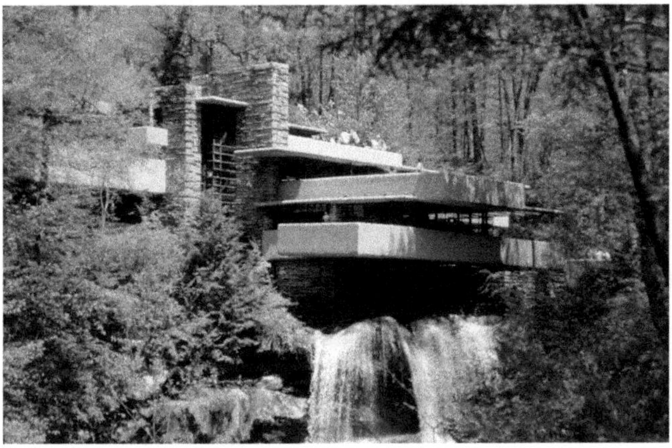

Fig. 10.1b: *Falling Water*.
Credit: CINARK.

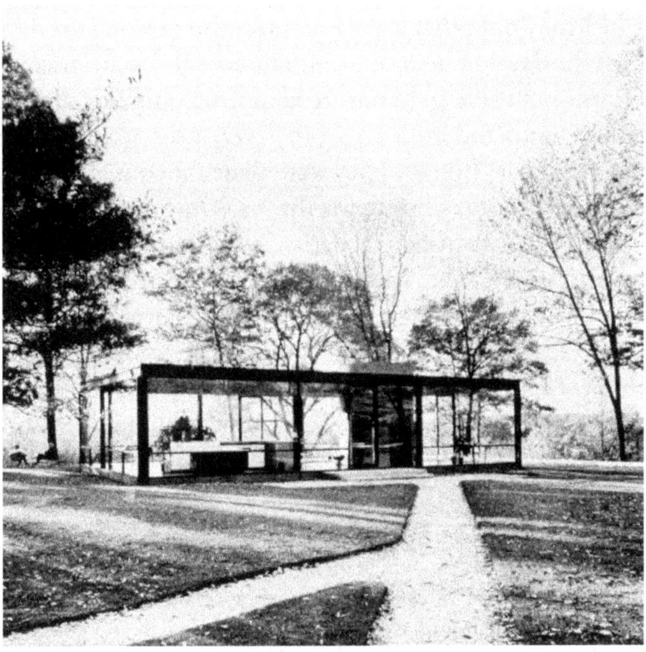

Fig. 10.1c: Johnson's *Glass House*.
Credit: Lise Bek.

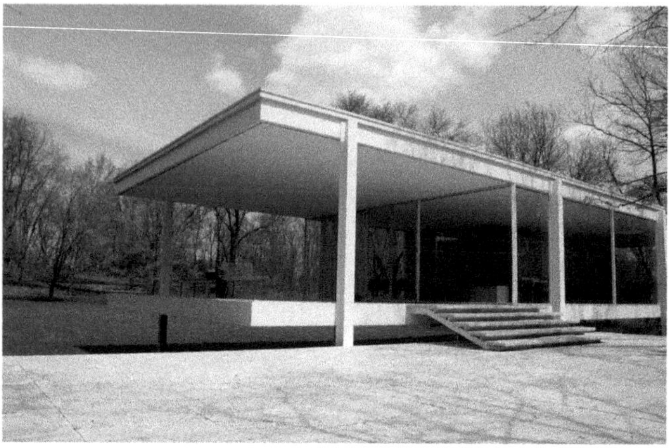

Fig. 10.1d: *Farnsworth House.*
Credit: CINARK.

There can be little doubt that these four houses are among the most important works in the development of twentieth-century domestic architecture, and their prominent role in literature about the domestic architecture of modernism serves to underline this. However, interestingly, none of these four houses are primary homes. They were all designed as *second homes. Villa Savoye* served as a country house for the wealthy Savoye family, who had their principal residence in central Paris. *Falling Water*, or the 'Kaufmann's Residence' as it is also called, served as a weekend retreat for the successful Pittsburgian businessman Edgar Kaufmann. Furthermore, although *Glass House* was said to be 'Philip Johnson's own home', it was in fact his second home. Finally, *Farnsworth House* was designed as a weekend retreat for Edith Farnsworth, who lived in Chicago, ninety kilometres away.[2]

2 In Scandinavia as well, designing holiday homes was an important and challenging architectural assignment in which all of the big modernist architects were involved. In Denmark, Arne Jacobsen designed a holiday home for himself by Sejrø Bay (*Sejrøbugten*) in 1938. Similarly in Sweden, Gunnar Asplund designed a holiday home for himself in 1937, and, in Finland, Alvar Aalto entered the fray back in 1928 when the cultural magazine Aitta arranged a competition to develop a new type of holiday home. Aalto felt free to experiment with new forms when designing for the

The above begs two obvious questions. Firstly, why did modernist domestic architecture seem to develop most prominently, and in its purest form, in the second home? I have addressed this question in earlier articles, which describe the residents' perceptions of life in the second home[3] and how these perceptions are expressed in and influence its architecture.[4] Secondly, why is the fact that these houses were built as second homes overlooked or neglected repeatedly in the literature? In what follows, I will try to find some answers to these questions by focusing on the relationship between principal homes and second homes in Denmark. As I will show, it appears that Danish second homes are generally overlooked and over-shadowed by the principal home. Perhaps the point is that life in the holiday home is a secret, invisible life?

Development of Danish Holiday Home Areas

First, let me define some important concepts. Existing international literature often uses the term 'second home'. Second homes are properties which are owned or rented for the purpose of temporary residence, for people who have their everyday residence elsewhere.[5] In Denmark second homes are typically built near to the sea and for recreational purposes.[6]

---

competition and won two out of the three categories. He later designed *Experimental House*, which was a holiday home, for himself.

3 Kirsten Gram-Hanssen and Claus Bech-Danielsen, 'Sommerhuset – om at komme ud og væk og være sammen'. Paper presented at NSBB, Nordisk Samfundsvidenskabelig By- og Boligforsker konference, Denmark (2009).

4 Claus Bech-Danielsen and Kirsten Gram-Hanssen, 'Second homes – another life in another Suburbia: A study on architectural design and cultural ideals related to Danish summerhouses', *Nordic Journal of Architectural Research* 1/2011 (2012), 7–23.

5 Mark Shucksmith, 'Second Homes: A New Framework for Policy', *Town Planning Review* 54 (1983), 174–93.

6 Gunther Tress, 'Development of Second-Home Tourism in Denmark', *Scandinavian Journal of Hospitality and Tourism* (April 2002), 109–22.

Second homes in Denmark are known as 'summerhouses', and these will be my focus in this chapter.

The majority of Danish summerhouses are located in areas specially designated for second-home residential use. This is due to Danish national and regional spatial planning, which since 1974 has divided Denmark into different zones according to use: urban zones, agricultural zones and recreational zones. Summerhouses may only be built in recreational zones. One of the reasons the Danish Planning Act designates special summerhouse areas is to protect the plant and animal life of these areas, which often hold unique qualities. These areas are used seasonally, during weekends and on holidays, and are therefore more or less depopulated in the remaining parts of the year. The summerhouse areas are thus different from the common residential areas, in that they periodically change character and are subject to a special cyclical rhythm.

Architecturally, while following a rather similar stylistic paradigm, Danish summerhouses also stand out from permanent homes in a number of aspects. For example, they are generally smaller than permanent homes (on average they are half the size) and they are very often built of wood. The architectural tradition and the cultural conventions linked to Danish summerhouses were shaped in part by a specific historical development and I will outline this below.

Historical Development: Two Suburbs

Liselund on the island of Møn is often identified as an important building and park when speaking of Danish summerhouses.[7] *Liselund* was constructed from 1792 to 1795 and it reveals an obvious inspiration from Marie

7 Dahlkild Nan and Flemming Skude, 'Fritidens huse', *Architectura* 20 (1998) 7–38; Kim Dirckinck-Holmfeld and Finn Selmer, *Arkitekternes sommerhuse* (Copenhagen: Danish Architectural Press, 2007); Søren Vadstrup and Katrine Martensen-Larsen,

Antoinette's romantic garden at Versailles in the way the island's natural landscape has been moulded into a romantic landscape. Much devotion has been given to Rousseau's ideals about the simple shepherd's life in harmony with nature and many authors agree that these ideals are still prevalent in perceptions of Danish summerhouse life,[8] mediated by the developing sentiments in the nineteenth century emphasising the medical advantages of seaside life in general, as well as the early twentieth-century vitalist body culture in which an informal, outdoor and recreational lifestyle evolved, one which characterises Danish summerhouse life to this day.

Similar ideals about health and outdoor life came to shape urban development, where the dramatic urbanisation of the industrial period brought with it strong anti-urban sentiment. During the cholera epidemic of 1853 in Copenhagen, which was at the time still a walled city with no subterranean sewer system, the city came to be seen – and experienced – as a locus of contagion.[9] As a preventive measure, people living in the most disease-prone buildings were moved to camps in the fields outside Copenhagen. Hope of recovery was associated with the fresh air in the open landscape outside the city. These temporary camps can be seen as a first stage in the development of the Danish suburbs. The same year saw the erection of the first residential buildings in the fields outside Copenhagen. The Association of Danish Doctors hired the Danish architect Gottlieb Bindesbøll to build homes suitable for healthy living in natural surroundings. With the Association's housing project, the urban borders were dissolved and the city began to spread out into the countryside, marking the genesis of the suburb.

This trend continued with the urban development of the twentieth century. The planners of the modern city wanted to break with the historical city centre as laden with prestige. They turned their eyes to the horizon and created residential areas on the periphery of the city, which offered light

---

Sommerhuset (Copenhagen: Gyldendal, 2008); Lisbeth Balslev Jørgensen, *Danmarks Arkitektur. Enfamiliehuset* (Copenhagen: Gyldendal, 1979).

8 Dahlkild and Skude, 'Fritidens huse'; Dirckinck-Holmfeld and Selmer, *Arkitekternes Sommerhuse*.

9 Karin Lützen, *Byen tæmmes. Kernefamilie, Sociale Reformer og Velgørenhed i 1800-tallets København* (Copenhagen: Hans Reitzels Forlag, 1998).

and air and plenty of opportunity for recreation in the green landscape. Most of the homes in the suburbs in Denmark were built as single-family houses, a trend that gathered momentum, especially in the 1960s and the 1970s, when the general level of wealth increased in earnest in Denmark. During these two decades, as many as 430,000 single-family houses were built in Danish suburbs.

The construction of summerhouses took place primarily during this same period,[10] boosted by the general increase in wealth that allowed the Danish middle class to realise its dreams of a second home. Furthermore, increased use of motor vehicles propelled the development, as both the Danish summerhouse areas and access to the detached houses of the suburbs were reliant on the car.

While throughout the twentieth century, urban development mainly took place on the city's perimeter, that is, in the suburbs, which were acclaimed for their qualities of light, fresh air and green surroundings, the summerhouse areas were developed even further away from the city centre, but focusing on the very same qualities. Thus, there were two coexisting movements away from the city and into rural surroundings; a movement into the suburbs and a movement into the summerhouse areas. Both of these movements were movements away from the noisy and busy city life.

One might mistakenly think that one part of the city population moved into the green suburbs, while another group of people remained in the city, choosing instead to buy a summerhouse that could provide them with recreational opportunities. However, this is not the case. One of the paradoxes of the success of summerhouses in Denmark is the fact that the owners of single-family houses in the suburbs are strongly overrepresented among Danish summerhouse owners. Thus, three out of four summerhouse owners in Denmark live in single-family homes or terraced houses in the suburbs.[11] This becomes no less of a paradox when looking at

10 Anne-Marie Hjarlager, *Udviklingsdynamikker i Sommerhussektoren* (Copenhagen: Center for Housing and Welfare, 2009).

11 Hans Skifter Andersen and Mark Vacher, *Sommerhuse i Danmark. Hvem har dem og hvordan bruges de?* 2009 <http://boligforskning.dk/sites/default/files/cbvnotat%20 sommerhuse%20_2_.pdf> accessed 17 october 2013.

the way many Danish summerhouses and summerhouse-areas are designed. Many of the most recently established Danish summerhouse areas resemble little copies of the typical Danish suburb, with single-family houses with gardens and following a similar architectural stylistic paradigm. Since it is largely the same people who own houses in both areas, one might wonder what motivates these people to have two houses that are so much alike?

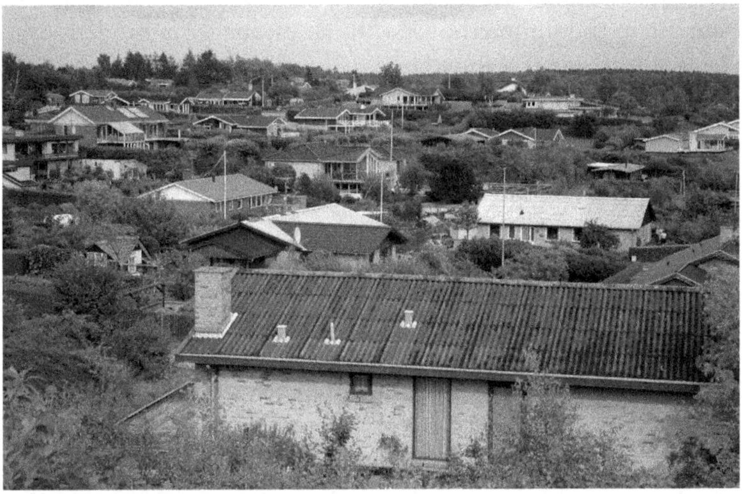

Fig. 10.2: Danish summerhouses and summerhouse-areas are designed as little copies of the typical Danish suburb, with single-family houses with gardens and following a similar architectural stylistic paradigm. Credit: Claus Bech-Danielsen.

The expansion of Danish summerhouse areas and of suburban areas with single-family houses therefore represents two simultaneous movements; both aiming at the open horizon and rural surroundings and both created by the same people. And the movement was extensive; there are approximately 220,000 summerhouses in Denmark today.[12] It is therefore surprising that this part of the Danish building stock has received so little attention. The

12 In comparison, there are 2.1 million dwellings in Denmark.

subject is only modestly described in existing literature and local government interest in the summerhouse areas is also limited.[13] This was evident when a number of municipal planners were interviewed[14] about Danish summerhouse areas: even the municipalities with the greatest number of summerhouses have no real policy for the development of these areas.

The summerhouse owners are not necessarily unhappy about this. As will emerge from the following discussion, many summerhouse owners associate life in the summerhouse with an escape from modern everyday life where everything is planned in detail and they like to see the summerhouse as a 'hidden place' or a 'secret cottage'. Being out of sight seems to be a good thing, when you live in a summerhouse.

The Qualities of the Summerhouse

As part of a research project, we conducted a number of qualitative interviews with summerhouse owners in order to understand the qualities of the summerhouse which, in their opinion, their residents most appreciate and which separate the summerhouse from the principal home.[15] These surveys form the basis for the following descriptions.

As described above, the idea prevails that summerhouse living allows for a life-style that is healthier than urban life. Although many summerhouse owners today in fact live their everyday lives in the green suburbs, many of

13 Also considerable elements of the Danish building regulation do not apply to summerhouses. For example, requirements for accessibility for the elderly and disabled people.

14 The interviews where carried out in spring 2009 in connection with a research project about Danish summerhouse architecture and life.

15 A total of twelve qualitative interviews were conducted in spring 2009. For a more detailed methodological description of the surveys conducted, we refer to other articles: Gram-Hanssen and Bech-Danielsen, 'Sommerhuset'; Bech-Danielsen and Gram-Hanssen, 'Second Homes'.

them still consider the summerhouse as a place to live a healthy life. Several families thus expressed the idea that they associate life in the summerhouse with physical recreation and healthy living. For example, fresh air is described as a fundamental quality of the summerhouse area and several of the interviewees said fresh air is the reason they sleep better in their summerhouses than in their permanent home. They also have better appetites in the summerhouse, presumably because of the fresh air and long walks. One family said they bought their summerhouse because their son is suffering from asthma and they are convinced he is considerably better when in the summerhouse.

As a part of healthy lifestyle, many of the interviewees also see their summerhouse as a place they can destress. In this context, the calm and quietude characterising most of the interviewees' summerhouses are important. 'It is unbelievable that it can be so quiet,' one interviewee tells us. However, it is important that specific types of sound are absent, because as one woman says: 'There are the birds, of course, but otherwise the peacefulness is very evident'. Others stress the dark nights as a contrast to the city's electric lights, which they say seem false. The summerhouse must be without the traces and sounds of modern everyday life.

That much of the activity in the summerhouse takes place in the open air is also part of the notion of healthy summerhouse living. 'You spend much more time outside, here. At least, I know, I spend more time outside here than I do at home,' one man says, explaining the difference between life in the summerhouse and life in the permanent home. Many of the interviewees also mention that they often eat outdoors at the summerhouse and that they use the terrace even on cooler days by simply wearing more clothes for the occasion. They could choose to do this at home as well, as they acknowledge – but they don't.

The outdoor space is therefore an important part of the summerhouse. In fact, making use of outdoor space at the summerhouse may be required, because most summerhouses are not very big. Whereas the average Danish single-family house is 139m^2,[16] the average Danish summerhouse is 72m^2.[17]

16 Jesper Bo Jensen, *Parcelhuset i fremtiden – Fakta og tendenser* (Copenhagen: Bolius, 2008).

17 Hjarlager, *Udviklingsdynamikker i sommerhussektoren*.

This has a direct bearing on the life lived in the summerhouse. The children's rooms, for example, are so small they are unsuited for play, and thus in the summerhouse the bedrooms are only used for night rest. The rest of the time the bedrooms are empty, and the family is gathered in the living room or in the outdoor spaces. The small summerhouses therefore support the family life that many of the interviewees stress as being an important quality of the summerhouse. For example, one boy, aged twelve, said that his family was 'more of a family in the summerhouse', because they are forced to be closer there.

The limited space is one of the reasons the open kitchen so quickly became a popular feature of the summerhouse. Casual holiday living is another reason. In the summerhouse, the housewife will not accept having to cook dinner behind a closed kitchen door.[18] One woman, who has an open kitchen both in her summerhouse and in her permanent residence, speaks enthusiastically about her summerhouse kitchen because it allows her to be a part of everything that goes on: not just because the kitchen, the living room, and the terrace are spatially connected, but also because the small summerhouse is a manageable size.

It is important that the summerhouse is manageable, because life here has to be simple. Thus, life in the summerhouse involves an element of *basic living*. This does not necessarily mean that life in the summerhouse has to be primitive, with cold showers and old-fashioned toilets; it's about living a life that consists of only the most basic qualities, without any disturbing factors. 'There is no laundry, no cleaning and clearing up,' says one woman, and more or less all of the interviewees express similar viewpoints, i.e. that an important part of being in the summerhouse is to get away from the duties and tasks always lurking in the permanent home. In the summerhouse, residents can relax with a clear conscience because the duties of daily life have been temporarily forgotten.

As suggested above, the attitude toward cleanliness is different in the summerhouse. 'It's not like you have a cleaning obsession here,' one woman explains, and she agrees with others that cleaning is more important

18 Alastair Gordon, *Weekend Utopia. Modern living in the Hamptons* (New York: Princeton Architectural Press, 2001).

in the permanent home. It is completely allright to have spruce needles on the floor in the summerhouse; it's all a part of living close to nature. You can also be a little more relaxed about your personal hygiene in the summerhouse, according to one summerhouse owner. It is not as if she completely neglects her personal hygiene in the summerhouse, 'it's just not that important.'

There are several such examples of how life in the summerhouse is far easier because residents are more willing to let go, and have other expectations of themselves and each other. This is an important reason why almost all of the interviewees in the study entertain far more guests in their summerhouses than in their permanent residences. When we asked one woman whether it was easier to have guests over in the summerhouse she responded: 'Yes it is, actually. Because it is as if it is less conventional, I think. Guests can go ahead and make their own sandwiches if they want. I would probably look twice if they got up and did that at home.' Several of the female interviewees state that they feel less obligated to play the role of the perfect host in the summerhouse, and that, similarly, they don't expect to be waited on so much when they are the guest in other people's summerhouses. The roles are reversed in the summerhouse. Everyday habits are broken, and people live the simple life. However, despite the fact that summerhouse residents entertain more guests in the summerhouse, they do not want to have a dishwasher installed. The dishwasher, along with other domestic appliances, is linked to the stressful modern life from which they escape by going there.

The summerhouse residents are also less strict about meal times. 'When we are at the summerhouse, we just go ahead and eat whenever we are hungry', several of the interviewees say, and in other areas as well, summerhouse residents have alternative attitudes to time. For example, one woman explains that she feels 'a bit outside time' when at her summerhouse, while another woman says she feels time is 'fluid'. One man explains how taking off his wristwatch is one of the first things he does when he arrives at his summerhouse. He also explains how in everyday life at home he has no time to himself. 'Anyway, my wristwatch is part of my work life. I think it's this part of my life that I take off,' he explains. To be independent of a watch reminding you of the time is part of the relaxation of life in the summerhouse.

A man who has an academic job explains that books are entirely absent from his summerhouse. In his permanent home there are books everywhere. In the summerhouse, he wants there to be no books to remind him of his work. However, this does not mean that life lived in the summerhouse is devoid of activity. Several of the interviewees state that part of the relaxed life in the summerhouse involves do-it-yourself building and construction projects. One man, who holds a managerial position in his work life, involving mainly administrative and human resource tasks, explains that he relaxes when he is outdoors doing physical work around the summerhouse. Tools are a permanent part of the family's kit for the summerhouse, because the summerhouse is where the man lives out another side of himself; as a handyman. Work is allowed in the summerhouse, as long as the duties of everyday life are absent.

The children also get away from life at daycare, school and after-school activities. 'Having to come up with things to do is challenging for them', several of the parents say, meaning this positively. The children we spoke with were also enthusiastic about the summerhouse. One boy explains how he invents entirely different games at the summerhouse. He is currently building a 'fitness centre' in the backyard out of rope and branches. He would never have done that in the garden at home, he explains. Play Station and other toys from the permanent home are not brought along to the summerhouse, and friends from school are not there either. In this way, children's lives in the summerhouse become other lives.

Adults too are forced to come up with other things to do than at home. 'Actually, there is not much else one can do than sit down and read a book,' one woman says, and according to one man the main attraction of his summerhouse neighbourhood is 'the peace and quiet; the fact that nothing happens'. Nothing happens in the summerhouse. The basic quality of the summerhouse appears to be that activities are *not* taking place and that things are *not* there. Thus, the most important quality of the summerhouse is absence: the absence of noise, space, entertainment, domestic appliances, phones, street lightning, an internet connection, computer games, watches and appointments, paid work, and the habits and conventions of everyday life. In the summerhouse the residents rid themselves of the lives they live in their permanent homes.

Second Lives

As I have outlined, life lived in the summerhouse is a second life, different from the one lived at home. For example, one woman describes how the move back and forth between the permanent house and the summerhouse can feel somewhat intense, because she feels that she is living very different lives in the two houses. Another woman explains that life cannot continue where they left it two weeks ago until the bags have been unpacked. Finally, one woman, who has 45km between her permanent house and her summerhouse, thinks it's fantastic to have access to two such different lives within such a short distance.

Time off spent at the summerhouse has become so insulated[19] that second homes are rather second lives. During the drive to the summerhouse, the summerhouse residents make a mental switch, they go from one condition to another, and while staying in the summerhouse, they establish a *cul de sac* in time in which they live their second life. They leave the duties of their everyday lives behind in their permanent home and live out their dream of a life close to the family and to nature.

Interestingly, studies of the housing preferences of Danes conclude that there is a huge difference between their dream houses and actual choices of house. Many Danes, who live in the single-family houses of the suburb, dream of having a small country house with land and room for livestock and hobby activities.[20] And yet, in reality they buy a house that is close to supermarkets, schools and daycare, children's playmates, public transport, and so on.[21] They step out of the dream and are caught up by the realities of the everyday world.

19 The division between worklife and leisure life in modern society has a physical expression in Danish summerhouse areas with the spatial zoning between summerhouse areas, the recreational zones, and residential areas.

20 Thorkild Ærø, *Boligpræferencer, Boligvalg og Livsstil*, PhD dissertation (Hørsholm: Danish Building Research Institute, 2002).

21 Thorkild Ærø, *Boligpræferencer, boligvalg og livsstil.*

From this perspective, the suburban areas of single-family houses with gardens, and the summerhouse areas, cannot only be considered as the suburbs of worklife and leisure life respectively. Rather, the summerhouse areas are the suburbs of dreams, whereas the suburbs of single-family houses negotiate a compromise with the realities of life at work. The residents of the summerhouses live out their dreams there, at a distance from the disturbances of everyday life. This distance between the two houses is described as important by several of the interviewees. For instance, several of the interviewees explain that it would be downright comical if the two houses were situated in the same area, so that shopping when staying at the summerhouse would have to be done in the same shops used on a daily basis. It would be very difficult to play out the dream life in surroundings belonging to everyday life. When meeting your neighbour, you would suddenly wake up from your dream and see yourself stubbly and wearing a jogging suit, an old sweater and rubber boots – the typical rural and casual summerhouse attire.

Therefore, summerhouse residents stick desperately to their dreams, even when things from everyday life sneak up on them in the summerhouse area. We experienced this a couple of times during our interviews, for example, when a summerhouse owner talked about the peace and quiet of the summerhouse while a plane came in to land in the nearby airfield, and when a neighbour started his chainsaw. The interviewee oddly managed to ignore these noises, just as when someone tries to wake you up from a lovely dream and you try desperately to cling on to your dream state.

The Free Modern Life: An Illusion?

In light of the above discussion, perhaps we can more easily understand why so many of the epoch-making homes of modernism are summerhouses. In the design of the summerhouse, the modernists could really free themselves from the conventions of the past and the present. They could rid themselves of traditional thinking and the mundane. In the development of the summerhouse, they could establish their dream of a *tabula rasa*, free from ties to a historical and urban context. Here they could steer free of the compromises that constitute everyday life. In other words, in the design of the summerhouse the architects of modernism could develop the dream of a modern and liberated life.

This conclusion probably explains why the existence of these houses as summerhouses is so often overlooked. Because when we are reminded that these houses were meant for temporary recreational use, we see that they do not meet the demands of a complex everyday life. We see that the architect's establishment of a *tabula rasa* takes place in a time-pocket kept free from reality. We see that the notion of a free life without commitments is an illusion.

Probably something similar is in play when Danish summerhouses are more or less intentionally overlooked as being a part of Danish suburbs. They are hardly considered to form a part of the built-up reality. As described above, municipal planners spend very little time on summerhouse developments, and summerhouses are only included to a limited extent in Danish building and construction statistics. This was evident when, recently, I was a part of the steering group in a research project that was to map the Danish suburb. I reminded the group that the Danish summerhouse areas constitute part of the suburbs all being developed as a physical frame for our welfare society, and although everyone in the group agreed with this, Danish summerhouses were not included in the final report. Danish summerhouses still live their own secret lives; they are a dream that is forgotten the moment residents leave and return home to their everyday lives. Perhaps this is for the best, because if the summerhouses remained too vivid in our minds, maybe this would reveal that our permanent homes do not live up to our dreams.

As a result, the summerhouses stay hidden away out there in the landscape. When the residents have left their houses, these are closed down, and time in the summerhouses is brought to a standstill. For many of the interviewees, closing down the summerhouse involves a long series of tasks that are almost like a ritual. This is reflected in the design of many summerhouses, and particularly so in the guest house that the Danish architect Vilhelm Wohlert designed for Niels Bohr's summerhouse in 1958. On the southern-facing façade of the house, large wooden panels serve to cover the patio along the house. When the house is left behind, the wooden panels are closed in front of the large glass windows, causing the house to resemble a closed box. The house lies in the landscape like a child holding its hands in front of its eyes in the hope that this will make it invisible. And there is much to suggest that Danish summerhouses have succeeded in this wish.

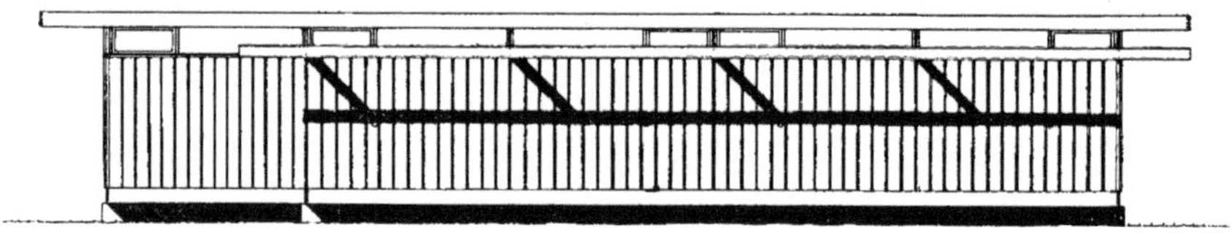

Fig. 10.3: The guest house at Niels Bohr's summerhouse in Tibirke. The seasonal use of the house is expressed in the southern façade: it opens up at summertime, and at wintertime the house is closed like a wooden box (Architect: Vilhelm Wohlert).

Bibliography

Andersen, Hans Skifter, and Mark Vacher, *Sommerhuse i Danmark. Hvem har dem og hvordan bruges de?* 2009 <http://boligforskning.dk/sites/default/files/cbvnotat%20sommerhuse%20_2_.pdf>

Ærø, Thorkild. *Boligpræferencer, Boligvalg og Livsstil*, PhD dissertation (Hørsholm: Danish Building Research Institute, 2002).

Bech-Danielsen, Claus, and Kirsten Gram-Hanssen, 'Second homes – another life in another Suburbia: A study on architectural design and cultural ideals related to Danish summerhouses', *Nordic Journal of Architectural Research* 1/2011 (2012), 7–23.

Dahlkil, Nan, and Flemming Skude, 'Fritidens huse', *Architectura* 20 (1998) 7–38.

Dirckinck-Holmfeld, Kim, and Finn Selmer, *Arkitekternes sommerhuse* (Copenhagen: Danish Architectural Press, 2007).

Gordon, Alastair, *Weekend Utopia. Modern living in the Hamptons* (New York, Princeton Architectural Press, 2001).

Gram-Hanssen, Kirsten, and Claus Bech-Danielsen, 'Sommerhuset – om at komme ud og væk og være sammen'. Paper presented at NSBB, Nordisk Samfundsvidenskabelig By- og Boligforsker konference, Denmark (2009).

Hjarlager, Anne-Marie, *Udviklingsdynamikker i Sommerhussektoren* (Copenhagen: Center for Housing and Welfare, 2009).

Jensen, Jesper Bo, *Parcelhuset i fremtiden – Fakta og Tendenser* (Copenhagen: Bolius, 2008).

Jørgensen, Lisbeth Balslev, *Danmarks Arkitektur. Enfamiliehuset* (Copenhagen: Gyldendal, 1979).

Lützen, Karin, *Byen tæmmes. Kernefamilie, Sociale Reformer og Velgørenhed i 1800-tallets København* (Copenhagen: Hans Reitzels Forlag, 1998).

Selmer, Finn, 'En anden verden', *Arkitektur* DK 6/2005 (2005), 354–61.

Shucksmith, Mark, 'Second Homes: A New Framework for Policy', *Town Planning Review* 54 (1983), 174–93.

Tress, Gunther, 'Development of Second-Home Tourism in Denmark', *Scandinavian Journal of Hospitality and Tourism* (April 2002), 109–22.

Vadstrup, Søren, and Martensen-Larsen, *Sommerhuset* (Copenhagen: Gyldendal, 2008).

ANNIE RING

11 Cool Critique Versus Hot Spectatorship: Jelinek/Haneke's Voyeur around Vienna, a Return

Some months after Elfriede Jelinek won the Nobel Prize for Literature in 2004, a member of the Swedish Academy that awards the prize resigned. The quality for which the prize was granted, Jelinek's skill in 'revealing the absurdity of society's clichés and their subjugating power',[1] was also the criterion upon which Knut Ahnlund resigned, writing to the Svenska Dagbladet that Jelinek's uncompromisingly explicit prose represented no less than 'violent pornography'.[2] As inaccurate as Ahnlund's comment was, his reference to pornography – that most notorious medium of 'making-visible' – nonetheless earns it a critical return in this chapter, which is concerned with the representation of voyeurism in Jelinek's novel of 1983, *Die Klavierspielerin* (*The Piano Teacher*), and in Michael Haneke's prize-winning movie adaptation of the novel, *La Pianiste* (*The Piano Teacher*) of 2001. Taking my lead from episodes where pornography proper features as an object of the attention of their shared protagonist, Erika Kohut, I revisit these core works of recent Austrian literary and visual culture in the company of some of the most respected scholarship on pornography from the 1980s to the present day. My aim here is to demonstrate how pornography's powerful visuals – and the range of responses, both hot and cool, they can elicit – offer a challenging resource for reflection on broader contemporary practices of spectatorship, and of critique.

1 'The Nobel Prize in Literature 2004', *Nobelprize.org* <http://www.nobelprize.org/nobel_prizes/literature/laureates/2004/> accessed 25 June 2013.

2 Luke Harding, 'Nobel winner's work is violent porn, says juror', *The Guardian* (12 October 2005) <http://www.guardian.co.uk/world/2005/oct/12/books.booksnews> accessed 25 June 2013.

In Angela Carter's definition, pornography is 'art with work to do'.[3] One of the most instrumental visual genres, pornography is pornography when it elicits from its viewer a bodily response of pleasure. Though far from pornography – indeed Jelinek has responded to critics that her novel is 'the opposite of pornographic'[4] – the text's key events are harrowing, and include a borderline incestuous mother-daughter relationship, the daughter's genital self-mutilation and a rape. Haneke's visual rendition of her plot undoubtedly moves viewers psychically, and perhaps indeed corporeally. Meanwhile both works include, respectively, narrative descriptions or short clips of pornography. Yet these samplings of pornography, and the texts' other explicit episodes, have work to do that is quite other than that identified by Carter. Soon after the film was released, Jelinek compared herself and Haneke to 'scientists studying the life of insects'.[5] More recently still, Haneke has stated: 'Ich möchte immer das Misstrauen des Zuschauers in das filmisch Gezeigte nähren' [I wish always to nourish the spectator's mistrust in what a film shows].[6] These, then, are artist-scientists, who make visible the taboo phenomena of modernity in order to encourage not pleasurable voyeurism, but the unpleasurable affect that can facilitate a critical agency.

A single woman in her late thirties, teaching at a Vienna conservatoire and living at home with her mother, Professor Erika Kohut presents as both performer and teacher of a cool, distanced critique. The 'souveräne Leistung' [sovereign achievement],[7] which her student Walter Klemmer identifies in her musical performances, also extends into a performance of

3 Cited in Victoria Best and Martin Crowley, *The New Pornographies: Explicit Sex in Recent French Fiction and Film* (New York and Manchester: Manchester University Press, 2007), 5.

4 Elfriede Jelinek, 'Interview: *The Piano Teacher*' <http://www.afc.at/jart/prj3/afc/main.jart?rel=de&reserve-mode=active&content-id=1164272180506&tid=1158748423955&artikel_id=3817> accessed 10 July 2013.

5 Ibid.

6 Karin Schiefer and Michael Haneke, 'Über *Das Weisse Band*', in Karin Schiefer, ed., *Filmgespräche zum Österreichischen Kino* (Vienna: Synema, 2012), 8.

7 Stefan Grissemann, ed., *Die Klavierspielerin: Drehbuch, Gespräche, Essays* (Vienna: Sonderzahl, 2001), 46.

persona that Erika executes: a persona that is deliberately sovereign and separate. Yet the novel's closely focalised third-person narrative, and the film's sustained visuals of Erika's (Isabelle Huppert's) facial expressions and gestures, betray her giving herself over to the consuming pleasures of video pornography and live striptease. These challenging works show Erika's self-styled sovereignty at war with a concurrent drive to participate in the visual and sexual cultures around her. The limits and the potential of such contained collaboration – in particular, Erika's efforts to maintain critical distance while being moved by strong voyeuristic pleasures – are at stake in the following pages. Following Erika, we begin on the streets of Vienna.

Critical Spectatorship: *Die Klavierspielerin*

In Jelinek's novel, Erika represents a lone spy among a mass of consumers who feast on the video and live visual pleasures on offer around the city. Erika's self-image, by contrast, is that of a tightly contoured subject, upon whom only 'das Flaumgewicht der Kunst' [the featherweight of art] may settle.[8] It is claimed that she detests '[d]as Kreatürlich-Körperliche' [the creaturely corporeal],[9] an experience of animal fleshiness that characterises the bodies of others. Yet Erika is concurrently drawn to the attractions of the Prater leisure park, of Vienna's shopping precincts, and of the movie theatres, all sites where the body's creaturely activities are clearly on display. In the first half of the novel, Erika successfully maintains her separation from other human creatures by remaining unmoved by what she sees. At first, she observes the viewing behaviour of visitors to X-rated cinemas, including among them one of her students from the conservatory. Erika's posture of disciplinary supervision in these sites is compatible with the

8 Elfriede Jelinek, *Die Klavierspielerin* (Hamburg: Rowohlt, 2005), 95/*The Piano Teacher*, trans. Joachim Neugroschel (London: Serpent's Tail, 1999), 90.

9 Ibid., 94/90; translation amended.

ethos of the conservatory, whose high culture is reproduced in strict musical forms and educational routines. At their next meeting, Erika punishes (or rewards?) the student she spotted in the cinema with an especially harsh lesson on Bach.

Not only observing the behaviour of others, Erika also turns her gaze upon the technologies of viewing to which the subjects of her surveillance have access. Thus she watches the technical process of a live peepshow in the Turkish area of Vienna, where customers pay to view women stripping under the arches of a railway viaduct: 'Der Münzschlitz wird beschickt, das Fenster klickt, und rosiges Fleisch erscheint' [The coin goes in, the window goes up, and rosy flesh comes out].[10] Erika's observation captures the fleshiness of the *Schlitz* [slit] into which the consumer's coins are *beschickt*, or loaded, all the while maintaining a cool curiosity, one that equally characterises her visit to the adult cinema. Here, Erika does not give herself over to watching a film that, we learn, she has in any case seen before, at an out-of-the-way venue where she would be recognised as a regular customer. Instead her attention lingers upon the city-centre cinema's all-male audience, before focusing on the women actors on screen, whose faces are 'vor Schmerz' and 'vor Freude gezogen' [twisted in pain/in joy], and one who 'zuckt, um kein gutes Ziel zu bieten' [jerks around to avoid offering a good target].[11] Erika observes the participation of certain actresses, and the attempt made by one to separate herself from the performance of which she forms a part.

There is something scholarly in Erika's observations of the city's pornographic processes. Readers learn that: 'sie, sich in die einander verkrallten Leute verbeißend, ergründen will, was nun dahintersteckt' [Erika, absorbed in these ensnarled people, would like to get at the bottom of this business].[12] Thus, through her Professor of the piano, Jelinek pre-empted the analyses of pornography that would develop in the late 1980s out of feminist and film criticism, beginning with Linda Williams' identification of a 'frenzy of the visible' by which hard-core heteroporn revealed sexual acts and experiences

10 Ibid., 52/48.

11 Ibid., 109/106.

12 Ibid., 111/107.

that were lacking from other cinematic genres.[13] In Williams' argument, the extreme screening of the body that hard-core pornography performs is accompanied by another kind of screening, namely concealment. Part of the remit of this Carterian 'art with work to do' is to render invisible the labour behind the images. Accordingly, as Williams stressed in 2004, one of the roles of academic work on pornographic cinema has been to draw attention to 'the choreography of performing and labouring bodies' that the onscreen event of pornography hides from view.[14]

Erika, as proto-pornography theorist, discerns the labour behind the film's hard choreography. Hence her insight in the adult cinema that: 'In den Pornofilmen wird allgemein mehr gearbeitet als im Film über die Welt der Arbeit' [In porno flicks, people work harder than in movies about the workaday world].[15] Articulating the Marxist sensibility of her reading of the pornography, the male actor is described as a 'gelernte Mechaniker, [der] bearbeitet das kaputte Auto, das Werkstück Frau' [trained mechanic, [who] works on the woman, a damaged car].[16] Erika's critical eye captures the unequal distribution of gender roles, as the man works actively upon a feminine body that waits passively to be penetrated or, in the S&M flick on show that evening, struck by the repetitive blows of whip or crop. Erika observes the labouring and gendering of these bodies, and she conjectures that the 'ausgefransten Laienschauspieler' [frazzled amateur actors] must dream of appearing on other screens in quite other genres.[17]

In these passages, Jelinek makes Erika a critical participant in the visual pleasures of pornography and striptease, a voyeur who can maintain an analysis of what she sees. Moreover, this distanced surveillance is revealed as something that Erika has learned at home and transferred onto the city streets. Tellingly, she carries her deceased father's binoculars with her. Meanwhile,

13 Cf. Linda Williams, *Hard Core: Power, Pleasure, and the 'Frenzy of the Visible'* (Berkeley: University of California Press, 1999).

14 Linda Williams, ed., *Porn Studies* (Durham, NC and London: Duke University Press, 2004), 5.

15 Jelinek, *Die Klavierspielerin/The Piano Teacher*, 110/106.

16 Ibid.

17 Ibid., 110/107.

analeptic subchapters uncover a childhood in which adolescent sexual curiosity was suppressed in favour of a strict routine of musical diligence. These flashbacks frame Erika's viewings not only as supervisory missions, but as opportunities to indulge a curiosity prohibited at home. Perhaps therefore, despite their problematic gender politics, pornography and striptease can offer Erika some sexual agency and enjoyment. In his film of the novel, Haneke stresses these hotter aspects, those of curiosity and enjoyment, in Erika's voyeurism. Moreover, in line with Haneke's own critical project, the focus moves in the film to the risks that accompany such affective states.

Mimetic Spectatorship? Haneke's Collaborative Voyeurs

Haneke's French-language film of Jelinek's novel was released in 2001, and awarded the Grand Prix du Jury in Cannes, along with Best Actor Awards for Isabelle Huppert as Erika and Benoît Magimel as Walter. The peepshow episode is absent from the screenplay, and Erika's regular visits to pornography cinemas are condensed into a single visit to an adult store that offers single-occupancy video booths with a choice of pornography clips. The repetitive quality of Erika's city walks is nonetheless captured in a recurrent straight-on angle shot of her exiting the conservatory's glass doors. On the other hand, the element of supervision so prominent in the novel is reduced, so that Erika's espionage around Vienna's streets is transformed into private viewing. Thus in her trip to the adult store, while Erika has an eye upon the other shoppers, it is she who draws more attention, as a rare female visitor to this male-occupied space. Admittedly, Erika's surveillance of live sex from the bushes of the Prater is not removed, but only translated into a tour on foot of a drive-in cinema where she can watch a couple having sex in a car. Yet the film downplays Erika's supervisory role overall, repositioning her instead as a consumer of sexual spectacles. In this way, Haneke can emphasise a concern central to his cinematic project, that of a troublingly mimetic quality to visual consumerism.

Haneke's feature film of 1992, *Benny's Video*, showed the eponymous character killing a young girl after watching a rental video in which a pig is slaughtered. The concern that spectators might mimic the violence that they observe on screens around them aligns Haneke with the second-wave feminist critique of pornography, pioneered by the legal theorist Catharine MacKinnon, who claimed that pornography 'contributes causally to attitudes and behaviors of violence and discrimination'.[18] MacKinnon advocated banning pornographic images in order to prevent their reproduction in the everyday sexual practices of uncritical consumers. Lacking communication with their families and peers, both Benny and Erika seem at especially high risk of uncritical viewing, a behaviour that surely recurs with most frequency where pornography's images and scenarios do not represent a pleasurable entertainment or perverse exception within sexual life, but instead the central, or even only, image of what sex is and can be.

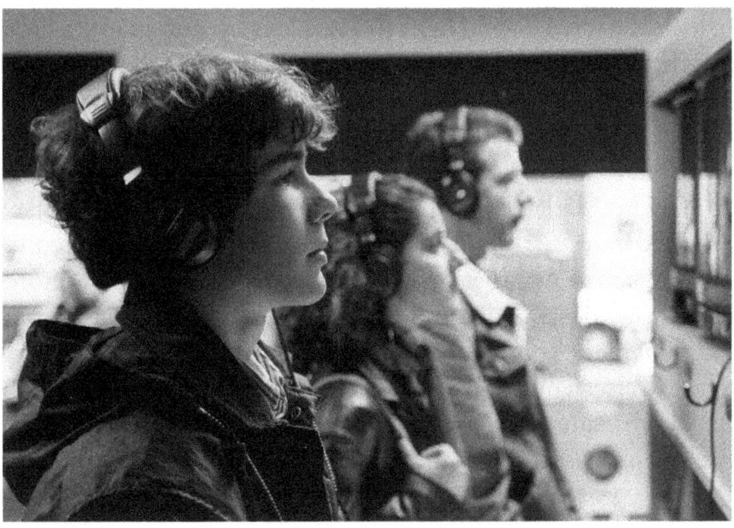

Fig. 11.1: *Benny's Video*: Cool spectatorship.
Credit: WEGAfilm © 1992.

18 Catharine MacKinnon, *Toward a Feminist Theory of the State* (Cambridge, MA: Harvard University Press, 1989), 196.

In 2009, the British film scholar Catherine Wheatley praised *La Pianiste* as the most successful yet of Haneke's film projects that have sought to 'position [...] the spectator as an ethical subject'.[19] She describes the cool detachment with which Erika watches the pornography clip in her video booth. Even as she breathes in the smell from a previous user's discarded tissue, Erika's face is 'impassive, her very reaction an inversion of the excesses of masturbation'.[20] Wheatley's reading finds in Erika a role-model for how critical cinemagoers might approach the images that Haneke screens. Yet Erika's later behaviour suggests that her cool spectatorship – perhaps like the still, calculating gaze of Benny in the earlier film – gives way to certain forms of mimicry of what she has seen.

In her booth, Erika selects a short clip in which a woman performs oral sex on a man. The camera alights three times upon the video screen, taking in the actress's throat as she lies in a prone position, and a partial view of the male genitals. The intervening reverse-shots show Erika's face, onto which the screen's cold light flickers. Her eyes and mouth twitch in what might be impassivity, or perhaps an unconscious immersion in the images on screen. Before she has picked up the tissue, the first reverse-shot shows Erika watching with her lips slightly parted, as if she were viewing with thirsty curiosity an act whose execution she wishes to mimic. Accordingly, for Mark Chapman, Erika watches the pornography 'like a student engaged in research' and later makes use of its 'pedagogical content'.[21] Indeed, Haneke's introduction of this clip, replacing the whipping and stripping scenes described in the novel, enables him to suggest a mimetic reproduction in the episodes taken from the novel wherein Erika performs oral sex on Walter, and to relate these acts to what she has seen in the video booth. All subsequent sex in which Erika consensually engages in the film includes fellatio. This is a slight adaptation when it comes to Erika and

19 Catherine Wheatley, *Michael Haneke's Cinema: The Ethic of the Image* (Oxford: Berghahn, 2009), 9.

20 Ibid., 133.

21 Mark Chapman, '*La Pianiste*: Michael Haneke's Aesthetic of Disavowal', *Bright Lights Film Journal* 74 (2011) <http://brightlightsfilm.com/74/74piano_chapman.php> accessed 22 February 2013.

Walter's first sexual encounter, in the bathroom, where in the novel Erika applies hands, nails, and briefly her teeth to Walter's penis, and only in the later cleaning-cupboard scene engages in sustained oral sex. The film's repetition and extension of oral sex in Erika's live sex-life works to signal that a pornographic 'lesson' has been transmitted.

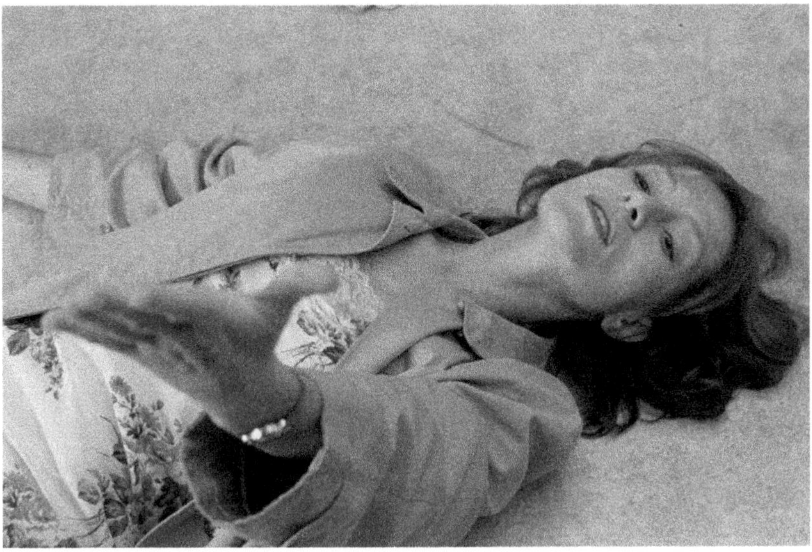

Figure 11.2: *Die Klavierspielerin*. Does Erika mimic the prone pose of the pornography actress?
Credit: WEGAfilm © 2001.

On the other hand, pornography is not the only medium through which Erika learns to conduct herself. More powerful than the television that blares constantly in the Kohuts' apartment is the relationship that plays out in armchairs before it. Haneke's concern with the mimicry of violence continued into *The White Ribbon* of 2009, which depicts a series of violent acts as the results of social learning in pre-World War One rural Germany. Here it is not screen images but sexual abuse and sadistic punishment that are transmitted into the children's treatment of animals, adults, and one another. In this sense, the critical message of Haneke's œuvre surpasses a social-learning theory of screen media, to suggest that violent images do not generate, but instead make visible and perhaps release from latency, behaviours that are already being learned in homes, schools, and churches far from the X-rated cinema. By the same token, the pig-slaughter clip might influence the earlier character Benny's behaviour, but his parents' willingness to help in the concealment of his crime suggests a culture of violence that pre-exists his trip to the video store, and which Benny indicts by finally framing his parents for the original act as well as its cover-up.

Pornography proper occupies only a very brief segment of the running time of *La Pianiste*, and it plays a rather unexceptional role in Erika's routine. Instead, more shock is generated by her sadistic teaching at the conservatoire, her relationships with Walter and her mother, and the acts of self-harm that leave blood running down the side of a bathtub or seeping into her pale clothing. Rather than a central cause, pornography appears here as only one of many symptoms of a sick society – and one that is perhaps less harmful, for its visibility, than other abuses. On the other hand, the repetitions and re-iterations through which mainstream pornography functions, and its resultant affective power, make it a powerful cipher through which both novel and film can depict the precarious balancing acts that their protagonist plays, between positions of domination and submission, and between hot immersion and cool critique.

Critical Repetitions? Pornography's Reproduction and the (Re)turns of Drive

For Sarah Schaschek, pornography's defining generic feature is its seriality, the repetition of the stock sex acts and plot events that keep its users coming back for more.[22] Repetition is also a modernist aesthetic technique, for instance in Jelinek's compelling repetition of verbs of touch and spectatorship

22 Cf. Sarah Schaschek, *Pornography and Seriality: The Culture of Producing Pleasure* (New York: Palgrave, 2014).

such as 'bohren' [boring] and 'sehen' [seeing] that create a furious and heady prose,[23] and the traumatic revisiting of violent or self-destructive acts in her plot. Themes and figures recur across her œuvre, too, including the controlling S/Mother and the Jewish father who survived the Holocaust and was committed to an asylum late in life. Haneke, meanwhile, has made repeated use of actors Ulrich Mühe, Susanne Lothar, and Huppert, who in *Amour* (2012) is shown gazing out of a window beside a piano in a rear-angle shot almost identical to one of Erika at the conservatory. The extreme case of self-referential repetition comes in Haneke's shot-for-shot US remake in 2008 of his suspense thriller *Funny Games* (1997). Such repetitions set Jelinek's readers and Haneke's viewers to tasks of interpretation that contrast starkly with the repeat-enjoyment of the canonical pornography viewer.

Yet, it is in their representation of pornography that both the novel and the film engage in their most telling repetitions. The Erika of the novel visits an adult cinema that she has attended before in order to catch the screening of a film that has been screened before in another cinema across the city. In Haneke's film, though condensed, a kind of repetition can be found in the video clips from which Erika must choose in her booth, which uniformly depict straight couples in acts of either oral or vaginal penetration, the former an act that Erika then chooses to repeat in her own sex life. Such plot and screen repetitions are reflected in the imagery of hoops, loops and ties that structure Erika's S&M fantasy that she communicates in a letter to Walter, imagery that is particularly pronounced in the novel. The destructive loops of experience become visceral metaphor in her request, for instance, that Walter bind her in spools of wet rope that will tighten as they dry, and gag her with the looping shapes of a 'Gummischlauch' [rubber hose] and with 'Strumpfhosen' [panty hose], while wearing a 'Dreieckbadehose' [bikini].[24] The bikini itself would reproduce her male cousin's 'Minibadehose' [mini-swimsuit],[25] a looping construction that barely concealed the body it was designed to bind.

23 Jelinek, *Die Klavierspielerin/The Piano Teacher*, 109–10/105–6.

24 Ibid., 227/223.

25 Ibid., 42/39.

Erika adorns herself with 'Ketten, mit Manschetten, mit Gürteln, mit Schnürungen' [chains, cuffs, belts, cordings],[26] looping props that evoke the circling structure of the repetition-compulsion that Freud discovered in the late years of his practice, and which Žižek updates for his post-Freudian readings of contemporary life as 'the endless repetitive cycle of wandering around in guilt and pain'.[27] The repetition-compulsion's cyclical form offers a geometric template for Erika's evening perambulations, and for the obsessive return, in her instructions to Walter, to the circular props of her subjugation. Yet the post-Freudian reinterpretation, by Žižek and others, of the death drive as an excess of painful-pleasurable *jouissance*, may endow such compulsive repetition with a liberatory potential. *Jouissance* refers to a destructive pleasure that might be read as surpassing the duller repetitions of the pleasure principle as conservative love story. Hence the potential that Jennifer Moorman has located in online queer pornography, to re-appropriate the gestural language and media forms of mainstream heteroporn for a 'diversity of sexual expression' that may effect pornography's resignification.[28]

Admittedly, the pornography that Erika views is not queer, but instead fits Gubar's description during the 1980s debates of most pornography as a 'gender-specific genre produced primarily for men but focused obsessively on the female figure'.[29] However, there is a re-gendering of the gaze in Jelinek/Haneke's vision, one which could ally itself with Gertrud Koch's description of a feminine watching that can identify in pornography's repetitive images a 'flickering [...] shadow world of bodies' that varies from

26 Ibid., 205/202.

27 Slavoj Žižek, *The Ticklish Subject: The Absent Centre of Political Ontology* (London: Verso, 2000), 292.

28 Jennifer Moorman, 'Gay for Pay, Gay For(e)play: The Politics of Taxonomy and Authenticity in LGBTQ Online Porn', in Feona Attwood, ed., *Porn.com: Making Sense of Online Pornography* (New York: Peter Lang, 2010), 155.

29 Susan Gubar, 'Representing Pornography: Feminism, Criticism, and Depictions of Female Violation', in Susan Gubar and Joan Huff, eds, *For Adult Users Only: The Dilemma of Violent Pornography* (Bloomington: Indiana University Press, 1989), 48.

its originally phallic instrumentality.[30] Koch advocates a feminine spectatorship whose political effectiveness in looking anew at the instrumental imagery of pornography is enhanced by a playful, pleasurable element to the viewing encounter. Such an element is invoked by the original French and German titles of the two works considered here, which set up Erika as the *Pianiste* or *Spielerin* for whom play dominates all areas of life.

In her rebuttal of MacKinnon's pro-censorship approach to hard-core pornography, Judith Butler has considered how certain rhetorical gestures that communicate violence might be subject to 'reverse citation [...] the repetition of an originary subordination for another purpose, one whose future is partially open'.[31] On this model, if Erika's spectatorship of pornography does involve the mimesis that Haneke aims to emphasise in his œuvre, her oral-sexual copying can be read not only as a disempowering re-quotation of what she sees on screen. Like Butler's drag queen, or Žižek's pervert, Erika might be role-playing a 'too-literal identification' with a social code of domination and submission,[32] mimicking it so precisely that her performance renders it ridiculous. This would explain Walter's reaction of disgust at her letter. Erika's assertive request has not only surprised him by issuing from her expected feminine role of passivity. It has also exposed a hidden violence that underpins the culture of romance, a violence not usually rendered as explicit as in Erika's letter and in the jarring visual evidence of her S&M prop box.

Trapped in loops of domination at home and work, Erika practices a citational play that may potentially break the death-drive repetitions that it mimics. The risks of such play, however, are great. Walter rejects Erika, and readers learn that 'als Mensch kann er sie jetzt nicht mehr recht sehen' [he can no longer see her as a human being].[33] The rejection is only partial, however, as Walter later carries out certain of the acts that her letter

30 Gertrud Koch, 'On Pornographic Cinema: The Body's Shadow Realm', trans. Jan-Christopher Horak, *Jump Cut* 35 (1990), 28.

31 Judith Butler, *Excitable Speech: A Politics of the Performative* (New York: Routledge, 1997), 37–8.

32 Slavoj Žižek, *The Plague of Fantasies* (London: Verso, 2007), 14.

33 Jelinek, *Die Klavierspielerin/The Piano Teacher*, 218/215.

requested. Erika is unable to call the play to a halt when Walter breaks her nose and ribs and rapes her. It might appear that this is precisely what Erika was asking for. Readers of the novel are aware, however, of the vulnerability and the reverse-request underlying the letter, which she hopes will *not* be taken at its word: 'Bitte tu mir nicht weh, steht unleserlich zwischen den Zeilen' [Please don't hurt me; that's what's written illegibly between the lines].[34] Erika's rape articulates the limits of parodically re-playing the violent codes of conduct around her. It makes clear that, as long as it persists in citing anew the object of its critique, *détournement* remains a further turn of reproduction. Thus in the case of pornographic viewing, even Koch's non-phallic women who watch pornography will continue to encounter ever new iterations of their gender's degradation. The same problem concerns queer pornography's appropriation of heterosexual mainstream genres and gestures. Niels van Dorn has shown how even amateur queer pornography, free to represent whichever bodies and sexual acts it likes, continues to screen conservative scenarios.[35]

A practitioner of controlled *détournement*, Erika feels the limits of critical perversion in her body. For instance, when spying on the couples having sex outdoors, she urgently needs to empty her bladder. Her body is revealed here as one that precisely does not do what its sovereign 'owner' commands it to do, and while she pees against the side of the car in the film version, she is spotted by the objects of her surveillance, who turn their gaze upon her and chase her away. Her attempts to train her piano pupil Walter in her critical S/M project are riskier still. Walter is willing to repeat the cool conduct that Erika has taught him in his piano lessons and the didactic text of the letter: thus before the rape, he observes himself waiting 'ruhig und diszipliniert' [calm and disciplined] outside the Kohuts' apartment,[36] even as inside 'treten ihn seine Sinne in den Leib' [his senses are kicking him in the belly].[37] Erika's most diligent pupil, Walter learns

34 Ibid., 230/226.

35 Cf. Niels van Doorn, 'Keeping it Real: User-Generated Pornography, Gender Reification, and Visual Pleasure', *Convergence* 16 (2010), 411–30.

36 Jelinek, *Die Klavierspielerin/The Piano Teacher*, 265/260.

37 Ibid.

better than she could have imagined, and grievously applies to her the cool sadism that she set out to teach him in her erotic text. Cool conduct has switched here to uncontrolled repetition, and Erika's role turned from that of critical spectator to victim.

Conclusion: Hot Critique

As the Nobel committee identified, Jelinek's intransigent prose reveals patterns of personal and societal domination that would otherwise remain concealed. If her character Erika is a pervert – a sadist, masochist, or voyeur – she is one in millions in her society, whose hidden violence she repeats with a perverse clarity that makes everyday phenomena of sadism and submission visible. This clarity is especially pronounced in Jelinek's novel, where Erika represents a rare and relatively sovereign spectator of her society, safe until she picks a lover who fails to collaborate in her critical play. The Erika of the novel differs from the more collaborative watcher of Haneke's film, whose self-controlled surveillance is overtaken by mimetic reproduction of pornography's forceful images. Yet the works also bear witness to a viewpoint that can shift, as Erika encounters the different sexual spectacles on offer around the city. The ambulant repetition of her spectatorship permits Erika, in her two iterations, to reposition herself in relation to the images and acts that she observes, allowing these to appeal to her at times as objects of cool interest and at others as vehicles for her own drives. Admittedly these drives prevent her from fully resisting a visual medium that she might ethically or politically reject – and from protecting herself when pornography's images are reproduced live in Walter's drive to abuse her.

The problem of critical resistance also pertains to the form of these works of literature and cinema which, if they are to critique the phenomena of mediatised modernity, must also necessarily re-produce them. *Die Klavierspielerin* does not go so far as Jelinek's anti-porno of 1989, *Lust*, whose erotic prose eviscerates the factory-like productions that the author finds in the sexual relationships between men and women. Yet many of Erika's focalised sections, and above all the letter, which occupies thirteen pages, produce an S/M-erotic prose that might yet interpellate a body-response on the part of the reader. Equally, there is no guarantee that the sections of the novel focalised on Walter (which are few but powerful) will not elicit empathy among readers, the presentation of his inner thoughts possibly provoking a reaction in which his actions are perceived as justified by frustration.

Such a risk pertains perhaps more urgently to Haneke's use of diegetic pornographic footage in the video-booth, and the sex and rape scenes in the film. As well as wishing to nourish the suspicious viewer of his films, Haneke has also stated the less gentle aim, that his work 'vergewaltig[e] den Zuschauer zur Selbstständigkeit' [rape the viewer into autonomy],[38] a critical self-reliance that he hopes will arise from the shock effect of the images that he screens. The idea of autonomy resulting from violation is proven tenuous here by his chosen text, as Erika's self-mutilation at the close of both novel and film works at most as a desperate attempt to assert control amidst ongoing heteronomy. Meanwhile it is not clear whether cool camera-work and editing can prevent the rape scene from arousing Haneke's viewers – a risk that is especially urgent in his cinema that has devoted itself to criticising the mimetic danger of behaviours and images. As Best and Crowley have observed in their study of recent French-language texts, the inclusion of explicit sex in fiction and film can potentially breach 'aesthetic boundaries, contaminating its host with its base, bodily instrumentality'.[39] The risk for both novel and film is that their consumers will be contaminated, and begin to collaborate corporeally or phantasmatically with their explicit passages and images.

Yet the inclusion of pornography and other sexual voyeurism in these works itself fulfills a critical function: by including pornography, Jelinek

38 Stefan Grissemann and Michael Omaste, 'Herr Haneke, wo bleibt das Positive? Ein Gespräch mit dem Regisseur', in Alexander Horwarth, ed., *Der Siebente Kontinent: Michael Haneke und seine Filme* (Vienna and Zurich: Europaverlag, 1991), 205.

39 Best and Crowley, *The New Pornographies*, 3.

and Haneke acknowledge it as a vital medium of modernity, one that contemporary literature and cinema must therefore engage if they are to resonate with the reality of mass sensual life – and to critique it. Moreover, in her spectatorship that shifts from sovereignty to immersion, Erika offers a model for a spectatorship that can be critical *and* moved. A further model for such a moved spectatorship is provided once more by contemporary pornography theory. Recording her analysis of a project on unsolicited X-rated email, Susanna Paasonen describes not only the textual operations of the pornographic spam images, their modes of address, pictorial assembly, and inbuilt ideological and plot structures – but also the way in which the images operate upon her as their recipient. Together with the explicit images and passages from the *Piano Teacher* text and film, such insights from the most contemporary studies of pornography exemplify a mode of critique that does not protect or separate itself, but instead consents to be affected by what it encounters, to experience the range of (hot or cool) states that are made available by a text or image, and to allow them to reveal fantasies and behaviours that may be invisibly violent, or indeed counterintuitively pleasurable.

Bibliography

Anon., 'The Nobel Prize in Literature 2004', *Nobelprize.org* <http://www.nobelprize.org/nobel_prizes/literature/laureates/2004/> accessed 25 June 2013.

Best, Victoria, and Martin Crowley, *The New Pornographies: Explicit Sex in Recent French Fiction and Film* (New York and Manchester: Manchester University Press, 2007).

Butler, Judith, *Excitable Speech: A Politics of the Performative* (New York: Routledge, 1997).

Chapman, Mark, '*La Pianiste* Michael Haneke's Aesthetic of Disavowal', *Bright Lights Film Journal* 74 (2011) <http://brightlightsfilm.com/74/74piano_chapman.php> accessed 22 February 2013.

van Doorn, Niels, 'Keeping it Real: User-Generated Pornography, Gender Reification, and Visual Pleasure', *Convergence* 16 (2010), 411–30.

Grissemann, Stefan, ed., *Die Klavierspielerin: Drehbuch, Gespräche, Essays* (Vienna: Sonderzahl, 2001).

Grissemann, Stefan and Michael Omaste, 'Herr Haneke, wo bleibt das Positive? Ein Gespräch mit dem Regisseur', in Alexander Horwarth, ed., *Der Siebente Kontinent: Michael Haneke und seine Filme* (Vienna and Zurich: Europaverlag, 1991), 193–214.

Gubar, Susan, 'Representing Pornography: Feminism, Criticism, and Depictions of Female Violation', in Susan Gubar and Joan Huff, eds, *For Adult Users Only: The Dilemma of Violent Pornography* (Bloomington: Indiana University Press, 1989), 47–67.

Harding, Luke, 'Nobel winner's work is violent porn, says juror', *The Guardian* (12 October 2005) <http://www.guardian.co.uk/world/2005/oct/12/books.booksnews> accessed 25 June 2013.

Jelinek, Elfriede, 'Interview: *The Piano Teacher*' <http://www.afc.at/jart/prj3/afc/main.jart?rel=de&reserve-mode=active&content-id=1164272180506&tid=1158748423955&artikel_id=3817> accessed 10 July 2013.

——, *Die Klavierspielerin* (Hamburg: Rowohlt, 2005).

——, *The Piano Teacher*, trans. Joachim Neugroschel (London: Serpent's Tail, 1999).

Koch, Gertrud, 'On Pornographic Cinema: The Body's Shadow Realm', trans. Jan-Christopher Horak, *Jump Cut* 35 (1990), 17–29.

MacKinnon, Catharine, *Toward a Feminist Theory of the State* (Cambridge, MA: Harvard University Press, 1989).

Moorman, Jennifer, 'Gay for Pay, Gay For(e)play: The Politics of Taxonomy and Authenticity in LGBTQ Online Porn', in Feona Attwood, ed., *Porn.com: Making Sense of Online Pornography* (New York: Peter Lang, 2010), 155–67.

Paasonen, Susanna, 'Strange Bedfellows: Pornography, Affect and Feminist Reading', *Feminist Theory* 8 (2007), 43–57.

Schaschek, Sarah, *Pornography and Seriality: The Culture of Producing Pleasure* (New York: Palgrave, forthcoming 2014).

Schiefer, Karin & Michael Haneke, 'Über *Das Weisse Band*', in Karin Schiefer, ed., *Filmgespräche zum Österreichischen Kino* (Vienna: Synema, 2012), 6–11.

Wheatley, Catherine, *Michael Haneke's Cinema: The Ethic of the Image* (Oxford: Berghahn, 2009).

Williams, Linda, *Hard Core: Power, Pleasure, and the 'Frenzy of the Visible'* (Berkeley and Los Angeles: University of California Press, 1999).

——, ed., *Porn Studies* (Durham and London: Duke University Press, 2004).

Žižek, Slavoj, *The Plague of Fantasies* (London: Verso, 2007).

——, *The Ticklish Subject: The Absent Centre of Political Ontology* (London: Verso, 2000).

DEVIKA SHARMA

12 Visions of Punishment: On Susan Crile's Abu Ghraib Drawings*

A decade after their publication, why should we keep looking at the infamous torture images from the Abu Ghraib prison outside Baghdad? One reason to keep looking, analysing and discussing these images is that they may help us grasp central aspects of contemporary American penal culture, insofar as they provide insights into conditions not only for prisoners in American war prisons abroad, but for the more than two million people who are incarcerated in the US as well. The Abu Ghraib prison certainly differed significantly from state and federal prison systems within the US, not least because of an entirely different and complex jurisdiction, and its specificity should therefore not be ignored. Yet, as has been discussed by several commentators and socio-legal scholars in the wake of the Abu Ghraib scandal, the torture conveyed in the digital snapshots that became public seemed conditioned by a wider penal discourse developed in concurrence with correctional contexts within the United States.[1] Torture is evidently central to these images in terms of what they depict as well as in terms of

* Portions of this article first appeared in my book (in Danish) *Amerikanske Fængselsbilleder. Kunst, kultur og indespærring i samtidens USA* (Copenhagen: Tiderne Skifter, 2011), 105–35.

1 Michelle Brown, '"Setting the Conditions" for Abu Ghraib: The Prison Nation Abroad', *American Quarterly* 57/3 (2005); Allen Feldman, 'On the Actuarial Gaze: From 9/11 to Abu Ghraib', *Cultural Studies* 19/2 (2005); Judith Greene, 'From Abu Ghraib to America: Examining Our Harsh Prison Culture', *Ideas for an Open Society* 4/1 (2004); Mark Danner, *Torture and Truth: America, Abu Ghraib, and the War on Terror* (New York: New York Review Books, 2004). As for more general discussions of the particular 'Americanness' of the culture of humiliation and voyeurism exposed by the photos see Susan Sontag, 'Regarding the Torture of Others', *New York Times*

their very production and distribution. As journalist Mark Danner has suggested, even the act of taking the pictures served as a kind of torture, in the sense that the snapshots were visual vehicles for a multiplication in time and space of the shame and humiliation involved in the acts of torture themselves.[2] But central to the Abu Ghraib photos is, at the same time, a certain *non-exceptional*, non-covert, and visually highly dramatised culture of punishment, the same culture according to which the domestic prison system is organised in the US.

In Abu Ghraib, the prison guard was no unseen yet seeing person in a central surveillance position. Instead, the guards actively took part in a form of punishment sustained by shaming, degradation, and visual dramatisation. To align my argument with Michel Foucault's history of punishment, we could say that in Abu Ghraib the paradigmatic panoptic institution, the prison, proved hospitable to non-panoptic, theatrical practices of punishment. Not only did the guards locate themselves squarely within the photographic gaze, the distribution of the photos among fellow soldiers, family, and friends likewise effectively reversed the fundamental idea of the panopticon: as a result of this wide distribution, it was no longer a case of the few observing the many, but of the many observing the few. Accordingly, the power playing itself out in and through these images differed in various ways from the discrete power of discipline analysed by Foucault in *Discipline and Punish* (1975).

The visual dramatisation of punishment, as well as the production and publication of shame so crucial to the photos and the affective situations they convey, is central to contemporary American punishment. The current focus on afflicting shame is manifest in practices such as chain gangs, zebra-striped uniforms, and public databases of convicts, and moreover, recent years have seen a resurgence of what we may think of as *scarlet letter sentencing* in the guise of so-called *shaming penalties*. Over the last fifteen years, state courts have thus experimented with

(23 May 2004); and Slavoj Žižek, 'Move the Underground: What's Wrong with Fundamentalism?' 2005. <www.lacan.com> accessed 17 October 2013.

2 Danner, *Torture and Truth*, 19, 23.

imposing shame penalties for violations such as drunk driving, domestic violence, burglary and drug possession, by sentencing felons to wearing clothing stating their crimes, post signs announcing their convictions, or otherwise engage in humiliating rituals. In Oregon, a convicted sex offender was ordered to post signs beside his house and car saying 'Dangerous Sex Offender: No Children Allowed'.[3] In a plea bargain in Pennsylvania, a woman and her adult daughter were ordered to stand outside the courthouse holding signs reading 'I stole from a nine year-old girl on her birthday! Don't steal or this could happen to you!'[4] While such penalties are clearly meant as deterrents and as expressions of the moral values of the community, legal scholars and philosophers such as Martha Nussbaum and Jeffrey Abramson have poignantly argued that these alternative correctional practices risk becoming rituals of public humiliation, dehumanisation, and mob justice, not to mention the arbitrariness involved in the current legal administration of shame.[5] What is significant with regard to these strands of the current visual culture of punishment is that in contrast to the discrete surveillance techniques of the panopticon, such shaming penalties punish by virtue of public ridicule and stigmatisation. Here, punishment is not only meted out by the state, but by the humiliating gaze of the public. This gaze cannot

3 Jeffrey Abramson, 'Response to Professor Kahan', *Federal Sentencing Reporter* 12/1 (1999).

4 *Daily Mail* (5 November 2009) <http://www.dailymail.co.uk/news/article-1225561/Women-stole-giftcard-birthday-girl-9-hold-signs-shame-town-centre.html> accessed 17 October 2013.

5 Shaming penalties form part of a more general turn within American penal culture to marginalising and incapacitating individual and collective bodies. During the last three decades the American systems of crime reduction and penal justice have thus undergone a radical transformation, which may be roughly described as a passage from the disciplinary and rehabilitative model of the modern prison analysed by Foucault to a late modern practice of punishment prioritising risk management, safety, vengeance, and simple segregation. For an overview of this generally acknowledged transformation, see David Garland, *The Culture of Control: Crime and Social Order* (Chicago: Chicago University Press, 2001); and David Garland, ed., *Mass Imprisonment: Social Causes and Consequences* (London: Sage Publications, 2001).

be controlled by law, and this, in a sense, is the very essence of this kind of punishment. With the Abu Ghraib photos as radical icons of non-panoptic visual cultures of punishment, we can begin to register a general revival of theatricality in the current US culture of punishment to the extent that the panopticon today co-exists with correctional practices characterised by shaming and spectacle.[6]

Two larger stories, then, converge in these images. On the one hand, we find the story of American torture, the war on terror, and its policies. On the other, we find the story of apparently commonplace contemporary US practices of punishment. Taking as my starting point the American artist Susan Crile's series of pastel drawings and paintings, *Abu Ghraib: Abuse of Power*, my main focus in this chapter will be the precarious bodily states produced by practices of punishment that are profoundly shaming and essentially theatrical. As Judith Butler has pointed out, the Abu Ghraib photos show that in the world of the war prison, some humans qualify as humans, while others do not. According to Butler, these snapshots provide 'evidence that a break from the norm governing the subject of rights has taken place and that something called 'humanity' is at issue here'.[7] What is immediately significant in Susan Crile's interpretation of this universe is that her drawings do not exactly restore integrity to the frail bodies depicted or somehow bring back their humanity as something evident for us to contemplate. Rather, she investigates what the body is like when it has fallen out of the field of the human. In my discussion of this series of drawings, I will also touch upon their relation to the photographic source and to the genre of atrocity photography. Here, my suggestion is that one of the effects of reimagining and interpreting the world of the war prison through the medium of drawing is that these images, and the

6 It could be argued that theatrical elements of correctional practices always co-existed with panoptical surveillance techniques in the United States. For a discussion of the continuation of spectacular punishment, see for instance Brian Jarvis, *Cruel and Unusual: Punishment and US Culture* (London: Pluto Press, 2004).

7 Judith Butler, *Precarious Life: The Powers of Mourning and Violence* (New York: Verso, 2004), 78.

events to which they attest, break away from the fate of serving as emblems of the exceptional.[8]

Chalk

The collected works of Susan Crile fall into two distinct categories. On one side we find the contemplative abstractions that have formed the backbone of Crile's œuvre since the 1970s. This work is characterised by shared formal features borrowed from such diverse sources as patterns on snakeskin, mosaics, Persian carpets, and Italian architecture. From sharp geometrical shapes to more organic forms, we may think of Crile's work as an abstract kind of landscape painting – Crile herself calls her work 'eccentric geometrical abstraction'.[9] On the other side we find four markedly political series of drawings and paintings. In large oil panoramas the *Fires of War* series from the early 1990s depicts burning oil fields in Kuwait during the first Gulf War. The series *9/11* from 2002 is based on snapshots of Manhattan in the wake of the terrorist attack, while the series *In Our Name* (2010–11) examines confinement and abuse in settings such as Guantanamo. In her framing of the images of torture in *Abu Ghraib: Abuse of Power*, Susan Crile has focused primarily on the postures of and relations between the human figures. In several cases, she has eased the subjects out of their contexts, so that several of the drawings are not immediately recognisable as reproductions of the photographic source. Generally, since the direct gaze of the

8 The Abu Ghraib photographs of course by now have their own cultural history, traveling through diverse contexts of analysis and interpretation: art exhibitions, court-martials, critical commentary, popular culture, and research settings. A discussion of the relations between various framings and modes of reception falls outside the scope of this chapter.

9 I interviewed Susan Crile in December 2006, and this particular description of her own work dates from here. See my article (in Danish) 'Torturtegninger: Susan Criles manøvrer med mennesker' KRITIK 40/183 (2007), 129–36.

guards has been obstructed by Crile's cropping of the image, the sense of triumph and merriment is also absent from these drawings, if not similarly excised from our simultaneous memory of the photos themselves.

In *The Body in Pain* (1987), Elaine Scarry describes the various ways in which physical torture undoes the world of the prisoner. During torture, Scarry suggests, the prisoner becomes invisible to himself, because his idea of *being* a self falls apart. Simultaneously, the prisoner is in a sense invisible to the torturer, who does not *recognise* the humanity and suffering of the prisoner. When the correlates of the self are undone in this way, the body on the contrary becomes critically present, as Scarry notes. In the case of torture, it is precisely the goal of the torturer to render the body of the prisoner urgently present; to make the body 'emphatically and crushingly present by destroying it'.[10] In the process of torture the distance separating prisoner and torturer has become the greatest distance that can separate two human beings, and in this process of distancing, the prisoner is rendered, in Scarry's term, 'ghostly'.

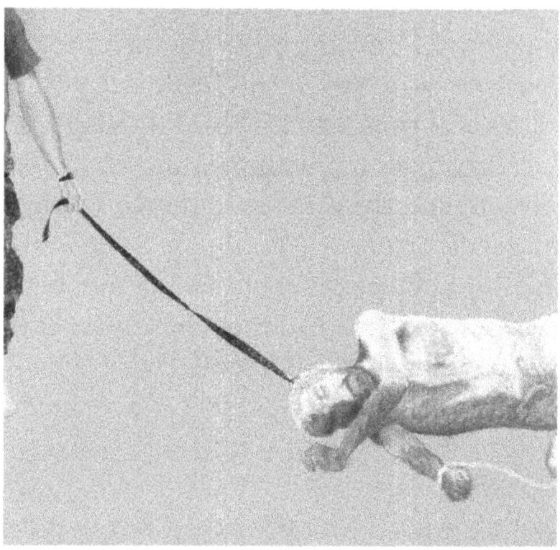

Fig. 12.1: Susan Crile. *Private England Dragging a Prisoner on a Leash*, 2005. White chalk, pastel and charcoal on paper. Credit: Susan Crile.

10 Elaine Scarry, *The Body in Pain: The Making and Unmaking of the World* (New York: Oxford University Press, 1987), 49.

Elaine Scarry's description of the paradoxical status of the body subjected to torture also sucessfully captures two of the most striking features of Susan Crile's Abu Ghraib drawings. Firstly, the impression that the prisoner has become partly invisible and ghost-like; secondly, the impression that the distance between the two types of human figures has become unbridgeable. Thus, in Crile's interpretation of the world of the Abu Ghraib prison, there exist two types of human bodies. On one hand we find a naked, skinny, and fragile body, and, on the other, we find a body protected by boots, gloves, and several layers of clothing, a body that seems heavy and massive. What these two bodily types have in common, however, is that they are exactly *types*: these bodies hold no evident personality, and the few faces not turned away or hidden behind hoods figure not as mirrors of the soul, but as surfaces fleetingly registering fear or even death.

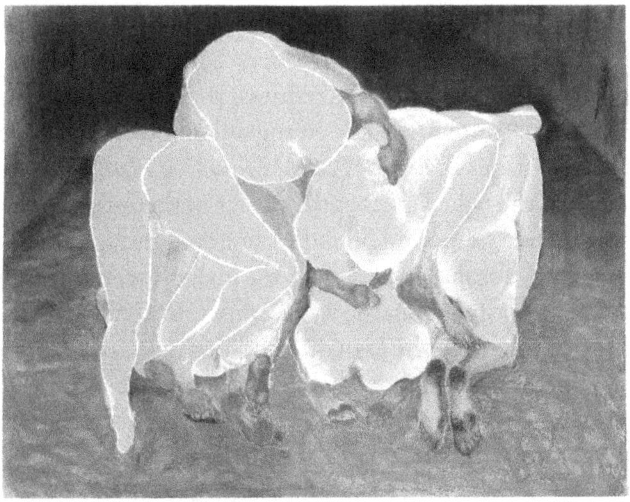

Fig. 12.2: Susan Crile. *Arranged: Naked Mound of Flesh*, 2005. Pastel and white chalk on paper. Credit: Susan Crile.

The white, chalk-like figure is the most distinctive element of these drawings. Here, the outline of the body of the prisoner is sketched out, but the material qualities of the chalk indicate that the limits of the body are fragile and might in fact be wiped out, as if softening up the prisoner implies softening up the self and its limits. In a catalogue for one of her exhibitions, Crile herself mentions that, to her, the white chalk symbolises among other things the figures mantled in ashes fleeing the World Trade Center after the terrorist attack in 2001.[11] From this point of view, the white chalk establishes a visual connection between these two emblematic moments in the war on terror; the terrorist attack and the Abu Ghraib scandal. At the same time, the white prisoners in Crile's drawings call forth associations with a legal and political phenomenon also related to the war on terror, namely the so-called *ghost detainees*. This term signals, of course, that these prisoners have become politically and legally invisible.

The tension between an acutely present body and a destroyed body – the tension which for Scarry characterises a situation of torture – is made tangible in the chalky qualities of the prisoner's bodies. On the one hand, the whiteness emphasises the outline of the body by making it stand out radiantly from the background of the picture. The whiteness thus accentuates the ecstatic presence of the prisoners' bodies *as* bodies, an insistent presence derived also from their nakedness. But on the other hand, these white bodies seem, simultaneously, strangely unbodily, incorporeal. Thus if we look at the image *Arranged: Naked Mound of Flesh*, it is striking how badly the flesh of the title describes the object of the image. Of course, the picture does represent a mound of bodies, but even though these bodies are absolutely exposed, absolutely unprivate, the image does not readily connote flesh. Rather, the bodies appear dry and empty. In Crile's work, the chalk simply resists representing the carnality and fleshiness of the human body.

As a means of rendering of the human figure, we often associate the white line of chalk with a crime scene and with the forensic framing of a body no longer present. The chalky figures in Crile's tableaux are utterly reduced to their bodies, which therefore appear strangely incorporeal. At a crime scene, a surface has taken the place of the body once framed by the white line of chalk; similarly, in several of Crile's pictures we see bits of surface and space through the partly transparent figure, so that the limit

11 Susan Crile, *Abu Ghraib: Abuse of Power*. Exhibition catalogue (New York: The Bertha and Karl Leubsdorf Art Gallery, 2006).

between interior and exterior collapses. The prisoners' bodies in Crile's drawings attest to precisely such a bodily vacancy. These bodies are not exactly dead, but they are nevertheless somehow absent – from themselves, from our common repertoire of images of the human body. With regard to our normal ideas of the carnal body, Crile's drawings seem to suggest that the human body shelters a profound un-bodiliness, which shows exactly when the body has been reduced to sheer body.

Few images in the Abu Ghraib series present us with an impression of space like that in *Arranged: Naked Mound of Flesh*. What is significant here is the fact that Crile does not use this spatial effect in order to indicate a space for human activity. Rather, the depth in the image signals a vacuum effect, the lines leading into a condensed darkness, the space appearing to be a void. The spatial effect in the image thus connotes a kind of black hole, as if the prison space mirrored the legal void engulfing the prisoners.

Theatres of Shame

In an essay titled 'Neighbors and Other Monsters' (2005), Slavoj Žižek has discussed the relation between self-exposure and shame in a way that seems helpful when trying to understand the implications of the current revival of theatricality in US penal culture. We are currently witnessing, Žižek suggests, a tragicomic reversal of Jeremy Bentham's plans for (and George Orwell's later concerns about) a panoptic society: 'Today, anxiety arises from the prospect of *not* being exposed to the Other's gaze all the time, so that the subject needs the camera's gaze as a kind of ontological guarantee of his or her being,' Žižek writes.[12] For instance, according to Žižek, the contemporary ubiquitous and shameless use of webcams signals

12 Slavoj Žižek, 'Neighbors and Other Monsters', in Slavoj Žižek, Eric L. Santner and Kenneth Reinhard, eds, *Neighbors: Three Inquiries in Political Theology* (Chicago: The University of Chicago Press, 2005), 180.

that today we share a constant need to feel a gaze confirm our existence as subjects. As one of various possible shameless subject positions, Žižek mentions what he calls 'the perverse sadist'. The perverse sadist is not primarily interested in causing the other physical harm. Rather, the sadist's aim is to make the other ashamed of enjoying the situation forced upon him or her. The sadist makes himself an instrument, so to speak, for the other's unbearable realisation of his or her enjoyment of humiliation.

In the context of the Abu Ghraib images, I find Žižek's account relevant not as a possible psychology of the torturers, but as a micro-sociology of shame and shamelessness. Regarding the photos from Abu Ghraib, his observations are productive in at least two ways. Firstly, the photos confirm that, as we have already noted, the basic anti-panoptic structure evident in the perpetual self-exposure emphasised by Žižek has indeed engaged the exemplary panoptic institution, the prison. Secondly, the photographs suggest that theatrical self-exposure might invite, as its reflection, a theatrical exposure of others, as implied by Žižek's account of perverse sadism. In these photos we see that the effort of the guards to appear on a stage and before a public presupposes a theatrical framing of the other. Starting from these photos, one can then distinguish between two forms of perverse sadism, which are here joined in a kind of alliance. One form is active and, in a sense, shameless, while the other form is passive and shameful.

Elaine Scarry notes that during torture, the body of the prisoner is transformed into a weapon against the prisoner himself. The senses, the needs of the body, and its ways of touching itself: all of these bodily capacities are turned against the prisoner's own body.[13] If we place Scarry's description of the transformation of a body into a self-destructive weapon in tandem with Žižek's account of perverse sadism, we have, I would like to suggest here, a framework for understanding the complex mixture of shame, shamelessness, and torture characterising the events in Abu Ghraib as they are represented by the notorious photographs and interpreted in Crile's drawings. For if a scene of torture constitutes a purely antagonistic relation between two persons, as Scarry suggests, we see that here this

13 Scarry, *The Body in Pain*, 48.

antagonistic relation is meant to be internalised, through shaming, in the prisoner himself. Thus, in this sense, the forced masturbation in Crile's *In Line to Perform* shows a line of bodies becoming their own enemies: the forced sexual acts depicted in both photographs and drawings indicate that the prisoner's potential enjoyment of the humiliating acts were central to the torture.

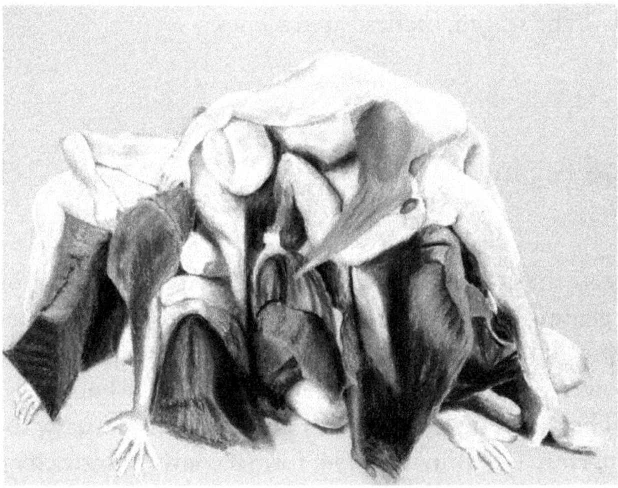

Fig. 12.3: Susan Crile. *Naked, Piled, Hooded Prisoners, Flesh to Flesh*, 2005. White chalk, pastel and charcoal on paper. Credit: Susan Crile.

In these drawings, Susan Crile has paid more attention to the conditions of the fragile figures than to the soldiers' posing for the camera. Therefore we do not see Charles Graner and Sabrina Harman with their arms around each other in the background of *Naked, Piled, Hooded Prisoners, Flesh to Flesh*. In other words, Crile has focused on the passive and shameful side of perverse sadism. When looking at this painting, the theatrical aspect of the arrangement is striking: the pile of bodies looks like a group of performers in one last clever constellation before the fall of the curtain. In drawings such as *Arranged: Naked Mound of Flesh* and *Naked, Piled, Hooded Prisoners*, the fact that Crile has omitted the guards and their cheery gaze into the camera provides the viewer with the sense that the pile of bodies is somehow a staged arrangement in honour of him or her. In this way, Crile's framing is also a de-framing – reconfiguring the structures of seeing by erasing the direct gaze into the camera – opening up new ways of interpreting these images while simultaneously raising questions about our, the viewers', part in the alliance between shame and shamelessness performed before us. If Crile has in several instances withheld the guards' right to be seen, to be included in the field of vision, she has not spared her viewers the sense of complicity in the staged, orchestrated scenes.

Seeing and Feeling

We can situate the graphic snapshots from the Abu Ghraib prison squarely within the genre of war trophy photography. As Hilary Roberts notes of this genre, trophy photographs are 'generated by photographers of a dominant military power, often without official sanction or the knowledge of those depicted. The initial purpose of such photographs is usually to serve as a form of souvenir'.[14] Within the wider formal context of atrocity photography, a recurrent critical discussion considers the horror and grief provoked, or not provoked, by atrocity photography and the actions to which such affective response may or may not give rise. Taking up Susan Sontag's well-known skepticism regarding the power of images to do more than move us in passing, Judith Butler suggests in *Frames of War* that responding affectively to images of the suffering of others may very well carry critical and political significance. Without responsiveness, no sense of responsibility; without a sense of responsibility, no political change, Butler argues. But responsiveness to the suffering of others requires that these others appear as potential subjects of mourning for us, the viewers of the image. And

14 Hilary Roberts, 'War Trophy Photographs: Proof or Pornography?', in Geoffrey Batchen, Mick Gidley, Nancy K. Miller and Jay Prosser, eds, *Picturing Atrocity: Photography in Crises* (London: Reaktion Books, 2012), 202.

'*grievability*' as an assigned quality is tacitly regulated by both the actual discursive and visual frames used to represent suffering, and by more general cultural norms. As a function of such interpretive frames, grievability is glaringly unevenly distributed globally, and a contemporary critique of power ought therefore, Butler suggests, to invest itself in rendering visible the interpretive frames through which certain lives and the suffering of these human lives appear irrelevant.

What is at stake then in the reconstructions and cropping of Susan Crile's interpretation of the atmosphere of the war prison? What do we do with what we see here; where do we store it? Peggy Phelan suggests that the Abu Ghraib photographs are traumatic in the sense that they both document and produce a certain blindness, a failure of seeing.[15] But Crile's drawings are not exactly traumatic, they do not travel by way of shock, and if they call on us to act, their call is not primarily of a familiarly horrifying, sickening, and outrageous kind. Does this mean that these drawings fail to render the fragile bodies grievable, and that they thus present the viewer with a morally indifferent framing of suffering? My suggestion is that the remarkable affective flatness of these tableaux in comparison with the photographic snapshots that inspire them – the slowing and cooling down of the horror, shamelessness, and pain produced by both the softness of the chalk and pastel on paper and the cropping of the images – is indeed an invitation to look and feel differently, but not indifferently. The effect of this cooling down is not, I would argue, one of unresponsiveness or ethical apathy. On the contrary, the affective work initiated by Crile's drawings is to make us feel the framework through which distant, suffering bodies are most often made to appear irrelevant to the Western media consumer. Here, since the triumphant gaze of the guards is in several cases erased, we do not get to *see* this interpretive framework in action. Instead we get to *feel* the chilling effects of the typically dehumanising framing of distant others and their apparently irrelevant pain, because we are deprived of the

15 Peggy Phelan, 'Atrocity and Action: The Performative Force of the Abu Ghraib Photographs', in Geoffrey Batchen, Mick Gidley, Nancy K. Miller and Jay Prosser, eds, *Picturing Atrocity: Photography in Crises* (London: Reaktion Books, 2012), 55.

opportunity to feel the strong pangs of shock, compassion, and indignation that we have come to expect from our confrontation with images of atrocity, and from these prison motifs in particular. Crile's Abu Ghraib drawings do not draw heavily on our morally suitable feelings. Instead of turning away in horror, we are invited to stay with the event and its reflections. This aesthetic strategy, of making the images *bearable*, is not, however, a strategy of acceptance, of glossing over or covering up. It is, on the contrary, a strategy that effectively prevents these images from becoming emblems of the exceptional.

Literary scholar Sianne Ngai has coined the term 'noncathartic aesthetics' in order to describe art and literature that is about or produces small, unprestigious feelings, or seems to withstand the emotional outlet of its viewers and readers as well as of its subjects.[16] According to Ngai, such ignoble, amoral or merely hesitant feelings share a diagnostic potential in so far as they testify to social experiences of obstructed agency and passivity. As I understand them, Susan Crile's Abu Ghraib drawings are exactly non-cathartic in their aesthetic configuration, and if their hesitance to evoke strong emotions testifies to experiences of obstructed agency and unwelcome passivity, it is to experiences of passivity on behalf of both these painfully typified, exposed, and exploited bodies and on behalf of ourselves, the viewers of the images. In other words, this is not an aesthetic that pacifies, but rather one that actively interprets the conjunction of several experiences of passivity, however asymmetrical these experiences are.

Perhaps the passivity and obstructed agency interpreted here is also that of atrocity photography itself as a mode of thinking and sensing the world. Crile herself seems to suggest as much, writing in a catalogue text that:

> Photos have become such a part of the fast expendable information age we live in that they have created a glut, where the sheer mass and volume of photographic images have made the eye the most overused sense. Drawing, the use of chalk and charcoal, the texture of paper, speaks to our sense of touch. Touch slows down the hungry and impatient appetite of the eye [...].[17]

16 Sianne Ngai, *Ugly Feelings* (Cambridge, MA: Harvard University Press, 2005).

17 Crile, *Abu Ghraib: Abuse of Power*, 7.

Slowing down our way of looking seems to me an accurate description of the effect of *Abu Ghraib: Abuse of Power*. This is not a question of posing drawing against photography, touching against seeing, or thinking against feeling, but of thinking with the senses, slowly touching that which is seen. But most importantly, perhaps, this less impatient aesthetic moves us beyond the questions of 'What do I feel?' and 'Do I feel enough?' These drawings are not 'powerful' in the sense of lifting us out of ourselves in confrontation with spectacular trauma and exception. Yet their slowness and their foregrounding of passivity invite new structures of looking at a familiar scene of suffering, structures producing in turn alternative responses, alternative senses of responsibility.

Circulating Bodies and Images

In a study of political violence in Northern Ireland, media scholar Allen Feldman shows how marginalised, invisible groups in a given society may serve as vehicles for distributing messages and values central to that particular society. Feldman illustrates this point by describing two photographs. The first depicts one of the Parisian sandwich men described by Walter Benjamin as emblematic of the spectacle of commodification. The sandwich men walked the streets of Paris in the 1930s bearing advertising boards mounted on the fronts and backs of their bodies. Ironically, Feldman notes, the sandwich men were often homeless or in other ways living on the absolute margins of the capitalist economy they simultaneously embodied and boosted. The second photo from the same period depicts a German Jew marching between two policemen. His pants and shoes have been taken from him; instead he carries a placard announcing that he is Jewish and that he has no complaints about the Nazis.[18] Both of these

18 Allen Feldman, *Formations of Violence: The Narrative of the Body and Political Terror in Northern Ireland* (Chicago: The University of Chicago Press, 1991), 7.

images, Feldman argues, show ways in which the marginalised body can serve as spectacular medium. The sandwich man and the placard-bearing Jew act as political 'texts', ideological screens permitting 'the state and the crowd to exchange messages on the reciprocal constitution of otherness and community. The body as a social type and not an individual is being walked through these streets'.[19]

Feldman's description of the ways in which marginalised bodies may circulate as vehicles for communicating and disseminating important societal messages is a fruitful framework for understanding the dramatic element of both the Abu Ghraib photos and the current use of shaming penalties in the United States. In both cases, the risk-bearing bodies are visually marked as political texts announcing their own unworthiness, even their inhumanity. These bodies are marginalised, yet they are not politically superfluous. Rather, the shameful and publicly circulated penal bodies act as performers of a distinct political landscape; they become spatial units of power. And the power that these bodies are at once subjected to and manifest is not a discretely disciplining power, but a power whose devices include shame, visual drama and entertainment.

Susan Crile's interpretation of the Abu Ghraib universe suggests that shaming acts of torture committed there profoundly affected the body's bodiliness. The human body became a typified, transparent body. At once present and absent, the body in these images seems empty, just as the law subjecting the body seemed empty. Here, the 'bodylessness' of the body corresponds to the lawlessness of law. Moreover, Crile's drawings invite ways of responding to these acts that follow extended routes into our affective infrastructures by producing new structures of seeing suffering.

In the late modern instances of scarlet letter punishment, the offender is realised as criminal not only in the eyes of the public, but by the eyes of the public. As the photos from Abu Ghraib made painfully clear, we need to examine more closely the relationship between law and visual practices of shaming that are thought to be effective exactly because they cannot be controlled by the law. In Abu Ghraib a handful of lower rank soldiers

19 Feldman, *Formations of Violence*, 8.

acted as instruments of punishment. With the re-emergence of shaming penalties and other forms of punishment based on theatres of humiliation, the performer of punishment in the contemporary US has to some extent become identical with the ordinary American citizen.

Bibliography

Abramson, Jeffrey, 'Response to Professor Kahan', *Federal Sentencing Reporter* 12/1 (1999).

Butler, Judith, *Frames of War* (New York: Verso, 2009).

——, *Precarious Life: The Powers of Mourning and Violence* (New York: Verso, 2004).

Crile, Susan, *Abu Ghraib: Abuse of Power*. Exhibition catalogue (New York: The Bertha and Karl Leubsdorf Art Gallery, 2006).

Danner, Mark, *Torture and Truth: America, Abu Ghraib, and the War on Terror* (New York: New York Review Books, 2004).

Feldman, Allen, *Formations of Violence: The Narrative of the Body and Political Terror in Northern Ireland* (Chicago: The University of Chicago Press, 1991).

Foucault, Michel, *The Culture of Control: Crime and Social Order in Contemporary Society* (Chicago: Chicago University Press, 2001).

——, *Discipline and Punish: The Birth of the Prison* [1975] (New York: Random House, 1995).

Garland, David, ed., *Mass Imprisonment: Social Causes and Consequences* (London: Sage Publications, 2001).

Greene, Judith, 'From Abu Ghraib to America: Examining Our Harsh Prison Culture', *Ideas for an Open Society* 4/1 (2004), 2–4.

Ngai, Sianne, *Ugly Feelings* (Cambridge, MA: Harvard University Press, 2005).

Nussbaum, Martha, *Hiding from Humanity: Disgust, Shame, and the Law* (Princeton, NJ: Princeton University Press, 2004).

Phelan, Peggy, 'Atrocity and Action: The Performative Force of the Abu Ghraib Photographs', in Geoffrey Batchen, Mick Gidley, Nancy K. Miller and Jay Prosser, eds, *Picturing Atrocity: Photography in Crises* (London: Reaktion Books, 2012).

Roberts, Hilary, 'War Trophy Photographs: Proof or Pornography?', in Geoffrey Batchen, Mick Gidley, Nancy K. Miller and Jay Prosser, eds, *Picturing Atrocity:Photography in Crises* (London: Reaktion Books, 2012).

Scarry, Elaine, *The Body in Pain: The Making and Unmaking of the World* (New York: Oxford University Press, 1987).

Sharma, Devika, *Amerikanske fængselsbilleder. Kunst, kultur og indespærring i samtidens USA* (Copenhagen: Tiderne skifter, 2011).

——, 'Torturtegninger. Susan Criles manøvrer med mennesker', *KRITIK* 40/183 (2007), 129–36.

Sontag, Susan, 'Regarding the Torture of Others', *New York Times* (23 May 2004).

Žižek, Slavoj, 'Move the Underground: What's Wrong with Fundamentalism?', 2005 <http://www.lacan.com> accessed 22 May 2014.

——, 'Neighbors and Other Monsters', in Slavoj Žižek, Eric L. Santner and Kenneth Reinhard, eds, *The Neighbor: Three Inquiries in Political Theology* (Chicago: The University of Chicago Press, 2005).

PART IV

Screens, Cameras and Surveillance

zURBS
Prelude IV

At every point the city offers surprises to your view [...] 'Happy the man who has Phyllis before his eyes each day and who never ceases seeing the things it contains,' you cry regret at having to leave [...] But it so happens that, instead, you must stay in Phyllis and spend the rest of your days there. Soon the city fades before your eyes [...]. Many are the cities like Phyllis, which elude the gaze of all, except the man who catches them by surprise.

—ITALO CALVINO, *Invisible Cities*

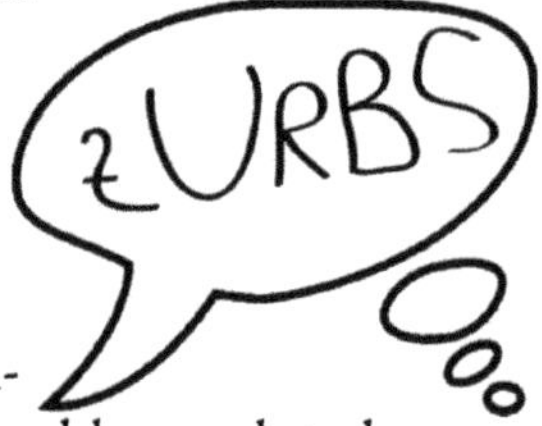

Watching and interpreting our city can be seen as a means of transforming and reconfiguring it: they are actions that could confirm or modify the invisible distribution of the sensible. Therefore urban settings should enable people to be active as interpreters, storytellers, and translators, rather than merely being passive observers. Urban settings should open up to allow people to appropriate the story of the city, and to make their own story of it. However, this way of looking should not be confused with seeing only what one chooses to see, or with identifying what one sees with the truth or a given reality. Rather we should remain

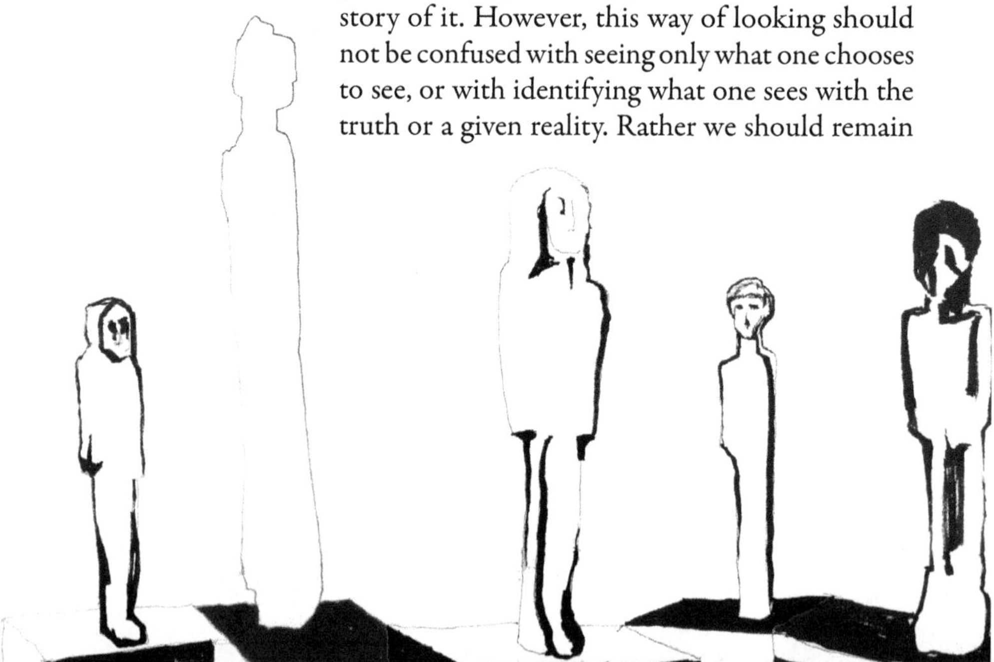

HAPPY THE MAN WHO NEVER CEASES SEEING THE THINGS THE CITY CONTAINS

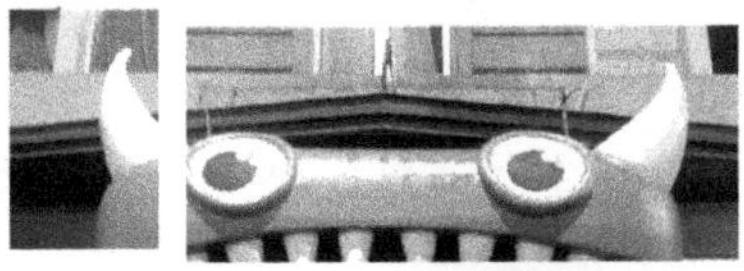

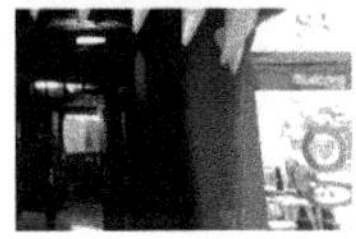

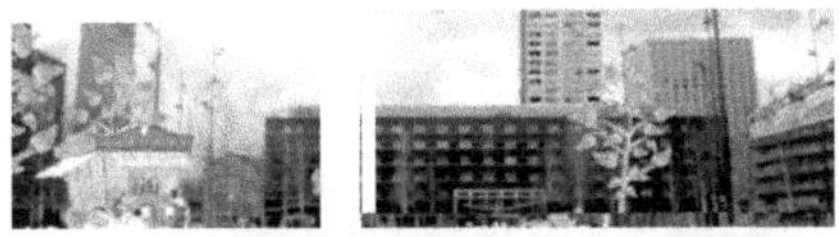

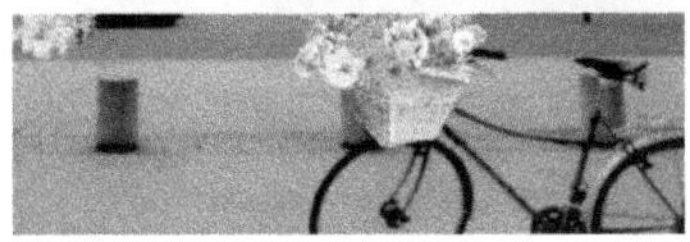

open to the gaze, acknowledging that it is not about seeing things as they are, but seeing things as they could be.

This way of seeing the city may make room for our co-producing and appropriating new spatial realities, informing an understanding of urban space as defined by a radical openness productive of diverse and multiple outcomes, rather than as one fixed and given urban reality.

Space then, could open up and tell you its unexpected stories: the chewed pieces of gum so frequently spit out in the street are joining forces to become a reverse universe of gum-stars. The cobblestones hope to play a role in the next big revolution. The surveillance company and TV shop are best friends, since they have been trading images in nursery. Traffic signs are proud of being travel itineraries and journals. The kiosk passionately studies art magazines and strives to become a museum of colourful and tasty little things. The shopping mall hates being a luxury prison for wealthy criminals – it would rather be a zoo.

How would your surroundings change if you looked at them differently?

SUSANNE WIGORTS YNGVESSON

13 To See the World as It Appears: Vision, the Gaze and the Camera as Technological Eye

> My basic view of things is – not to have a basic view of things. From having been exceedingly dogmatic, my views on life have gradually dissolved. They don't exist any longer ...
>
> —INGMAR BERGMAN[1]

> [B]ut Thou, O Lord [...] didst turn me round towards myself, taking me from behind my back where I had placed me, unwilling to observe myself; and setting me before my face [...] And if I sought to turn mine eye from off myself, and trustedst me before my eyes, that I might find out mine iniquity, and hate it.
>
> —ST AUGUSTINE[2]

The Vision and the Gaze

A Brief Introduction

In this chapter, my aim is to take a phenomenological point of view toward the 'hard core' usage of surveillance technology, and particularly the ocularcentric ones. In so doing, my analysis will demonstrate aspects of seeing

1 Stig Björkman, ed., *Bergman on Bergman. Interviews with Ingmar Bergman* (New York: Da Capo P. 1993), 17.

2 St Augustine, *The Confessions of St. Augustine* (New York: Signet Classics, 2001), VIII.7.16.

and technology that are interdisciplinary, and contribute to the complexity of the subject of what it is to see, and what happens in different sorts of relations when we see, either through the camera lens, through our own eyes, or with an 'inner eye'. Maurice Merleau-Ponty's thoughts on visibility and invisibility are particularly fascinating and useful to me in this investigation, since he strives to dismantle the distinction between subject and object, a problem Jean-Paul Sartre and other Western philosophers have struggled with since René Descartes.

In this chapter, Merleau-Ponty's arguments about seeing as a mode of perception will be discussed and related to the camera as a viewing apparatus. The questions I address will include that of whether we should differentiate between surveillant and non-surveillant modes of vision. If so, what is the basis of this distinction? Does the apparatus enhance perception in any way, or is it rather a question of the intentionality behind its use? How does 'the flesh', in Merleau-Ponty's sense of the concept, influence the experience of the relation between the apparatus and our bodies? Moreover, how may our understanding of an 'open' visibility versus a 'categorised' visibility influence our understanding of surveillance?

I concentrate on two main subjects: first, a mode of seeing between physical people in a room as they appear despite the camera; second, as they appear through the camera lens to us as observers – categorised as objects or as people who 'come out of the picture'.

A New Reality?

In one of his most famous films, *Fanny and Alexander* (1982), Ingmar Bergman deals with the question of seeing and with objects and people being illuminated or exposed by their environments and social surroundings. One scene in particular illustrates the way in which something invisible becomes visible, seen not with the biological eye, but in a kind of vision of something real yet hidden. Oscar Ekdahl, the father of Fanny and Alexander, sneaks into the children's bedroom on Christmas Eve, a few hours before the church service on Christmas morning. He asks the children what they are doing, explaining that he had heard their whispering from the next room. He learns that Alexander has been exploring the cinematograph, a magic camera, which projects a moving picture onto the wall. Although picture and camera seem unconnected, there is an invisible link that joins machine, light and projection.

Ekdahl begins to tell a story about an unprepossessing chair – rickety, wooden and faded. 'This is a chair,' he declares, 'but not just any old chair.' He lifts it onto the table and shines the lamp on it. The children are curious. 'But don't be deceived,' he continues: 'This is the most valuable chair in the world.' As their father whispers, the children gather round and he asks 'Do you see the mysterious light shining from this little chair?', 'Why does it shine in the dark?' 'It's a secret. Whoever betrays it will die', the father explains. The children nods and swear to keep the secret.

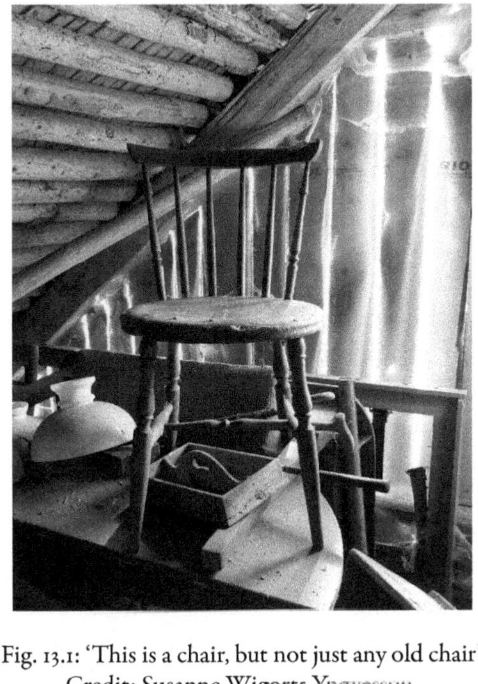

Fig. 13.1: 'This is a chair, but not just any old chair'.
Credit: Susanne Wigorts Yngvesson.

Bergman moves the camera towards the chair from an angle below the table, and then, as the story is related, moves into a close-up on the children's faces, as if to suggest that the truth can be seen reflected in the eyes of those who believe what they are being told. The father explains to the children how this chair once upon a time belonged to an empress of China. After spending her entire life on that particular chair, she died and was buried, still sitting on the chair. For 2,000 years, she sat in her burial chamber until some thieves came and gave her a blow that reduced her to dust. The chair is made of a metal available only in China at a depth of 59,000 metres. It has a special aura that makes it glow in the dark. 'Now the most precious chair in the world belongs to you,' whispers the father, and gently lifts the chair from the table. While he is telling the story, the chair becomes the most valuable chair in the world from the children's point of view, as it does for the film's audience.

While the father speaks in the film a new vision of what is perceived as reality is induced. The words contribute to an image of seeing the objects in a new way. This new vision 'happens' both within the film as a story but also for the audience watching that scenery behind the curtain of the camera lens.

Phenomenology as a Way to Discover Realities

I have begun with this example of the visible and the invisible because it raises issues both of what is seen and how one sees. My aims in this chapter are, firstly, to identify the inner logic of seeing, using the ontology and dialectic of perception developed by Merleau-Ponty, and, secondly, to investigate how seeing as a categorisation of objects, that is human beings, can be related to CCTV-surveillance. With regard to this second aim, my goal is to relate an inner logic of seeing to CCTV-cameras as a categorisation of seeing or watching. By 'inner logic', I mean a system of interpretation, a grammar of understanding – in this case, what can be called the 'culture' of surveillance. I make a distinction between seeing and watching, where seeing is considered a 'broader form of' perception than watching, i.e., watching is to look or search for something particular.

My principal philosophical source is Merleau-Ponty's last work, *The Visible and the Invisible*. Although incomplete at the time of his death in 1961, it is regarded as Merleau-Ponty's most important work after *Phenomenology of Perception* (1945). There is some debate among philosophers about the relation between these two works, particularly about the issue of phenomenology versus ontology in Merleau-Ponty's philosophy. I take Merleau-Ponty to be arguing for phenomenology as well as ontology. Merleau-Ponty's relevance for the present context thus lies in his arguments about perception as a phenomenological experience. Using the concept of 'situation', Merleau-Ponty develops a method of critical analysis – the 'hermeneutics of suspicion' – that seeks to expose the way in which abstract principles, that is, self-deception, attempt to cover the realities of the world. I will use this method to reveal what I understand to be the inner logic of surveillance. Further, Merleau-Ponty did not think of philosophy as a science in the sense of a positivist one, since he regarded positivism as a science inherited from a Cartesian dichotomy that he wanted to leave behind. Rather, he worked with a theory which involved him in the process; as 'the set of questions wherein he who questions is himself implicated by the question'.[3] Using this critical philosophical method, I shall seek to highlight different interpretations of the practices of seeing and watching as these relate to surveillance.

As noted, my principal source for this investigation is *The Visible and the Invisible*, not least because of its author's particular interest in the phenomenology of vision, a term he uses in his later writings in preference to the word 'perception' so central to his earlier work.[4] Although I will consider perception mainly as 'seeing', Merleau-Ponty investigates perception in relation to all senses. However, I argue, that in *The Visible and the Invisible*, he explores seeing and vision largely to the exclusion of other sensory experiences.

3 Maurice Merleau-Ponty, *The Visible and the Invisible* (Evanston: Northwestern University Press, 1968), 27.

4 Merold Westphal, 'Situation and Suspicion in the Thought of Merleau-Ponty: The Question of Phenomenology and Politics', in Galen A. Johnson, ed., *Ontology and Alterity in Merleau-Ponty* (Evanston Illinois: Northwestern University Press, 1990), 168.

To See the World as It Appears

To appear in the world or in front of another person – to see the world appear – is a relational act. The meeting between myself and the world is relational, whether I see the world as either a physical manifestation or in my imagination. To appear is not the same as *to be*. Seeing is not just a particular act of seeing or being seen by another. Everything visible is in principle open to a stranger's gaze, but as Merleau-Ponty argues, the *perception* of others is not placed in concrete bodies or particular spaces. This argument recalls George Berkeley's (1685–1753) idea about distance which cannot be seen, only experienced, since distance is a matter of objects being close or far away. But to understand distance only through the eye, without the experience, is impossible. We could know distance 'no more than we would pretend to judge a man's thoughts by his pronouncing words we had never heard before'.[5]

Merleau-Ponty describes the process of seeing as a birth: 'The other is born from my side'.[6] Seeing as a pre-conscious act is not an act that occurs in front of me as a perception. It is happening in every moment that *I* exist, just as Sartre proposes that the self is an ongoing project in the world. It is not alien to me, but comes from an experience of exteriority. Following Sartre, Merleau-Ponty argues that this experience reveals the world outside me to be nothingness, since 'I do not *know* the others, in the strong sense that I *know* myself',[7] and since in the eyes of others I must seem to be the same kind of nothingness, what Merleau-Ponty calls 'negintuition'. This is to say, nothingness inexists wherever being is. Such 'negintuition' is related to Sartre's 'négatité', that is, negativity as an integral part of the structure of human activities. Contrary to Sartre, however, Merleau-Ponty argues that we, as humans, are not just the sum of our choices, but also 'something else', 'an other who is not a thing'.[8]

5 George Berkeley, 'An Essay Towards a New Theory of Vision' [1709], in *Berkeley's Philosophical Writings* (New York, London: Collier Books, 1965, §2, 20.

6 Maurice Merleau-Ponty, *The Visible and the Invisible*, 59.

7 Ibid., 61.

8 Ibid., 61.

Merleau-Ponty's metaphor of being born from my side comes from the account in Genesis of how God created woman using Adam's rib, for whom she becomes 'bone of my bones and flesh of my flesh'.[9] They are one, but not the same: similar but different. Human beings come from nothingness into being, into the world that God, according to Genesis, created through His Word and vision, albeit not as a process of cause and effect. God sees what God creates, and God also sees what still does not exist: nothingness. Nothingness and Being belong together and are not opposites; rather they belong, side by side, to the same Being. The *ex nihilo*-argument has been interpreted as a dualistic world-view, but Merleau-Ponty opens up another possibility, one that, as I will show, is also relevant for my argument here.

Merleau-Ponty proposes a four-part system of relations between the self and others in the world through a phenomenological vision: 'my being for me, my being for the other, the being for itself of another, and his being for me'. These aspects of vision are relations of Being and Nothingness. In many ways his schema corresponds to Sartre's distinction between three categories of being – being in-itself, being for-itself, and being for-others – although Merleau-Ponty argues that the main experience of the gaze of the Other is not shame, but an 'intersection of my universe with that of another'.[10]

Both Sartre and Merleau-Ponty talk about the awareness of perception in different situations, but their interpretations differ in a strong sense with regard to the intentions and effect of the gaze. Sartre argues that to perceive is to *look at*, and to be the object of the gaze is to be conscious of *being looked at*. The effect of that gaze is to be aware that I am vulnerable. The gaze causes an effect that is not in the first instance that of seeing an object, but an awareness of one's situatedness in the world: 'I can not in any case escape from – *I am seen*'.[11] For Merleau-Ponty the gaze and visualisation represent not a frightening closedness, but openness. Indeed, he argues that it is 'through other eyes we are for ourselves fully visible'.[12] Sartre's theory of

9 Genesis 2:23.

10 Maurice Merleau-Ponty, *The Visible and the Invisible*, 80.

11 Jean-Paul Sartre, *Being and Nothingness. An Essay on Phenomenological Ontology* [1943], (London, New York: Routledge, 2003), 282.

12 Maurice Merleau-Ponty, *The Visible and the Invisible*, 143.

the gaze has been interpreted as 'a narcissistic fear of splitting the body from the self'. This argument is developed from a revolt against an omniscient God whom Sartre recognises as having an 'absolute look', a look that is not negotiable.[13] Merleau-Ponty has criticised Sartre on this point; for Merleau-Ponty, the gaze can be open or closed, yet it is not so distinctly invested with power as it is for Sartre. Another way to describe the difference between their theories of the gaze, suggested by Martin Jay, would be to define Merleau-Ponty's standpoint as aletheic, that is, a condition of unclosedness that implies sincerity, and not something passively unfinished, and Sartre's as 'hostile to any redemptive notion of vision' and an 'ocularphobia'.[14]

A relation can, according to Merleau-Ponty, be described as open or closed. The philosophical question is not whether the world as it appears exists or not, 'we are asking what it is for it to exist'.[15] Perception starts with a pre-consciousness of what we identify when we perceive, a pre-consciousness that is not separate from human reality but part of it. This is not the opposite of consciousness or awareness; it is a part of the same world yet different. Pre-consciousness confers upon these perceptions a degree of doubt. The purpose of doubt here is to remain open to the gaze, to an awareness that we do not have to identify perceptions with things 'as they are', or 'the constructed significations whose terminal product one supposes the world and the things to be'. In shutting down the gaze, we categorise the world and make it into an object without a 'horizon of brute being and of brute mind'.[16]

The paradox of doubt and of thinking the negative is that we cannot say that the negative is for itself, isolated from positive being. Sartre, too, identifies two aspects of human reality, the in-itself and the for-itself, as constituting the ontological root of human ambiguity. Every given factual moment manifests our situation, in Sartre's sense of the situation as the only thing that gives humans freedom. This aspect of freedom for Sartre include also experiences of something transcendent, which is an experience

13 Martin Jay, *Downcast Eyes. The Denigration of Vision in Twentieth-Century French Thought* (Berkeley, London: University of California Press, 1994), 277.

14 Ibid., 275f.

15 Maurice Merleau-Ponty, *The Visible and the Invisible*, 96.

16 Ibid., 97.

of the fluid and dynamic for-itself. For Sartre, the consequence of this ambiguity is freedom. For Merleau-Ponty, doubt itself is the answer, a flow of constant change which means that nothing perceived can ever be completed or fully explained:

> For it is quite obvious that there is pure negation only in principle and that the existent For Itself is encumbered with a body, which is not outside if it is not inside, which intervenes between the For Itself and itself.[17]

The process of perceiving or seeing with an 'open' gaze is somehow to realise or experience that there is no direct contradiction between the objects I see and the I who sees them. Things 'attract my look' in the relation, and thereby reveal their complicity.[18] Here, in the world as it appears, Merleau-Ponty also regards the imaginary as 'not an absolute unobservable' because it *is* incarnated in the world.[19] What he describes as an imaginary incarnated in the world as it appears can be interpreted as a process of creating from bodily experience – or bodily experience as a creation of the imagination.

However, Merleau-Ponty is not an immaterialist or dualist in a Cartesian sense. For him, the imaginary world is incarnated in the flesh of the world. It is an experience of belonging to the same system of being. In its incarnation, the flesh of the world appears as thing, world, and history. In the relation between me and the other, the gaze is predetermined in the body to be a 'mirror of me as I am of him'; seeing another involves not two images but 'one sole image'. This means, for example, that awareness of myself and distance from the other is not contradictory; rather, each is the reverse of the other.[20] Merleau-Ponty argues for a holistic perception of the world, in contrast to a Cartesian dualistic and objectivist worldview that he believes has for centuries distorted the possibilities of perceiving world as it is. And yet, within this holistic worldview, Merleau-Ponty offers different interpretations of the functions of visions and bodily experiences. I will return to these in due course.

17 Ibid., 68.
18 Ibid., 76.
19 Ibid., 77.
20 Ibid., 82–3.

To close one's vision is an act of totalisation. The starting point of pre-existing experience must instead be a belief in a 'there is': '[O]ne does not arouse being from nothingness, *ex nihilo*; one starts with an ontological relief where one can never say that the ground be nothing'.[21] The open gaze is dialectical and does not completely identify itself with itself, since dialectical thought is always 'proceeding toward the opposite term'.[22] Dialectical thought, according to Merleau-Ponty, is not philosophy; rather, the process is one of intuitive, self-reflexive critical thinking, an awareness that any *thesis* about that which is identified is a form of idealisation. Being is 'bound wholes where signification never is except in tendency'.[23]

One of Merleau-Ponty's central ideas is that the body is a kind of consciousness. There is nothing between my body and the flesh: 'Inside and outside are inseparable. The world is wholly inside and I am wholly outside myself'.[24] Pace the Cartesian view of consciousness as structured, there is no subject and object. *It* or *you* belong to the same world as *I*. This idea prompts an interesting question about me and my relation to the camera (or any technology that surrounds me): what is happening in the relation between the *I* and the camera? Is the camera also a part of my flesh?

The Camera as Technological Eye: Seeing the World Through a Camera Lens

Allow me to return briefly to the scene in *Fanny and Alexander* described earlier, in order to think about the possibility of eternity in the film. Through the camera lens, and the frame it produces, people are fixed. The single camera cannot, any more than a single human eye, see the whole picture or

21 Ibid., 88.

22 Ibid., 90.

23 Ibid., 94.

24 Maurice Merleau-Ponty, *Phenomenology of Perception* [1945], (London, New York: Routledge, 2002), 407.

the world behind the camera, that is, the world that the director (or God, or someone in a position of surveillance) chooses not to show. Once people are depicted, and the film is developed from the negative (assuming it is not a digital film), they are stuck in a repetitive status quo – or, in the case of CCTV, framed but unseen, unless there is a particular reason to show them. Oskar can tell his story as many times as the audience is willing to hear and see it, while the people outside the frame grow up, have children, and die. Allan Edwall, the actor who plays the father, died in 1997, but those still alive in the world 'outside' the film can see him in the film in a state of a technological eternity. He actually also dies in the picture as Oskar, but show himself to the children several times from 'the other side'. We see Allan Edwall in the film even after 1997, and yet it is not he, he has left behind a shell within the frame of an *I* – a shell of Being and Nothingness.

The Gaze as Producer of Shame or Integration into the World?

What is happening with the perceptions the film produces? We see the people filmed; they do not see us; they are there, yet they are elsewhere: 'films have the *appeal* of a presence and of a proximity', to quote film theorist Christian Metz, who provides a phenomenological interpretation of films and perception.[25] Metz makes a fascinating point about how we experience movement as something real, more so than a still photograph: 'Movement is insubstantial. We see it, but it cannot be touched, which is why it cannot encompass two degrees of phenomenological reality, the "real" and the copy.'[26]

Another possible clue lies in the perspective offered by Merleau-Ponty and Sartre on the process of seeing as always entailing alienation of the viewer from the one being seen – in Sartre's terminology, alienation of the subject from the object. Such alienation forms part of the gaze, with or without the camera. In his critique of Sartre, Merleau-Ponty refers to emptiness and the exterior of the self. For Merleau-Ponty, however, such

25 Christian Metz, *Film Language. A Semiotics of the Cinema* (Chicago: The University of Chicago Press), 4.

26 Ibid., 8.

emptiness is not frightening but a kind of being, which integrates me into the world. It is a basic condition of being seen in the world:

> I have to be this emptiness, to make it be in the world, I take up again on my own account my body and my situation and the other's gaze which I see posed on this exterior that is me. For me there is no activity and presence of another; there is on my part the experience of a passivity and of an alienation which I recognize concern me, because, being nothing, I have to be my situation. [...] [T]he other's gaze which suddenly congeals me adds to my universe no new dimension – it only confirms for me an inclusion in being which I knew from within.[27]

Merleau-Ponty agrees that shame can be an effect of the gaze, but argues there must be more to it. Where Sartre understands the gaze as a polarisation between subject and object, Merleau-Ponty regards it as entailing the possibility of an intersubjective phenomenon: the experience of being one among many in the world sharing the same experience. The criterion for an experience to be intersubjective is that it has to be symmetrical, but since self-consciousness is asymmetrical, Merleau-Ponty cannot understand this experience other than as two sides of one and same phenomenon.[28] For Merleau-Ponty, this intersubjective condition would not change if we added a camera or another apparatus to the perception, any more than spectacles influence the intersubjectivity of the gaze; in this relation, the apparatus is not aware of itself. Instead it gives us, in Metz's words, 'the feeling that we are witnessing an almost real spectacle'.[29] The camera does not see; rather, it is used for seeing or watching – an apparatus is a prosthesis in an Aristotelian sense; as an extension of the experiences and capabilities of the body.

It is the intention of the camera user that influences the symmetry or asymmetry of the perception. In a very immediate sense, using a camera can influence the relation in a situation in which someone holds the camera in front of them, since their eyes are hidden from the other who is, so to speak, 'veiled' by the camera – and the awareness of being photographed will make you perform in front of it. This is in line with the way the French literary theorist and philosopher Roland Barthes describes his own experience of

27 Maurice Merleau-Ponty, *The Visible and the Invisible*, 70–1.

28 Maurice Merleau-Ponty, *Phenomenology of Perception*, 394.

29 Christian Metz, *Film Language*, 5.

the awareness of being photographed, as a kind of theft or transformation beyond his control:

> I feel myself observed by the lens, everything changes: I constitute myself in the process of 'posing', I instantaneously make another body for myself, I transform myself in advance into an image. This transformation is an active one: I feel that the Photograph creates my body or mortifies it, according to its caprice.[30]

Sartre relates a similar experience from his childhood when he performed in front of the camera or under the gaze of his parents. Faced by a (real or imaginary) camera, he recalls, 'I would stop moving, I would lean forward, I was a runner getting set, the little birdie about to spring from the camera'. But his sense of the absolute look was not restricted to the camera. It was primarily a sense of power so strong as to warrant description as a panoptic experience, that is, an experience of being subject to an array of gazes: 'I had learned to see myself through their [his parents'] eyes [...] When they were not present, they left their gaze behind, and it mingled with the light'.[31]

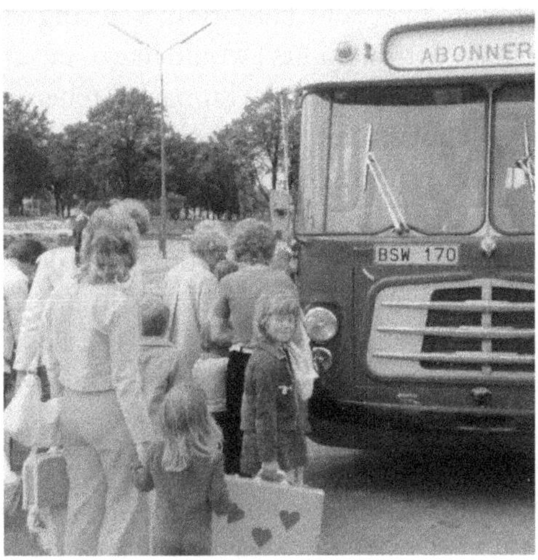

Fig. 13.2: Performing in front of the camera? On my way to summer camp. Credit: Sig-Britt Wigortsson.

30 Roland Barthes, *Camera Lucida* (London: Vintage Classics, 2000), 10–11.

31 Quoted in Martin Jay, *Downcast Eyes*, 279.

Frightening or otherwise, what Sartre here describes is also an experience of being categorised, either as an individual or as a member of a particular group. At family gatherings, the camera is used to store memories of that particular moment. When made aware of the camera, people try to look relaxed; they perform for it. In contrast, in the first instance at least, closed-circuit cameras are located in a public space either to record criminal actions or to register surroundings or people. Their purpose is to foster a sense of public safety as well as to collect evidence, should a criminal act occur. What we see through the camera lens is thus related to whatever we are already looking for. The camera is often used for categorising the visible. In his account of the genealogy of punishment, Michel Foucault confirms this conclusion: 'A glance at the new art of punishing clearly reveals the supersession of the punitive semio-technique by a new politics of the body.'[32]

Once an individual is registered by a surveillance system there can be reason to investigate the intentions of an action, because such intentions will categorise one's perception of what is being seen. One can describe it, with Merleau-Ponty, as an act of totalisation, a closing act of one's vision. This is one of the main critical points I would like to raise when it comes to the technological eye or the gaze of the human watcher: it is programmed to see something particular, and therefore it closes off vision. The moral and ethical consequences of this could mean that people and bodies will be dominated by the inner logic of surveillance. Some examples here might be ID cards, check-points, passports, and the social control they add. To prove to the world that your identity is what you proclaim it to be, you need an ID. The particular card, though, is just the tip of the iceberg as it also reveals other data about you. David Lyon describes the relationship between screen and identification as 'stretched screens'; screens that look beyond the surface of the body and its movements.[33]

This kind of seeing already has an order or a 'political technology'. It is mapped. The surveillor or originator of the gaze has decided what to

32 Michel Foucault, *Discipline and Punish. The Birth of the Prison* [1977], (New York: Vintage Books, 1995), 103.

33 David Lyon, *Identifying Citizens. ID Cards as Surveillance* (Cambridge: Polity Press, 2009), 85.

see, and thus the political technology of surveillance will close the gaze for the 'invisible' or the unexpected objects of vision. Such 'closed' categorised viewing is in some respects similar to the point of view of a fundamentalist in that it is a way of seeing only what one chooses to see. Indeed, it is also fundamentalist in how the viewer identifies what she sees with the truth 'as it is' – identifying that which is being observed with a perceived 'reality'. It is a perception that diminishes the world as 'what it is for it to exist'.[34]

The Camera and the Creational Act

It is not the camera in the first instance that constructs a particular way of seeing; it is, rather, the situatedness of the viewer that enables or prevents sight, and guides it towards a particular way of seeing that is related to a political technology or an inner logic of photographing or surveillance. Moreover, the camera is also not neutral in its intent. The design of the apparatuses and the places they are installed or used speak a political language of semiotic and cultural awareness.

However, as the scene from *Fanny and Alexander* suggests, the camera can also reveal a world that initially seems to be ordinary or mapped. In this creative act, both words and believers make possible a vision of the chair as the most valuable object in the world. 'The movie spectator is absorbed, not by "has been there", but by a sense of "There it is"'.[35] Merleau-Ponty elaborates this idea in his phenomenology of perception and seeing, as a process of dispensing with categories and fundamentalist approaches:

> The analytic of Being and Nothingness is the seer who forgets that he has a body and that what he sees is always beneath what he sees, who tries to force the passage toward pure being and pure nothingness by installing himself in pure vision, who makes himself a visionary, but who is thrown back to his own opacity as a seer and to the depth of being.[36]

34 Maurice Merleau-Ponty, *The Visible and the Invisible*, 96.

35 Christian Metz, *Film Language*, 6.

36 Maurice Merleau-Ponty, *The Visible and the Invisible*, 77.

Merleau-Ponty describes a kind of awareness of seeing, that is, an action of placing oneself 'above' or 'outside' the perceptional experience. He also compares this kind of seeing with madness: I am exploring the world itself even as I enter a world that 'do[es] not coexist without me'.[37] Even though it is a process of change, we do not leave ourselves (even if this were possible) but, rather, install ourselves 'in pure vision'. We become an active part of the seeing; we become visionaries even as we learn that our faculty of vision cannot be mastered. It is being and nothingness at one and the same time – not as opposites but in parallel.

The camera is similar to the biological eye, or God's eye, in the matter of perspective, since both are able to behold the world 'from behind'. Regardless of where a perceiver is situated, or where she is present in the world, she can be said to be 'inviting' the environment to interact. She meets the world she perceives as it is presented to her: 'The world is always around me and never simply before me'; and 'It is true that I see what I do see only from a certain angle, and I concede that a spectator differently placed sees what I can only conjecture'.[38] Merleau-Ponty does not discuss the gaze of the camera or the possibility of considering an apparatus as a perceiver, but I believe his claims about perspective can reasonably be applied to the camera, since we are here considering the world and all that is in it as a part of all of our perceptions, though it would be wrong to say that Merleau-Ponty ascribes consciousness to an apparatus. It is rather a kind of phenomenological prosthesis that brings the world to the person, who is both perceiver and sender of perceptions. Metz touches on this point when he writes about the spectator and the film as a medium:

> The spectator is indeed 'disconnected' from the real world, but he must then connect to something else and accomplish a 'transference' of reality, involving a whole affective, perceptual, and intellective *activity*, which can be sparked only by a spectacle resembling at least slightly the spectacle of reality.[39]

37 Ibid., 75.

38 Maurice Merleau-Ponty, *Phenomenology of Perception*, 394.

39 Christian Metz, *Film Language*, 11–2.

Like the eye, the camera is often calibrated to particular objects where some things are seen and others are hidden from our conscious vision. Indeed, Merleau-Ponty argues that perceptions of the world are subject to certain preconditions, such as the accessibility of objects moving within the space of the subject's perceptual field. Not everything is possible in perception, because the subject needs a relation to the world that is congruent with its capacities in order to interact with it.[40] This interpretation of perception is both similar to and different from the eye's and the camera's 'gaze'. The first of these differences is that the camera can enlarge details invisible to the human eye; the second is that it can freeze particular 'settings' for later study, which then form part of a new perception; the third is that the gaze of the camera stays at the surface and it shows something with a kind of distance to the object, while the human eye has the option of engaging the gaze. Unlike the Aristotelian, Merleau-Ponty does not use the notion of teleology. One reason for this, I suspect, is that he proposes a holistic worldview, independent of the object-subject dichotomy or any view of events as an interaction of cause and effect, despite treating perceptions as comprehensible and sometimes, if not always, conditioned by intentionality.

This raises the question of whether the camera creates new realities in the world itself. Do vampires exist? Of course they do: we see them on the screen. Do terrorists exist? Yes, of course: there is a category of human beings who act against states and people in a particular fashion and are thus by definition 'terrorists'. The surveillance system has a particular grammar of security and terrorism (and several other subjects) that are categorised according to particular objects and rules. But if no one ever saw or experienced vampires or terrorists, would they nonetheless exist? Rather than simply replying in the negative, our response must take into account what a thing is when it is *visible*. As for objects made visible, are the procedures for the visibility a moral matter of responsibility? In this sense, the camera is an apparatus that not only observes the world, but enables a person or a data programme to create perceptions of visions and fantasies, such that

40 Komarine Romdenh-Romluc, *Merleau-Ponty and Phenomenology of Perception* (London, New York: Routledge, 2011), 85.

they become parts of our perceptions of the world as it appears. The camera makes it possible to extend the visible through the archive of the 'here and now'. In this sense, surveillance techniques are not merely an issue of registration and observation, they are an act of constructive creation, directed by the inner logic of surveillance.

Bibliography

Augustine, *The Confessions of St. Augustine*, trans. Edward Bouverie Pusey (New York: Signet Classics, 2001).

Barthes, Roland, *Camera Lucida*, trans. Richard Howard (London: Vintage Classics, 2000).

Berkeley, George, 'An Essay Towards a New Theory of Vision' [1709], in *Berkeley's Philosophical Writings* (New York, London: Collier Books, 1965).

Björkman, Stig, ed., *Bergman on Bergman. Interviews with Ingmar Bergman* (New York: Da Capo P. 1993).

Foucault, Michel, *Discipline and Punish. The Birth of the Prison* [1977], trans. Alan Sheridan (New York: Vintage Books, 1995).

Jay, Martin, *Downcast Eyes. The Denigration of Vision in Twentieth-Century French Thought* (Berkeley, London: University of California Press, 1994).

Lyon, David, *Identifying Citizens. ID Cards as Surveillance* (Cambridge: Polity Press, 2009).

Merleau-Ponty, Maurice, *Phenomenology of Perception* [1945], trans. Colin Smith (London, New York: Routledge, 2002).

——, *The Visible and the Invisible*, trans. Alphonso Lingis (Evanston: Northwestern University Press, 1968).

Metz, Christian, *Film Language. A Semiotics of the Cinema*, trans. Michael Taylor (Chicago: The University of Chicago Press).

Romdenh-Romluc, Komarine, *Merleau-Ponty and Phenomenology of Perception* (London, New York: Routledge, 2011).

Sartre, Jean-Paul, *Being and Nothingness. An essay on phenomenological ontology* [1943], trans. Hazel E. Barnes (London, New York: Routledge, 2003).

Westphal, Merold, 'Situation and Suspicion in the Thought of Merleau-Ponty: The Question of Phenomenology and Politics', in Galen A. Johnson, ed., *Ontology and Alterity in Merleau-Ponty* (Evanston, IL: Northwestern University Press, 1990).

DAVID MURAKAMI WOOD

14 Vanishing Surveillance: Ghost-Hunting in the Ubiquitous Surveillance Society[1]

The twenty-first century is seeing a rapid transformation of our societies into pervasive or ambient ubiquitous surveillance societies. Ubiquitous surveillance ('ubisurv') depends on 'ubiquitous computing ('ubicomp'). The gradual infiltration of computing and communications devices into increasingly mundane objects, structures and living things, is one of the key technological enablers of ubiquitous surveillance.

There are many individual technological developments one could give as examples, from geodemographic and geolocation systems to the complex augmented reality environments created by artists. However, surveillance becoming ubiquitous is not simply the proliferation of intensely but narrowly seeing 'oligoptica';[2] it is also a question of the way in which surveillance is less obvious even as it increases: surveillance is vanishing.

This chapter argues that the increasing ubiquity of technologies of visibility, coupled with the vanishing of the technologies themselves, represents a change in the place of the visual in Western culture, and with it,

1 This paper is based on work originally commissioned by the Canadian federal Office of the Privacy Commissioner (OPC). This chapter is an expansion of the original position paper (Murakami Wood 2011), which can be found here and which is used with the permission of the OPC: <http://www.priv.gc.ca/information/research-recherche/2011/wood_201107_e.asp>. The author would also like to acknowledge the contribution of colleagues in the Department of Aesthetics and Communication at the University of Aarhus, Denmark, for their responses to an earlier version of this paper during my all too brief time there, and in particular, Kasper Schiølin, who alerted me to Sara Danius' paper.

2 Bruno Latour, *Reassembling the Social: An Introduction to Actor-Network-Theory* (Oxford: Oxford University Press, 2005).

challenges to knowledge and politics. In the modern period, the visual gradually assumed a central and privileged place, and the idea that understanding something is secondary to its viewing became dominant.[3] As modern subjects, we are acculturated into this sense that vision matters, that seeing something is the prelude to grasping its meaning, and hence to constructing a politics.

As Danius remarks, following Jonathan Crary,[4] 'the model of vision that modernism deploys, whether implicitly or explicitly, takes as its point of departure the immanence of the individual body, not the Cartesian, noncorporeal, and transcendental model of vision', and Crary's history of techniques of vision argues that a great deal of modernity has been obsessed with making visible through technology that which would otherwise be invisible and internal.[5] This makes for a particular relationship between seeing and knowledge. Martin Jay has developed the notion of the 'scopic regime', a particular assemblage of historical, social and political forces that serve to configure the basic (already complex) biological bases of vision in certain directions.[6] Surveillance technologies are in many ways exemplary of this: as Majid Yar[7] and Jonathan Finn[8] have observed, the prevalence of visual imagery related to the products of video surveillance constitute the contemporary scopic regime.

However, I would argue that it is not simply the products of surveillance that help construct such a scopic regime. Bentham's Panopticon was

3 Martin Jay, *Downcast Eyes: The Denigration of Vision in Twentieth-Century French Thought* (Berkeley: University of California Press, 1993); Sara Danius, 'Novel Visions and the Crisis of Culture: Visual Technology, Modernism, and Death in *The Magic Mountain*', *boundary 2*, 27/2 (2000), 177–211.

4 Jonathan Crary, *Techniques of the Observer: On Vision and Modernity in the Nineteenth Century* (Cambridge, MA: MIT Press, 1990).

5 Danius, 'Novel Visions'.

6 Jay, *Downcast Eyes*.

7 Majid Yar, 'Panoptic Power and the Pathologisation of Vision: Critical Reflections on the Foucauldian Thesis', *Surveillance & Society* 1/3 (2003), 254–71.

8 Jonathan Finn, 'Seeing Surveillantly: Surveillance as Social Practice', in Aaron Doyle, Randy Lippert and David Lyon, eds, *Eyes Everywhere: The Global Growth of Camera Surveillance* (London: Routledge, 2012), 69–78.

chosen by Foucault[9] as his diagram of the disciplinary society because it was precisely the most obvious application of a technology of visibility to the invisibilities of the social and personal (or interior) realms. By rendering the exterior of the subject permanently visible, the interior life would be opened and, it was hoped, reformed. Much is made of the asymmetry of visibility in the design of the Panopticon. Foucault writes of the uncertainty created by the inability of the prisoner to the see if there is a guard in the watchtower. But it is the visibility of the watchtower that creates the preconditions for any sense of what the subject is to do, not the invisibility of the guard. The guard tower represents a watching authority in a modern world in which the necessity of 'believing one's own eyes' has replaced the numinous sense of being under the constant eye of an invisible god.

In forms of post-panoptic surveillance, like open street video surveillance systems, this simple visual element remains: one cannot normally see the watchers, but one can see the cameras. These cameras can be clearly seen mounted on walls and ceilings or on dedicated poles or fittings – they are obvious and visible. In many nation states, they are made more visible still by legally mandated colouration or, more commonly, signage informing users of the space who is responsible for their surveillance.[10] Indeed, a common argument is that cameras should be made as visible as possible if the claims about their preventative effects are true, although this argument if often made as much satirically as genuinely, for there seems to be relatively little evidence for the preventative efficacy of video surveillance.[11]

As Frosh has argued, 'photography is best grasped not as a medium of visual communication, but as a manifest performance of the power to

9 Michel Foucault, *Discipline and Punish: The Birth of the Prison* (London: Penguin, 1977).

10 Mark Cole, 'Signage and Surveillance: Interrogating the Textual Context of CCTV in the UK', *Surveillance & Society* 2/2–3 (2004), 430–45; Randy Lippert, 'Signs of the surveillant assemblage: Privacy regulation, urban CCTV, and governmentality', *Social & Legal Studies* 18/4 (2009), 505–22.

11 See Brandon Welsh and David P. Farrington, *Making Public Places Safer: Surveillance and Crime Prevention* (Oxford: Oxford University Press, 2009).

make visible.'[12] Indeed, I would argue this of any surveillance technology or technology of visibility, although certainly not of all vision.[13] The scopic regime of the late twentieth and early twenty-first centuries, insofar as it can be characterised by the predominance of surveillance, has been made up of a combination of publicly consumed images (surveillance products) and of the visual performance, perception and imagination of surveillance at work (cameras and other visible surveillance technologies).

The visibility of these surveillance technologies would seem to be linked to three forms of power/knowledge: firstly, consciousness of being watched; secondly, and indirectly, knowledge of how to hold the operators of the systems to account; and finally, the ability to develop informed decisions about political and social action. However, as the era of visible surveillance technologies comes to an end, this change in scopic regimes heralds transformations of our ways of knowing, and therefore of our abilities to hold to account, to regulate, and to make informed political decisions about surveillance.

Vanishing Surveillance

Contemporary surveillance systems have been characterised as 'surveillant assemblages,'[14] or actor-networks[15] consisting of multiple heterogeneous elements, material, social, natural, and so on. With digitisation we have already seen the vanishing of parts of surveillance systems[16] through the

12 Paul Frosh, 'The Public Eye and the Citizen-Voyeur: Photography as a Performance of Power,' *Social Semiotics* 11/1 (2001), 43.

13 See Yar, 'Panoptic Power'.

14 Kevin D. Haggerty and Richard V. Ericson, 'The Surveillant Assemblage', *British Journal of Sociology* 51/4 (2000), 605–22.

15 Kirstie Ball, 'Elements of Surveillance: A new Framework and future Directions', *Information, Communication & Society* 5/4 (2002), 573–90.

16 Stephen Graham, and David Wood, 'Digitizing Surveillance: Categorization, Space, Inequality', *Critical Social Policy* 23/2 (2003), 227–48.

'black-boxing' of the inner workings of such systems,[17] in particular the storage, analysis and sorting of data, or dataveillance.[18] Binding all the other elements together is the ability to deal with ever-larger amounts of data (now referred to with a strange combination of hype and understatement as 'big data') in databases. These range from the simple single computers or intranets of police and local governments to the huge 'server farms' of private corporations like Google, Apple, Microsoft and Facebook as these gradually become the default option for personal data storage through cloud computing, and to the 'data warehouses' of major state surveillance organisations like the US Federal Bureau of Investigation's Investigative Data Warehouse (IDW), which aims to suck in data on crime and criminals, as well as crime threats and potential criminals, from all over the world, including CCTV footage,[19] and finally, to the US National Security Agency's massive Utah data centre.[20] The data analytic processes that take place to sort, sift, and connect such data, from internet traffic patterns to social networks to faces in the crowd, also take place largely invisibly, and often beyond the boundaries of jurisdictions that may be concerned about the effects on their citizens.

Although I will return to these last aspects later, this chapter concentrates on the vanishing of the sensor elements of surveillance systems. There are many ways in which sensor systems are vanishing, but for the sake of clarity, I identify four further trends. The first is simply that surveillance technologies are getting smaller, whilst increasing in power and range of capabilities. The second is that surveillance technologies are more mobile, whilst remaining connected. The third is that surveillance technologies increasingly mimic other things, and finally and relatedly, surveillance

17 Bruno Latour, *Science in Action: How to follow Scientists and Engineers through Society* (Cambridge, MA: Harvard University Press, 1987).

18 Roger Clarke, 'Information Technology and Dataveillance', *Communications of the ACM* 31/5 (1988), 498–512.

19 Electronic Frontier Foundation (EFF), Report on the Investigative Data Warehouse. April 2009.

20 James Bamford, 'The NSA Is Building the Country's Biggest Spy Center (Watch What You Say)', *Wired* Threat Level blog (15 March 2012).

systems may be camouflaged or even be 'everything', in the sense that whole landscapes might hide or actually be surveillance systems.

1. Size matters: One of the most basic technical trajectories is the decreasing size of many individual components of surveillance systems, in particular, the sensors. This is important because, as Donna Haraway has remarked, 'miniaturization has changed our experience of mechanism'.[21] One example is the Radio Frequency Identification (RFID) microchip. While small, RFID chips have until recently been relatively visible, even when implanted into living beings. However, workable sensors are now being developed that function at ever-smaller scales. Dust Networks,[22] a spin off company of the University of California at Berkeley has been producing 0.2mm^2 chips since the early 2000s, and these devices are designed to work as distributed, wireless, multi-functional sensor platforms for a variety of applications. These 'motes' made by Dust Networks are already starting to look large in comparison with the tiny RFID chips made by Hitachi of Japan, which has now demonstrated working examples at 0.025 mm^2, the smallest working sensors currently known.[23] It does not seem unlikely that such chips will continue to decrease in size.

Once again, these technologies will come to seem rather primitive in a few years' time. Imaging devices have become more sophisticated. Cameras have been developed that can fit on the head of a pin, albeit with poor resolutions.[24] At border crossing points, we have seen the increasing deployment of body-scanners (or virtual strip searches), following a number of incidents of attempted terrorism using concealed explosives. So far such equipment is bulky, and indeed is designed, at least partly, to create a theatrical atmosphere in which the passenger is made conscious

21 Donna Haraway, 'A Cyborg Manifesto: Science, Technology and Socialist-feminism in the Late Twentieth Century', in *Simians, Cyborgs and Women: The Reinvention of Nature* (New York: Routledge, 1991), 149–82.

22 Since 2011, part of Linear Technology <http://www.linear.com/products/wireless_sensor_networks> accessed 17 October 2013.

23 <http://thefutureofthings.com/news/1032/hitachi-develops-worlds-smallest-rfid-chip.html> accessed 17 October 2013.

24 *boingboing*, 'Tiny Camera fits on head of pin' (6 July, 2011).

of security and surveillance procedures. However, research is pointing in directions indicating that the bulky visibility of body scanning may not be necessary. Terahertz wave technology, currently one of the least popular of the three main imaging technologies employed for body scanning, has now been shown to be able to work well, at least theoretically, in much smaller devices.[25] The output is of video standard and could be built into arrays using standard silicon CMOS technology. In other words, it would be something that could be added onto small, cheap and portable equipment. The New York City Police Department has already been testing portable terahertz-wave scanning systems in the streets in early 2013.[26] The era of cheap video cameras with body-scanning capability may not be far away. What this means is that there is no longer any technological reason why sensor systems, including cameras, need to be the relatively visible objects that we are used to. This kind of change in size is not unprecedented, but the jump in scale which is now occurring is of a different order.

2. Nowhere to run: The decreasing size of surveillance technologies has allowed surveillance to become increasingly portable and more covert. This is also enabled by wireless networking. However, the vanishing of surveillance is also encouraged by new types of surveillance platforms that can use vertical mobility to be more distant and able to 'get away'. The militaries of the USA, Israel, the United Kingdom and India, amongst many others, now rely heavily on Unmanned Aerial Vehicles (UAVs) for reconnaissance (as well as for warfighting operations).[27] However, UAVs are not restricted to the battlefield: police forces in many jurisdictions are already purchasing camera-equipped drones for urban surveillance operations, and drones are already used for a number of public activities outside

25 *MIT Technology Review*, Physics arXiv Blog, 'Terahertz Transistor Could Usher in Era of Cheap Surveillance Video Cameras' (20 July 2009).

26 *New York Daily News*. 'NYPD Commissioner says department will begin testing a new high-tech device that scans for concealed weapons' (23 January 2013).

27 Government Accountability Office (GAO), UNMANNED AIRCRAFT SYSTEMS (18 September, 2012).

of policing, from the real-estate sector to monitoring forest cover.[28] These 'Micro-' 'or Mini-' 'UAVs' (or MAVs) tend to be small, lightweight (some are compact enough to 'fit in backpacks') and easily operated, in many cases may resemble hobbyist remote-control kit aircraft, and are already available to private citizens at low prices.[29]

3. 'Is it a bird, is it a plane?': MAVs, through their mobility, may be able to bypass the laws on signage for video surveillance (although they have had problems with civil aviation regulations, at least in the UK). However, they are still visible. Current developments may change this. The major area of research and development expansion in mobile surveillance devices is in biomimetic technologies.[30] Biomimetics are machines that imitate naturally occurring animals or plants. The most common biomimetic devices tend to be birds, snakes, and insects. The US company AeroVironment recently demonstrated a working, partially radio-controlled and partially autonomous robotic 'Nano Hummingbird'.[31] Technion, the Israeli Institute of Technology, has been developing a 'snakebot', a camera that moves like a snake, and could, it says, be used for search and rescue in collapsed buildings and so on.[32] These devices are therefore not necessarily surveillance devices in themselves, but 'platforms' that could be used for both surveillance and weapons deployment. That this is undoubtedly an aim is shown by the funding of such research: for example, AeroVironment is funded largely by the US Defense Advanced Research Projects Agency (DARPA).

Biomimetics are not necessarily aimed primarily at disguising surveillance, but rather designed to adapt or model all kinds of natural behaviours.

28 Neil Ungerleider, 'Unmanned Drones Go From Afghanistan To Hollywood', *Fast Company* (15 February 2012); Lian Pin Koh, and Serge A. Wich, 'Dawn of drone ecology: low-cost autonomous aerial vehicles for conservation', *Tropical Conservation Science* 5/2 (2012), 121–32.

29 Daniel Terdiman, 'Your very own drone to follow you home', *CNET* (11 May, 2013).

30 This is also part of a wider trend towards the instrumentalisation of nature within the surveillant assemblage, considered by Haggerty and Trottier (forthcoming).

31 AreoVironment Inc. <http://www.avinc.com/> accessed 30 May 2013.

32 Associated Press, 15 June 2009 <http://www.youtube.com/watch?v=1JnQL7mjspg> accessed 30 May 2013.

The trend here is towards what paranoids have long believed – that anything could be a surveillance device. Clearly there are many technological obstacles to overcome. In the case of the Nano Hummingbird, the drawback as far as those who would want a truly covert device are concerned is its sound – it really does hum, and rather noticeably.

4. 'If you go down to the woods today ...': While the camouflaging and rendering of all kinds of devices or systems made invisible by covering or concealing them has a long history, particularly in military settings, the tiny, distributed, network and digital qualities of contemporary sensor systems allows a more thorough concealment that can essentially turn anything that appears to be 'normal' landscape, whether urban or rural, into a surveillance system. One particularly interesting example is the Israeli company, G-Max, which makes security geotextiles, cables, and surfaces that passively detect pressure or motion. For example, its 'buried cable intrusion detection sensor', can operate under 'all types of ground, concrete, asphalt roads, runways, vegetation, between trees, mountain terrain and even under water, snow and ice',[33] and 'can distinguish between actual intruders and stray animals, fish, birds, a floating leaf, bits of paper or vegetation.'

The combination of ubiquitous computing and massive everyday data collection, infrastructural sensor systems, and 'natural' landscapes means that we can no longer know for sure whether we are or whether we are not under surveillance, by whom, or why. Moreover, while in the past it was possible to adopt another identity in order to escape the oppressive natural surveillance of intimate rural communities, and while it might still be possible to leave behind the surveilled urban environment of the present, such options to avoid surveillance by changing location could very well be lost.[34]

33 G-Max Security Systems <http://www.g-max-security.com/Items/Item.aspx?Id=153&Cat=P> accessed 30 May 2013.

34 David Murakami Wood, 'Surveillance and Globalization', in Kirstie Ball, Kevin Haggerty and David Lyon, eds, *The Routledge Handbook of Surveillance Studies* (London: Routledge, 2012).

Ghost-Hunting in the Ubiquitous Surveillance Society

There are many questions that arise from the changing scopic regime, the simultaneous ubiquity and vanishing of surveillance I have outlined. This chapter began with the suggestion that if an era of visible surveillance is coming to an end, potentially so too is our ability to know, to hold to account, to regulate, and to make informed political decisions about surveillance. Whilst not dismissing this concern, I would argue that the coming of an era of ubiquitous, mobile, (near) invisible surveillance devices changes both the spatiality and the temporality of the perception of surveillance. It generates uncertainty and it unsettles. How might one try to understand the underlying anxieties generated by the new visibility of subjects coupled with the vanishing of surveillance? Such anxieties comprise the equation of knowledge with what can be seen or represented; the inability to cope effectively with the rapid rescaling and increasing complexity of social information processes; the terror of public performance; and the increasingly inescapable fear (or realisation) that sovereign individuality is, and has always been, a myth.

With the proliferation of passive, background, infrastructurised surveillance systems, combined with fast-moving, often disguised, robotic surveillance devices, we moving away from the conventional visibilities that we have in the relatively short period of their widespread use come to associate with surveillance systems. We are also moving from a machine-readable world[35] to a world that can *only* be fully interpreted, navigated, and inhabited by machines. Our visual window onto future surveillance might be the flickering wing of a hummingbird glimpsed out of the corner of one eye, or things never seen at all, only imagined. When combined with invisible but continuous dataveillance, it may come to seem as though surveillance has no direct effect on our lives or has vanished entirely, but this would only be because surveillance had been successfully black-boxed

35 Rob Kitchin and Martin Dodge, *Code/space: Software and Everyday Life* (Cambridge, MA: MIT Press, 2011).

and punctualised into an actor-network or assemblage, whose components are beyond our immediate perception and understanding.

The qualities of a scopic regime of vanishing surveillance are therefore perhaps more amenable to understanding based on Freud's concept of the 'uncanny' (*unheimlich*)[36] and Derrida's connected notion of 'haunting',[37] rather than the more conventional ways of analysing such developments based on, for example 'the industrialization of the social',[38] or a new kind of institutionalisation.[39] Vidler defined the uncanny of the nineteenth century as a generalised condition related to urban living.[40] However, I would argue that its location in the metropolitan was actually merely symptomatic of the underlying roots of the uncanny, which were related to the sociotechnical acceleration and the inability of humans to feel at home in the world as it is and is becoming (hence its strong connection to nostalgia). This sense of the uncanny is captured in Mori's coining of the phrase 'uncanny valley' to indicate the emotional-perceptual space that opens when humans are confronted with the artificial other: human-like robots.[41] In this sense, vanishing surveillance is uncanny because we are confronted by things that may not (only) be what they appear, animals that may not (only) be animals, and environments in which we can never be fully 'at home' and which may be acting against our desires.

Vidler describes Derrida's use of 'haunting' as a postmodern uncanny. Derrida understands all texts as being haunted, by memory and by the ghosts of previous writings,[42] and Nolan and Levesque have noted the

36 Sigmund Freud, 'The Uncanny', *The Standard Edition of the Complete Psychological Works of Sigmund Freud* 17 (London: The Hogarth Press 1952 [1919]), 219–52.

37 Jacques Derrida, *Specters of Marx: The State of the Debt, the Work of Mourning and the New International*, trans. Peggy Kamuf (London/New York: Routledge, 1994).

38 Nigel Thrift and Shaun French, 'The automatic production of space', *Transactions of the Institute of British Geographers* 27/3 (2002), 309–35.

39 Michalis Lianos, 'Social Control after Foucault', *Surveillance & Society* 1/3 (2003), 412–30.

40 Anthony, Vidler, *The Architectural Uncanny: Essays in the Modern Unhomely* (Cambridge, MA: MIT Press, 1992).

41 Masahiro Mori, 'The Uncanny Valley', *Energy* 7/4 (1970), 33–35.

42 Derrida, *Specters of Marx*.

potential relevance of Derrida with regard to internet surveillance,[43] since much of what constitutes surveillance on the net is 'buried, encrypted, fragmented and largely lost to easy viewing'.[44] These are exactly the qualities that I have suggested are now increasingly applicable to surveillance in general. Derrida's concept of haunting also has another significant aspect: the relationship to 'truth'. Haunting is about fragments, lies, and uncertainty, as much as it is about accurate memory. While ubisurv may lead to the idea of a total record, in fact this is often merely the multiplication of 'oligoptica', systems that see the particular.[45] So whilst 'surveillance' may be everpresent, there is not a single watching authority: just as there is no tower in the post-panopticon, there is also no single guard. Instead, there is the fragmentary presence of multiple ghostly and possibly non-human watchers. When what is watching us vanishes, it is likely not to be disappearing into the 'sunshine' of 'nothing but signals' Haraway ironically summons up,[46] but rather into the haunted darkness of unknowing.

This situation cannot possibly give rise to any particular kind of singular subjectivity, or the more moral modern citizen, as hoped for by Bentham.[47] Instead, subjects are as fragmented and ghostly as the watchers, 'dividuals' who come together only spatiotemporally when they appear to present a particular threat or profit profile. Otherwise, so long as predictable

43 Jason Nolan and Michelle Levesque, 'Hacking human: data-archaeology and surveillance in social networks', *ACM SIGGROUP Bulletin* 25/2 (2005), 33–7.

44 Even the recent revelations of Edward Snowden about pervasive telecommunications surveillance by the American National Security Agency and its allies do not challenge this general conclusion as the 'Five Eyes' system is only one type of intelligence system, not even representing all state surveillance systems amongst one groups of nations, and this is before one considers non-state surveillance. And, what we know from the Snowden revelations does not represent anything like a total picture of what the NSA and its allies do. In many ways, the number of documents about multiple programs provides an illusion of a comprehensive view.

45 Latour, *Reassembling the Social*.

46 Haraway, 'Cyborg Manifesto', 153.

47 Gilles Deleuze, 'Postscript on the Societies of Control', *October* 59, 3–7; Lianos, 'Social Control after Foucault'.

safe and profitable patterns are observed, nothing happens and nothing is 'seen'.

This scopic regime, haunted by possible futures as much as by fragmented presents and always-ready-to-be-reconstructed pasts, provides no place for politics, because it provides no place for knowledge. In her analysis of the place of vision in Thomas Mann's pre-eminent modern novel, *The Magic Mountain* (1924), Sarah Danius highlights a crucial moment, in which the hero, Hans Castorp, is examining an X-ray of his cousin's body, and 'suddenly understands that he beholds the symbol of life itself, the core of the human being: the heart.'[48] His cry of 'Yes, yes! I see it [...] My God, I see it!' is exemplary of how vision functions in modernity, and indeed of the way in which surveillance is intended to reveal truths about the world, which are then amenable to categorisation, and analysis:

> Proposing that seeing is reading, the episode indicates that vision depends on a language that names what is seen. A new epistemic space is opened up, a space produced by an epistemological reorganization of the interior of the human body.[49]

Surveillance has engendered the continuous opening of new epistemic spaces, each prompting a new gasp of 'I see'. However, if this opening is continuous, revelation becomes mundane. What is seen no longer generates knowledge, merely data, and is taken for granted until it vanishes. It seems that what is happening at present is that total and continuous transparency through the generation of data is increasingly detached from the production of knowledge. Data is becoming 'bigger', and more data of all kinds, including the visual, are collected, stored and generating, even with sophisticated analytics, much of the information may never be amenable to any kind of applied intelligence[50] but will merely form a vast ocean of largely unknown, uninterpreted and perhaps unknowable data, on which floats a thin layer of knowledge. So, instead of a clear and

48 Danius, 'Novel Visions'.

49 Ibid.

50 Mark Andrejevic, *Infoglut: How Too Much Information Is Changing the Way We Think and Know* (London/New York: Routledge, 2013).

coherent understanding, we are haunted by fragmentary and contingent meanings, and the production of the visual is no longer amenable to visual understanding, to being fully seen.

There are also political questions here: how can we respond to the vanishing of surveillance? It is already clear that politicians and the law lag behind the progress of technological development. There are few politicians with the scientific or technical knowledge to understand or assess developments in this area, and in addition, with the dominance of neoliberal economic thinking, technological development is an area often seen as something that should be left entirely to the market or to 'experts' like technology developers, security professionals and police, and in which government should involve itself as little as possible.[51] This attitude unfortunately feeds back into the general technological ignorance of policy-makers, and is also compounded by the different temporalities involved in rapid technological innovation on the one hand, and much slower legislative development on the other. It also increases the opacity of the development process to the public, and means that the politics of ubisurv increasingly vanishes behind the closed doors of security experts, mid-level producer groups, programmers and specialist internet webzines, or books only likely to be read by the already technologically literate.[52]

There are many options for regulation, from doing nothing and accepting the transparency of the individual to the introduction of new laws banning particular kinds of surveillance technologies and/or practices. For example, several cities in the USA have already passed anti-drone ordinances and one might adopt such a solution in the case of personal body-scanning cameras. Hard regulation does have an attractive symbolic dimension, but it would encourage shadow markets in banned surveillance technologies, and would require a corresponding expansion in the

51 See Colin Crouch, *Post-Democracy* (Cambridge: Polity Press, 2004); Peter Miller and Nikolas Rose, *Governing the Present: Administering Economic, Social and Personal Life* (Cambridge: Polity Press, 2008).

52 Susan Leigh Star, *The Cultures of Computing* (Oxford: Blackwell Publishers, 1995).

deployment of specialist detection systems even to confirm the presence of banned invisible technologies.

Without new hard regulation, regulators could still adopt maximalist interpretations of existing remits to protect privacy, or work with quasi-regulatory technological solutions such as Privacy by Design and other interventions at the R&D stage. There are successful examples of this, most notably the camera 'click' sound required for all digital cameras manufactured in Korea and Japan, introduced in the wake of scandals about covert 'upskirt' photography, or the reversing alarms on large vehicles, which one could see being applied in the case of mobile cameras but would not be so feasible in the case of distributed network of sub-microscopic sensors.

Finally, market solutions, which put a value on anonymity, non-locatability and disconnection, might result in the widespread availability of anti-surveillance technology and also in research into anti-surveillance devices, such as real-time video erasure[53] and light-bending materials that create a form of invisibility.[54] However, if market forces entirely determined the distribution of privacy and transparency, this would be likely to harm the already vulnerable, and to empower the already relatively powerful, extending existing divisions and inequalities.

Why wait for regulation? There is already a conflict in many countries between citizen and police use of visual technologies, especially in the use of counter-surveillance or sousveillance used to 'watch the watchers' or to collect evidence of brutality, corruption, and misbehavior. Such forms of watching are also increasingly likely to make use of the same kinds of covert and less visible technologies of monitoring. This route is likely to lead down the path to transparency becoming socially normative. Genuine popular anti-surveillance does exist in the form of camera destruction and threats to shoot down micro-UAVs, but the politics of such anti-surveillance is as diverse and problematic as the politics of surveillance. However, direct

53 Ray Kurzweil, '"Diminished reality" software removes objects from video in real time', *Kurzweil* blog (14 October, 2010).

54 Andrea Di Falco, Martin Ploschner and Thomas F Krauss, 'Flexible metamaterials at visible wavelengths', *New Journal of Physics* 12 (2010).

attacks on cameras can help keep them visible: one of the main reasons why cameras are still visible despite being smaller is because their housings are getting more bulky in order to provide greater protection against tampering and destruction, especially when they are more accessible (e.g. on public transportation).

However, within the new scopic regime, such forms of overt destruction rely on exactly what is vanishing: the ability to see the materials involved in surveillance and then to act. As surveillance disappears into black boxes and is punctuated in networks, it is the networks themselves that form the terrain for resistance. State military organisations, in redefining hacking as 'cyber-war' and 'cyber-crime', have already attempted to deem such actions beyond the pale of acceptable political activity. And indeed, armed resistance to US hegemony has attempted to hijack surveillance systems: in 2009 it was revealed that insurgents in Iraq used $26 'Skygrabber' satellite TV interception tools to capture live video feed from US military surveillance drones.[55] Thus far, artists and political hackers have tended to concentrate on rendering visible the powerful but invisible, whether it be Michelle Teran, showing how one can intercept multiple wireless signals carrying networked video surveillance in cities with her *Parasitic Video Interceptor* (2008),[56] Wikileaks' challenge to state secrecy, or Anonymous-offshoot KnightSec's online revelation of the alleged identities of rapists in the USA and Canada.

Such piggybacking and subversion still relies on the affordances of the sociotechnical networks that they subvert, critique, or oppose. However, in rendering visible what is becoming or has become invisible, they produce new possibilities for hunting the ghosts of surveillance and for revelatory moments when 'I see!', when the ghostly presence resolves itself into the intelligible, when the uncanny is rendered ordinary. These moments of seeing, increasingly, will not be of the same type as before. Just as dataveillance has come to dominate surveillance, so forms of understanding based on interpreting and manipulating data are already forming the basis of a

55 *Wall Street Journal*, Insurgents Hack U.S. Drones (17 December 2009).

56 Ubermatic website <http://www.ubermatic.lftk.org/blog/?p=205> accessed 30 May 2013.

new scopic regime that is in the process of replacing more conventional visual surveillance, and the politics of this scopic regime rely on a different kind of visual literacy. As the early examples given above show, it is not necessarily the case that such seeing and politics will be the province of educated, privileged white men. Rather than intentional empowerment through technology defeating the digital divides which have accentuated material inequalities, it may well be that resistance to control will play a more significant role in generating new forms of understanding.

Bibliography

Andrejevic, Mark, *Infoglut: How Too Much Information Is Changing the Way We Think and Know* (London, New York: Routledge, 2013).

Associated Press, 15 June 2009 <http://www.youtube.com/watch?v=1JnQL7mjspg> accessed 30 May 2013.

Ball, Kirstie, 'Elements of surveillance: a new framework and future directions', *Information, Communication & Society* 5/4 (2002), 573–90.

Bamford, James, 'The NSA Is Building the Country's Biggest Spy Center (Watch What You Say)', *Wired* Threat Level blog (15 March 2012) <http://www.wired.com/threatlevel/2012/03/ff_nsadatacenter/> accessed 30 May 2013.

Boingboing, 'Tiny Camera fits on head of pin' (6 July 2011) <http://boingboing.net/2011/07/06/tiny-camera-fits-on.html> accessed 30 May 2013.

Clarke, Roger, 'Information Technology and Dataveillance', *Communications of the ACM* 31/5 (1988), 498–512.

Cole, Mark, 'Signage and Surveillance: Interrogating the Textual Context of CCTV in the UK', *Surveillance & Society* 2/2–3 (2004), 430–45.

Crary, Jonathan, *Techniques of the Observer: On Vision and Modernity in the Nineteenth Century* (Cambridge, MA: MIT Press, 1990).

Crouch, Colin, *Post-Democracy* (Cambridge: Polity Press, 2004).

Danius, Sara, 'Novel Visions and the Crisis of Culture: Visual Technology, Modernism, and Death in *The Magic Mountain*', *boundary 2*, 27/2 (2000), 177–211.

Deleuze, Gilles, 'Postscript on the Societies of Control', *October* 59 (1992), 3–7.

Derrida, Jacques, *Specters of Marx: The State of the Debt, the Work of Mourning and the New International*, trans. Peggy Kamuf (London, New York: Routledge, 1994).

Di Falco, Andrea, Martin Ploschner and Thomas F Krauss, 'Flexible metamaterials at visible wavelengths', *New Journal of Physics* 12 (2010).

Electronic Frontier Foundation (EFF), Report on the Investigative Data Warehouse. April 2009 <https://www.eff.org/issues/foia/investigative-data-warehouse-report> accessed 30 May, 2013.

Finn, Jonathan, 'Seeing Surveillantly: Surveillance as Social Practice', in Aaron Doyle, Randy Lippert and David Lyon, eds, *Eyes Everywhere: The Global Growth of Camera Surveillance* (London: Routledge, 2012), 69–78.

Fisher, Jill A., and Torin Monahan, 'Tracking the social dimensions of RFID systems in hospitals', *International Journal of Medical Informatics* 77/3 (2008), 176–83.

Foucault, Michel, *Discipline and Punish: The Birth of the Prison* (London: Penguin, 1977).

Freud, Sigmund, 'The Uncanny', *The Standard Edition of the Complete Psychological Works of Sigmund Freud* 17 [1919] (London: The Hogarth Press 1952), 219–52.

Frosh, Paul, 'The public eye and the citizen-voyeur: Photography as a performance of power', *Social Semiotics* 11/1 (2001), 43–59.

Government Accountability Office (GAO), UNMANNED AIRCRAFT SYSTEMS: Measuring Progress and Addressing Potential Privacy Concerns Would Facilitate Integration into the National Airspace System (18 September 2012) <http://www.gao.gov/assets/650/648348.pdf> accessed 30 May 2013.

Graham, Stephen, and David Wood, 'Digitizing Surveillance: Categorization, Space, Inequality', *Critical Social Policy* 23/2 (2003), 227–48.

Haggerty, Kevin D., and Richard V. Ericson, 'The Surveillant Assemblage', *British Journal of Sociology* 51/4 (2000), 605–22.

Haraway, Donna, 'A Cyborg Manifesto: Science, Technology and Socialist-feminism in the Late Twentieth Century', in *Simians, Cyborgs and Women: The Reinvention of Nature* (New York: Routledge, 1991), 149–82.

Jay, Martin, *Downcast Eyes: The Denigration of Vision in Twentieth-Century French Thought* (Berkeley: University of California Press, 1993).

Kitchin, Rob, and Martin Dodge, *Code/space: Software and Everyday Life* (Cambridge, MA: MIT Press, 2011).

Koh, Lian Pin, and Serge A. Wich, 'Dawn of drone ecology: low-cost autonomous aerial vehicles for conservation', *Tropical Conservation Science* 5/2 (2012), 121–32.

Kurzweil, Ray, '"Diminished reality" software removes objects from video in real time', *Kurzweil* blog (14 October 2010) <http://www.kurzweilai.net/diminished-reality-software-removes-objects-from-video-in-real-time> accessed 30 May 2013.

Latour, Bruno, *Reassembling the Social: An Introduction to Actor-Network-Theory* (Oxford: Oxford University Press, 2005).

——, *Science in Action: How to follow scientists and engineers through society* (Cambridge, MA: Harvard University Press, 1987).

Lianos, Michalis, 'Social Control after Foucault', *Surveillance & Society* 1/3 (2003), 412–30.

Lippert, Randy, 'Signs of the surveillant assemblage: Privacy regulation, urban CCTV, and governmentality', *Social & Legal Studies* 18/4 (2009), 505–22.

Lyon, David, *Surveillance Studies: An Overview* (Cambridge: Cambridge Polity Press, 2007).

MIT Technology Review, Physics arXiv Blog, 'Terahertz Transistor Could Usher in Era of Cheap Surveillance Video Cameras' (20 July 2009) <http://www.technologyreview.com/blog/arxiv/23871/> accessed 30 May 2013.

Miller, Peter, and Nikolas Rose, *Governing the Present: Administering Economic, Social and Personal Life* (Cambridge: Polity Press, 2008)

Monaghan, Jeffrey, and Kevin Walby, '"They Attacked the City": Security intelligence, the Sociology of Protest Policing and the Anarchist Threat at the 2010 Toronto G20 summit', *Current Sociology* 60/5 (2012), 653–71.

Mori, Masahiro, 'The Uncanny Valley', *Energy* 7/4 (1970), 33–5.

Murakami Wood, David, 'Towards Spatial Protocol: The Topologies of the Pervasive Surveillance Society', *Augmented Urban Spaces: Articulating the Physical and Electronic City* (Aldershot: Ashgate, 2008), 93–106.

——, 'Vanishing Surveillance: Why Seeing What is Watching Us Matters', Ottawa: Office of the Privacy Commissioner (OPC), Canada 2011 <http://www.priv.gc.ca/information/research-recherche/2011/wood_201107_e.asp> accessed 30 May 2013.

New York Daily News, 'NYPD Commissioner says department will begin testing a new high-tech device that scans for concealed weapons' (23 January 2013) <http://www.nydailynews.com/new-york/nypd-readies-scan-and-frisk-article-1.1245663> accessed 30 May, 2013.

Nolan, Jason, and Michelle Levesque, 'Hacking human: data-archaeology and surveillance in social networks', *ACM SIGGROUP Bulletin* – Special issue on virtual communities 25/2 (2005), 33–7.

Price, Giles, 'The visual documentation of public protest: G20, London, 2009', *Crime, Media, Culture* 7/1 (2011), 99–101.

Star, Susan Leigh, *The Cultures of Computing* (Sociological Review Monograph), (Oxford: Blackwell Publishers, 1995).

Terdiman, Daniel, 'Your very own drone to follow you home', *CNET* (11 May 2013) <http://news.cnet.com/8301-11386_3-57584024-76/your-very-own-drone-to-follow-you-home/> accessed 30 May, 2013.

Thrift, Nigel, and Shaun French, 'The automatic production of space', *Transactions of the Institute of British Geographers* 27/3 (2002), 309–35.

Ungerleider, Neil, 'Unmanned Drones Go From Afghanistan To Hollywood', *Fast Company* (15 February 2012) <http://www.fastcompany.com/1816578/unmanned-drones-go-afghanistan-hollywood> accessed 30 May 2013.

Vidler, Anthony, *The Architectural Uncanny: Essays in the Modern Unhomely* (Cambridge, MA: MIT Press, 1992).

Wall Street Journal, 'Insurgents Hack U.S. Drones' (17 December, 2009) <http://online.wsj.com/article/SB126102247889095011.html> accessed 30 May 2013.

Welsh, Brandon, and David P. Farrington, *Making Public Places Safer: Surveillance and Crime Prevention* (Oxford: Oxford University Press, 2009).

Yar, Majid, 'Panoptic Power and the Pathologisation of Vision: Critical Reflections on the Foucauldian Thesis', *Surveillance & Society* 1/3 (2003), 254–71.

NANNA BONDE THYLSTRUP

15 The Invisibilities of Internet Censorship

Digital Censorship

The emergence of new forms of censorship is the dark side of the digital revolution.[1] While digitisation has revolutionised communication, it has also facilitated escalations in both surveillance and censorship practices.[2] The use of filtering software has thus become a common response both to controversial online content such as pornography, violence and hate speech, as well as to less obviously problematic content, in particular if this is judged as a threat to established norms.[3]

In a certain sense, digital censorship resembles traditional political and religious forms of censorship. This is not surprising since the word 'revolution', if we understand the term etymologically, must entail a sense

1 Ronald Deibert et al., *Access Denied: The Practice and Policy of Global Internet Filtering* (Cambridge, MA: MIT Press, 2008); Ronald Deibert et al., *Access Contested: Security, Identity, and Resistance in Asian Cyberspace Information Revolution and Global Politics* (Cambridge, MA: MIT Press, 2012); Ronald Deibert et al., *Access Controlled: The Shaping of Power, Rights, and Rule in Cyberspace* (Cambridge, MA: MIT Press, 2010).

2 Matt Buchanan, 'The NSA's Prism Remains Opaque', *The New Yorker* (13 June 2013); Leo Kelion, 'Censoring Facebook: Social Network's Violent Video Dilemma', *BBC News* (9 May 2013); Brian Ries, 'Bea Arthur's Boobs Got Us Booted From Facebook', *The Daily Beast* (16 May 2013); *New York Times*, 'Hate Speech on Facebook', *New York Times* (May 31 2013).

3 William H. Dutton, Anna Dopatka, Ginette Law and Victoria Nash, *Freedom of connection, freedom of expression: the changing legal and regulatory ecology shaping the Internet* (Paris: UNESCO, 2011). Richard Rosenberg, 'Controlling access to the Internet: The role of filtering', *Ethics and Information Technology* 3/1 (2001), 35–44.

of circularity.[4] Yet digital technology also has distinguishing features that set it apart from all previous socio-technological inventions. It has therefore enabled the dramatic inversion of cultural, political and legal infrastructures, which in turn has created a 'cultural lag' between censorship as cultural-legal concept and socio-technological practice. This chapter shows how current epistemological concepts of censorship and the legislative frameworks that protect citizens against censorship are challenged by new, and often opaque, digital censorship assemblages.

Invisible Infrastructures

Understanding how digital censorship practices work, and how they differ from traditional forms of censorship, necessitates an examination of the infrastructures of digital censorship. Infrastructures is here understood to encompass both basic physical and organisational structures and more abstract entities such as protocols (human and computer) and standards.[5]

While the impact of infrastructures on society in general, and on democratic processes in particular, seems only to increase, they tend to become increasingly invisible mundane background operations.[6] In this

4 Reinhart Koselleck, *Futures Past: On the Semantics of Historical Time* (New York: Columbia University Press, 2004).

5 Geoffrey C Bowker et al., 'Toward Information Infrastructure Studies: Ways of Knowing in a Networked Environment', in Jeremy Hunsinger, Lisbeth Klastrup, and Matthew Allen, eds, *International Handbook of Internet Research* (Dordrecht: London, Springer, 2010), 97.

6 Jeremy Hunsinger, 'Toward a Transdisciplinary Internet Research', *The Information Society* 21/4 (2005), 277–9; Jeremy Hunsinger, 'Broadening Possibilities by Expanding the Theoretical Richness of the Social Construction of Technology', *Social Epistemology* 19/2–3 (2005), 255–59; Susan Leigh Star and Karen Ruhleder, 'Steps towards an Ecology of Infrastructure: Complex Problems in Design and Access for Large-scale Collaborative Systems', *1994 ACM Conference on Computer Supported Cooperative Work* (Chapel Hill: North Carolina, USA, 1994), 253–64;

way, the notion of digital information infrastructures, and of digital censorship infrastructures, relates to theories of invisibility, and the challenge of coming to see and understand the infrastructures that influence our lives. This challenge has arisen with modernity's increase in sub-political practices occurring outside of the formal political system.[7] These practices are typically guided by a broad array of norms, rules and conventions, constructed around standards of infrastructure and developed by groups of people loosely identified as 'experts' and they often occur 'behind the scenes' or are made boring and unexciting as 'lists of numbers and technical specifications'.[8]

The deepening of sub-political infrastructures is especially seen in the emerging digital public spheres[9] that increasingly shape our lives and how we think. They tend to be regulated by corporations without direct government interference, and their information infrastructures are increasingly becoming invisible. Yet the invisibilities of digital infrastructures challenge not only the possibility of insight into regulation mechanisms, but also knowledge about the cultural forms that emerge in their shadows.[10]

These challenges can be met in different ways. One approach is to accept that 'the perception and experience of other beings (including computers) remains outside our grasp, yet available to speculation thanks to

---

Jeremy Hunsinger, 'Toward a Transdisciplinary Internet Research'; Jeremy Hunsinger, 'Broadening Possibilities by Expanding the Theoretical Richness of the Social Construction of Technology'.

7 Ulrich Beck, Anthony Giddens and Scott Lash, *Reflexive Modernization: Politics, Tradition and Aesthetics in the Modern Social Order* (Cambridge: Polity Press, 1994).

8 Jeremy Hunsinger, 'Knowledge and Cultural Production in the Context of Contemporary Capitalism: A Response to Wittkower', *Fast Capitalism* 4/1 (2008); Jeremy Hunsinger, 'Toward nomadological cyberinfrastructures', in Jeremy Hunsinger, Lisbeth Klastrup, and Matthew Allen, eds, *The International Handbook of Internet Research* (Dordrecht; London, Springer, 2010), 267–78; Star and Ruhleder, 'Steps towards an ecology of infrastructure'.

9 I use the concept of the digital public sphere to denote any kind of digital place that allows the user to express him- or herself either by behavioral patterns or speech.

10 Theodore G. Striphas, *The Late Age of Print: Everyday Book Culture from Consumerism to Control* (New York: Columbia University Press, 2009).

evidence that emanates from their withdrawn cores like radiation around the event horizon of a black hole',[11] as argued by Ian Bogost. Another is to conceptualise digital censorship as black boxes, whose inner workings are hidden from view even though the box itself may be visible.[12] This chapter employs a third, and related, approach; it examines the failures of algorithmic and human censorship, thus providing a sense of what they 'cannot' do.

What is Digital Censorship?

Traditionally defined, censorship is institutionalised pre- and post-publication control based on a binary opposition between the censor (the state, the church) and the censored (the individual, the citizen).[13] Scholars often associated with poststructuralism gave rise to a more complex conceptualisation of censorship as a structural a priori.[14] These arguments imagined speech not as the act of a sovereign subject, but as a practice formed socially in the individual. From this epistemological perspective, freedom of speech is a conceptual impossibility; the condition of speech's being free in the first place cannot be realised.

11 Ian Bogost, 'The New Aesthetic Needs to Get Weirder', *The Atlantic* (13 April 2012).

12 Alexander Galloway, 'Black Box, Black Bloc', in Benjamin Noys, ed., *Communization and its Discontents: Contestation, Critique, and Contemporary Struggles* (New York: Autonomedia, 2012), 237–52.

13 J. M. Coetzee, *Giving Offense: Essays on Censorship* (Chicago: University of Chicago Press, 1996).

14 See for instance: Pierre Bourdieu and John B. Thompson, *Language and Symbolic Power* (Cambridge, MA: Harvard University Press, 1991); Judith Butler, 'Ruled Out: Vocabularies of the Censor', in Robert C. Post, ed., *Censorship and Silencing: Practices of Cultural Regulation* (Los Angeles: Getty Research Institute for the History of Art and the Humanities, 1998), 247–60.

On face value, the poststructuralist positions appear to stand in direct contrast to the position of traditional, predominantly liberal, freedom of expression philosophers. Yet, a closer look reveals that key figures within this philosophical-ideological framework seemed to be working within the same framework of ideas of social control. John Stuart Mill, for instance, envisioned how extra-legal methods such as social control could police expressions, thus deterring disapproved-of conduct by using 'the super-added force of shame'.[15] Similarly, the French enlightenment *philosophes* sought to establish a form of *censure publique* by seizing control of the French language to render obsolete, distasteful, subversive or contrary ideas outside the acceptable realm of debate.[16] Bourdieu's reformulation of those theories of social control that can be found in the eighteenth and nineteenth centuries, for instance, thus crystallised and nuanced censorship both as a legal proceeding and a social practice.[17]

The poststructuralist conception of censorship is particularly well suited to today's privatisation paradigm because it allows for an epistemological shift in focus from state institutions to private actors. This move shows that far from eradicating censorship practices, digitisation and privatisation have just transposed them into new assemblages in which state censors are replaced, or supplemented, by a whole host of other actors such as users, algorithms and corporations. In addition, poststructuralist censorship theories facilitate a social understanding of digital public spheres, not only as technological constructions but also as spaces of structural censorship practices.

While private censorship is not a new phenomenon, it has taken on new dimensions on the internet, with its self-regulative practices that leave

15 John Stuart Mill, *Nature: The Utility of Religion and Theism* (London: Longmans, Green, Reader, and Dyer, 1874), 108; Joseph Hamburger, *John Stuart Mill on Liberty and Control* (Princeton, NJ: Princeton University Press, 1999).

16 Sophia Rosenfeld, 'Writing the History of Censorship in the Age of Enlightenment', in Daniel Gordon, ed., *Postmodernism and the Enlightenment: New Perspectives in Eighteenth-century French Intellectual History* (New York, London: Routledge, 2001), 117–45.

17 Bourdieu and Thompson, *Language and Symbolic Power*, 138.

ample space for self-censorship and corporate censorship.[18] In addition, it has reconfigured the notion of freedom of the user: while the reflexive and dialogical nature of digital public spheres seems at first glance to enhance the freedom of users, a closer look reveals that algorithmic mechanisms increasingly organise individuals according to certain hegemonic mechanisms through a process of interpellation whose impenetrability increases with its complexity.[19] The following sections of this chapter are thus devoted to the emerging assemblage of digital censorship actors and the practices they institute.

The New Censoring Actors

The notion of social media has infiltrated all forms of digital space, from news media to retail shops and search engines, giving the individual instant access to self-expression in a wide variety of digital settings, and effectively converting all forms of digital spaces to digital public spheres. These public spheres have introduced a series of intermediary institutions that differ markedly from the traditional institutions regulating speech, in that they are mostly private bodies. Since international treaties and covenants conceptualise freedom of expression as a right belonging primarily to the public sphere, this reassembling constitutes a potential erosion of the very legal infrastructure of freedom of expression, giving rise to the question: what happens to freedom of expression when the public sphere is increasingly colonised, or transposed to, the private sphere?

18 Robert Atkins, Svetlana Mintcheva and National Coalition against Censorship (US), *Censoring Culture: Contemporary Threats to Free Expression* (New York: New Press, 2006); Joe McNamee, 'The Slide from "Self-Regulation" to Corporate Censorship', 2013 <http://www.edri.org/files/EDRI_selfreg_final_20110124.pdf> accessed 3 March 2013.

19 Alexander Galloway, *Protocol: How Control Exists after Decentralization* (Leonardo: Cambridge, MA: MIT Press, 2004).

Digital public spheres hover somewhere in between the private and public realms, as quasi-public spheres subject to both public and private content controls, spanning multiple jurisdictions and differing social mores.[20] While they post-date principal international human rights treaties,[21] their status as privately owned spaces nonetheless challenge the ability of these same treaties to effectively ensure the kind of protection normally associated with the public sphere. Despite advancements in human rights jurisprudence to relate to modern-day governance, the public-private distinction still remains a threshold that must be overcome in each individual case, and both international and national courts have thus struggled to ensure that individuals are able to exercise their rights in these privately owned forums.[22]

The advent of social media has thus structurally changed publicity and knowledge governance, and the categories of public and private.[23] This

20 Jillian C. York, Robert Faris, Ronald Deibert and Rebekah Heacock, 'Policing Content in the Quasi-Public Sphere' (OpenNet Initiative, 2010).

21 Dominic McGoldrick, 'The Limits of Freedom of Expression on Facebook and Social Networking Sites: A UK Perspective', *Human Rights Law Review* 13/1 (2013), 125–51; Jacob Rowbottom, 'To Rant, Vent and Converse: Protecting Low Level Speech', *The Cambridge Law Journal* 71/02 (2012), 355–83.

22 Yet, as a recent significant case from the European Court of Human Rights suggests, this court's opinion may change if the very domain for public expression is effectively taken over by private entities 'notwithstanding the acknowledged importance of freedom of expression, it does not bestow any freedom of forum for the exercise of that right. While it is true that democratic, social, economic and technological developments are changing the ways in which people move around and come into contact with each other, the Court is not persuaded that this requires the automatic creation of rights of entry to private property, or even necessarily, to all publically owned property [...] where however the bar on access to property has the effect of preventing any effective exercise of freedom of expression or it can be said that the essence of the right has been destroyed, the Court would not exclude that a positive obligation could arise for the State to protect the enjoyment of Convention rights by regulating property rights. The corporate town, where the entire municipality was controlled by a private body, might be an example', Appleby and others v UK at para 47.

23 Wolfgang Schulz, 'New Public Spheres and How to Incorporate Them into Information Law', *The 1st Berlin Symposium on Internet and Society* (Alexander von Humboldt Institut für Internet und Gesellschaft, 2011).

structural change has resulted in a 'cultural lag',[24] where the legal regulation of social media no longer fit with the paradigms on which laws relating to freedom of expression have been built.[25]

Hence, digital public spheres remain governed by an amorphous rule of individual and collective power relations, as does the internet itself. While a large portion of the internet community emphasises the importance of self-regulation vis-à-vis what is presumed to be oppressive state regulation,[26] the scope of digital censorship and surveillance practices indicate that while direct state governance may be lessened in the digital sphere, censorship practices nevertheless persist, only in new forms and configurations.

In what follows, I identify two digital censorship practices – one clearly interventionist, the other of a more structural nature – that have arisen as effects of these structural changes.[27]

Interventionist Digital Censorship

Interventionist digital censorship is carried out in digital public spheres, typically when a user expresses something that violates the community guidelines of a given institution. As such, interventionist digital censorship aligns with traditional censorship practices, explicitly targeting unwanted expressions such as women's nipples or maps of Kurdistan on Facebook,

24 William Fielding Ogburn, *Social Change with Respect to Cultural and Original Nature* (Delta book; New York: Dell Pub. Co., 1966).

25 Dominic McGoldrick, 'The Limits of Freedom of Expression on Facebook and Social Networking Sites'.

26 Viktor Mayer-Schönberger, 'The Shape of Governance: Analyzing the World of Internet Regulation', *Virginia Journal of International Law* 43/3 (2003), 605–74.

27 These two categories are of course two sides of the same coin, but a distinction may nevertheless serve to nuance the various forms of suppressions that take place in the digital sphere.

copyrighted material on Google, pornography in Apple's online retail shops, etc. There are several agents involved in interventionist digital censorship, both human and non-human, and different degrees of intervention. For the sake of clarity, I reduce these numerous practices to three modes: censorship by corporate employees, censorship by algorithm, and user generated censorship.

The first mode of interventionist digital censorship is carried out by corporate employees. Facebook's User Operations team, for instance, consists of people who regulate users' complaints about content. This team is again subdivided into smaller groups such as the Hate and Harassment Team, which scrolls through streams of reports about bullying, harassment and hate speech, the Safety Team, which patrols for suicidal content, child exploitation and underage users, and the Authenticity Team, which looks into complaints of fake accounts. Due to the enormous workload, the average decision time for workers to determine whether content is appropriate or not is only a second or two.[28] With the growing amount of content, Facebook has also had to outsource regulation to third party agencies.[29]

Employees often rely on reports about content that violates community guidelines. These 'others' who make such reports are typically either algorithms or users. Facebook thus usually blocks content either because it has received a user generated complaint, or because it was flagged by an automated system. Hence, the second mode of digital interventionist censorship is censorship by algorithm, which is to say, by algorithms that are configured to detect potentially offensive material and behaviour, such as spam activity, pornography material and hate speech.[30] Many of these gatekeepers remain invisible until a failure occurs, typically when

28 Emily Bazelon, 'How to Stop the Bullies', *The Atlantic* (20 February 2013).

29 Adrian Chen, 'Inside Facebook's Outsourced Anti-Porn and Gore Brigade, Where "Camel Toes" are More Offensive Than "Crushed Heads"', *Gawker* (16 February 2012).

30 Chloe Albanesius, 'Facebook Reinstates Activists' Accounts After Spam Filter Glitch', *PC Mag* (22 August 2011); Mark Risher, 'Impermium: The Allied Front' <http://www.impermium.com/blog/the-dark-side-of social-protect-your-brand-from-abusive-social-spam/> accessed 13 June 2013.

algorithms have difficulties decoding context, e.g. defining what is 'art' instead of 'pornography'.[31]

The third mode of digital interventionist censorship is user generated. Many digital public spheres have designed and deployed tools to incorporate 'social' feedback into quality assurance algorithms. As a result, user generated censorship, strategic[32] as well as affective, has become an emergent practice. What defines this networked censorship practice is that it differs from normal censorship paradigms in which the censor holds some sort of official and sovereign power. Instead, we see here a new configuration of user power in the context of networked social intermediaries that can best be described as a distributed policing practice.

The three interrelated and synergistic modes of digital interventionist censorship outlined above show that digital information infrastructures have distributed the means and structures of interventionist informational removal. Yet most of these means and structures remain opaque to the user. Users rarely see the internally communicated rules that underpin externally communicated guidelines. Moreover, they only receive a brief notification upon removal of what is deemed to be indecent material.[33] In some cases the user's account is even blocked without further notice.[34]

The time constraint imposed on employees also means that the time available to double-check user reports is highly limited. Indeed, the outsourcing practices and mistakes suggest that employees are not necessarily in any more of an enlightened position than the user when it comes to evaluating acts of censorship. The same argument can be made for the algorithm side of the equation. Those responding to cases automatically flagged for follow-up do not necessarily understand why and on what basis

31 Tarleton Gillespie, 'Can an Algorithm be Wrong?', *limn*, 2 (2011).

32 Josh Halliday, 'Digg investigates claims of conservative "censorship"', *The Guardian* (6 August 2010).

33 Roland Simon-Schäfer and Walther Christoph Zimmerli, *Theorie zwischen Kritik und Praxis: Jürgen Habermas und die Frankfurter Schule* (Problemata: Stuttgart, Frommann Holzboog, 1975).

34 Marc Heckert, 'Wie ein Handy-Fan von Wolke Sieben fiel', *Aachener Zeitung* (February 1 2011).

the computer-generated censorship has reacted. Instead, an opaque presumption of fault is generated by the system, and only a secondary human finding – challenging this very code – can overrule the decision. This sort of open-loop system is often hailed to insure against erroneous decisions, but as shown in other areas it may equally exacerbate the problem.

While highly opaque, digital censorship structures do surface when systems fail. Facebook thus calculates with a certain margin of error when it comes to these distinctions.[35] Examples show how wide that margin is. In 2013, Paris' Jeu de Paume temporarily lost its account privileges after the museum posted an image from an exhibition on nude studies. Facebook removed the photo and disabled the institution's account for 24 hours, threatening to deactivate it entirely if the museum persisted in its nude postings.[36] In 2012, Facebook censored Gerhard Richter's *Ema* (1966) on the Pompidou Center's web page. When Facebook took down Richter's work, it was because the nude painting was mistaken for a photograph.[37] And in 2011, Facebook banned Gustave Courbet's *L'Origine du Monde* (1866).[38]

Facebook's practices are not unique, however; other digital public spheres have even stricter censorship practices. In the case of award-winning Danish author Peter Øvig Knudsen, for instance, both Apple and Facebook banned his works featuring images of naked hippies.[39] In another case, Microsoft's new cloud service SkyDrive disabled an account after the user stored and circulated images of Amedeo Modigliani's painting *Reclining Nude* (1917).[40] While the political and ethical problems these tendencies

35 John Seed, 'When Is a Nude OK on Facebook?', *Huffington Post* (24 May 2010).

36 Kate Deimling, 'Facebook Censors Paris's Jeu de Paume, Threatens to Deactivate the Museum's Account', *Blouin Artinfo* (6 March 2013).

37 Juliette Soulez, 'Facebook Censors Pompidou's Gerhard Richter Nude, Fueling Fight Over "Institutional Puritanism"', *Blouin Artinfo* (31 July 2012).

38 Alan Posener, 'Facebook verbannt weibliches Genital von Websites', *Die Welt* (15 April 2011).

39 Michael Posner, 'Nudity, E-books and Censorship: How Apple became Big Brother', *The Globe and Mail* (21 November 2012); Ritzau, 'Løkkegaard støtter Forfatter i Kamp mod Facebook', *Information* (11 June 2013).

40 Ingrid Lunden, 'Microsoft SkyDrive "Confuses Naked With Nude", Art Account Frozen', *paidContent* (17 January 2012).

give rise to are acknowledged on a political level, a legal solution has yet to be found.[41]

What these examples and modes of digital interventionist censorship practices show is that the transfiguration of public spheres into digital quasi-public spheres has not only hampered existing freedom of expression provisions, but also relegated censorship practices, rules and infrastructures to the automated actions of machines and placed them under a corporate veil, leaving them close to impenetrable and/or unintelligible for the user as well as corporate employees and other involved actors.

As the following section shows, a second kind of censorship of a more structural kind seems even more opaque. While these mechanisms – and their implications – may be harder to conceptualise than interventionist digital censorship, they are nevertheless just as powerful structures, which organise our ways of being and thinking just as deeply as, if not more than, interventionist digital censorship. As the following section shows, while these mechanisms do not actively prevent access, they do, however, create regimes of visibility and invisibility that act as a kind of distribution of what one recollects and does not recollect. One possible side effect is an environment in which the active co-shaping of online activity potentially limits the possibilities for confrontation with difference. Such an environment would, then, according to Rancière, effectively rule out the potential for politics.[42]

Structural Digital Censorship

In contrast to interventionist censorship, structural digital censorship does not actively remove content. It does, however, create regimes of visibility and invisibility. The question of structural digital censorship is thus not so

41 European Federation of Journalists, 'On Apple and de facto Censorship', in *EFJ General Meeting Resolutions*, 13–14.

42 Jacques Rancière, *Disagreement: Politics and Philosophy* (Minneapolis: University of Minnesota Press, 1999).

much about what the internet is hiding from the user per se as it is about the kinds of manipulations corporations and people use to create different kinds of regimes of visibility.

Digital public spheres (Amazon, Google, Facebook etc.) capture and collect increasing amounts of personal information at each visit, on the basis of which websites custom-design themselves to conform to our perceived preferences by means of algorithms.[43] These configurations are made possible by intelligent web systems that are said to facilitate situations of self-governance, in which a 'power over' attitude is superseded by a 'power with' approach that recognises that everyone is able to contribute to the production and organisation of, and navigation within, information.[44] Within this digital environment, web users are configured as empowered. This empowerment is felt as autonomy, inclusion and recognition, and is in particular facilitated by the ease with which users can curate, navigate, leave and enter various web information assemblages through a multitude of entry and exit points. Users create these entry and exit points by means of identifying nodes of connections themselves. Yet in this process they also release ever more information about themselves that is immediately captured and processed by a wide range of corporations and public institutions.[45]

While the digital environment allows one to disengage from the disciplinary system of analog knowledge systems, for instance through disintermediation of experts and algorithmic deterritorialisation of traditional taxonomic systems, the web user is nevertheless still administered, regulated and interpellated by a multiplicity of governing principles, from algorithms to commercial interests, as well as the movements of oneself and other users. These digital interpellative mechanisms form an ever-tighter grid

43 Eli Pariser, *The Filter Bubble: What the Internet is Hiding from you* (New York: Penguin Press, 2011).

44 Wendy Hui Kyong Chun, *Control and Freedom: Power and Paranoia in the Age of Fiber Optics* (Cambridge, MA: MIT Press, 2006).

45 Philip Agre, 'Surveillance and Capture: Two Models of Privacy,' in Noah Wardrip-Fruin and Nick Montfort, eds, *The New Media Reader* (Cambridge, MA: MIT Press, 2003), 740–60.

around the user: the needs and actions of users are increasingly preempted by protocological algorithms that preclude alternatives by partitioning results and gently inciting future movements in the manner of 'If you like this, you might also like …'

These intelligent web systems are thus not only censoring mechanisms in the sense that they curate content, but also take on a 'constitutive' role as discourse regulators, influencing what can be said by whom, to whom, how, and in what context. The advantage of these systems is that the sprawling web becomes seemingly navigable. The drawback is that such systems necessarily cut off certain options and possibilities on behalf of the user; the algorithmic operations thus imply that users are not only calculable, but that they can also be controlled.[46]

Hence, it has been argued that these algorithmic controls create a situation in which digital public spheres become 'echo chambers' that feed the *sein* of desires instead of the moral imperative of *sollen*, ultimately eliminating the possibility of dissensus and thus of politics.[47] Moreover, it seems important to note that the protocological organisational mechanisms not only *represent* desires, but also *predicate* the user's identity on certain hegemonic patterns by way of group interpellations, thus actively co-shaping what actors do.[48] Antoinette Rouvroy has thus noted how the algorithms that guide our paths perform a kind of 'algorithmic governmentality' that enclose users into predetermined pathways created by the past behavior of both the individual and the collective.[49]

46 Alain Desrosières, 'Mapping the Social World: From Aggregates to Individuals', *limn* 2 (2012); Yvonne Hofstetter, 'Ein totalitäres System', *Frankfurter Allgemeine* (9 June 2013).

47 Cass R. Sunstein, *Republic.com 2.0* (Princeton, NJ: Princeton University Press, 2007), 49; Jacques Rancière et al., 'Democracy, Dissensus, and the Aesthetics of Class Struggle: An Exchange', *Historical Materialism* 13/4 (2005), 285–301. Jacques Rancière, 'The Ethical Turn of Aesthetics and Politics', *Critical Horizons* 7/1 (2006), 1–20.

48 Alexander Galloway, *Protocol*, 115; Peter-Paul Verbeek, 'Artifacts and Attachment: A Post-Script Philosophy of Mediation', in Hans Harbers, ed., *Inside the Politics of Technology* (Amsterdam: Amsterdam University Press, 2005), 125–46, 125.

49 Antoinette Rouvroy, 'The End(s) of Critique: Data-Behaviourism Vs. Due-Process,' in Mireille Hildebrandt and Katja de Vries, eds, *Privacy, Due Process and*

The implications for these continual constructions of identities, and the structural censorship practices accompanying them, imply the emergence of a new kind of 'soft biopolitics',[50] which raises significant questions about the concepts of freedom and expression that inform the liberal conception of the public sphere. How may we understand these algorithmic discourse regulators as structural censorship mechanisms? Are they transparent enough, or should more criteria be revealed? And can other regimes of visibility be created through alternative algorithms?

Certainly, it can be plausibly argued that the new digital navigational techniques are more than a technical occurrence; rather, they signal a more general operative logic that creates a regime of anticipation in which invisible preemptive measures make interventionist acts of censorship obsolete.[51]

Conclusion: On Conspiracy, Invisibility and Censorship

The infrastructures of digital public spheres show that websites are never merely 'on the internet', but that they are mediated by certain systems and infrastructures. And examples in recent years have revealed that these infrastructures are far from neutral.

The ideals of transparency and access have consequently been challenged by those of (in)visibility and findability. And as the NSA scandal has shown, the liberating notions of decentralisation and self-governance brought on by digitisation practices has in many instances turned out to

---

the Computational Turn: The Philosophy of Law Meets the Philosophy of Technology (Abingdon: Routledge, 2013), 143–68.

50 John Cheney-Lippold, 'A New Algorithmic Identity: Soft Biopolitics and the Modulation of Control', *Theory, Culture & Society* 28/6 (2011), 164–81.

51 Brian Massumi, 'Potential Politics and the Primacy of Preemption', *Theory & Event* 10/2 (2007); Adrian Mackenzie, 'Programming subjects in the Regime of Anticipation: Software Studies and Subjectivity', *Subjectivity* 6/4 (2013), 391–405.

be shibboleths for other kinds of power (ab)uses. These revelations have given rise to a sense of paranoia about the intentions of 'the market', 'the state', and 'technology', a paranoia that is arguably a symptom of our times arising out of the evasive infrastructures of the internet and the world wide web, the many digital public spheres they host, the logics that guide them, and the practices they support.[52]

This chapter seeks to mitigate outright paranoia by making visible a fragment of the infrastructures of certain digital public spheres and the practices they institute, from deeper structural cultural programming practices to more obvious acts of censorship by employees, algorithms, and users. What this mapping shows is not so much a blueprint for conspiracy. Instead, it indicates a 'cultural lag' in which our epistemological notions of censorship and the political and legal frameworks to ensure accountability no longer correspond to technological infrastructures and private practices.

Individuals are increasingly consenting to surveillance and control in a Faustian bargain for their data and behaviour. And expressions are increasingly regulated outside the scope of international covenants and treaties. If this gap between our epistemological notions of censorship and the political and legal frameworks to ensure protection against it is to be lessened, a double-barreled reconceptualisation must take place, one that concurrently rethinks the notion of censorship and reevaluates the rights of individuals in privately operated public spheres.

Bibliography

Agre, Philip, 'Surveillance and Capture: Two Models of Privacy,' in Noah Wardrip-Fruin and Nick Montfort, eds, *The New Media Reader* (Cambridge, MA: MIT Press, 2003), 740–60.

52 Fredric Jameson, 'Cognitive Mapping', in Cary Nelson and Lawrence Grossberg, eds, *Marxism and the Interpretation of Culture* (Urbana: University of Illinois Press, 1988), 347–60.

Albanesius, 'Facebook Reinstates Activists' Accounts After Spam Filter Glitch', *PC Mag* (22 August 2011).

Atkins, Robert, and Svetlana Mintcheva, National Coalition against Censorship (US), *Censoring Culture: Contemporary threats to free expression* (New York: New Press, 2006).

Bazelon, Emily, 'How to Stop the Bullies', *The Atlantic* (20 February 2013).

Beck, Ulrich, Anthony Giddens and Scott Lash, *Reflexive Modernization: Politics, Tradition and Aesthetics in the Modern Social Order* (Cambridge: Polity Press, 1994).

Bogost, Ian, 'The New Aesthetic Needs to Get Weirder', *The Atlantic* (13 April 2012).

Bourdieu, Pierre and John B. Thompson, *Language and Symbolic Power* (Cambridge, MA: Harvard University Press, 1991).

Bowker, Geoffrey C., et al., 'Toward Information Infrastructure Studies: Ways of Knowing in a Networked Environment', in Jeremy Hunsinger, Lisbeth Klastrup and Matthew Allen, eds, *International Handbook of Internet Research* (Dordrecht: London, Springer, 2010), 97–117.

Buchanan, Matt, 'The NSA's Prism Remains Opaque', *The New Yorker* (13 June 2013).

Butler, Judith, 'Ruled Out: Vocabularies of the Censor', in Robert C. Post, ed., *Censorship and Silencing: Practices of Cultural Regulation* (Los Angeles: Getty Research Institute for the History of Art and the Humanities, 1998), 247–60.

Chen, Adrian, 'Inside Facebook's Outsourced Anti-Porn and Gore Brigade, Where "Camel Toes" are More Offensive Than "Crushed Heads"', *Gawker* (16 February 2012).

Cheney-Lippold, John, 'A New Algorithmic Identity: Soft Biopolitics and the Modulation of Control', *Theory, Culture & Society* 28/6 (2011), 164–81.

Chun, Wendy Hui Kyong, *Control and Freedom: Power and Paranoia in the Age of Fiber Optics* (Cambridge, MA: MIT Press, 2006).

Coetzee, J. M., *Giving Offense: Essays on Censorship* (Chicago: University of Chicago Press, 1996).

Deibert, Ronald et al., *Access Contested: Security, Identity, and Resistance in Asian Cyberspace Information Revolution and Global Politics* (Cambridge, MA: MIT Press, 2012).

——, *Access Controlled: The Shaping of Power, Rights, and Rule in Cyberspace* (Cambridge, MA: MIT Press, 2010).

——, *Access Denied: The Practice and Policy of Global Internet Filtering* (Cambridge, MA: MIT Press, 2008).

Deimling, Kate, 'Facebook Censors Paris's Jeu de Paume, Threatens To Deactivate the Museum's Accoun', *Blouin Artinfo* (6 March 2013).

Desrosières, Alain, 'Mapping the Social World: From Aggregates to Individuals', *limn* 2 (2012).

Dutton, William H., Anna Dopatka, Ginette Law and Victoria Nash, *Freedom of Connection, Freedom of Expression: The Changing Legal and Regulatory Ecology Shaping the Internet* (Paris, UNESCO, 2011).

European Federation of Journalists, 'On Apple and de facto censorship', in *EFJ General Meeting Resolutions* (13–15 May 2013), 13–14.

Galloway, Alexander, 'Black Box, Black Bloc', in Benjamin Noys, ed., *Communization and its Discontents: Contestation, Critique, and Contemporary Struggles* (New York: Autonomedia, 2012), 237–52.

——, *Protocol: How Control Exists after Decentralization* (Cambridge, MA: MIT Press, 2004).

Gillespie, Tarleton, 'Can an Algorithm be Wrong?', *limn* 2 (2011).

——, 'The Relevance of Algorithms', in Tarleton Gillespie, Pablo Boczkowski and Kirsten Foot, eds, *Media Technologies* (Cambridge, MA: MIT Press, 2013).

Halliday, Josh, 'Digg Investigates Claims of Conservative "Censorship"', *The Guardian* (6 August 2010).

Hamburger, Joseph, *John Stuart Mill on Liberty and Control* (Princeton, NJ: Princeton University Press, 1999).

Heckert, Marc, 'Wie ein Handy-Fan von Wolke Sieben fiel', *Aachener Zeitung* (1 February 2011).

Hofstetter, Yvonne, 'Ein totalitäres System', *Frankfurter Allgemeine* (9 June 2013).

Hunsinger, Jeremy, 'Broadening Possibilities by Expanding the Theoretical Richness of the Social Construction of Technology', *Social Epistemology* 19/2–3 (2005), 255–59.

——, 'Knowledge and Cultural Production in the Context of Contemporary Capitalism: A response to Wittkower', *Fast Capitalism* 4/1 (2008).

——, 'Toward Nomadological Cyberinfrastructures', in Jeremy Hunsinger, Lisbeth Klastrup and Matthew Allen, eds, *The International Handbook of Internet Research* (Dordrecht: London, Springer, 2010), 267–78.

——, 'Toward a Transdisciplinary Internet Research', *The Information Society* 21/4 (2005a), 277–79.

Jameson, Fredric, 'Cognitive Mapping', in Cary Nelson and Lawrence Grossberg, eds, *Marxism and the Interpretation of Culture* (Urbana: University of Illinois Press, 1988), 347–60.

Kelion, Leo, 'Censoring Facebook: Social Network's Violent Video Dilemma', *BBC News* (9 May 2013).

Koselleck, Reinhart, *Futures Past: On the Semantics of Historical Time* (New York: Columbia University Press, 2004).

Lunden, Ingrid, 'Microsoft SkyDrive "Confuses Naked With Nude", Art Account Frozen', *paidContent* (17 January 2012)

McGoldrick, Dominic, 'The Limits of Freedom of Expression on Facebook and Social Networking Sites: A UK Perspective', *Human Rights Law Review* 13/1 (2013), 125–51.

Mackenzie, Adrian, 'Programming Subjects in the Regime of Anticipation: Software Studies and Subjectivity', *Subjectivity* 6/4 (2013), 391–405.

McNamee, Joe, 'The Slide from "Self-Regulation" to Corporate Censorship', 2013 <http://www.edri.org/files/EDRI_selfreg_final_20110124.pdf> accessed 3 March 2013.

Madrigal, Alexis C., 'How Facebook Designs the "Perfect Empty Vessel" for Your Mind', *The Atlantic* (2 May 2013).

Massumi, Brian, 'Potential Politics and the Primacy of Preemption', *Theory & Event* 10/2 (2007).

Mayer-Schönberger, Viktor, 'The Shape of Governance: Analyzing the World of Internet Regulation', *Virginia Journal of International Law* 43/3 (2003), 605–74.

Mill, John Stuart, *Nature: The Utility of Religion and Theism* (London: Longmans, Green, Reader, and Dyer, 1874).

New York Times, 'Hate Speech on Facebook', *New York Times* (31 May 2013).

Ogburn, William Fielding, *Social Change with Respect to Cultural and Original Nature* (New York: Dell Pub. Co., 1966).

Pariser, Eli, *The Filter Bubble: What the Internet is Hiding from You* (New York: Penguin Press, 2011).

Phillips, David, and Klaus Wiegerling, 'Introduction to IRIE Vol. 8', *International Review of Information Ethics* 8/12 (2007), 4–6.

Posener, Alan, 'Facebook verbannt weibliches Genital von Websites', *Die Welt* (15 April 2011).

Posner, Michael, 'Nudity, E-books and Censorship: How Apple became Big Brother', *The Globe and Mail* (21 November 2012).

Rancière, Jacques, *Disagreement: Politics and Philosophy* (Minneapolis: University of Minnesota Press, 1999).

——, 'The Ethical Turn of Aesthetics and Politics', *Critical Horizons* 7/1 (2006), 1–20.

——, et al., 'Democracy, Dissensus, and the Aesthetics of Class Struggle: An Exchange', *Historical Materialism* 13/4 (2005), 285–301.

Ratto, Matt, 'Ethics of Seamless infrastructures: Resources and Future Directions', *International Review of Information Ethics* 8/12 (2007), 20–27.

Ries, Brian, 'Bea Arthur's Boobs Got Us Booted From Facebook', *The Daily Beast* (16 May 2013).

Risher, Mark, 'Impermium: The Allied Front' <http://www.impermium.com/blog/the-dark-side-of-social-protect-your-brand-from-abusive-social-spam/> accessed 13 June 2013.

Ritzau, 'Løkkegaard støtter Forfatter i Kamp mod Facebook', *Information* (11 June 2013).

Rosenberg, Richard, 'Controlling Access to the Internet: The role of Filtering', *Ethics and Information Technology* 3/1 (2001), 35–44.

Rosenfeld, Sophia, 'Writing the History of Censorship in the Age of Enlightenment', in Daniel Gordon, ed., *Postmodernism and the Enlightenment: New Perspectives in Eighteenth-century French Intellectual History* (New York: Routledge, 2001), 117–45.

Rouvroy, Antoinette, 'The End(s) of Critique: Data-Behaviourism Vs. Due-Process', in Mireille Hildebrandt and Katja de Vries, eds, *Privacy, Due Process and the Computational Turn: The Philosophy of Law Meets the Philosophy of Technology* (Abingdon: Routledge, 2013), 143–68.

Rowbottom, Jacob, 'To Rant, Vent and Converse: Protecting Low Level Speech', *The Cambridge Law Journal* 71/02 (2012), 355–83.

Schulz, Wolfgang, 'New Public Spheres and How to Incorporate Them into Information Law', *The 1st Berlin Symposium on Internet and Society* (Alexander von Humboldt Institut für Internet und Gesellschaft, 2011).

Seed, John, 'When Is a Nude OK on Facebook?', *Huffington Post* (24 May 2010).

Simon-Schäfer, Roland and Walther Christoph Zimmerli, *Theorie zwischen Kritik und Praxis: Jürgen Habermas und die Frankfurter Schule* (Stuttgart: Frommann Holzboog, 1975).

Soulez, Juliette, 'Facebook Censors Pompidou's Gerhard Richter Nude, Fueling Fight Over "Institutional Puritanism"', *Blouin Artinfo* (31 July 2012).

Star, Susan Leigh and Karen Ruhleder, 'Steps towards an Ecology of Infrastructure: Complex Problems in Design and Access for Large-scale Collaborative Systems', 1994 ACM Conference on Computer supported Cooperative Work, Chapel Hill, NC, 1994.

Striphas, Theodore G., *The Late Age of Print: Everyday Book Culture from Consumerism to Control* (New York: Columbia University Press, 2009).

Sunstein, Cass R., *Republic.com 2.0* (Princeton, NJ: Princeton University Press, 2007).

Verbeek, Peter-Paul, 'Artifacts and Attachment: A Post-Script Philosophy of Mediation', in Hans Harbers, ed., *Inside the Politics of Technology* (Amsterdam: Amsterdam University Press 2005), 125–46.

York, Jillian C., Robert Faris and Ron Deibert, 'Policing Content in the Quasi-Public Sphere (OpenNet Initiative, 2010).

HENRIETTE STEINER AND KRISTIN VEEL

16 Visible in Theory: Perceived Visibility as Symbolic Form – A Photo-Expedition into a Contemporary Urban Environment

The glass façade is commonly found in recently developed urban areas, suggesting an architectural typology in which transparency dominates. In modernist architecture such as Mies van der Rohe's famous *Farnsworth House* (1951), large glass panes were meant to create a direct link between the interior spaces and an ideal, unspoilt natural environment surrounding them. But few people live in natural surroundings. In contemporary Western culture, it is rather the urban environment that is the most typical human biotope; and in this context, the idea that the glass façade or panorama window facilitates direct communication between inside and outside becomes problematic. Glass, of course, not only allows someone to appreciate the surrounding environment, it also allows the gazes of others to penetrate the private sphere. Yet at the same time, even highly transparent architectures give rise to a spectrum of unexpected opacities. Hence a glass façade can also function as a reflective screen: what we think is visible is, in fact, often invisible, and vice versa. We propose that such situations can be understood as an aesthetic experience of 'perceived visibility', according to which visuality (seeing and being seen) is emphasised – but seldom realised – through a particular formal architectural language. We are concerned here with situations in which we are simply 'visible in theory'.

This chapter explores the aesthetic paradigm of perceived visibility as a particular form of seeing – and not seeing – that is deeply ingrained in the modern imagination, and which can be associated with three architectural typologies or concepts: the 'panopticon', the seemingly transparent 'glass façade', and the 'black box'. We understand the visual culture of perceived visibility as a 'symbolic form' in the tradition of Ernst Cassirer, and we approach these three typologies as 'concrete material signs' of this symbolic form.[1] Our aim is to show how the panopticon, the glass façade, and the black box respectively can be viewed as concrete architectural expressions that meet functional and site-specific needs, but which are also infused with a culturally charged, symbolic layer of meaning.

A symbolic form can be understood as an experiential and expressive framework, which also determines what is communicated. In this sense, we are exploring the cultural foundations for 'what we see' and 'how we see' when confronted with particular forms of contemporary urban architecture, and probing the visual culture this form of architecture embodies. We thus propose that architecture which embodies the symbolic form of perceived visibility gestures towards a more fundamental negotiation of the categories of the visible and the invisible in contemporary culture. This process can be illuminated by an investigation of concrete architectural settings.

Using a photo-expedition through the contemporary urban-planning context of Ørestaden in Copenhagen[2] as a case study, we explore how the material culture of contemporary architecture contributes to a reconfiguration of the visible and the invisible. We use this case study to read the formal architectural language, as well as the material and construction of

1 According to Cassirer, a symbolic form consists of three elements: a sensory sign, a spiritual meaning, and a spiritual energy, which describes how the other two are connected. Echoing Kant's concept of the schema, a symbolic form is characterised by the interaction of the transformative energy of the spirit and the concrete, perceptible sign. The concrete presents itself to the senses and can be perceived, but it is simultaneously linked to a spiritual meaning, which determines its form and perception. What Cassirer calls spirit may only be experienced when it manifests itself in something concrete. Likewise, something concrete can only be experienced and recognised when it is structured and has a meaning. Ernst Cassirer, 'Der Begriff der symbolischen Form im Aufbau der Geisteswissenschaften', in *Wesen und Wirkung des Symbolbegriffs* [1956] (Darmstadt: Wissenschaftliche Buchgesellschaft, 1977), 169–201.

2 The text can thus be regarded as site-specific in the sense used by Jane Rendell in her contribution to this volume. However, we also posit a general applicability that would make the same approach relevant to other architectural environments.

specific settings, in relation to the aesthetic tradition of Ørestaden's principal architectural paradigm, and to consider how the public and private, the visible and invisible, are renegotiated in this context. Seen in this way, Ørestaden provides an example of perceived visibility as a symbolic form in contemporary culture, and allows us to investigate, polemically, perhaps, concrete instances of its materialisation.[3]

Ørestaden, a New Urban Environment in Copenhagen

Our study focuses on the newly developed urban area of Ørestaden in Copenhagen, which stretches five kilometres from the old industrial harbour of Copenhagen across the island of Amager, where large building complexes have been erected on a previously unused field.[4] Reaching towards the southeast of Amager and towards Sweden on the other side of the Øresund strait, Ørestaden is close to Copenhagen's urban core, making this area an obvious choice for extending the capital. The political decision to use this area for development was made in 1992. Alongside the urban project of Ørestaden, local infrastructure has also been developed: in 2000, a railroad station and a bridge across Øresund to Sweden were opened, and in 2002, a lightweight urban train line, part of the Copenhagen metro, was put into use (see Figure 16.1). The most recent building boom in the area, in particular of residential buildings, was planned around the economic boom that peaked in 2008 just before the onset of the financial crisis.

3 We would like to thank Mikkel Gerken for accompanying us on this photo expedition and helping us to produce the images. Our approach and conceptual framework draws on a similar exploration of a building in Copenhagen harbour, described in Henriette Steiner and Kristin Veel, 'Living Behind Glass Facades: Surveillance Culture and New Architecture', *Surveillance & Society* 9/1–2 (2011), 215–32.

4 As opposed to the German topographies that Dora Osborne deals with in her chapter on German 'memory culture' in this volume, this piece of land is surprisingly unmarked by traces of the past, despite being heavily laden with history.

In 2013, Ørestaden had 8,500 inhabitants, and this figure is projected to reach 20,000 within the next decade.[5] It thereby constitutes a huge urban planning project, not only on a national scale, but also at the European level.

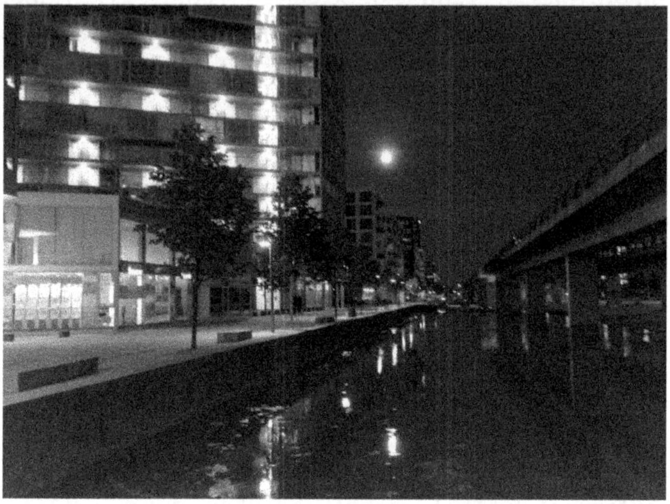

Fig. 16.1: 'Ørestad city' by night. The bridge on the right-hand side of the picture is for the lightweight train.
Credit: Kristin Veel.

The planners and architects of such new urban constituencies aim to create areas full of life, accommodating a large number of people and functions.[6] This suggests a response to the widespread criticism of the modernist urban paradigm according to which cities are dominated by the recurrence of similar high-rise buildings and by the separation of functions, whereby cities and the lives of their citizens are organised in four sectors; dwelling, work, leisure and infrastructure. This criticism has influenced architecture and planning discourse, especially since the 1980s.

5 <http://www.urbandanmark.dk/index.php/33-demografi-hovedstaden/900-1000-nye-beboere-i-orestad-pa-et-ar> accessed 9 August 2013.

6 See Udviklingsselskabet By & Havn, *Godt Begyndt – Et tilbageblik over Ørestads Udvikling* (Copenhagen: By & Havn, 2010), 5, 9.

Yet, despite this inherent form of resistance to modernist architectural planning practice, recently planned urban areas such as Ørestaden are often best described as representing a neo-modernist architectural paradigm.[7] For when we visit an urban environment such as Ørestaden, we are confronted with large-scale, largely mono-functional high-rise buildings presented in a reduced, functional (if sometimes 'spectacular') aesthetic that uses a rather limited inventory of cool materials (concrete, steel, glass, a little aluminium, the odd splash of colour). There are plenty of garages for parking, and an efficient infrastructure, which in the case of Ørestaden is seen paradigmatically in the Copenhagen Metro (see map, Figure 16.2). The train line emerges from its unseen underground location in the central district of Copenhagen and sweeps through Ørestaden, elevated on a bridge. Apart from large institutions such as university campuses or large company headquarters like the National Danish Broadcasting Company, there are only few institutional structures. People mainly shop in the shopping centre appropriately named 'Fields', which has been dubbed 'Scandinavia's biggest shopping centre'.[8]

As a structure, Ørestaden seems far removed from contemporary, nostalgically inclined urbanistic attitudes, such as New Urbanism, where block-structures, squares and piazzas are reintroduced into the urban fabric.[9] In fact – and this is already indicated in the terms of the original competition, which suggested building a new city 'from scratch' on a barren field – it seems closer to Le Corbusier's Plan Voisin of 1927. In his modernist urban plan for Paris, Le Corbusier set a radical new paradigm, suggesting the centre of Paris should be bulldozed and replaced with a rational pattern of high-rise structures. Today, the area of Ørestaden makes a monumental impression, where huge architectural structures are isolated in the vast nothingness of

7 See Birgitte Bundesen Svarre and Pia Rost Rasmussen, 'Byen set fra oven – Michel de Certeau og planerne for Ørestad', in Henrik Reeh et al., ed., *Rumlig Kultur* (Copenhagen: Museum Tusculanum Press, 2012). For a more general discussion of the neo-modernist paradigm in the 1990s, see Claus Bech-Danielsen and Jens Schjerup Hansen, eds, *Modernismens Genkomst* (Copenhagen: Arkitektens Forlag, 2001).

8 Udviklingsselskabet By & Havn, *Godt Begyndt*, 31.

9 The latter more organic development of previous industrial sites is explored in Mark Vacher's chapter in this volume.

empty space and communicate with each other by means of their common aesthetic orientation.[10] We argue that this sense of coherence in terms of urban planning, aesthetic expression and sociality makes Ørestad a kind of urban 'environment'.[11] The vast fields surrounding the development make the buildings visible from far away. They produce a clear line, which, in the Danish context, marks an extreme horizontal contrast to the tall developments of new architectural icons that have already become popular sites of architectural tourism, in particular projects by the architectural practice Bjarke Ingels Group (BIG).

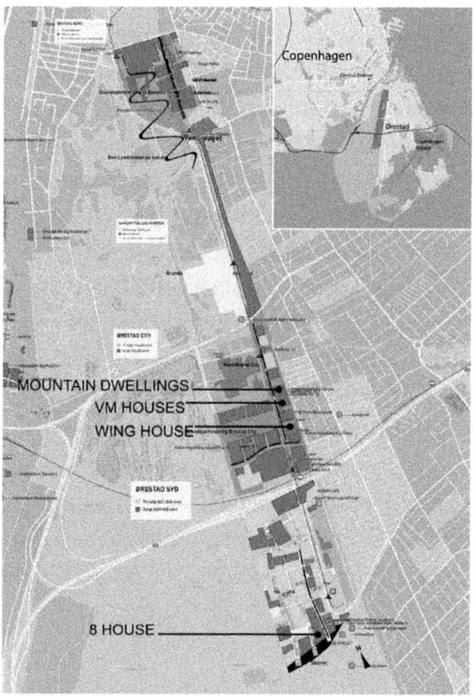

Fig. 16.2: Map of Ørestad, highlighting the main institutions and sites, the Copenhagen Metro and the relationship of Ørestad to central Copenhagen (small map). Credit: By & Havn.

10 Svarre and Rasmussen, 'Byen set fra oven', 144–6.

11 Other types of urban environments are explored in this book in the chapter by Henrik Reeh.

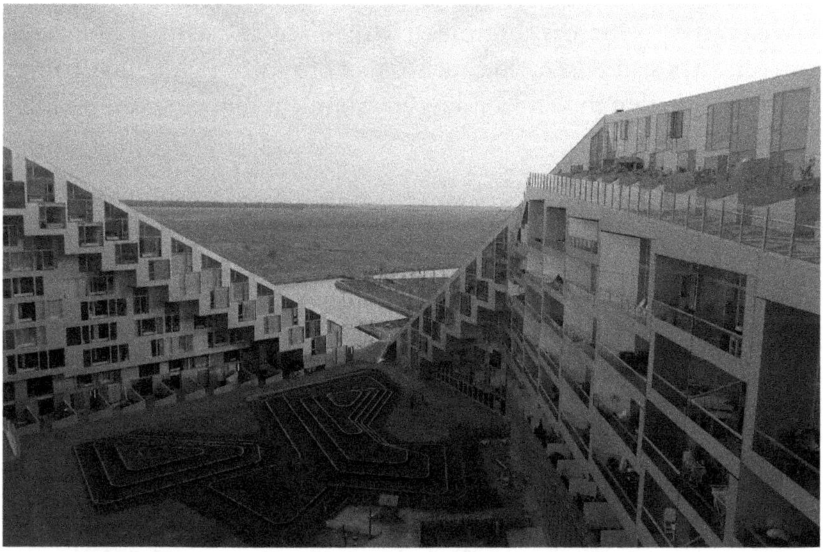

Fig. 16.3: Inner courtyard of *8 House*, BIG (2010), from the top floor of the building. Credit: Mikkel Gerken.

This picture (Figure 16.3) reveals the stunning view towards the large surrounding fields from the residential building *8 House* BIG, which won the category for best housing project at the World Architecture Festival in 2011. The building complex, with its large, semi-open structure and use of materials that reflect the sun, constitutes a deconstructed courtyard structure and pitches its oblique form against the flatness of the adjacent 'Amager common'.

The Panopticon: Surveying the Field

As Le Corbusier's drawing (Figure 16.4) illustrates, in modernist architecture the desire for a direct link between inside and outside, for transparency, can be seen as an attempt to re-establish contact between the urban dweller and nature, a relationship lost in the modern city. Here we see how, in the high-rise building, man is reduced to a kind of Cartesian eye, which because of its elevated position, is confronted with 'space' and nature. Conversely, however, a Miesian glass façade, such as that of Farnsworth House, conveys the impression that the surrounding environment flows into the building.

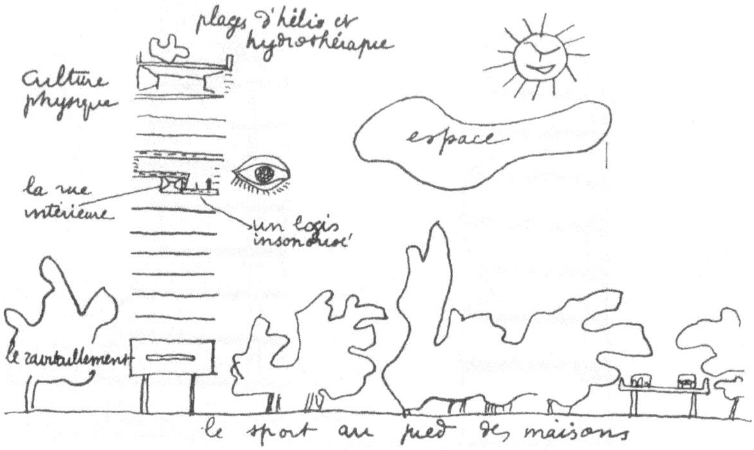

Fig. 16.4: Le Corbusier, Section of the Ville Radieuse, c. 1924.
Credit: FLC/PROLITTERIS, 2013.

Yet when this form of thinking is brought to bear on urban architecture in denser contexts than Le Corbusier's completely freestanding high-rise building, or Mies van der Rohe's secluded holiday home, we may find unexpected situations of visibility. The glass façade opens itself to our inquisitive gaze. Thus, we might ask whether the panopticon, one of the key architectural forms embodying modern culture's desire to see, control and surveil, can be regarded as the flipside of this use of transparent glass in architecture.

As can be seen from the view above the inner courtyard of *8 House*, what came to mind when we visited was precisely the spatial form of the panopticon. This can be seen clearly when a spectator is introduced into the inner courtyard (Figure 16.5). The father of the panopticon, the Enlightenment philosopher, Jeremy Bentham (1748–1832), worked on the assumption that visibility would reform the criminal. His infamous panopticon prison structure featured prison cells filled with light and placed along the inner curvature of a circular building.[12] These cells could be seen by the warden at any time from his position in a watchtower at the centre of the building complex. Since the prisoners did not know when they were being watched, they were forced to act as if they were being observed at all times. In this sense, the panopticon embodies an extreme variant of what we have called 'perceived visibility', insofar as the gaze from the outside eventually becomes internalised and expected by the inmates. According to Bentham's reformist principle, the prisoners would internalise the panoptic gaze and be able to re-enter society in a reformed state: the panopticon was supposed to control the wild forces of human nature.

The logic of the panopticon can be heard in the dictum 'if you've got nothing to hide, you've got nothing to fear', and is still inherent to the way transparency is often positively connoted today. Different allusions to transparency – whether through architectural constructions or other technologies that give access to data, or reveal internal processes to the public – are crucial to the way corporations and institutions like to picture themselves.[13] When it comes to residential architecture, this is also echoed in contemporary culture, insofar as people consider themselves absolutely modern and exceptionally open minded when living behind large glass windows.[14] By implication, potential exposure equals security, sociality, and a morally superior position. In this case, perceived visibility carries with it an early version of the modern reformist credo. As the photo suggests, insofar as a building such as *8 House* embodies the logic of the panopticon, it reveals itself as a concrete material sign that makes evident the cultural logic of the visuality that it fosters. In this way *8 House* gestures towards perceived visibility as a symbolic form.

12 See Devika Sharma's chapter for a consideration of the panopticon structure in relation to contemporary prisons.

13 Steiner and Veel, 'Living Behind Glass Facades'.

14 See the anthropological interviews with people living in similar buildings in other Copenhagen locations in Marie Stender, 'Glashuse til Debat: En Nation af Vindueskiggere', *ARKFOKUS: Tidsskrift for Arkitektur, Design, By og Land* 10 (2006), 10–15.

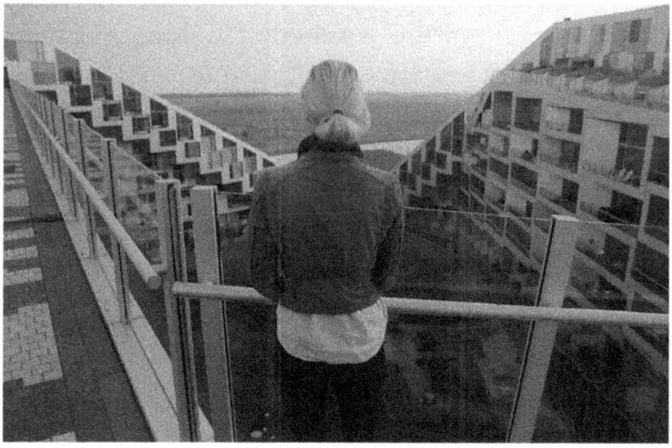

Fig. 16.5: Viewer's perspective of the inner courtyard of *8 House*, BIG (2010). Credit: Mikkel Gerken.

The building complex comes to indicate – possibly inadvertently – the idea of a transparent way of living, despite the enclosed appearance of the inner façade. It constantly prompts us to ask whether we are seen by someone. The answer to this question seems to oscillate between 'yes', 'no', and 'potentially', which brings us a step further towards understanding how perceived visibility is negotiated in the present context.

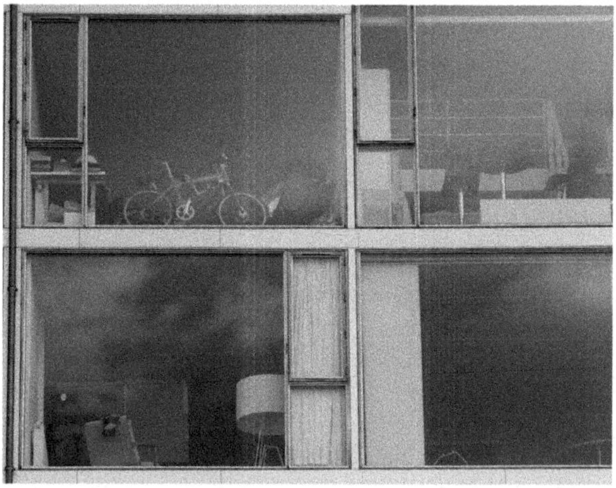

Fig. 16.6: View of interior, *VM Houses*, Plot (2005). Credit: Mikkel Gerken.

Under certain light conditions, glass surfaces reveal life inside a building as part of a layered urbanity. When we are allowed to see into the interior, we find inhabitants who seem highly aware that they are – potentially – always being watched.[15] As we know from anthropological fieldwork, people are very aware that they can be seen by others – and vice versa – and that everyone has an opinion about their neighbours' choice of decor.[16]

Looking into a residential building in Ørestaden, *VM Houses* by Plot, the first housing complex to be erected in the Ørestad development (Figure 16.6), we see what appear to be two deliberate strategies in response to this situation. Either this awareness of being seen from without is incorporated in the home through a carefully decorated aesthetic, and a perfect arrangement of objects, people, and movements; or there is an equally conscious display of indifference to the gaze. We see the untidiness of lived life – children's toys, bicycles, multicoloured curtains and potted plants, but such objects in fact serve to barricade our view into the deeper, more private recesses of the flat.[17] Yet no matter which strategy of living is displayed, the panoptic effect seems to be present.

In contrast to the panoptic prison, where visibility is one-directional (the warden can observe the inmates at any given time, while remaining invisible to the prisoners), the self-disciplinary potential of a glass façade like this works both ways. The power relation embodied in the categories of visibility and invisibility is constantly interchangeable: here we are dealing with something that can best be described as an intermingling of the exhibitionist pleasure in being seen and the voyeur's wish to remain hidden,[18] which envelops the surroundings in a disciplinary, panoptic gaze. Performance and visuality are thus closely linked, and are key terms for understanding the mode of living in environments like the *VM Houses* by Plot, where the walls of the home are made of thin, transparent glass surfaces. Moving from the idea of the panopticon to that of the glass façade, we will now consider in more detail how the symbolic form of perceived visibility is materialised through the use of glass in the urban environment of Ørestad.

15 See Mechtild Widrich's chapter in this volume on glass architecture and voyeurism.

16 See Stender, 'Glashuse til Debat'.

17 See Claus Bech-Danielsen's chapter in this volume on the desire to live invisibly.

18 See Annie Ring's chapter in this volume for a more careful consideration of the voyeur.

Imagined Transparency: Screen Reflections

Like the panopticon, the choice of the glass façade in many of the new buildings in Ørestaden also carries modernist connotations. Almost a hundred years ago, large glass panes were introduced as an important feature of avant-garde modernist architecture. Large windows are meant to create a direct link between the interior spaces and an ideal, unspoilt environment that surrounds them.[19] An obvious question to ask, therefore, is to what degree the potential transparency of more recent structures also bear witness to a return of the ideological connotations underlying the variant of modern architecture that integrates large glass surfaces into its structure, and to what extent we may regard this as another material sign of perceived visibility.[20]

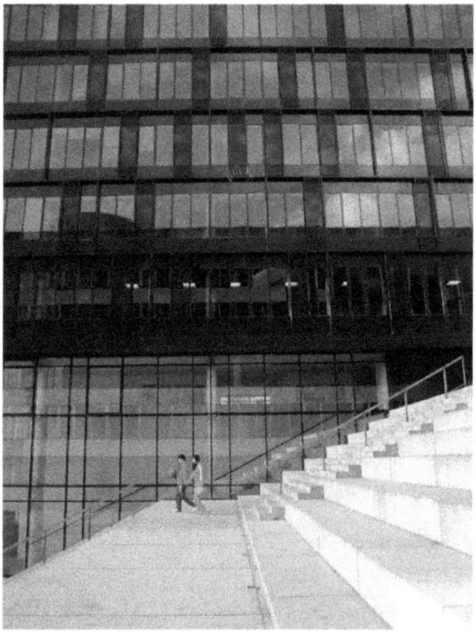

Fig. 16.7: Façade, *Winghouse*, Henning Larsen Architects (2010). Credit: Mikkel Gerken.

19 Martin Tschanz, 'Bildhaftigkeit oder räumliche Verschränkung. Wie Fenster innen und aussen trennen oder verbinden', *werk, bauen+wohnen* 9 (2007), 4–9.

20 Bech-Danielsen, *Modernismens Genkomst*.

According to Anthony Vidler, modern architecture's love affair with transparency[21] has always worked mainly on an immaterial level:

> Modernity has been haunted, as we know very well, by a myth of transparency: transparency of the self to nature, of the self to the other, of all selves to society, and all this represented, if not constructed from Jeremy Bentham to Le Corbusier, by a universal transparency of building materials, spatial penetration, and the ubiquitous flow of air, light and physical movement. [...] On another level, transparency opened up machine architecture to inspection – its functions displayed like anatomical models, its walls hiding no secrets; the very epitome of social morality.[22]

In many contemporary institutional or commercial buildings, glass is used to signal the morally superior position of that particular corporation; the dictum 'if you've got nothing to hide, you've got nothing to fear' is again a common reference point. But as we see for instance in Figure 16.7, a photograph of the façade of *Winghouse* by Henning Larsen Architects (2010) taken on a sunny evening in May 2013, this is often an over-statement. Glass façades often appear thick and dark – or darkened – like a brick wall. In these developments, the see-through effect of a glass façade remains merely potential, a connotation of glass.

Just as striking as the actual transparency of *VM House* (see Figure 16.6), is the fact that even highly transparent architectures give rise to particular kinds of opacity, reflections or blurry zones of greyness. In fact, it is only possible to see through a glass façade under very particular light conditions. Most of the time, it looks like a solid surface – what we glimpse of the interior is minimal.

Thus only rarely does the actual appearance of transparent surfaces *from the outside* completely reveal a private interior, or produce a direct connection between the interior and its surroundings. Even a glass box only appears completely transparent in particular weather and light conditions, and mainly at night. Under other circumstances, glass displays reflective qualities, which might make it look like a screen onto which the surroundings of the building are reflected, thus doubling their appearance. When the material quality of the glass façade (that potentially allows us to see

21 See also Lorens Holm's contribution to this volume for an in-depth discussion of transparency.

22 Anthony Vidler, *The Architectural Uncanny* (Cambridge, MA: MIT Press, 1999), 217–8.

through the structuring surfaces of a building) gives rise to features that are not transparent, the transparency in such contexts is thus often an imagined one – we see how, as a concrete material sign, the glass façade gestures towards perceived visibility as a symbolic form. When we are dealing with glass façades in contemporary urban environments, we need to bear in mind that the negotiation of transparency happens mainly at an imagined and discursive level, and that we need to conceive of the visual culture of these environments in different terms, as one of constant potential or imagined revelation, rather than of complete, unrestricted exposure.[23]

Black Box – Into the Camera

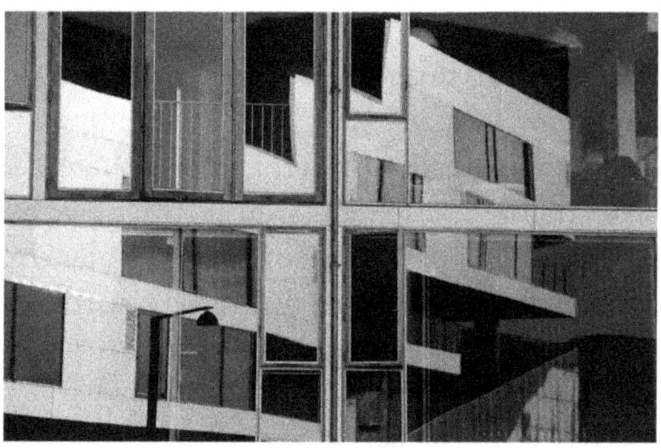

Fig. 16.8: Façade, *VM Houses*, Plot (2005).
Credit: Mikkel Gerken.

23 Inquiries into the theme of transparency relate to a large interdisciplinary field, the precise boundaries of which cannot be set out here. Key text are: Deborah Barnstone, *The Transparent State: Architecture and Politics in Postwar Germany* (London: Routledge, 2005); Ufuk Ersoy, 'The Fictive Quality of Glass', *ARQ* 11 (2007), 237–43; Anette Fierro, *The Glass State: The Technology of the Spectacle, Paris, 1981–98* (Cambridge, MA: MIT Press, 2006); Detlef Mertins, 'The Enticing and Threatening Face of Prehistory: Walter Benjamin and the Utopia of Glass', *Assemblage* 29 (1996), 6–23; Werner Oechslin, 'Einführung', in Colin Rowe and Robert Slutzky, eds, *Transparenz* (Basel: Birkhäuser Verlag, 1997).

The symbolic form of perceived visibility can also be understood in terms of the black box. In Figure 16.8 we see the same façade as pictured in Figure 16.5. The photograph was taken at the same time of day, but from a slightly different angle, which means much of the interior of the flats is no longer visible. Instead, the reflective properties of glass become evident, and we see the surrounding milieu – the context in which we are situated, and possibly even our own reflections.[24] The building becomes impenetrable, functioning like a black box and reflecting our gaze back on ourselves.

At the entrance to the car park under one of the other well-known residential buildings in Ørestad, *VM Mountain* by BIG and PLOT from 2008, there is a surveillance camera (Figure 16.9). It represents a kind of perceived visibility not dissimilar to that of a glass building or panopticon-like architectural structure, but embodied in a different kind of technology. The camera is a reminder of the panoptic effect of the surveillant eye. It emphasises the visibility of the external gaze, which we accept precisely because of its disciplinary potential. Living here, more or less visibly behind the glass façades, one might still fear those outside who do have something to hide, and therefore feel more at ease when a CCTV camera is in operation.

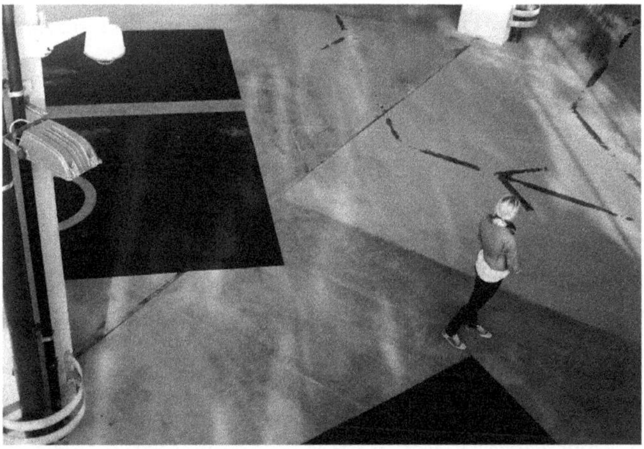

Fig. 16.9: Entrance to car park, *VM Mountain*, Plot (2008). Credit: Mikkel Gerken.

24 See Slavko Kacunko's chapter on the mirror in this volume.

Even though it is a more recent technology, the surveillance camera still carries connotations of the panopticon of the late eighteenth century. But at present, the camera has become what Bruno Latour would call 'blackboxed', that is, imperceptible, as a consequence of its ubiquity in contemporary culture:[25]

> Black-boxing: an expression from the sociology of science that refers to the way scientific and technical work is made invisible by its own success. When a machine runs efficiently, when a matter of fact is settled, one need focus only on its inputs and outputs and not on its internal complexity. Thus, paradoxically, the more science and technology succeed, the more opaque and obscure they become.[26]

Here, we contend, architecture itself appears as a black box, and this reveals a third set of qualities linked to perceived visibility as a symbolic form.

When technology runs smoothly, we no longer need to focus on its complexity; we are simply interested in its inputs and outputs.[27] In the case of the surveillance camera, for example, we are only concerned with the actions we perform in front of it (input), and the images it creates (output), and not with its technology, or the particular cultural logic it embodies.[28] However, precisely this process of 'blackboxing' influences the way we might perceive the camera as a material sign that gestures towards larger cultural issues. If we turn again to the concrete setting of the parking garage with a camera, the surveillance camera is 'blackboxed' insofar as the camera is no longer a foreign element. We (who consider ourselves to have nothing to hide) do not think twice about it. In this case, perceived visibility is met with indifference by the 'actors' involved.

According to Jean-Paul Sartre, becoming conscious of the gaze of the other means becoming conscious of oneself and one's place in the world as an object. For Sartre, this involves an infringement of the freedom of

25 See David Murakami Wood's chapter in this volume on vanishing surveillance.

26 Bruno Latour, *Pandora's Hope: Essays on the Reality of Science Studies* (Cambridge, MA: Harvard University Press, 2001), 304.

27 Nanna Bonde Thylstrup deals with the invisible censorship that takes place inside the black box in her contribution to this volume.

28 See also Murakami Wood on ubisurv in this volume.

the individual – suddenly one has to see oneself as an object through the eyes of the other.[29] However, as indicated above, in the case of these glass façades that invite the gaze of the other into the private realm of the apartment, the gaze does not seem to pose a threat to the individual; it is rather a means of communication with a (perceived) audience. It turns living into a performance of individuality and of indifference to exposure.[30] The inhabitants reveal everything at the same time as they do not really reveal anything: the human subject has itself been blackboxed.[31]

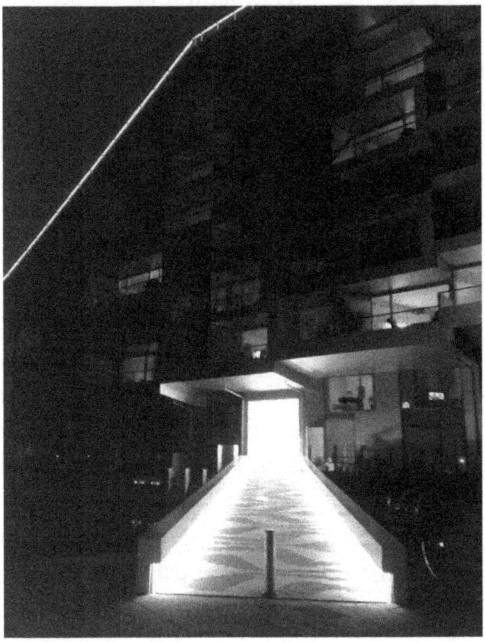

Fig. 16.10. Exterior view of the inner courtyard of *8 House*, BIG (2010) at night. Credit: Mikkel Gerken.

29 See also Susanne Yngvesson's contribution in this volume for a discussion on Satre's conception of the gaze.

30 See Stender, 'Glashuse til Debat', and Steiner and Veel, 'Living Behind Glass Facades'.

31 See for instance the artist Hassan Elahi's artwork *Tracking Transcience*, which also plays with these notions, <http://trackingtransience.net/>.

The same can be argued when, at night and on a larger scale, we see lit buildings perform a communication with light as a deliberate strategy (Figure 16.10). Here we seem to be dealing with a new understanding of urbanity, which does not operate symbolically, according to previous power structures, but as a concrete light-polluting manifestation that says nothing more than: 'we are here!' The building has thus indeed become a black box. We are not really interested in what goes on inside – in its internal complexity – but in what is projected onto its surface, the manifestation of its presence, and the performed presence of its inhabitants. We see a shift, from 'nothing to hide, and nothing to fear', to 'nothing to hide and nothing to see'.

On an even larger scale, we might see the whole urban environment of the Ørestad development as a black box. The security camera reminds us that this particular urban environment works according to particular social rules and standards, and instigates a line of separation between itself and the more heterogeneous 'other' of the surrounding urban context, of Amager in particular, and of Copenhagen in general. This is not only emphasised architecturally and topographically in the way Ørestad is neatly separated from the rest of the city (see Figure 16.2), but also in the way that Ørestad as a whole may be regarded as a particular 'environment', constituted by a particular gaze from above.[32] From this perspective, one can regard the intended large-scale beauty of the development as merely another aspect of the visual culture of transparency or, perhaps more correctly, the perceived visibility it embodies.

These effects tell us that seemingly contradictory conceptions of visibility and invisibility exist side by side in this kind of urban environment. They are not mutually exclusive, but should be regarded as cultural phenomena that reveal something fundamental about what it means to inhabit contemporary urban space, as well as something about perceived visibility as a symbolic form. We believe perceived visibility is a significant concept,

32 See also Svarre and Rasmussen, 'Byen set fra oven', for their discussion of the urban planning strategy of Ørestad in relation to the conceptual apparatus of Michel de Certeau.

and it pertains, as we have shown, to various different aspects of contemporary urban culture.

Visible in Theory: Towards a Conclusion

In this final chapter we have explored the visual culture of contemporary urban environments using the example of Ørestad in Copenhagen. Starting with the hypothesis that perceived visibility may be regarded as a significant symbolic form of the visual culture fundamental to such environments, we have traced its materialisation in three concrete architectural forms that are each indicative of a particular cultural logic of visuality: the panopticon, the glass façade, and the black box. These three examples not only allow us to explore Ørestad topgraphically, they also imply a movement from the beginnings of modern architectural thinking, exemplified in the reformist ideology underlying the panopticon, via the imagined form of transparancy that preceded this logic. This is a logic found most prominently in modernist architecture, as well as in its reappearance in the neo-modernist architectural paradigm – a paradigm that can be seen in many buildings of Ørestaden and is echoed in its underlying planning logic pointing to contemporary culture's ambiguous relation to visual culture. This ambiguous relation is played out through technologies which, under the condition of our own late modernity, are themselves subject to the process of 'blackboxing'. In this way, we have indicated the powerful effect of perceived visbility as a symbolic form that allows us to develop precise strategies for understanding current negotiations between the visible and the invisible in contemporary culture. Our exploration of Ørestaden offers a way of approaching architectural settings, where, despite the presence of elements that aspire towards openness, visuality, and the transparancy that is so heavily imbued with positive connotations also in contemporary culture, it becomes apparent that we are merely 'visible in theory'.

Bibliography

Barnstone, Deborah, *The Transparent State: Architecture and Politics in Postwar Germany* (London: Routledge, 2005).

Bech-Danielsen, Claus, and Jens Schjerup Hansen, eds, *Modernismens Genkomst* (Copenhagen: Arkitektens Forlag, 2001).

Cassirer, Ernst, 'Der Begriff der symbolischen Form im Aufbau der Geisteswissenschaften', in *Wesen und Wirkung des Symbolbegriffs* [1956] (Darmstadt: Wissenschaftliche Buchgesellschaft, 1977), 169–201.

Christensen, Hans, *Housing in Denmark* (Copenhagen: Centre for Housing and Welfare, 2007).

Colomina, Beatriz, *Privacy and Publicity* (Cambridge, MA: MIT Press, 1996).

Corrodi, Michelle and Klaus Spechtenhauser, *Lichteinfall* (Basel: Birkhäuser Verlag, 2008).

Ersoy, Ufuk, 'The Fictive Quality of Glass', *ARQ* 11 (2007), 237–43.

Fierro, Anette, *The Glass State: The Technology of the Spectacle, Paris, 1981–98* (Cambridge, MA: MIT Press, 2006).

Galloway, Alexander, *Black Box, Black Bloc*, in Benjamin Nyes, ed., *Communization and its Discontents: Contestation, Critique, and Contemporary Struggles* (New York: Minor Compositions, 2011).

Isenstadt, Sandy, 'The Rise and Fall of the Picture Window', in Barbara Miller Lane, ed., *Housing and Dwelling – Perspectives on Modern Domestic Architecture* (London, New York: Routledge, 2007), 298–306.

Latour, Bruno, *Pandora's Hope: Essays on the Reality of Science Studies* (Cambridge, MA: Harvard University Press, 1999).

Mertins, Detlef, 'The Enticing and Threatening Face of Prehistory: Walter Benjamin and the Utopia of Glass', *Assemblage* 29 (1996), 6–23.

Oechslin, Werner, 'Einführung', in Colin Rowe and Robert Slutzky, eds, *Transparenz* (Basel: Birkhäuser Verlag, 1997).

Overy, Paul, *Light, Air and Openness* (London: Thames and Hudson, 2007).

Schivelbusch, Wolfgang, *Licht Schein und Wahn* (Berlin: Erco Edition, 1992).

Schmid, Christian, 'A New Paradigm of Urban Development for Zurich & The New Metropolitan Mainstream', in Raffaele Paloscia, ed., *The Contested Metropolis* (Basel: Birkhäuser Verlag, 2004), 237–46, 253–60.

Steiner, Henriette and Kristin Veel, 'Living Behind Glass Facades: Surveillance Culture and New Architecture', in *Surveillance & Society* 9/1–2 (2011), 215–32.

Stender, Marie 'Glashuse til Debat: En Nation af Vindueskiggere', in *ARKFOKUS: Tidsskrift for Arkitektur, Design, By og Land* 10 (2006), 10–5.

Svarre, Birgitte Bundesen, and Pia Rost Rasmussen, 'Byen set fra oven – Michel de Certeau og planerne for Ørestad', in Henrik Reeh et al., ed., *Rumlig Kultur*, (Copenhagen: Museum Tusculanum Press, 2012).

Teuwsen, Peer, 'Land der Klotze', *Die Zeit* (22 July 2010).

Tschanz, Martin, 'Bildhaftigkeit oder räumliche Verschränkung. Wie Fenster innen und aussen trennen oder verbinden', *werk, bauen+wohnen*, 9 (2007), 4–9.

Udviklingsselskabet By & Havn, *Godt Begyndt – Et tilbageblik over Ørestads Udvikling* (Copenhagen: By & Havn, 2010).

Vidler, Anthony, *The Architectural Uncanny* (Cambridge, MA: MIT Press, 1999).

Notes on Contributors

CLAUS BECH-DANIELSEN is a Professor at Aalborg University, where he has for some years been Coordinator of Architectural Research at the Danish Building Research Institute. He has served as Research Director at the Institute, and is now Head of the Danish Centre for Housing Research, and Editor in chief of the *Nordic Journal of Architectural Research*. Bech-Danielsen has published several books in different languages. He holds different positions of trust in the Scandinavian research community, and at the moment he is the chairman of two Danish Think Tanks. Bech-Danielsen has received awards for his work, among them The Danish Business Research Prize from The Danish Business Research Academy.

NANNA BONDE THYLSTRUP is a PhD Fellow at the Department of Modern Culture and Communication, University of Copenhagen. Thylstrup's dissertation outlines and examines the politics of mass-digitised archives. She has furthermore published and given lectures on digital censorship, digital archives and the geopolitics of information.

LORENS HOLM is Reader in Architecture and Director of the Geddes Institute for Urban Research at the University of Dundee. He has taught at the Architectural Association, the Bartlett, the Mackintosh, and Washington University in St Louis. His teaching/research focuses on the threads that link architecture to philosophy, history, psychoanalysis, and machines. Publications include *Brunelleschi Lacan Le Corbusier: Architecture Space and the Construction of Subjectivity* (Routledge, 2010). His papers have appeared in *The Journal of Architecture*, *Perspecta*, *Critical Quarterly*, *Architecture Theory Review*, and *Assemblage*.

SLAVKO KACUNKO (PhD, Dr. habil.) is Professor of Art History and Visual Culture at the University of Copenhagen. Key foci of his research include Processual Arts, Visual Studies and its Boundaries, History of

Aesthetical Discourse and the interdisciplinary study of bacteria. Kacunko is the author of *Spiegel. Medium. Kunst* (Fink, 2010) and *Closed Circuit Videoinstallationen* (Logos, 2004), described as a 'milestone in the history of media art', while his *Marcel Odenbach. Konzept, Performance, Video, Installation* (Chorus, 1999) was described as an 'art history pioneer achievement' in the field of video art.

CHARLES LOCK has been the Professor of English Literature at the University of Copenhagen since 1996. From 1983 he taught at the University of Toronto where he was appointed Full Professor in 1993. He received his DPhil from Oxford in 1982 for a dissertation on John Cowper Powys, and is now the Editor of the *Powys Journal*. In 1979 he was awarded Oxford University's Laurence Binyon Prize in the History of Art, and has published extensively on visual semiotics, petroglyphs, and Byzantine icons. Much of his recent work has been dedicated to contemporary poets, notably Geoffrey Hill and Anne Blonstein.

NINA LUND WESTERDAHL grew up on the island of Bornholm, Denmark. This isolation might have fostered her interest in cities, and dreams of how life could be lived elsewhere. Thus, after studying architecture in Copenhagen and city development and conservation in Tanzania, she moved to Zurich. Nina is an architect/urbanist/artist/human (in reversed order of prioritisation), and joined the just-founded zURBS in February 2012. She aims to raise public awareness by exploring, collecting, and sharing the wonders of everyday city life.

DAVID MURAKAMI WOOD, educated at Oxford and Newcastle, is currently Canada Research Chair (Tier II) in Surveillance Studies at Queen's University in Canada. From 2013–14, he was a Japan Society for the Promotion of Science Invitation Fellow at Kwasei Gakuin University and Visiting Professor at Meiji University, in Japan. He is a widely published specialist in the sociology and geography of surveillance and security in cities from a global comparative perspective, with a particular focus on Japan, Brazil, Canada and the UK. He is also a leading organiser in the field of surveillance studies as the Editor-in-Chief of the international, open-access, peer-reviewed journal, *Surveillance & Society*, as well as a consultant and in-demand media commentator on surveillance issues.

BERND NICOLAI is Professor of Architectural History and Cultural Heritage at Bern University, Department of Art History. His research focuses on art and architecture in the middle ages and its development after the industrial revolution. Among numerous articles and books on architecture and cultural transfer, he has published *Moderne und Exil, Deutschsprachige Architekten in der Türkei 1925–55* (Verlag für Bauwesen, 1998), and *Modernity and Early Culture* (co-edited, Peter Lang, 2012).

DORA OSBORNE is Leverhulme Early Career Fellow in German at the University of Edinburgh. She completed her PhD at the University of Cambridge in 2008 and has published a monograph on the prose work of W. G. Sebald and Christoph Ransmayr. Her research focuses on questions of trauma and postwar memory. Her current project looks at the relationship between memory and the archive in contemporary Germany, particularly in literature and visual culture.

HENRIK REEH, PhD in comparative literature, is Associate Professor of Humanistic Urban Studies and Modern Culture in the Department of Arts and Cultural Studies, University of Copenhagen. He is director of Urban Culture Lab at the University's Faculty of Humanities, and the Danish director of 4Cities – Erasmus Mundus Master Course (4Cities.eu). Author of books on urbanity, art in public space and cultural theory, Reeh's *Ornaments of the Metropolis: Siegfried Kracauer and Modern Urban Culture* was published by the MIT Press. After completing a volume on Venice, he is finishing a book on architectural experience in Daniel Libeskind's Jewish museums. Reeh is also a photographer.

JANE RENDELL is a writer whose work crosses architecture, art, feminism, history and psychoanalysis. She has developed concepts of 'critical spatial practice' (2002–6) and 'site-writing' (2007–10) through such authored books as *Site-Writing* (I B Tauris, 2010), *Art and Architecture* (IB Tauris, 2006), and *The Pursuit of Pleasure* (Continuum, 2002). Recent texts have been commissioned by artists such as Jasmina Cibic, Apollonia Susteric and transparadiso, and institutions such as FRAC Centre, Orléans, and Hamburger Bahnhof, Berlin. She is currently working on a new book concerning transitional spaces in architecture and psychoanalysis. She is Professor of Architecture and Art at the Bartlett, UCL. <http://www.janerendell.co.uk/>

ANNIE RING is Research Fellow and Acting Director of Studies in German at Emmanuel College, Cambridge. She also teaches undergraduate and graduate courses in film, literature, and cultural studies at the Faculty of Modern and Medieval Languages, University of Cambridge. She has published essays on literary portrayals of the East German secret police (the 'Stasi'), on Kafka and pleasure and on French women's writing after May 1968. Her monograph, about the writing of German unification, is forthcoming with Bloomsbury.

CECILIE SACHS OLSEN is co-founder of zURBS and PhD researcher at Queen Mary University of London. Her research revolves around questions of how art can be used as a framework to analyse and re-imagine space and politics. Cecilie studied Urban Studies in Brussels, Vienna, Copenhagen and Madrid, and Theatre and Performance Studies at the University of Copenhagen. She has been working as a Research Assistant at the Institute of Critical Theory at Zurich University of the Arts, as well as at the research project Urban Breeding Grounds at the Chair of Architecture and Urban Design, ETH Zurich.

DEVIKA SHARMA is Assistant Professor of Modern Culture at the University of Copenhagen. She is the author of *Amerikanske fængselsbilleder: Kunst, kultur og indespærring i samtidens USA* [*American Prison Imagery: Arts, Culture, and Incarceration in the Contemporary U.S.*] and the co-editor (with Frederik Tygstrup) of *Structures of Feeling*, a volume exploring the significance of affectivity for the study of culture (De Gruyter, 2014). She is currently working on a monograph on contemporary humanitarian culture, focusing specifically on images of Africa as vital to humanitarian feeling culture.

HENRIETTE STEINER is Associate Professor at the Section for Landscape Architecture and Planning at the University of Copenhagen in Denmark. She graduated with a PhD from the Department of Architecture at the University of Cambridge in 2008, after which she worked for five years as a Research Associate at the Department of Architecture at the ETH Zurich in Switzerland. She is author of *The Emergence of a Modern City – Golden Age Copenhagen 1800–50* (Ashgate, 2014) and co-editor of *Memory Culture and the Contemporary City – Building Sites* (Palgrave Macmillan, 2009) and *Rumlig Kultur/Spatial Culture* (Museum Tusculanum Press, 2012).

SABETH TÖDTLI grew up in Zurich, Switzerland, and studied architecture in Zurich and Glasgow. Working as project leader on the conversion and extension of a housing complex, she came to realise how the social and economic processes of cities interest her more than the house as an object. She went on to study urbanism in Brussels, Vienna, Budapest, Copenhagen and Madrid. Back in Zurich, she co-founded the social-artistic urban laboratory zURBS, and has been working at the interface of city development, artistic practices and social issues ever since – in theory as well as, mainly, in practice.

MARK VACHER is an Associate Professor at the SAXO Institute, University of Copenhagen. A cultural analyst specialising in housing issues and urban anthropology, his work is inspired by phenomenological theories on the perception of time and space and by post-structuralist theories on consumption. He has conducted fieldwork in a variety of urban settings in Europe and North Africa focusing on gentrification and urban transformations and their impact on private homes and dwellings, as well as on public domains and transportation systems.

KRISTIN VEEL is Postdoctoral Research Fellow at the Department of Arts and Cultural Studies, University of Copenhagen. She completed her PhD at the University of Cambridge, German Department. Her research interests are focused on the impact of information and communication technology on the contemporary cultural imagination, with a particular interest in issues of information overload and surveillance and the way in which these are negotiated in film, art and literature. She has published the monograph *Narrative Negotiations: Information Structures in Literary Fiction* (Vandenhoeck & Ruprecht, 2009) and is co-editor of the collected volume *The Cultural Life of Crises and Catastrophes* (de Gruyter, 2012).

MECHTILD WIDRICH (MPhil University of Vienna, PhD Department of Architecture, MIT) is Assistant Professor of Contemporary Art History at the School of the Art Institute Chicago. Her research focuses on ephemeral practices in relation to the built environment and on global art geographies. Recent publications are *Performative Monuments. The Rematerialisation of Public Art* (Manchester University Press, 2014), and texts in the *Journal of Architectural Historians* (JSAH), *Art Journal*, *Grey Room*, *The Drama Review* (TDR), *Performance Art Journal* (PAJ), *Log* and *thresholds*. Mechtild is member of the academic advisory council of the Jewish Museum Vienna.

SUSANNE WIGORTS YNGVESSON is Associate Professor in Ethics at Uppsala University and Senior Lecturer at Stockholm School of Theology, Sweden. Her research concerns ethical and moral aspects of surveillance, media ethics, sexual ethics, theological ethics and human rights, especially freedom of thought, conscience and religion. During 2009–13 she was an expert in the European network LiSS (Living in Surveillance Societies). Her main ongoing research project is *Ethics of Vision*, which concerns phenomenological and theological analyses of vision in relation to surveillance and moral philosophy.

zURBS wants to make people look at and rethink their cities in new and different ways. By working with a wide range of urban citizens through a social-artistic approach, zURBS aims to pose alternatives to how we live together in our cities (=the social), through creative and imaginative processes (=the artistic). Thus, zURBS organises projects, workshops, interventions, and lectures, in collaboration with a wide range of national and international organisations.

Index

CULTURAL HISTORY AND LITERARY IMAGINATION

EDITED BY CHRISTIAN J. EMDEN & DAVID MIDGLEY

This series promotes inquiry into the relationship between literary texts and their cultural and intellectual contexts, in theoretical, interpretative and historical perspectives. It has developed out of a research initiative of the German Department at Cambridge University, but its focus of interest is on the European tradition broadly perceived. Its purpose is to encourage comparative and interdisciplinary research into the connections between cultural history and the literary imagination generally.

The editors are especially concerned to encourage the investigation of the role of the literary imagination in cultural history and the interpretation of cultural history through the literary text. Examples of the kind of issues in which they are particularly interested include the following:

- The material conditions of culture and their representation in literature, e.g. responses to the impact of the sciences, technology, and industrialisation, the confrontation of 'high' culture with popular culture, and the impact of new media;

- The construction of cultural meaning through literary texts, e.g. responses to cultural crisis, or paradigm shifts in cultural self-perception, including the establishment of cultural 'foundation myths';

- History and cultural memory as mediated through the metaphors and models deployed in literary writing and other media;

- The intermedial and intercultural practice of authors or literary movements in specific periods;

- The methodology of cultural inquiry and the theoretical discussion of such issues as intermediality, text as a medium of cultural memory, and intercultural relations.

Both theoretical reflection on and empirical investigation of these issues are welcome. The series is intended to include monographs, editions, and collections of papers based on recent research in this area. The main language of publication is English.

Vol. 1 Christian Emden & David Midgley (eds): Cultural Memory and Historical Consciousness in the German-Speaking World Since 1500. Papers from the Conference 'The Fragile Tradition', Cambridge 2002. Vol. 1.
316 pp., 2004. ISBN 3-03910-160-9 / US-ISBN 0-8204-6970-X

Vol. 2 Christian Emden & David Midgley (eds): German Literature, History and the Nation. Papers from the Conference 'The Fragile Tradition', Cambridge 2002. Vol. 2.
393 pp., 2004. ISBN 3-03910-169-2 / US-ISBN 0-8204-6979-3

Vol. 3 Christian Emden & David Midgley (eds): Science, Technology and the German Cultural Imagination. Papers from the Conference 'The Fragile Tradition', Cambridge 2002. Vol. 3.
319 pp., 2005. ISBN 3-03910-170-6 / US-ISBN 0-8204-6980-7

Vol. 4 Anthony Fothergill: Secret Sharers. Joseph Conrad's Cultural Reception in Germany.
274 pp., 2006. ISBN 3-03910-271-0 / US-ISBN 0-8204-7200-X

Vol. 5 Silke Arnold-de Simine (ed.): Memory Traces. 1989 and the Question of German Cultural Identity.
343 pp., 2005. ISBN 3-03910-297-4 / US-ISBN 0-8204-7223-9

Vol. 6 Renata Tyszczuk: In Hope of a Better Age. Stanislas Leszczynski in Lorraine 1737-1766.
410 pp., 2007. ISBN 978-3-03910-324-9

Vol. 7 Christian Emden, Catherine Keen & David Midgley (eds): Imagining the City, Volume 1. The Art of Urban Living.
344 pp., 2006. ISBN 3-03910-532-9 / US-ISBN 0-8204-7536-X

Vol. 8 Christian Emden, Catherine Keen & David Midgley (eds): Imagining the City, Volume 2. The Politics of Urban Space.
383 pp., 2006. ISBN 3-03910-533-7 / US-ISBN 0-8204-7537-8

Vol. 9 Christian J. Emden and Gabriele Rippl (eds): ImageScapes. Studies in Intermediality.
289 pp., 2010. ISBN 978-3-03910-573-1

Vol. 10 Alasdair King: Hans Magnus Enzensberger. Writing, Media, Democracy.
357 pp., 2007. ISBN 978-3-03910-902-9

Vol. 11 Ulrike Zitzlsperger: ZeitGeschichten: Die Berliner Übergangsjahre. Zur Verortung der Stadt nach der Mauer.
241 pp., 2007. ISBN 978-3-03911-087-2

Vol. 12 Alexandra Kolb: Performing Femininity. Dance and Literature in German Modernism.
330pp., 2009. ISBN 978-3-03911-351-4

Vol. 13 Carlo Salzani: Constellations of Reading. Walter Benjamin in Figures of Actuality.
388pp., 2009. ISBN 978-3-03911-860-1

Vol. 14 Monique Rinere: Transformations of the German Novel. *Simplicissimus* in Eighteenth-Century Adaptations.
273pp., 2009. ISBN 978-3-03911-896-0

Vol. 15 Katharina Hall and Kathryn N. Jones (eds): Constructions of Conflict. Transmitting Memories of the Past in European Historiography, Culture and Media.
282pp., 2011. ISBN 978-3-03911-923-3

Vol. 16 Ingo Cornils and Sarah Waters (eds): Memories of 1968. International Perspectives.
396pp., 2010. ISBN 978-3-03911-931-8

Vol. 17 Anna O' Driscoll: Constructions of Melancholy in Contemporary German and Austrian Literature.
263pp., 2013. ISBN 978-3-0343-0733-8

Vol. 18 Martin Modlinger and Philipp Sonntag (eds): Other People's Pain. Narratives of Trauma and the Question of Ethics.
252pp., 2011. ISBN 978-3-0343-0260-9

Vol. 19 Ian Cooper and Bernhard F. Malkmus (eds): Dialectic and Paradox. Configurations of the Third in Modernity.
265pp., 2013. ISBN 978-3-0343-0714-7

Vol. 20 Kristina Mendicino and Betiel Wasihun (eds): Playing False. Representations of Betrayal.
355pp., 2013. ISBN 978-3-0343-0867-0

Vol. 21 Guy Tourlamain: *Völkisch* Writers and National Socialism. A Study of Right-Wing Political Culture in Germany, 1890–1960.
394pp., 2014. ISBN 978-3-03911-958-5

Vol. 22 Ricarda Vidal and Ingo Cornils (eds): Alternative Worlds. Blue-Sky Thinking since 1900.
343pp., 2015. ISBN 978-3-0343-1787-0

Vol. 23 Henriette Steiner and Kristin Veel (eds): Invisibility Studies. Surveillance, Transparency and the Hidden in Contemporary Culture.
388pp., 2015. ISBN 978-3-0343-0985-1

Lightning Source UK Ltd.
Milton Keynes UK
UKHW020627200422
401775UK00005B/166

9 783034 309851